Finite Mathematics

for Business, Social Sciences, and Liberal Arts

Louis M. Rotando   Westchester Community College

D. Van Nostrand Company

New York Cincinnati Toronto London Melbourne

For Elia, Matthew, and Carrie . . .
with special thanks to my parents,
Edith and Louis I. Rotando.

(30 28 −13 8 32 28 −34 17 78 −66 29 144)

D. Van Nostrand Company Regional Offices:
New York   Cincinnati

D. Van Nostrand Company International Offices:
London   Toronto   Melbourne

Library of Congress Catalog Card Number: 79–66275
ISBN: 0–442–25760–0

Published by D. Van Nostrand Company
135 West 50th Street, New York, N.Y. 10020

10 9 8 7 6 5 4 3 2 1

Preface

This text is intended for a finite mathematics course where it is desirable to have a variety of elementary applications. The wealth and variety of applications make it possible to adapt the book to the needs and interests of students majoring in business, social science, economics, or the liberal arts.

The text assumes that the student has a working knowledge of elementary algebra; students having one or two years of high-school mathematics will be able to benefit from its use. The book does not require a student to have mastered every topic in basic algebra; often a review of elementary techniques is incorporated within a presentation or example.

The material is uniquely "teachable" in that the discussion and examples readily lend themselves to classroom presentation. I have presented appropriate examples and clearly organized solutions. In many cases, solutions have clarifying diagrams and boxed-in comments or details to enhance the student's understanding. The exercise sets occasionally include problems marked by an asterisk or a double-asterisk, which are either more difficult or especially challenging.

Although the topics covered are contemporary, the mathematical style is traditional. I have tried to avoid notational excesses and overzealous theoretical generalizations. In most cases theorems are motivated by discussion or example, and proofs are usually omitted.

Throughout I have provided optional sections and problems with which instructors may enrich the basic material. Special examples and materials include topics in recreational logic, astronomy, medical diagnosis, casino gambling, business and economics models, population forecasting, sociometric models, and computer programming.

Particular care has been taken to make the Simplex Method understandable. The algorithm is first explained for "standard" linear programming problems in order to avoid the difficulties that may arise in nonstandard linear programming problems. These special cases are categorized and explained with illustrative examples in a separate section.

The text is flexible enough so that material can be organized in several ways. A solid, four-credit, one-semester course could include all of the chapters in the order in which they are presented in the book, possibly omitting Chapters 7 (Linear Equations and Inequalities), and 12 (Essentials of Precalculus). A three-credit, one-semester course having some students with weaker backgrounds could be handled in the following way:

Chapters 4 (Basic Counting Techniques-Indirect Methods), 5 (Discrete Probability with Applications), 6 (Special Problems in Probability and The Binomial Theorem), 7, 8 (A First Look at Linear Programming), 9 (Matrix Algebra), and 10 (Applying Matrices to Linear Programming)

A three-credit, one-semester course having students with stronger backgrounds might include Chapters 4, 5, 6, 8, 9, 10, and 11 (Matrix Games with Applications). Courses designed specifically for business students (who may ultimately have to study calculus) might include Chapters, 7, 8, 9, 10, 11, and 12. Quite often social science students take a course specifically designed to prepare them for statistics; a preparatory course of this kind could include Chapters 1 (Logic), 2 (Special Problems in Logic), 3 (Sets), 4, 5, and 6.

Chapters 1, 2, or 3 are not necessary to the study of subsequent material. Chapter 7 can be safely omitted for strong students, but I have found it useful for students with weaker backgrounds in basic algebra and graphing. Chapter 12 is a tight-knit review of elementary functions for those who may wish to use it as a "bridge" to calculus.

I wish to express my appreciation to the individuals who helped with the development of this text; to my students for their suggestions while class-testing this material; and to the following reviewers for their valuable comments, criticisms, and organizational suggestions: Ellen E. Casey, Massachusetts Bay Community College; Walter Feibes, Western Kentucky University; John B. Fraleigh, University of Rhode Island; David A. Klarner, State University of New York at Binghamton; Peter Nichols, Northern Illinois University; Richard Semmler, Northern Virginia Community College. Special thanks go to Ed Lugenbeel and the excellent editorial and production staff at D. Van Nostrand Company for their encouragement and hard work.

Finally I would also like to extend my thanks to my family and friends who, although they were neglected while I was writing this book, somehow provided a mysterious and wonderful source of inspiration for the effort.

Louis M. Rotando

Contents

1

Logic

> Logic supplies us with steps whereby we may
> go down to reach the water.
>
> Isaac Watts

1. Introduction to Logic

One reason for studying logic in a formal or symbolic way is that
we may have a means of correctly analyzing the process of arriving
at inescapable conclusions from stated premises. Examine the structure
of the following statements:

Premise 1   If a figure is a rectangle, then it is a quadrilateral.
Premise 2   This figure is not a quadrilateral.

Conclusion   This figure is not a rectangle.

Although we recognize the truth of premise 1, we have no idea whatso-
ever about the truth or falsity of premise 2, since it is unclear what
"this figure" refers to. Nevertheless, we are pretty certain that the
conclusion follows naturally from the given premises. Most of us would
be certain even if we did not know the meaning of the words "figure,"
"rectangle," and "quadrilateral." We could separate the structure of
the argument from the meaning of many of the words in the following
way:

If $\underline{x}$ is an $\underline{A}$, then $\underline{x}$ is a $\underline{B}$.
This $\underline{x}$ is not a $\underline{B}$.

This $\underline{x}$ is not an $\underline{A}$.

In this latter form, we recognize immediately the *validity* of the structure
as something distinct from the factual truth or falsity of the statements
involved. In this chapter we will develop an algebraic process that
will permit us to determine the validity of arguments; without such
an algebra, some logical processes would be difficult to analyze.

We will be using letters like p, q, r, and s to represent statements,
not numbers. Instead of using arithmetic symbols, we will use symbols
such as $\wedge$, $\vee$, $\sim$, and $\rightarrow$, which express relations between statements
in a thinking process. Thus we shall attempt to study certain kinds
of thinking by using symbols to help clarify our analysis.

Statements We will limit our analysis to sentences and phrases that are clear and unambiguous, which means that we will exclude sentences that are paradoxical or that have syntactical ambiguities. We cannot analyze a logical process containing forms like "I am lying right now" or "the skies are not cloudy all day." "I am lying right now" is a paradox in which truth implies falsity and vice versa; "the skies are not cloudy all day" is ambiguous because we cannot determine whether the sentence describes a whole day without clouds or, perhaps, part of a day without clouds. Certain types of exclamations and poetic language forms must also be excluded from discussion.

In the logical analysis we will limit ourselves to sentences that are also statements.

> **Definition 1.**   A statement is a declarative sentence that is either true or false, but not both simultaneously.

Example 1

Which of the following are statements?

a. $17 + 5 = 22$
b. $18 + 4 = 65$
c. Go away!
d. All zorches are lollypopped.
e. Westchester Community College is a fine place to learn.
f. $x^2 - 6x + 3 = 0$
g. San Francisco is a large city.
h. Do you think we can leave now?
i. It is raining now.
j. No fox terrier can play a trombone.

Solution
a. True statement
b. False statement
c. An exclamation, not a statement
d. Meaningless, it is impossible to decide whether it is true or false, not a statement
e. Could be disagreement concerning the truth or falsity, not a statement
f. Cannot be classified as true or false, not a statement
g. True statement
h. Interrogative sentence, not a statement
i. Statement (truth will depend on time and place)
j. True statement

A statement is said to be *compound* if it contains two or more statements as component parts. Thus "if the sun is shining, then I must be careful not to get sunburned" and "either I will go to the movies or else I will stay home" are examples of compound statements.

Exercise 1.1   1.   Which of the following are statements?

     a.   If $x = 5$, then $x + 6 = 11$.
     b.   The sun is hotter than the earth.
     c.   It is raining, but I am not wet.
     d.   Right triangles are beautiful.
     e.   Don't run!
     f.   A triangle is a right triangle if and only if the sum of the squares of the legs equals the square of the hypotenuse.
     g.   Hickory dickory dock.
     h.   A quadrilateral with equal diagonals is a rectangle and conversely.
     i.   Only policemen carry guns.

2.   Which of the statements in Problem 1(a)–(i) are compound?

3.   Explain the syntactical ambiguity that prevents the following sentence from being classified as a statement: Metals are abundant.

4.   Explain the paradox (first identified by Bertrand Russell) inherent in the following sentence that prevents it from being classified as a statement: The barber in town shaves everyone who does not shave himself.

1.2   Three Basic Connectives

If the letters p and q both represent statements, then there are three important logical *connectives* in our algebra of propositions: negation ("not"), conjunction ("and"), and disjunction (inclusive "or"). They are symbolized in the following way:

Algebra	*Translation*
$\sim p$	"*not p*" or "it is false that p"
$p \wedge q$	"p and q"
$p \vee q$	"p or q, possibly both"

The three propositions summarized above will be considered true under certain circumstances and false under others. We will define the *truth value* of a simple statement to be its truth (T) or falseness (F). When statements are compound and are linked with connectives, we must be equally precise about whether they are true or false. We must include all possible combinations of truth and falsity of the component statements. We summarize our definitions of the connectives by *truth tables* listing the various T-F combinations. In each truth table are listed symbols of the statements we are examining. Under them, on the left, are the possible combinations of truth and falseness, and on the right, the consequent truth and falseness of compound statements, with connectives.

Definition 2

Negation

p	$\sim p$
T	F
F	T

The negation of p always has a truth value opposite to p itself.

Conjunction

p	q	$p \wedge q$
T	T	T
T	F	F
F	T	F
F	F	F

The conjunction of p and q is true only when p is true and q is true.

Disjunction

p	q	$p \vee q$
T	T	T
T	F	T
F	T	T
F	F	F

The disjunction of p and q is false only when p is false and q is false.

Example 1

Let p represent "it is cold" and let q represent "it is raining." Write the following statements in symbolic form.

a. It is both cold and raining.
b. It is cold or it is not raining.
c. It is false that it is either raining or cold.
d. It is cold but it is not raining.

e. It is neither raining nor cold.

f. It is not the case that it is either cold or raining.

Solution   a. $p \wedge q$ b. $p \vee \sim q$ c. $\sim(q \vee p)$

d. $p \wedge \sim q$ e. $\sim q \wedge \sim p$ f. $\sim(p \vee q)$

Example 2

Write the logical negation (denial) of each of the following statements.

a. All dogs are animals.

b. Some reptiles are four-footed.

c. Some people who study hard do not pass the course.

d. No ducks waltz.

e. It is both cold and raining.

Solution   a. Some dogs are not animals.

b. It is false that some reptiles are four-footed. Alternatively: No reptiles are four-footed.

c. All people who study hard pass the course.

d. Some ducks waltz.

e. It is false that it is both cold and raining. Alternatively: It is either not cold or it is not raining.

Example 3

Let p represent "it is raining" and q represent "the streets are wet." Write a verbal translation (simplified if possible) for each of the following.

a. $\sim p \vee q$ b. $\sim(\sim p)$ c. $\sim p \wedge \sim q$

d. $p \vee \sim p$ e. $\sim(p \wedge q)$ f. $\sim(p \vee q)$

g. $\sim(\sim p \wedge \sim q) \vee p$

Solution   a. It is not raining or the streets are wet.

b. It is raining.

c. It is not raining and the streets are not wet.

d. It is raining or it is not raining.

e. It is not the case that it is raining and the streets are wet. Alternatively: It is not raining or the streets are not wet.

f. It is not the case that it is either raining or the streets are wet. Alternatively: It is not raining and the streets are not wet.

g. It is raining or the streets are wet.

Remark
Concerning
the Connective
"or"
The way we have defined the inclusive "or" symbol ∨ may not always agree with the meaning implied by current English usage. For example, if someone says "I will either go to the movies or I will go to a discotheque," the statement probably implies that the person will do one or the other but not both. A correct algebraic translation must therefore be presented in a more complicated way. This could be accomplished by writing an *exclusive* "or" as

$$(p \lor q) \land \sim(p \land q)$$

In our study of logic, however, we will consistently interpret the symbol $p \lor q$ to be *inclusive*, by which it is understood that both alternatives p and q may be true. In a special statement where the exclusive "or" is clearly implied, we can represent the statement by using the algebraic translation indicated above.

Exercise 1.2   1.   List the four T-F combinations (from memory) for the conjunction and disjunction truth tables below and complete the truth tables.

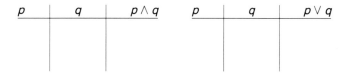

p	q	$p \land q$	p	q	$p \lor q$

2. Translate each of the following into symbolic logic.

   a. p or not q
   b. p or q or r
   c. p or q, and r
   d.   not p and not q, or r
   e. p or q or both p and q
   f. p or q but not both simultaneously
   g. p and q, but not q and not r

3. Write the logical negation (denial) of each of the following statements.

   a.   Either we will study or we will go to the movies.
   b.   Harold is dashing and Cheryl is charming.
   c.   Joe Smith is a socialist but not a communist.
   d.   All astronauts are brave.
   e.   Some buses are made in Italy.
   f.   Some vehicles made in Italy are buses.

g. Some positive numbers are not rational.

h. No fathers are mothers.

4. Let p represent "Donald is rich" and q represent "Malcolm is intel-lectual." Write a verbal translation (simplified if possible) for each of the following.

a. $p \lor \sim q$ b. $\sim[\sim(\sim p)]$ c. $\sim p \lor \sim q$

d. $p \land \sim p$ e. $\sim(p \land q)$ f. $\sim(\sim p \lor q)$

g. $\sim(\sim p \lor \sim q) \land p$

5. Where x and y are integers, let p represent "x is an even integer" and q represent "y is a perfect square integer." Translate each of the following into symbolic form.

a. x is even and y is not a perfect square.

b. x is odd and y is a perfect square.

c. Either y is a perfect square or x is even.

d. Either y is a perfect square or x is odd, but not both.

e. It is false that x is even and y is a perfect square.

f. It is false that x is odd or y is a perfect square.

g. It is false that it is false that it is false that x is odd.

1.3 Conditional and Biconditional Connectives—Equivalence

Two additional connectives are required to complete the set of symbols for propositional logic.

Consider the following statement: "If I earn enough money today, then I will go to the movies in the evening." The statement is not a direct assertion about whether or not the person involved will actually earn money or go to the movies. Thus the statement is a *conditional*.

We will be strict in our interpretation of such statements. We will not infer from the statement that if money is not earned, the speaker will not go to the movies since it is quite possible that a friend could lend the money for the movies anyway. The statement merely says that if money is earned, the speaker will go to the movies, and nothing more.

The conditional in the above example will be symbolized as follows:

$$p \rightarrow q$$

where p represents "I earn enough money today" and q represents "I will go to the movies in the evening."

Statements such as the above can be read as "if p, then q" or "p is sufficient for q." $p \rightarrow q$ is called a *conditional statement*. We will now consider the definition of this type of statement by examining an agreed-upon truth table.

Definition 3

		p	q	$p \rightarrow q$
Case 1		T	T	T
Case 2		T	F	F
Case 3		F	T	T
Case 4		F	F	T

Cases 1 and 2 seem to make sense. Cases 3 and 4 may seem a bit peculiar at first. Why should we define $p \rightarrow q$ to be true if statement p is false? There are actually some good reasons for Case 3 and Case 4 definitions (one of these can be found in an exercise at the end of this section). However, to simplify matters we will say that if the hypothesis p is false, then we cannot prove the conditional to be false; therefore we will define it to be true. Although this may appear totally arbitrary, two simple examples from algebra may help to illuminate the definition.

Consider the statement "If $2 = 3$, then $5 = 5$." Such an assertion could be proved true in the following way:

$$
\begin{array}{l}
2 = 3 \\
\underline{3 = 2} \quad\quad \text{Add "equals to equals"} \\
5 = 5
\end{array}
$$

This simple example illustrates that it is always possible to find a way of logically deriving a true conclusion from a false hypothesis.

Also consider the statement "if $2 = 3$, then $11 = 17$." There are probably an infinite number of ways of proving the conclusion from the false premise $2 = 3$. One way might be the following:

$$
\begin{array}{l}
2 = 3 \\
3 = 2 \\
2 = 3 \quad\quad \text{Square both sides of } 2 = 3 \\
\underline{4 = 9} \quad\quad \text{Add the corresponding sides} \\
11 = 17
\end{array}
$$

In this case we have logically deduced a false conclusion from a false hypothesis. It is possible to prove almost any conclusion from a false premise, and therefore we agree to define such cases to be true.

The various language forms equivalent to the $p \rightarrow q$ statement can be summarized as follows:

(i)   If p, then q.
(ii) p is sufficient for q.
(iii) q, if p.
(iv) p, only if q.
(v) q is necessary for p.

Although at first glance (iv) and (v) appear confusing, an example will illustrate these and all of the above cases. Suppose our implication was the statement, *If a geometric figure is a rectangle, then it is a quadrilateral.* This statement could be equivalently reworded as in these examples.

For a geometric figure to be a quadrilateral, it is sufficient that it be a rectangle.
A geometric figure is a quadrilateral, if it is a rectangle.
A geometric figure is a rectangle, only if it is a quadrilateral.
It is necessary that a figure be a quadrilateral in order for it to be a rectangle.
All rectangles are quadrilaterals.

The last statement reveals that it is possible, with a slight rewording, to make a conditional statement out of a "categorical" statement. Thus statements such as "all A's are B's" can be changed into the equivalent conditional form, "If x is an A, then x is a B." We will point out in a later section that certain categorical forms are also equivalent to each other. It is perhaps appropriate to mention now, however, that the statement "no A's are non-B's" is equivalent to "all A's are B's." Thus the following two forms are the same:

No rectangles are nonquadrilaterals.
All rectangles are quadrilaterals.

It is useful to remember these last two forms in order to convert categorical statements into if-then forms whenever it is useful to do so.

Another important connective is the biconditional, which records two relations between statements p and q. Consider the statement

I will go to the movies this evening if and only if I earn the money today.

This sentence has two conditional statements built into it, which we can separate into:

(i)   If I go to the movies this evening, it will be because I earned the money today.

(ii)   If I earn the money today, I am going to the movies this evening.

We will symbolize statements of the type "p if and only if q" in the following way:

$$p \leftrightarrow q$$

We understand this to mean "if p, then q" and "if q, then p." Splitting the biconditional into two conditional statements this way can be justified by means of a truth table; but first we need to define the circumstances under which a biconditional is true and under which it is false.

> **Definition 4**   A biconditional is true if and only if statements p and q have exactly the same truth value.

p	q	$p \leftrightarrow q$
T	T	T
T	F	F
F	T	F
F	F	T

Example 1

Show, by means of a truth table, that $p \leftrightarrow q$ has exactly the same truth value as $(p \rightarrow q) \wedge (q \rightarrow p)$ for each T-F combination that is possible for p and q.

Solution

p	q	$p \leftrightarrow q$	$(p \rightarrow q)$	$\wedge$	$(q \rightarrow p)$
T	T	T	T	T	T
T	F	F	F	F	T
F	T	F	T	F	F
F	F	T	T	T	T

Since the truth values (in boxes) that result for the two algebraic forms are identical in all cases, the forms are considered *equivalent*.

There are other, equivalent, verbal forms for the biconditional statement. $p \leftrightarrow q$ is also identical to the following forms:

(i) p if and only if q.
(ii) q if and only if p.
(iii) p is a necessary and sufficient condition for q.
(iv) q is a necessary and sufficient condition for p.

It is easy to translate the above because even if we inaccurately inter-change p and q, we will still have an equivalent form!

Example 2

Let p represent "n is divisible by 4" and q represent "n is divisible by 2," where it is understood that n is an integer. Write a verbal transla-tion for each of the following:

a. $p \to q$ (also prove this statement)
b. $q \to p$ (disprove this statement)
c. $\sim p \to \sim q$
d. $\sim q \to \sim p$
e. $p \leftrightarrow q$

Solution a. If n is divisible by 4, then n is divisible by 2. We prove this by the following: Since n is divisible by 4, n can be written $n = 4m$, where m is an integer. But $4m = 2(2m)$; hence n is divisible by 2.

b. If n is divisible by 2, then n is divisible by 4.
   This statement is false: 14 is divisible by 2, but 14 is not divisible by 4.

c. If n is not divisible by 4, then n is not divisible by 2.
d. If n is not divisible by 2, then n is not divisible by 4.
e. n is divisible by 4 if and only if n is divisible by 2.

Note that (d) appears to be the same as (a), but (c) and (e) are incorrect and can be disproved.

If we think carefully about $p \to q$ and $\sim q \to \sim p$ in the previous exam-ple, we may intuit that the two forms are equivalent. Although we have mentioned the word "equivalent" previously, we will state a pre-cise definition that will permit us to establish the equivalence (or none-quivalence) of various propositional forms, including the ones in the previous example.

> **Definition 5**   If two propositions a and b (they may be simple or compound) have identical truth values for each and every T-F combination, then a and b are *logically equivalent*, and we write $a \equiv b$.

Example 3

Using a truth table, prove the logical equivalence of the statements $p \to q$ and $\sim p \vee q$.

Solution Since we have two letters in our propositions, there are four possible T-F combinations.

p	q	$p \to q$	$\sim p$	$\sim p \vee q$
T	T	T	F	T
T	F	F	F	F
F	T	T	T	T
F	F	T	T	T

The T-F values for the two (boxed) forms are identical; thus the two forms are said to be logically equivalent.

Example 4

Using a truth table, show that the propositions $p \to (q \to r)$ and $(p \to q) \to r$ are not logically equivalent.

Solution Since we have three letters in our propositions, there are $2 \times 2 \times 2 = 8$ possible T-F combinations.

p	q	r	$p \to$	$(q \to r)$	$(p \to q)$	$\to r$
T	T	T	T	T	T	T
T	T	F	F	F	T	F
T	F	T	T	T	F	T
T	F	F	T	T	F	T
F	T	T	T	T	T	T
F	T	F	T	F	T	F
F	F	T	T	T	T	T
F	F	F	T	T	T	F

In this situation the resulting T-F values for the two forms are not identical in two of the cases. Thus the propositional forms are not equivalent. Hence, there is nothing "associative" about conditionals; or, generalized to symbols, $p \to (q \to r) \not\equiv (p \to q) \to r$.

Important variations in the structure of a proposition, in which some, but not all, of the variations are equivalent to the original proposition, occur so often that they are given special names. They are listed below.

$p \to q$	Proposition
$q \to p$	Converse
$\sim p \to \sim q$	Inverse
$\sim q \to \sim p$	Contrapositive

Suppose, for argument's sake, we assume the truth of the proposition

If it rains, then I shall get wet.

We can clarify the wording of the converse, inverse, and contrapositive by writing these three forms in the following way:

Converse   If I get wet, then it must have rained.

Inverse   If it does not rain, then I shall not get wet.

Contrapositive   If I don't get wet, then it must not have rained.

As simple as it must seem, we can explain why the converse and inverse are not logically equivalent to the original proposition (which we assume is true). If it does not rain, it does not necessarily follow that I will not get wet: someone might squirt me with a garden hose. However, it appears that the contrapositive of the proposition says the same thing (in different words) as the proposition itself.

The above example shows that a proposition and its converse are not logically equivalent. In some cases, a converse may happen to be true; however the truth of a converse is independent of the truth of the original proposition. In everyday English usage, we have to be careful to distinguish between a proposition and its converse; this distinction is often confused by intelligent people!

Example 5

We are given any conditional proposition and its converse, inverse, and contrapositive. Using truth tables, establish which of the forms are logically equivalent.

Solution

p	q	$\sim p$	$\sim q$	$p \rightarrow q$	$q \rightarrow p$	$\sim p \rightarrow \sim q$	$\sim q \rightarrow \sim p$
T	T	F	F	T	T	T	T
T	F	F	T	F	T	T	F
F	T	T	F	T	F	F	T
F	F	T	T	T	T	T	T

Two pairs of the propositional forms are equivalent to each other. A proposition is equivalent to its contrapositive, and the converse of a proposition is equivalent to its inverse. Further thought helps us to see that (this sounds confusing at first) the converse and inverse are contrapositives of each other.

Example 6

Which of the following sentences are equivalent to each other? Which are converses of each other?

a. If I eat oysters, then I will get sick.
b. If I eat oysters, then I will not get sick.

   c. If I do not get sick, then I have not eaten oysters.
   d. If I do not get sick, then I have eaten oysters.
   e. If I get sick, then I have not eaten oysters.
   f. If I do not eat oysters, then I will get sick.
   g. All times when I eat oysters are times when I get sick.

Solution The above statements can be translated into algebraic forms by letting p represent "I eat oysters" and q represent "I will get sick." Then we have

   a. $p \to q$
   b. $p \to \sim q$
   c. $\sim q \to \sim p$
   d. $\sim q \to p$
   e. $q \to \sim p$
   f. $\sim p \to q$
   g. $p \to q$

By comparing the propositions in algebraic form and examining the relationships between them, we can determine which are equivalent and which are converses. We see that (a), (c), and (g) are equivalent; (b) and (e) are contrapositives of each other and thus are equivalent; (b) and (d) are converses of each other; (e) and (f) are converses of each other; and (d) and (f) are equivalent to each other. These results may be summarized in the form of a map:

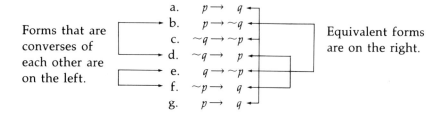

Forms that are converses of each other are on the left.   Equivalent forms are on the right.

          a. $p \to q$
          b. $p \to \sim q$
          c. $\sim q \to \sim p$
          d. $\sim q \to p$
          e. $q \to \sim p$
          f. $\sim p \to q$
          g. $p \to q$

Exercise 1.3   1. Using simple algebraic techniques, demonstrate that the conditional statement "if $4 = 3$, then $12 = 6$" is true.

          2. Let p represent "a triangle is a right triangle" and q represent "$a^2 + b^2 = c^2$." Translate each of the following statements into algebraic propositional forms using the correct conditional or biconditional forms.

             a. If $a^2 + b^2 \neq c^2$, then a triangle is not a right triangle.
             b. If a triangle is a right triangle, then $a^2 + b^2 = c^2$.
             c. If $a^2 + b^2 = c^2$, then a triangle is a right triangle.
             d. It is necessary that $a^2 + b^2 = c^2$ for a triangle to be a right triangle.

    e. It is sufficient that $a^2 + b^2 = c^2$ for a triangle to be a right triangle.

    f. A triangle is a right triangle only if $a^2 + b^2 = c^2$.

    g. A necessary and sufficient condition for a triangle to be a right triangle is that $a^2 + b^2 = c^2$.

3. Using a truth table, show that a conditional statement and its converse are not equivalent.

4. Using a truth table, show that the inverse of a conditional statement is equivalent to the converse of the statement.

5. By means of a truth table, show that the proposition p is logically equivalent to the proposition $p \lor (p \land q)$.

6. Using truth tables, prove that

    a. $p \leftrightarrow q \equiv (\sim p \lor q) \land (p \lor \sim q)$
    b. $\sim(p \to q) \equiv p \land \sim q$
    c. $\sim(p \to q) \neq \sim p \to \sim q$

7. Using eight T-F combinations, establish that

$$(\sim p \to q) \land (\sim r \to \sim q) \equiv \sim [(\sim q \to \sim p) \land (q \to \sim r)]$$

8. Prove the contrapostive of the following statement: If mn is even, then either m or n is even, where m and n are integers. Does this proof establish a proof of the original proposition? Is the converse also true and does it require a separate proof?

9. Which of the following sentences are equivalent to each other? Which are converses of each other?

    a. If I feel happy, then I will dance.
    b. If I do not dance, then I am not happy.
    c. I always dance when I am happy.
    d. I am always happy when I dance.
    e. If I dance, then I am not happy.
    f. If I feel happy, then I will not dance.
    g. If I don't dance, then I'm happy.
    h. If I'm not happy, then I don't dance.
    i. I only dance when I'm happy.
    j. I'm only sad when I'm not dancing.

10. We certainly would want the proposition $p \to (p \lor q)$ to be true under all circumstances. Make a truth table for this proposition and explain why the results help to justify the truth-table definition for $p \to q$ (see p. 9).

1.4 Tautologies, Contradictions, and Important Equivalences

A *tautology* is a compound statement that is true for all possible T-F combinations of the component propositions. The simplest example is $p \vee \sim p$, which is obviously true under all circumstances.

A *contradiction* is a compound statement that is false for all possible T-F combinations of the component propositions. An example is $p \wedge \sim p$, which is always false.

Example 1

Show that $(p \wedge q) \rightarrow (p \vee \sim q)$ is a tautology.

Solution

p	$\wedge$	q	$\rightarrow$	p	$\vee$	$\sim q$
T	T	T	T	T	T	F
T	F	F	T	T	T	T
F	F	T	T	F	F	F
F	F	F	T	F	T	T

Example 2

Show that $(p \rightarrow q) \leftrightarrow (p \wedge \sim q)$ is a contradiction.

Solution

p	$\rightarrow$	q	$\leftrightarrow$	p	$\wedge$	$\sim q$
T	T	T	F	T	F	F
T	F	F	F	T	T	T
F	T	T	F	F	F	F
F	T	F	F	F	F	T

At this stage it must seem to the reader that there ought to be a better way to establish equivalence than by means of truth tables. It certainly does seem redundant to be writing down the same kinds of T-F combinations when certain algebraic forms occur again and again. We will try to circumvent this problem by recognizing and summarizing some of the most important equivalences that occur in propositional logic. Some of these will be used later for simplifying logical arguments, which is important in determining when common implications and uncommon, complex arguments are valid. These equivalences can all be proved using truth tables. In fact some of them are already familiar to us. The student should try to verify some of the less familiar ones by using truth tables. The equivalences are listed and identified either by commonly used names or by purpose.

Table of Equivalent Propositional Forms

Commutative law	$p \vee q \equiv q \vee p$
	$p \wedge q \equiv q \wedge p$
Associative law	$p \vee (q \vee r) \equiv (p \vee q) \vee r$
	$p \wedge (q \wedge r) \equiv (p \wedge q) \wedge r$
Idempotent law	$p \vee p \equiv p$
	$p \wedge p \equiv p$
Complementation law	$p \wedge \sim p \equiv c^*$
	$\sim t^* \equiv c$
	$\sim(\sim p) \equiv p$
	$\sim c \equiv t$
Law of the excluded middle	$p \vee \sim p \equiv t$
Identity law	$p \vee c \equiv p$
	$p \vee t \equiv t$
	$p \wedge c \equiv c$
	$p \wedge t \equiv p$
Absorption law	$p \vee (p \wedge q) \equiv p$
	$p \wedge (p \vee q) \equiv p$
De Morgan's law	$\sim(p \vee q) \equiv \sim p \wedge \sim q$
	$\sim(p \wedge q) \equiv \sim p \vee \sim q$
Equivalent form of a conditional	$(p \rightarrow q) \equiv \sim p \vee q$
Negation of a conditional	$\sim(p \rightarrow q) \equiv p \wedge \sim q$
Equivalent forms for biconditional	$(p \leftrightarrow q) \equiv (p \rightarrow q) \wedge (q \rightarrow p)$
	$\equiv (\sim p \vee q) \wedge (\sim q \vee p)$
Negation of a biconditional	$\sim(p \leftrightarrow q) \equiv (p \wedge \sim q) \vee (q \wedge \sim p)$
Distributive law	$p \vee (q \wedge r) \equiv (p \vee q) \wedge (p \vee r)$
	$p \wedge (q \vee r) \equiv (p \wedge q) \vee (p \wedge r)$

* t represents a tautology and c represents
a contradiction

Example 3

Using the table of equivalent forms, simplify each of the following propositional forms. In each case identify the law(s) utilized.

a. $\sim(\sim p \vee \sim q) \wedge q$
b. $\sim(p \rightarrow \sim q) \wedge \sim q$
c. $\sim p \vee (\sim p \wedge q)$

Solution

a. $\sim(\sim p \vee \sim q) \wedge q$
$\equiv (p \wedge q) \wedge q$ De Morgan's law
$\equiv p \wedge (q \wedge q)$ associative law
$\equiv p \wedge q$ idempotent law

b. $\sim(p \rightarrow \sim q) \wedge \sim q$
$\equiv \sim(\sim p \vee \sim q) \wedge \sim q$ Equivalent form for a conditional

$$\equiv (p \wedge q) \wedge \sim q \qquad \text{De Morgan's law}$$
$$\equiv p \wedge (q \wedge \sim q) \qquad \text{associative law}$$
$$\equiv p \wedge c \qquad \text{complementation law}$$
$$\equiv c \qquad \text{identity law}$$

In this case the compound proposition is a contradiction.

c. $\sim p \vee (\sim p \wedge q)$
$$\equiv (\sim p \vee \sim p) \wedge (\sim p \vee q) \qquad \text{distributive law}$$
$$\equiv \sim p \wedge (\sim p \vee q) \qquad \text{idempotent law}$$

In this case, if the distributive law is applied again, the result is not a simpler version, merely a different one.

In some cases it may be easier to verify a statement using a truth table. However, it is usually more efficient to utilize the laws (or theorems) presented in the table of equivalent forms. You have to be clever, indeed, to prove the absorption law without a truth table, but it can be done. The reader who is challenged by this should by all means attempt it!

Exercise 1.4 1. Using truth tables, prove that the following are tautologies.

a. $[(p \to q) \wedge \sim q] \to \sim p$
b. $[(p \to q) \wedge (q \to r)] \to (p \to r)$

2. Show that the following are *not* tautologies.

a. $[(p \to q) \wedge q] \to p$
b. $[(p \to q) \wedge \sim p] \to \sim q$

3. Using truth tables, prove that the following are contradictions.

a. $p \wedge (\sim p \wedge q)$ \qquad\qquad b. $(p \to q) \wedge (p \wedge \sim q)$

4. Using truth tables prove the following.

a. De Morgan's law   b. Absorption law
c. Distributive law

5. Simplify the following compound propositions using the table of equivalent forms.

a. $(p \vee t) \wedge (p \vee c)$ b. $(p \to q) \vee p$ c. $\sim(\sim p \vee q)$
d. $\sim(p \to q) \wedge q$ e. $p \wedge (\sim p \vee q)$ f. $\sim(p \leftrightarrow q) \vee (q \wedge \sim p)$
g. $(p \vee q) \wedge (p \vee \sim r)$ h. $(p \wedge r) \vee (p \wedge \sim r)$

6. One way the absorption law is listed in the table is in the form $p \vee (p \wedge q) \equiv p$. Using algebraic techniques obtained from the table, prove this law without truth tables. (*Hint:* On the right side, start by letting $p \equiv p \wedge t$ and then letting $t \equiv q \vee t$.)

7. In the distributive law, replace ∧ by the arithmetic operation for multiplication and replace ∨ by the arithmetic operation for addition. If *p, q,* and *r* represent real numbers, which of the statements are always true?

1.5   Arguments—Valid and Fallacious

In everyday life we come up against propositional forms that are good examples of arguments. What we mean by an "argument" will be easier to say after we have looked at a few examples. Consider the following line of reasoning:

> Only marijuana users end up using heroin.
> Therefore if you use marijuana, you will
> end up using heroin.

Even if we accept the first premise as true, the thought process seems somehow incorrect: the conclusion does not inescapably follow from the first premise. We can translate the language of the above into a clearer form. The word "only" obfuscates the meaning of the first premise. The first premise does not correctly translate into "all marijuana users end up using heroin," since the word *only* has the effect of reversing the sense of the proposition. We can, however, translate the statement into "if a person uses heroin, then that person was once a marijuana user." We can simplify the argument by letting *p* represent "you use heroin," and *q* represent "you use marijuana." Then the argument has the following algebraic structure:

$$(p \rightarrow q) \rightarrow (q \rightarrow p)$$

which is a conditional statement that is not true in all cases. We then say the argument is invalid.

In the previous example, we are not questioning the truth or falsity of the premise. We are examining, however, whether or not the entire conditional is true under all circumstances.

We will examine a second example of an argument that is not explicitly stated but that can be inferred from a set of given statements. Consider the following ficticious advertisement:

> Beautiful houses are painted with nonfading paint.
> We know you want your house to be beautiful, so use
> Birch paints. They simply don't fade.

The first statement tells us that if your house is beautiful, then it is painted with nonfading paint. We are also told that Birch paints will not fade. What the argument seems to prove is that if you use a nonfading paint, such as Birch, your house will be beautiful. This may or may not be the case. A dilapidated shack, for example, will not benefit very much from a nice coat of nonfading paint. Algebraically we can write the argument in the following way:

$$[(p \rightarrow q) \wedge q] \rightarrow p$$

where p represents "your house is beautiful" and q represents "your house is painted with nonfading paint." A simple truth table will assist us in proving the argument is invalid.

[(p	→	q)	∧	q]	→	p
T	T	T	T	T	T	T
T	F	F	F	F	T	T
(F)	T	T	T	T	F	F
(F)	T	F	F	F	T	F

Note that the circled letters F tell us that if your house is not beautiful to begin with, it may be for reasons that have little or nothing to do with the fact that the house lacks a coat of nonfading paint. The conditional is therefore false, and the argument is invalid.

At this point it is appropriate to define what we mean by an *argument*.

Definition 6   An *argument* is a conditional that connects the conjunction of a set of statements called premises (or hypotheses) to another statement called the conclusion.

An argument thus has the form

$$[F_1(p, q, r, \ldots) \wedge F_2(p, q, r, \ldots) \wedge \ldots \wedge F_n(p, q, r, \ldots)] \rightarrow G(p, q, r, \ldots)$$

A *valid* argument is one in which the conditional is a tautology: the conclusion inescapably follows from the given set of premises. We agree to nothing *a priori* about the truth or falsity of any of the premises; we are interested rather in the truth of the conditional. If for some T-F combination of the component statements, the conditional is false, the argument is *invalid* or *fallacious*.

We do realize that valid arguments are most fruitful when the premises are, in fact, true. In this circumstance the conclusion is also true. At times, however, it is instructive or amusing to analyze arguments that have false or nonsensical premises to help us focus on the validity of the argument, rather than on the truth or falsity of the conclusion.

Common Forms of Valid Arguments Of the countless valid forms for arguments we shall summarize some of the more common and important ones. The written organization of a form may be notated horizontally, such as $[(p \rightarrow q) \wedge p] \rightarrow q$. When translating verbal arguments, it is also useful to organize the structure vertically, such as

Premise 1	$p \rightarrow q$
Premise 2	p
Conclusion	q

It should be well understood that premises are linked by the conjunction $\wedge$, and when taken together they must yield the conclusion.

Commonly used valid forms for arguments, as well as typical fallacious forms, are listed in the following table.

Table of Arguments

Valid forms		Invalid forms (fallacies)	
$p \rightarrow q$ p q	$p \rightarrow q$ $\sim p \rightarrow \sim q$ $p \leftrightarrow q$	$p \rightarrow q$ q p	$p \vee q$ p q
$p \rightarrow q$ $\sim q$ $\sim p$	$p \leftrightarrow q$ p q	$p \rightarrow q$ $\sim p$ $\sim q$	$p \rightarrow q$ $q \vee r$ $r \rightarrow \sim p$
$p \rightarrow q$ $q \rightarrow r$ $p \rightarrow r$	$p \leftrightarrow q$ q p	$p \rightarrow q$ $r \rightarrow q$ $p \rightarrow r$	$p \rightarrow (q \vee r)$ p r
$p \vee q$ $\sim p$ q	$p \leftrightarrow q$ $\sim p$ $\sim q$	$p \vee q$ p $\sim q$	$p \rightarrow q$ $(q \wedge r) \rightarrow s$ $p \rightarrow s$
$p \wedge q$ p q	$p \leftrightarrow q$ $\sim q$ $\sim p$	$p \rightarrow q$ $p \rightarrow r$ $q \rightarrow r$	$p \rightarrow q$ $\sim p \vee q$ $q \rightarrow p$
$p \rightarrow q$ $q \rightarrow p$ $p \leftrightarrow q$		$p \wedge q$ $\sim p$ q	

We can prove each of the valid forms using a truth table. For each of the invalid forms, it is possible to find some (at least one) combination of T-F values under which the conditional is false.

To analyze simple arguments we use what we know about equivalences, refer to the table, and recognize whether certain of them are valid or fallacious. In other cases, however, we may have to apply to an argument the ultimate test, a complete truth table.

In translating verbal statements into algebraic forms we must be careful with certain confusing word forms. The fact that they are confusing is sometimes used by the unscrupulous to deliberately muddy an illogical argument in order to arrive at a certain desired conclusion. Be careful with the following:

Confusing expressions	Correct translation
"p but q"	$p \wedge q$
"neither p nor q"	$\sim p \wedge \sim q$
"p unless q"	$q \rightarrow \sim p$
"p because q"	$q \rightarrow p$
"p only if q"	$p \rightarrow q$
"p is sufficient for q"	$p \rightarrow q$
"p is necessary for q"	$q \rightarrow p$

Example 1

Analyze the validity of the following argument.

> If this is a good course, then it is worth taking.
> Either the grading is lenient, or the course is
> not worth taking. But the grading is quite severe.
> Therefore this is not a good course.

Solution Let p represent "this is a good course," q represent "it is worth taking," and r represent "the grading is lenient." The argument then has the form:

$$p \rightarrow q$$
$$r \vee \sim q$$
$$\underline{\sim r}$$
$$\sim p$$

Since $r \vee \sim q$ and $\sim r$, it does follow that $\sim q$. The contrapositive of $p \rightarrow q$ is $\sim q \rightarrow \sim p$. Thus

$$\sim q \rightarrow \sim p$$
$$\underline{\sim q}$$
$$\sim p$$

and the argument is valid.

*Alternate
solution*

{[(p	→	q)	∧	(r	∨	~q)]	∧	(~r)}	→	p
T	T	T	T	T	T	F	F	F	T	F
T	T	T	F	F	F	F	F	T	T	F
T	F	F	F	F	T	T	F	F	T	F
T	F	F	F	F	T	T	F	T	T	F
F	T	T	T	T	T	F	F	F	T	T
F	T	T	F	F	F	F	F	T	T	T
F	T	F	T	T	T	T	F	F	T	T
F	T	F	F	F	F	T	F	T	T	T

and the argument is valid.

Example 2

Show that the following argument is invalid:

For the candidate to win, it is sufficient that she carry New York. She will carry New York only if she takes a weak stand on affirmative action programs. She will take a strong stand on affirmative action programs. Therefore she will lose.

Solution Let p represent "the candidate will win," q represent "the candidate will carry New York," and r represent "the candidate will take a weak stand on affirmative action programs."
The argument can be analyzed as follows:

$$q \to p$$
$$q \to r$$
$$\underline{\sim r}$$
$$\sim p$$

We can deduce $\sim q$; we cannot deduce $\sim p$. Thus the argument is invalid. It is also possible to demonstrate that the argument is invalid by showing that for some particular combination of T-F values, the conditional is false.

Example 3

At the time of the burglary, Gordon said he was in the plant. Davis, however, said that Gordon was at home, 20 miles from the plant at that time. If Davis was not lying, then Gordon was not in the plant. On the other hand, if Gordon was lying, then either Davis was telling the truth or Gordon was guilty of the crime. But Gordon was, in fact, lying. Is Gordon guilty of the crime? Prove your contention.

Solution Let p represent "Gordon was in the plant," q represent "Davis was telling the truth," r represent "Gordon was lying," and s represent "Gordon is guilty of the crime." The statements translate algebraically as follows:

$$p$$
$$q \rightarrow \sim p$$
$$r \rightarrow (q \vee s)$$
$$r$$

From the first and second statements, we can properly deduce $\sim q$. From the third and fourth statements, we can properly deduce $(q \vee s)$. Taking these last two statements together, we have

$$\sim q$$
$$q \vee s$$

from which it is a valid conclusion that s is true. Thus Gordon is guilty of the crime.

Example 4

State a correct logical negation (denial) for each of the following statements:

a. If it snows, then the ground will be white.
b. Rectangles have equal diagonals.
c. Only rectangles have equal diagonals.
d. He took a plane and arrived in Newark.
e. If you're happily distracted and you're panting with expectation and excitement, then you have symptoms of infatuation.
f. If we take a trip to Las Vegas, then we'll enjoy it if we don't worry about finances.
g. The square of an integer is even if and only if the integer is even.

Solution a. We can negate a conditional in the following way:

$$\sim(p \rightarrow q) \equiv \sim(\sim p \vee q) \equiv p \wedge \sim q$$

So the negation of the statement could be written as "It will snow and the ground will not be white."
b. Some rectangles do not have equal diagonals.
c. Some figures with equal diagonals are not rectangles.
d. Either he did not take a plane or he did not arrive in Newark.

e.   You are happily distracted, panting with expectation and excitement, and you do not have symptoms of infatuation.

f.   We take a trip to Las Vegas and we don't worry about finances and we don't enjoy it.

g.   Either the square of an integer is even while the integer is odd, or else the square of an integer is odd while the integer is even.

Example 5

What valid conclusion follows from the following set of algebraic premises?

$$p \rightarrow q$$
$$\sim(\sim s \wedge r)$$
$$\sim r \rightarrow \sim q$$
$$\sim s \vee t$$

Solution If we convert all of the statements into conditionals, the statements will appear as follows:

$$p \rightarrow q$$
$$\sim(\sim s \wedge r) \equiv s \vee \sim r \equiv \sim s \rightarrow \sim r \equiv r \rightarrow s$$
$$\sim r \rightarrow \sim q \equiv q \rightarrow r$$
$$\sim s \vee t \equiv s \rightarrow t$$

We then place the premises in the following order:

$$p \rightarrow q$$
$$q \rightarrow r$$
$$r \rightarrow s$$
$$s \rightarrow t$$

We see that $p \rightarrow t$ is a valid conclusion using all of the premises.

Example 6

Prove the following argument is valid by proving the contrapositive of the statement:

$$\text{Hypothesis} \quad \text{Conclusion}$$
$$[(p \wedge q) \rightarrow r] \rightarrow [p \rightarrow (q \rightarrow r)]$$

Solution Negating the conclusion, we write

$$\sim[p \rightarrow (q \rightarrow r)]$$
$$\equiv p \wedge \sim(q \rightarrow r) \qquad \text{negate the first conditional}$$
$$\equiv p \wedge (q \wedge \sim r) \qquad \text{negate the second conditional}$$

$$\equiv (p \wedge q) \wedge \sim r \qquad \text{use the associative property}$$
$$\equiv \sim[\sim(p \wedge q) \vee r] \qquad \text{use De Morgan's law}$$
$$\equiv \sim[(p \wedge q) \rightarrow r] \qquad \text{change the disjunction to}$$
$$\qquad\qquad\qquad\qquad\qquad \text{a conditional}$$

We arrive at the negative of the hypothesis. The contrapositive is established; therefore the original form of the argument is valid.

Exercise 1.5 1. Find (if there is one) a valid conclusion for each of the following arguments.

a. $p \rightarrow q$ b. $p \rightarrow q$ c. $p \rightarrow (q \vee r)$ d. $p \rightarrow (q \wedge r)$

    $q \rightarrow r$ $\sim p$ $\sim q \wedge \sim r$ $\sim r$

2. Explain why the following song is a tautology:

> *Mein Hut, der hat drei Ecken,*
> *Drei Ecken hat mein Hut;*
> *Und hat er nicht drei Ecken,*
> *So ist er nicht mein Hut.*

3. Determine whether each argument is valid or fallacious.

a. $p \rightarrow q$ b. $p \vee q$ c. $p \rightarrow q$

    $q \rightarrow r$ $\sim p$ $\sim p \leftrightarrow q$

    $\sim r$ q q

    $\sim p$

d. $p \vee \sim q$ e. $\sim p$ f. $\sim(p \rightarrow q)$

    $r \vee \sim p$ q $p \rightarrow \sim q$

    $\sim r \rightarrow \sim q$ $p \rightarrow q$

4. Analyze the following advertisement from the point of view of logic. Does the conclusion inevitably follow from the assumed truth of the premises?

If your teeth are decaying, it's either because you haven't brushed regularly or you haven't been visiting your dentist. If you use Dream toothpaste with Floreve according to the manufacturer's label, then you'll brush after each meal every day. Use Dream toothpaste. Then your teeth won't decay!

In problems 5 through 8, determine the validity of the given arguments.

5. If someone is a communist, then that person is also a socialist. Pringle is not a communist.

Pringle is not a socialist.

6. The ground will be white if and only if it snows.
   The ground is not white.
   _____

   It did not snow.

7. Only insecure men are unpopular with women.
   All unhappy men are insecure.
   You are an unhappy man.
   _____

   You are unpopular with women.

8. A woman will get pregnant unless she uses birth control.
   Shirley will either use birth control or else forget the consequences.
   Shirley got pregnant.
   _____

   Shirley forgot the consequences.

9. Either Gordon's sentence will be light or he will implicate Boyle in the crime. But Gordon cannot implicate Boyle without exposing Mrs. Gordon's guilt. In any case Gordon's sentence will be heavy. And if Davis will not be convicted of perjury, then Mrs. Gordon's guilt will not be exposed. Will Davis be convicted of perjury?

10. Find the best conclusion using all the premises.
    Harold Jones has no integrity.
    If a politician is to remain in office, then he or she must have integrity and ability.
    _____

11. Find the best conclusion using all the premises.
    No female students at Yale are traditional.
    Only stupid people never have guilty feelings.
    All nontraditional students are intelligent.
    _____

12. What valid deductions can be made given the following assumed facts.

    a. Either Lord Chesterfield murdered with a gun, the maid murdered with a hatchet, or the butler did it with poison.
    b. If the maid did it with a hatchet, then Lord Chesterfield was lying during the investigation.
    c. If Lord Chesterfield murdered with a gun, the shot would have been heard.
    d. If the groundskeeper was not involved, then the butler definitely did not commit the murder with poison.
    e. Lord Chesterfield was telling the truth.
    f. No shot was heard.

13. Use a contrapositive argument to verify the following valid argument:

    Hypothesis   Conclusion

    $$[p \to (q \to r)] \to [(p \land q) \to r]$$

14. Comment on the following argument.

    If the radio won't work on your car, then either the battery is dead or the speaker wire is disconnected or an internal radio part is burned out or shorted. The lights on the car do work. Now if the speaker wire is disconnected or an internal part of the radio is burned out, then the test meter will read no resistance. The meter reads resistance. So if an internal part of the radio is not shorted, then the meter isn't operating properly, because the radio isn't working.

15. Prove each of the following biconditional arguments of the type *reductio ad absurdum*.

    a. $(p \to q) \leftrightarrow [(p \land \sim q) \to (r \land \sim r)]$ b. $p \leftrightarrow [\sim p \to (q \land \sim p)]$

16. Express each proposition in terms of disjunction and negation symbols only.

    a. $p \to (p \lor q)$ b. $[(p \to q) \land \sim q] \to \sim p$
    c. $[(p \land q) \land p] \to q$ d. $\{[p \to (q \land r \land s)] \land \sim q\} \to \sim p$

*17. Analyze the argument.

    If more work results in a higher salary, then the contract will be signed. There will either be no trainees or additional time will be allowed. It is not the case that there will be more work and no trainees. If we do not have higher salaries, then there will be additional time allowed. Therefore, the contract will be signed.

18. Assume that the following statements are true.

    Some people are artistic.
    Any person is either artistic or unartistic.
    Any person is either emotional or unemotional.
    All artistic people are emotional.

    State whether, on these assumptions, the assertions below are true, false, or undetermined. Prove your answer in each case.

    a. All unartistic people are unemotional.
    b. Some emotional people are artistic.
    c. None but unartistic people are unemotional.
    d. Any emotional person is not unartistic.

19. Answer questions (a) and (b) with respect to the views attributed to George and Esta below. Justify your answers.

    George denies that no sincere person is a politician.
    Esta denies that only sincere persons are politicians.
    George and Esta, however, agree that some politicians are sincere.

    a. Is George consistent in holding the views attributed to him?
    b. Is Esta consistent in holding the views attributed to her?

20. Comment on this advertisement: "Beautiful women dress beautifully and yes they know how to smell beautiful too. Use Rafael cologne."

Special Problems in Logic

> Syllogism is of necessary use, even to the lovers of truth, to show them the fallacies that are often concealed in florid, witty or involved discourses.
>
> John Locke

2.1 Logic Applied to Switching Networks

We have all been in houses in which there is a light fixture illuminating a stairway. The light fixture is generally controlled by two switches, one located at the bottom of the stairway and another at the top. Before walking upstairs we might flip the downstairs switch to position A and turn the light on; when we arrive upstairs we may flip the upstairs switch to position A and turn the light off. If a second person walks up the stairs and flips the downstairs switch to position B, she will turn the light on again; when she reaches the top of the stairs the light will go off if she flips the upstairs switch to position B.

How is it that in position A a single switch sometimes has the light on and sometimes off? Remarkably, the theory of propositional logic developed in the previous chapter can be applied to switching networks and will help to solve this and related problems. Switching networks are also one of the essential technical components of digital computers.

A switching network is a set of wires and switches connecting two terminal points A and B. Some combinations of open (off) switches and closed (on) switches will permit current to flow from A to B; other combinations will not.

There are four basic terms which should be understood at the outset: switch open, switch closed, series circuit, and parallel circuit. These are shown in the diagram below in Figure 2.1.

We can practically guess at a correct association between simple switching networks and the logic of propositions. In (a), if we associate a statement with switch p in the open position, we can say the statement is false (current will not flow). In (b), if we associate a statement with switch p in the closed position, we say the statement is true (current will flow). In the series circuit (c), the compound statement $p \land q$ is true, and current will flow if and only if switches p and q are both closed. In the parallel circuit (d), the compound statement $p \lor q$ is true, and current will flow if and only if either switch p or switch q is closed.

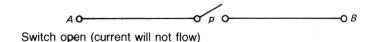

Switch open (current will not flow)

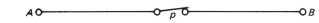

Switch closed (current will flow)

Series circuit (current will flow if and only if both switches p and q are closed)

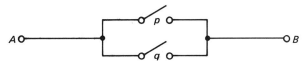

Parallel circuit (current will flow if and only if either switch p or q is closed)

There is also an analogy between certain circuits and logical tautologies and contradictions. Suppose we have two switches in parallel, built so that when one is open the other is closed and vice versa. We label the switches p and $\sim p$ in the following figure.

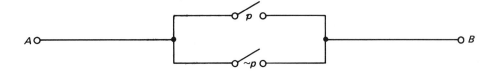

If either p or $\sim p$ is open, current will flow. The corresponding logical statement is $p \lor \sim p$, which we recall is the tautology of the excluded middle. It is always true for every T-F combination.

It is possible to show that current will flow in a network for every closed-open switch combination if and only if the corresponding logical compound statement is a tautology. Current will never flow in a network for every closed-open switch combination if and only if the corresponding logical compound statement is a contradiction. The following illustrates a simple contradiction:

Current in the network will never flow because when p is closed $\sim p$ is open, and when $\sim p$ is closed p is open. We verify this with a truth table:

p	$\wedge$	$\sim p$
T	F	F
F	F	T

The compound proposition is never true because when p is true $\sim p$ is false, and when $\sim p$ is true p is false.

We can associate the logical "and" with the series circuit, and the logical "or" with the parallel circuit. Since conditionals and biconditionals can be written in terms of disjunctions or conjunctions, it is possible to validate arguments by designing associated switching circuits!

Example 1

Under what conditions will current in the following circuit flow? Test your answer by means of a truth table. Can you design another equivalent circuit?

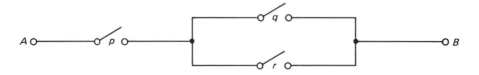

Solution Note that p is in series with the parallel circuit involving q and r. It is clear that current will flow if and only if p is closed and either q or r is closed. This means that if p is open or if q and r are both open, current will not flow.

We can further analyze the situation by using the associated logical statement $p \wedge (q \vee r)$ and examine its corresponding truth table.

p	∧	(q	∨	r)
T	T	T	T	T
T	T	T	T	F
T	T	T	F	T
T	F	F	F	F
F	F	T	T	T
F	F	T	T	F
F	F	F	T	T
F	F	F	F	F

Current will flow if and only if *p* is closed (true)
and either *q* or *r* is closed (true).

Equivalently, we can use the distributive property

$$p \wedge (q \vee r) \equiv (p \wedge q) \vee (p \wedge r)$$

to obtain an alternate interpretation, that current will flow if and only if (i) *p* and *q* are closed or (ii) *p* and *r* are closed. This means that the original network is equivalent to the following circuit.

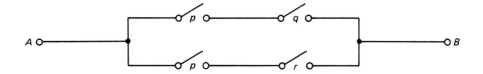

Example 2

Simplify the network shown. Verify using a truth table.

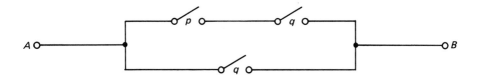

Solution We have $(p \wedge q) \vee q \equiv q$ by the absorption property. Therefore the circuit is equivalent to

Note that the column under the last *q* is identical to the column under the disjunction in the following truth table.

(p	∧	q)	∨	q
T	T	T	T	T
T	F	F	F	F
F	F	T	T	T
F	F	F	F	F

Example 3

Using the algebra of propositions, simplify the following network.

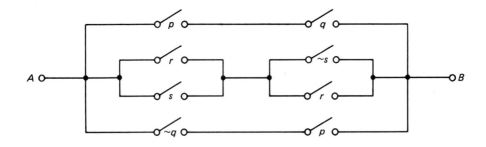

Solution $(p \wedge q) \vee [(r \vee s) \wedge (r \vee \sim s)] \vee (\sim q \wedge p)$

$\equiv (p \wedge \sim q) \vee (p \wedge q) \vee [(r \vee s) \wedge (r \vee \sim s)]$ commutative laws

$\equiv p \wedge (q \vee \sim q) \vee [r \vee (s \wedge \sim s)]$ distributive laws

$\equiv (p \wedge t) \vee (r \vee c)$ excluded middle and complementation laws

$\equiv p \vee r$ identity laws

Thus the network shown is equivalent to a very simple circuit:

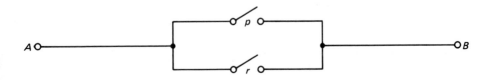

Example 4

Convert the following valid argument into a propositional form involving conjunctions and disjunctions. Draw a network and explain the connection between a valid argument and the corresponding circuit.

$$[(p \rightarrow q) \wedge \sim q] \rightarrow \sim p$$

Solution Recall that a conditional can be converted into an equivalent form using $(p \rightarrow q) \equiv \sim p \lor q$. Then all four of the following expressions are equivalent:

(i) $[(p \rightarrow q) \land \sim q] \rightarrow \sim p$
(ii) $[(\sim p \lor q) \land \sim q] \rightarrow \sim p$
(iii) $\sim [(\sim p \lor q) \land \sim q] \lor \sim p$
(iv) $[(p \land \sim q) \lor q] \lor \sim p$

The last statement can be translated into the following network:

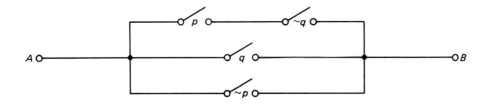

Careful thought demonstrates that current must always flow through this circuit, i.e., the argument is a tautology and is valid. This means that statement (iv) could be simplified algebraically to the tautology letter t, and the circuit above could be redesigned as a simple wire that would always allow current to pass.

Exercise 2.1 1. Design a simple switching network that will turn a light on if at least one of three switches p, q, and r is closed.

2. Convert the following network into an algebraic statement:

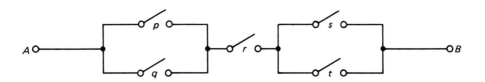

3. Translate the following algebraic statement into a network:

$$[p \land (p \lor \sim q)] \lor (\sim p \land q)$$

4. Change the biconditional $p \leftrightarrow q$ to an equivalent compound statement using conjunctions and disjunctions. Draw a network corresponding to $p \leftrightarrow q$. Under what conditions will the current flow through the network?

5.   Simplify the following network to only two switches:

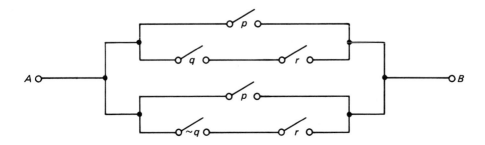

6.   Show that the following two networks are equivalent:

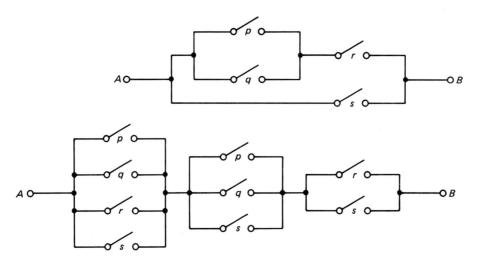

7.   Design a switching network that could be used to verify the following argument. Does the network show the argument is valid?

$$[(p \rightarrow q) \wedge p] \rightarrow q$$

8.   Can you show that the first network is equivalent to the second
"bridge" circuit?

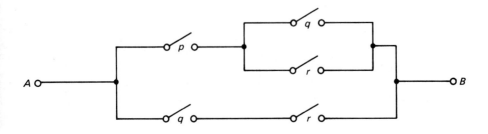

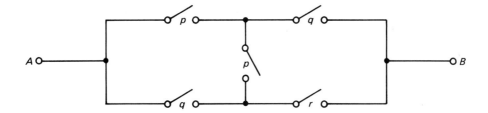

9. At the bottom of such a stairway as we described in the beginning of this chapter is a switch p (which also controls switch $\sim p$). At the top of the stairway is a switch q (also controlling $\sim q$). Find a switching network using p, $\sim p$, q, and $\sim q$ that can control one light from two different directions. *Hint:* we want the following result:

p	q	$\sim p$	$\sim q$	Network
T	T	F	F	F (open)
T	F	F	T	T (closed)
F	T	T	F	T (closed)
F	F	T	T	F (open)

2.2 Categorical Statements and the Syllogisms of Lewis Carroll

There are arguments, commonly used, we are not equipped to handle using only the propositional algebra previously developed. We can not, for example, translate the statement

(i)   Some citizens are independent thinkers

into the form of a conditional because reference is made to an *indefinite* number of citizens (the statement does not assert that all citizens are independent thinkers). We could diagram statement (i) as follows:

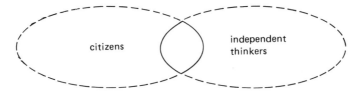

If the statement had been written as "all citizens are independent thinkers," we could have translated this into an equivalent conditional form

(ii)   If a person is a citizen, then that person is an independent thinker.

A diagram for statement (ii) could be drawn as follows:

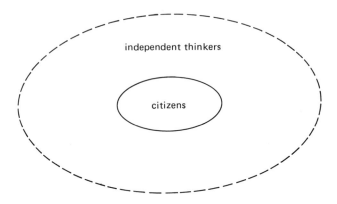

independent thinkers

citizens

Statements (i) and (ii) are not equivalent. Statement (i) is referred to as an *existential* (or particular) form because it asserts that there exists at least one citizen who is an independent thinker. Statement (ii), however, says nothing about the existence of citizens. It merely says that if someone is a citizen, then that person is an independent thinker.

We shall discuss four basic types of statements. They are listed below with respective diagrams and designations. The diagrams are slight modifications of those used by the Swiss mathematician, Leonard Euler.

Four basic categorical statements

Positive universal	All *A*'s are *B*'s.	*B* *A*
Positive existential	Some *A*'s are *B*'s (there exists at least one *A* which is a *B*).	*A* *B*
Negative existential	Some *A*'s are not *B*'s (there exists at least one *A* which is not a *B*).	*A* *B*
Negative universal	No *A*'s are *B*'s.	*A* *B*

In the two existential forms, a pair of overlapping circles represents either an indefinite partial inclusion or an indefinite partial exclusion. Solid circles represent all of the elements in a term (such terms are called *distributed*), and dotted or partially dotted circles represent indefinite numbers of the elements of a term (these are called *undistributed* terms). In solving a logical problem diagrammatically, we shall not be concerned with identifying distributed terms, but we shall use the concept later when we look at rules for syllogisms that do not depend on diagrams. We shall therefore draw all subsequent diagrams with solid circles.

A Lewis Carroll Puzzle Syllogism Solved by Euler Diagrams   Lewis Carroll, author of *Alice's Adventures in Wonderland,* was the Reverand Charles Lutwidge Dodgson, a mathematical lecturer of Christ Church. In *Symbolic Logic and the Game of Logic,* he included a number of puzzles and syllogisms that possess some of the madness that characterized the book about Alice. We will present a complete solution to the following problem.

Example 1

Find the "best" conclusion, that is, the one that utilizes all of the premises.

> p No ducks waltz.
> q No officers ever decline to waltz.
> r All my poultry are ducks.

Solution   By premise p, the set of ducks is totally disjoint from the set of waltzers:

By q, the set of officers cannot be outside the set of waltzers. Therefore it is inside the set of waltzers, and we have:

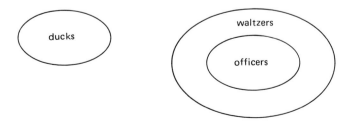

By *r* the set of "my poultry" is contained within the set of ducks, and we have:

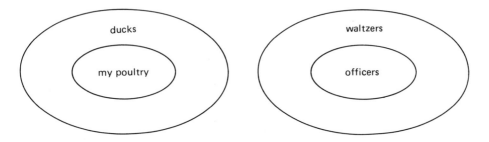

Thus the set of "my poultry" is totally disjoint from the set of officers. The best conclusion is, "None of my poultry are officers" or, equivalently, "no officers are my poultry."

It is not silly to consider nonsensical syllogisms such as the one above. When handling such puzzles we are forced into considering the *structure* of the argument. We are not side-tracked by the truth or falsity of the statements, and we are not aided or hindered by whether or not the argument seems plausible. If we develop the ability to solve nonsense syllogisms, we will improve our skills in recognizing more realistic arguments and their validity or fallaciousness.

It would be helpful if we considered a few arguments containing existential statements to see how they can be solved using diagrams. We should point out that any and all diagrams that are consistent with the premises must also fit the conclusion if the argument is to be valid. If we can draw one picture consistent with the premises and conclusion and also draw a second picture consistent with the premises and *not* consistent with the conclusion, the argument or syllogism is invalid.

Example 2

All four-footed beasts are animals, and some animals are carnivorous. It must follow that some four-footed beasts are carnivorous. (If this argument is spoken forcefully, it "sounds" valid.) Prove that it is invalid.

Solution Rewrite the problem in syllogistic form and draw a diagram.

> All four-footed beasts are animals.
> Some animals are carnivorous.
> _____
> Some four-footed beasts are carnivorous.

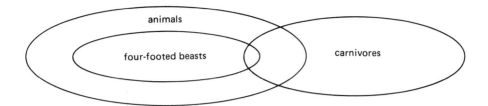

The diagram, consistent with both premises, shows that the conclusion does not hold. Thus the argument is *invalid.* One might object to this result by observing that the following diagram

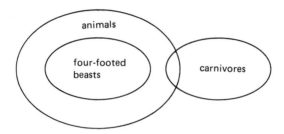

justifies the conclusion and is consistent with the premises. We would answer that, in every possible diagram, the conclusion must follow in order for the argument to be valid. Only inescapable conclusions are valid conclusions.

Example 3

All tulips are beautiful, and some rocks are not beautiful. Therefore some rocks are not tulips. (This argument may seem whimsical and, to some readers, invalid.) Prove that it is valid.

Solution   All tulips are beautiful.
Some rocks are not beautiful.
_____

Some rocks are not tulips.

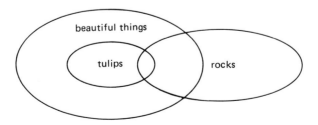

The diagram shows the argument is valid because, no matter how we draw the set corresponding to rocks, there must exist at least one rock outside the class of beautiful things. Thus there must be at least one rock that is not a tulip. (The realistic fact that no rocks are *ever* tulips is irrelevant to the validity of the argument.)

Rules for Determining the Validity of Syllogisms Having Two Premises Many syllogisms can be proved invalid without the aid of diagrams with an alternate method for proving validity. To understand the rules for this method and to apply them, we must recognize in the premises, the *distributed* terms, the terms referring to entire classes of objects (see p. 41). These are circled below in the four basic forms.

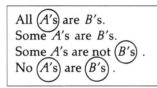

With these terms and the following five rules we can determine whether or not a syllogism is valid. If any one rule is violated, the syllogism is invalid.

Rules for syllogisms (two premises)

1. If one premise is negative, the conclusion must be negative.
2. If both premises are negative, there is no valid conclusion.
3. If both premises are universal, the conclusion must be universal.
4. The term common to both premises must be distributed at least once.
5. If a term is distributed in the conclusion, it must be distributed in the premises.

Example 4

All cats are animals.
Some cats are dogs.

Some dogs are animals.

Solution Valid since all the rules are satisfied.

Example 5

All cowboys are people.
No ranchers are cowboys.

No people are ranchers.

Solution Invalid since the term "people" is distributed in the conclusion but not in the premises.

Example 6

No children adore monsters.
No ogres adore children.

No ogres adore monsters.

Solution Invalid since there can be no valid conclusion if both premises are negative.

Example 7

All four-footed beasts are animals.
Some animals are carnivorous.

Some four-footed beasts are carnivorous.

Solution Invalid because the term "animals" is common to both premises but is undistributed in both.

Example 8

No old misers are cheerful.
Some old misers are thin people.

Some cheerful people are not thin.

Solution Invalid because the term "thin people" is distributed in the conclusion but not in either premise.

Example 9

All my sisters have colds.
No one can sing who has a cold.

Some of my sisters can't sing.

Solution Invalid, since if both premises are universal the conclusion must be universal.

In government, law, philosophy, mathematics, and political science, it is often important to be able to interpret language precisely. Sometimes this means being able to convert statements into various equivalent forms or being able to write a precise negation or denial of a statement. To clarify the logic of a detailed and lengthy argument it may be necessary to change the form and sequence of various categorical statements. Unscrupulous people may alter the forms of statements and try to create shades of meaning which the reader or listener will infer but which the author has no intention of explicitly stating with thoroughness and clarity. For these reasons, we are including a table of equivalent forms for statements. The table can also be used to solve the difficult syllogisms and puzzles appearing at the end of this section.

Useful forms of categorical statements

Statement	Equivalent forms	Negation (or denial)
All *A*'s are *B*'s.	All non-*B*'s are non-*A*'s. No *A*'s are non-*B*'s. No non-*B*'s are *A*'s.	Some *A*'s are not *B*'s.
Some *A*'s are *B*'s.	Some *B*'s are *A*'s. Some *A*'s are not non-*B*'s. Some *B*'s are not non-*A*'s.	No *A*'s are *B*'s.
Some *A*'s are not *B*'s.	Some non-*B*'s are not non-*A*'s. Some *A*'s are non-*B*'s. Some non-*B*'s are *A*'s.	All *A*'s are *B*'s.
No *A*'s are *B*'s.	No *B*'s are *A*'s. All *A*'s are non-*B*'s. All *B*'s are non-*A*'s.	Some *A*'s are *B*'s.

The denial of a universal statement is an existential statement, and the denial of an existential statement is a universal statement. We should also mention two tricky word forms that occur in our language because we must be very careful with their use.

Two tricky word forms

Statement	Correct translation
Only *A*'s are *B*'s. (Also expressed, None but *A*'s are *B*'s.	All *B*'s are *A*'s.
All except *A*'s are *B*'s. (Also expressed, All but *A*'s are *B*'s.	All non-*A*'s are *B*'s, *and* No *B*'s are *A*'s.

Example 10

Which statements are equivalent and which are contradictory?

   a. Only cruel people are intolerant.
   b. All non-cruel people are tolerant.
   c. Some intolerant people are not cruel.
   d. None but intolerant people are cruel.
   e. No cruel people are tolerant.
   f. All cruel people are intolerant.
   g. Some cruel people are not intolerant.

Solution Letting C represent "cruel people" and T represent "tolerant people," the statements translate as follows:

   a. All non-T's are C's $\equiv$ All non-C's are T's.
   b. All non-C's are T's.
   c. Some non-T's are non-C's $\equiv$ Some non-C's are not T's.
   d. All C's are non-T's.
   e. No C's are T's $\equiv$ All C's are non-T's.
   f. All C's are non-T's.
   g. Some C's are not non-T's.

We see that (a) and (b) are equivalent and (c) is their denial. Also (d), (e), and (f) are equivalent and (g) is their denial.

Example 11

The following exceptive legal statement is actually a conjunction of two distinct statements. State each of them clearly and distinctly.

All verbal contracts except the ones unverifiable by the party of the second will be considered unenforceable by the United States Government.

Solution Since "All except A's are B's "translates into the two statements (i) "All non-A's are B's," and (ii) "No A's are B's," we have for our solution

All verbal contracts verifiable by the party of the second will be considered enforceable by the United States Government.

No verbal contracts unverifiable by the party of the second will be considered enforceable by the United States Government.

Exercise 2.2 In problems 1–8, determine if the arguments below are valid or invalid using Euler diagrams.

1. Healthy stomachs have neutralized stomach acids.
   Tummy Tabs will neutralize stomach acids.

   Tummy Tabs produce healthy stomachs.

2. All pigs are fat.
   No one fed on soup is fat.

   No one fed on soup is a pig.

3. All these flowers are red.
   Some geraniums are red.

   Some flowers are geraniums.

4. No firemen are dreaded by children.
   All dentists are dreaded by children.

   No dentists are firemen.

5. It is false that some metals are scarce.
   Gold is a metal.

   Gold is not scarce.

6. No quadrilaterals are triangles.
   Some quadrilaterals are parallelograms.

   Some parallelograms are not triangles.

7. All reptiles are animals.
   Some reptiles are not fish.

   Some fish are not animals.

8. All rational numbers are real.
   No integers are irrational.

   Some integers must be real.

9. Establish the validity (or invalidity) of Problems 1–8 (above) by using the rules for syllogisms found on page 44.

10. Explain why the following nonstandard syllogism is invalid.

    > A good number of government employees are persons capable of being bribed. Barton Carfagno is a government employee. Therefore it is quite likely that he is capable of being bribed.

11. For each of the following sets of premises, supply a valid conclusion

    a. Some men are wise.
       No wise person is dishonest.

       ---

    b. All crows are black.
       Some crows can fly.

       ---

12. Which statements are equivalent to each other? Which statements are negations of each other?

    a. Only men capable of true intimacy are husbands of happy women.

> Anything that arrests cancerous tumors in a sample
> of white mice will also arrest my malignancy,

and the rules for syllogisms (or an Euler diagram) will verify the validity of the argument. However, the doubtfulness of the assumed premise makes us doubt the truth of the conclusion even though the argument is valid.

Example 3

Communism is immoral, and this is communism!

The conclusion "this is immoral" is, in this example, left unexpressed. The value of such types of enthymemes for purposes of innuendo are well known to demagogues and some politicians. This particular enthymeme, however, is considered valid as the diagram that follows will show.

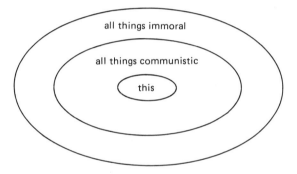

Example 4

All crooks end up behind bars. Therefore John will end up behind bars.

The implied premise, that John is a crook, might have seemed altogether too rude and nasty for it to have been stated explicitly. Since we find that the inferred premise would complete a valid argument, the enthymeme is valid.

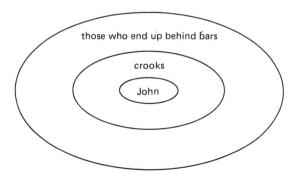

Example 5

People wanting to lower their primal urges always fail to eat oysters. I notice with some amusement that you've been avoiding oysters. . . .

The humor in this sly "put-down" may be fine, but the logic is terrible. Implied is that the avoidance of oysters is being done because "You want to lower your primal urges." Consider the Euler diagram:

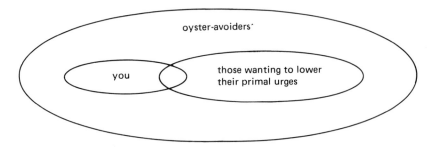

The diagram, consistent with the premises, indicates that the class "you" may not necessarily lie within the class of "those wanting to lower their primal urges." The enthymeme is therefore invalid.

Exercise 2.3   For each of the following enthymemes, determine the implied premise or conclusion that is missing. Then determine whether the enthymeme is valid or invalid. Use Euler diagrams to clarify your thinking.

1. You stole a wheelchair from an old lady! No one but a born thief would steal a wheelchair from an old lady.
2. Joe's TV set is broken again. Oh well, you get what you pay for.
3. When you had those new lenses fitted to your glasses, your reading skills improved. So I'm going to the optometrist too.
4. Democrats are always causing wars. So Carter will get us into a war before his term is out.
5. Communists base their theories on the writings of Karl Marx. I notice that so-and-so has been reading *Das Kapital*. Need I say more?
6. This medicine will cure my cough. Look, it cured my daughter's cough!
7. Women locked into dependency relationships with their boyfriends always end up unhappy. And let me tell you, Brenda is locked in. . . .

3

Sets

> God created infinity, and man, unable to under-
> stand infinity, had to invent finite sets.
> Gian-Carlo Rota

3.1 Introduction—Subsets and Equality of Sets

In Chapter 1 we examined an algebraic method for analyzing propositional logic, and in Chapter 2 we widened our view of logical thinking
by studying valid inferences made from categorical statements. In this
chapter we shall further extend our knowledge of categories or classes
or, in the language of this chapter, sets. Since we will develop an
algebraic system for sets just as we did for logic, it should not be
surprising that both systems are very closely related. We shall see
that there is a direct parallel between the connectives $\vee$, $\wedge$, $\sim$ and
the set-algebraic operations $\cup$, $\cap$, ', respectively.

It is not our purpose to present a study of sets that will touch on
foundations of modern mathematics. Rather we are introducing the
topic of sets to clarify certain areas to be studied in subsequent chapters.
A knowledge of sets will also help to explain the terminology and
notations for new concepts that might otherwise be confusing. Sets
will also be applied to survey analysis, an interesting and basic use
for set theory.

> A *set* is any well-defined collection of distinct objects.
> An object in a set is called a member or *element* of the set.

It is important to recognize that before anything significant can be
accomplished with a particular set it must be possible to determine
whether or not an object belongs to it. It is in this sense that we
mean a set must be "well-defined." It would not be possible to speak
meaningfully, for example, of the set of all elderly people even though
we have a vague idea about this classification. On the other hand,
the set of all individuals who have attained the age of 70 is a precisely
defined set because it is clear that a person is either a member of the
set or is not.

On occasion we encounter formulations that yield sets having no
members at all. The set of real numbers whose squares are negative

is such an example. Such sets are referred to as empty sets (or *null* sets) and are denoted by the Greek letter φ.

Generally we will use capital letters to designate sets and lower-case letters to designate elements of a set. Curved braces are used to surround the formulation of a set. Thus we can write

$$S = \{4, 5, 6, 7, 8, 9\}$$

as the formulation for the set of positive integers between 4 and 9 inclusive. By writing $6 \in S$ we mean that 6 belongs to the set S, and by writing $3 \notin S$ we mean that 3 does not belong to the set S. Two sets are considered equal (and we write $=$) if they have identical elements. Notice that it would be correct to write the above set S by utilizing an inequality:

$$\{x \mid 4 \leq x \leq 9, x \text{ is an integer}\}$$

this is read as the set of all elements x such that $4 \leq x \leq 9$, where x is an integer. Thus the vertical bar means "such that."

It is possible to specify sets having an infinite number of elements, such as the set of all even positive integers:

$$\{2, 4, 6, 8, \ldots\}$$

where the three dots after the last comma mean "and so forth."

Of course we do not wish to imply that all sets must have elements that are numbers. Quite often we will utilize sets that do not have numerical elements. We could refer, for example, to the set of 30-day months during the year:

$$\{\text{September, April, June, November}\}$$

A certain difficulty sometimes arises when we talk about the set of elements that are *outside* a particular set. In such cases usually, but not always, there is an implied limitation on the type of elements to be considered. Suppose, for example, we consider the set

$$T = \{a, e, i, o, u\}$$

and then we specify the set

$$T' = \{x \mid x \text{ is not a member of } T\}$$

It is not clear what T' refers to. Literally (perhaps fatuously) T' includes not only consonants but also donuts, trees, philosophies, galaxies and everything that is not an alphabetic vowel. Certainly the discussion is getting out of hand. To prevent ridiculously all-inclusive sets (which will not be useful anyway) from arising, there is usually a universal set, denoted U, that specifies limits of a discussion. Sometimes it is implied, but generally it is stated explicitly in order to avoid ambiguities. Thus it probably would be an improvement to write T' as follows:

$$T' = \{x \mid x \in T, x \text{ is a letter of the alphabet}\}$$

There will be cases, however, in which the student will have to use good judgment as regards an implied universal set for discussion.

Example 1

Which of the following are well-defined sets and which are not?

a. The set of superior students at this school
b. The set of all human beings hatched from eggs
c. The set of good-looking students in this class
d. The set of all cheap single men in the USA
e. The set of all single men who would not spend more than $5 on any date
f. The set of all women alive whose first name is Yvonne
g. The set of numbers between 6 and 10
h. The set of all even numbers divisible by 3

Solution
a. Not well-defined
b. Well-defined and empty
c. Not well-defined
d. Not well-defined
e. Well-defined
f. Well-defined
g. Not well-defined since it is unclear what kind of "numbers" are being considered
h. Well-defined

Example 2

Express each of the following sets in a different way:

a. $\{1, 2, 3, \ldots, 9, 10\}$
b. $\{x \mid x \text{ is an even integer between 1 and 17}\}$
c. $\{n \mid 5 \leq n < 10, n \text{ is an integer}\}$
d. $\{n \mid n^2 < 9, n \text{ is an integer}\}$
e. $\{p \mid p \text{ is a planet closer to the sun than the Earth}\}$
f. $\{n \mid n = 2m, m \text{ is a positive integer}\}$
g. $\{1, 5, 9, 13, 17, \ldots\}$

Solution a. $\{n \mid 1 \leqslant n \leqslant 10, n \text{ is an integer}\}$
      b. $\{2, 4, 6, 8, 10, 12, 14, 16\}$
      c. $\{5, 6, 7, 8, 9\}$
      d. $\{-2, -1, 0, 1, 2\}$
      e. $\{\text{Mercury, Venus}\}$
      f. $\{2, 4, 6, 8, \ldots\} = \{n \mid n \text{ is a positive even integer}\}$
      g. $\{n \mid n = 4m + 1, m \text{ is a non-negative integer}\}$

Example 3

Explain why the sets $S' = \{x \mid x \notin S\}$, $T' = \{x \mid x \notin T\}$, and $V' = \{x \mid x \notin V\}$ are not meaningful, where

$$S = \{\#, \&, \$, *\}$$
$$T = \{\text{Mars, 5, this piece of Halvah}\}$$
$$V = \{x \mid x \text{ is a number utilizing the symbol } 0\}$$

Solution In each set the universe of discussion must be specified in order for it to be clear which elements are not members of S, T, or V.

Subsets and Equality of Sets Suppose we have the following sets given: $A = \{a, b, c, f, z\}$, $B = \{a, b, c, d, e, f, y, z\}$, and $U = \{x \mid x \text{ is a letter of the alphabet.}\}$ Notice that every member of set A is also a member of set B. If the set U is regarded as the universe of discussion, then in *any* set of letters all members would also be contained in U. In cases such as these we say that A is a *subset* of B. Thus we have the following definition:

> **Definition 1**   Set A is a *subset* of set B if every element of set A is also contained in set B; in such cases we write $A \subset B$.

We shall note that in order to prove that a set A is not a subset of B, it will be necessary and sufficient to produce one element of A that is not in B. In this context, the empty set ϕ is a subset of any set since we cannot produce at least one element of set ϕ that is not in that set. We also note that any set is a subset of itself, and any set is a subset of the universe of discussion.

Example 4

List all of the possible subsets of the set $\{1, 2, 3\}$.

Solution There are eight possible subsets: $\{1\}$, $\{2\}$, $\{3\}$, $\{1, 2\}$, $\{1, 3\}$, $\{2, 3\}$, $\{1, 2, 3\}$, and ϕ.

Example 5

Consider the well-known mathematical sets given below. Which sets are subsets of each other?

Set of natural numbers $N = \{1, 2, 3, 4, \ldots\}$

Set of integers $I = \{\ldots, -3, -2, -1, 0, 1, 2, 3, \ldots\}$

Set of rational numbers $Q = \left\{ \dfrac{a}{b} \,\middle|\, a \text{ and } b \text{ are integers, } b \neq 0 \right\}$

Set of real numbers $R = \left\{ x \,\middle|\, \begin{array}{l} x \text{ is a number corresponding} \\ \text{to a point on a number line} \end{array} \right\}$

Solution   It is obvious that all natural numbers are integers. Since every integer n can be represented as the quotient of two integers (for example, $n/1$), all integers are rational. Finally we realize that all rational numbers correspond to points on a real number line; hence all rational numbers are real numbers. Therefore, we have the subset relationships

$$N \subset I \subset Q \subset R$$

The following diagrams may help to illustrate them:

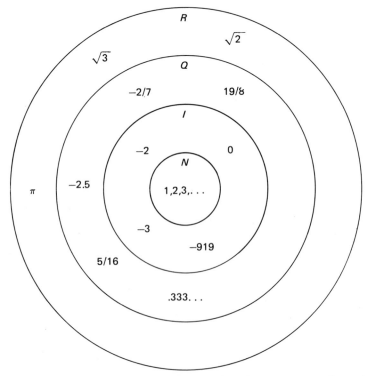

Set diagram for the real number system (illustrative elements shown in each set)

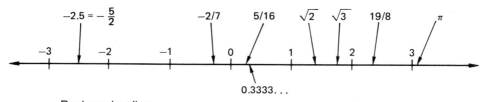

Real number line

Definition 2   Sets A and B are *equal* (written $A = B$), if $A \subset B$ and $B \subset A$.

It is clear that two sets can be equal if and only if they are identical.

Example 6

Are the following two sets equal or not?

$$A = \{x \mid x \text{ is a rectangle}\}$$

$$B = \{y \mid y \text{ is a quadrilateral with equal diagonals}\}$$

Solution Clearly every rectangle is a quadrilateral with equal diagonals; hence $A \subset B$. However, we can construct an isosceles trapezoid with equal diagonals that is not a rectangle; hence, $B \not\subset A$. Therefore $A \neq B$. Such a figure is shown below.

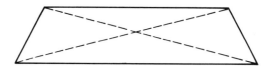

Theorems About Subsets Certain useful and basic properties of sets that are capable of proof are given here. Except for Theorem 4, these statements are so obvious that we will omit any formal proofs. The justification for Theorem 4 is contained in the last section.

Theorem 1	If $A \subset B$ and $B \subset C$, then $A \subset C$.
Theorem 2	For any set A, $A \subset A$.
Theorem 3	Given any set A and its associated universal set U, $A \subset U$.
Theorem 4	For any set A, $\phi \subset A$.

Exercise 3.1 1. Which of the following sets are well-defined and which are not?
   a. The set of people who are nice
   b. The set of living American teenagers
   c. The set of great presidents of the United States
   d. The set of individuals with socialist inclinations
   e. The set of persons who are obese
   f. The set of persons who weigh more than 200 pounds and who are less than 5'8" tall
   g. The set of rectangles with unequal diagonals

2. Specify a reasonable universal set that might be implied by each of the following set specifications.

   a. $\{2, 4, 6, 8, \ldots\}$
   b. The set of individuals who can play the "Revolutionary Etude" on the piano
   c. The set of planets closer to the sun than the Earth
   d. The set of rational numbers between 0 and 1 inclusive
   e. The set of individuals who have given birth to more than three children

3. Express each of the following sets in a different way.

   a. $\{2, 4, 6, 8, 10, 12, 14, 16, 18, 20\}$
   b. $\{x \mid x$ is a real number and x^2 is positive$\}$
   c. $\{x \mid x$ is a real number and x^2 is negative$\}$
   d. $\{n \mid n^2 \leq 4, n$ is an integer$\}$
   e. $\{p \mid p$ is a planet farther from the sun than the Earth$\}$
   f. $\{n \mid n = 2m + 1, m$ is an integer$\}$
   g. $\{2, 6, 10, 14, 18, \ldots\}$

4. Given that set $A = \{1, 2, 3, 4, 5\}$, list the elements of set $A' = \{x \mid x \notin A\}$ for each of the stated universal sets.

   a. $U = \{1, 2, 3, 4, 5, 6, 7, 8, 9, 10\}$
   b. $U = \{0, 1, 2, 3, 4, 5, 6, 7\}$
   c. $U = \{x \mid x$ is a natural number$\}$
   d. $U = \{x \mid x$ is an integer$\}$
   e. $U = \{x \mid x$ is a divisor of 120$\}$
   f. $U = \{x \mid x$ is a divisor of 30$\}$

5. List all of the possible subsets of set A. Then do the same for set B. Can you make a generalization regarding the number of subsets of a set of n elements?

$$A = \{1, 2\}$$
$$B = \{a, b, c, d\}$$

6. Give three examples of numbers in each of the following sets.
   a. The set of integers that are not natural numbers
   b. The set of rational numbers that are not integers

c. The set of real numbers that are not rational (these are called irrational numbers)

7. Repeating decimals are numbers such as the following:

$$0.\overline{333333}\ldots$$
$$0.\overline{132}\overline{132}\overline{132}\ldots$$
$$6.\overline{777777777}\ldots$$
$$23.\overline{000000000}\ldots$$
$$5,732.\overline{1785}\overline{1785}\overline{1785}\ldots.$$

in which the horizontal bars indicate that the decimal continues in a similar fashion with an endless succession of blocks of identical digits. Consider the following two sets: $Q =$ set of rational numbers and $D =$ set of real numbers expressible as repeating decimals. Show that 2/5, 2/7, 3/13, and 1/11 can be expressed as repeating decimals.

8. Which of the following conjectures would you make about sets Q and D in Problem 7?

(i) $Q \subset D$
(ii) $D \subset Q$
(iii) $Q = D$
(iv) $Q \neq D$

9. Are the following pairs of sets equal or unequal?

a. $\{1, 2, 3, 4\}$ and $\{x \mid x \text{ is a divisor of } 24\}$
b. $\{6, 7\}$ and $\{x \mid x \text{ is a root of } x^2 - 13x + 42 = 0\}$
c. $\{1, 2, 3\}$ and $\{x \mid x \text{ is a root of } x^3 - 6x^2 + 11x - 6 = 0\}$
d. ϕ and $\{s \mid s \text{ is a square with unequal sides}\}$
e. $\{p \mid p \text{ is a parallelogram}\}$ and
   $\{q \mid q \text{ is a quadrilateral with unequal diagonals}\}$

3.2 Set Operations—Venn Diagrams

There are several useful operations performed on sets that we have not yet discussed. These operations will be symbolized with notations that are new but easy to understand.

Consider the following universal set?

$U =$ set of all customers who entered any of Jimmy's department stores today

and let

$A =$ set of customers carrying Jimmy's charge cards

$B =$ set of customers carrying Palader cards

The following chart will help to introduce four new symbols.

Set	Symbol
Set of persons carrying *either* a Jimmy's charge card or a Palader card	$A \cup B$ (read "*A* union *B*")
Set of persons carrying both Jimmy's cards and Palader cards	$A \cap B$ (read "*A* intersection B")
Set of persons not carrying Jimmy's charge cards	A' (read "*A* complement")
Set of persons carrying Jimmy's charge cards and not carrying Palader cards	$A - B$ (read "*A* minus B" or "the complement of B relative to A")

The following definitions and diagrams will make things clear:

Definition 3 $A \cup B = \{x \mid x \in A \text{ or } x \in B\}$

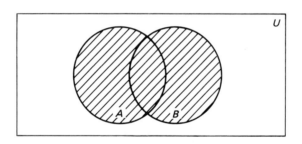

Notice that the union of two sets A and B consists of those elements that are in either A or B (possibly both). We understand this to mean that if an element belongs to both sets A and B, then it is only included *once* in the set $A \cup B$.

Definition 4 $A \cap B = \{x \mid x \in A \text{ and } x \in B\}$

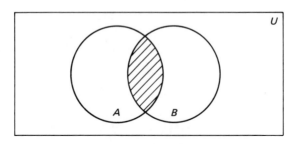

The intersection of two sets consists of those elements that lie on the regions that are overlapping or common to set A and set B.

Definition 5   Given a universal set U, then $A' = \{x \mid x \epsilon A\}$

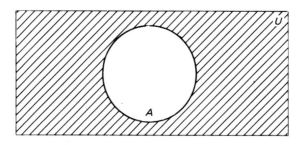

Again we must stress the importance of an explicit (or implied) universal set in order to discuss meaningfully the set of elements that lie outside a particular set.

Definition 6 $A - B = \{x \mid x \epsilon A \text{ and } x \epsilon B\}$.

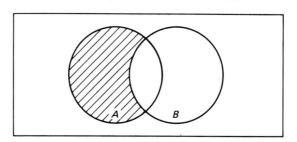

The complement of B relative to A (or simply, $A - B$) consists of those elements in A that are not in B.

Example 1

Given that $U = \{1, 2, 3, 4, 5, 6, 7, 8, 9, 10\}$, $A = \{2, 3, 4, 5\}$, and $B = \{4, 5, 6, 7, 8\}$, find

a. $A \cup B$ b. $A \cap B$ c. A' d. $A - B$ e. $B - A$

Solution a. $A \cup B = \{2, 3, 4, 5, 6, 7, 8\}$ (Note that we include not only elements that are in strictly one of the sets, *but also* elements, such as 4 and 5, that are in both. Thus in defining the union of two sets we use the word "or" in the inclusive sense.)

b. $A \cap B = \{4, 5\}$ (Here we only include elements common to both sets.)

c. $A' = \{1, 6, 7, 8, 9, 10\}$

d. $A - B = \{2, 3\}$

e. $B - A = \{6, 7, 8\}$ Observe that set "subtraction" is not commutative. In general, $A - B \neq B - A$.)

Example 2

For the same sets given above in Example 1, find

a. $(A \cup B)'$ b. $A' \cap B'$ c. $(A \cap B)'$ d. $A' \cup B'$

e. $A \cup \phi$ f. $A \cap \phi$ g. $(A - B) \cap (B - A)$

Solution a. $(A \cup B)' = \{x \mid x \; \epsilon \; (A \cup B)\} = \{1, 9, 10\}$

b. $A' \cap B' = \{1, 6, 7, 8, 9, 10\} \cap \{1, 2, 3, 9, 10\} = \{1, 9, 10\}$

c. $(A \cap B)' = \{1, 2, 3, 6, 7, 8, 9, 10\}$

d. $A' \cup B' = \{1, 6, 7, 8, 9, 10\} \cup \{1, 2, 3, 9, 10\} = \{1, 2, 3, 6, 7, 8, 9, 10\}$

e. $A \cup \phi = A$

f. $A \cap \phi = \phi$

g. $(A - B) \cap (B - A) = \{2, 3\} \cap \{6, 7, 8\} = \phi$

Example 3

Find $A \cap B$, where

$$A = \{x \mid x \text{ is a positive even integer}\}$$
$$B = \{y \mid y \text{ is a positive integral multiple of 5}\}$$

Solution

$$A = \{2, 4, 6, 8, 10, 12, 14, 16, 18, \ldots\}$$
$$B = \{5, 10, 15, 20, 25, 30, 35, 40, \ldots\}$$

Careful thought reveals that $A \cap B = \{10, 20, 30, \ldots\}$. Note that this result could also be obtained by representing A, B, and $A \cap B$ as follows:

$$A = \{x \mid x = 2m, \; m \text{ is a natural number}\}$$
$$B = \{y \mid y = 5n, \; n \text{ is a natural number}\}$$

then

$$A \cap B = \{z \mid z = 2(5n), \; n \text{ is a natural number}\}$$

Example 4

Two sets A and B are *disjoint* if $A \cap B = \phi$. Give some examples of disjoint pairs of sets.

Solution a.   The set of odd integers and the set of even integers

b.   The set of living teenagers and the set of individuals over age 65 collecting Social Security

c.   The set of rational numbers and the set of nonrepeating decimals (such as $\sqrt{2} = 1.414213562\ldots$ or $1.010010001\ldots$)

A large number of theorems can be proved using the definitions developed thus far, some with ease and some with difficulty. Except possibly for the distributive properties, the thoughtful student will find that intuition supports the truth of each assertion.

Theorem 5	$U' = \phi,\ \phi' = U$	
Theorem 6	$(A')' = A$	
Theorem 7	$A \cup A' = U,\ A \cap A' = \phi$	
Theorem 8	$A \cup A = A,\ A \cap A = A$	
Theorem 9	$A \cup U = U,\ A \cap U = A$	
Theorem 10	$A \cup \phi = A,\ A \cap \phi = \phi$	
Theorem 11	$A \subset (A \cup B)$	
Theorem 12	$(A \cap B) \subset A$	
Theorem 13	$\left.\begin{array}{l} A \cup B = B \cup A \\ A \cap B = B \cap A \end{array}\right\}$	commutative law
Theorem 14	$\left.\begin{array}{l} (A \cup B) \cup C = A \cup (B \cup C) \\ (A \cap B) \cap C = A \cap (B \cap C) \end{array}\right\}$	associative law
Theorem 15	$\left.\begin{array}{l} A \cap (B \cup C) = (A \cap B) \cup (A \cap C) \\ A \cup (B \cap C) = (A \cup B) \cap (A \cup C) \end{array}\right\}$	distributive law
Theorem 16	$A - B = A \cap B'$	
Theorem 17	$\left.\begin{array}{l} (A \cup B)' = A' \cap B' \\ (A \cap B)' = A' \cup B' \end{array}\right\}$	De Morgan's law

Example 5

Prove the second case of De Morgan's laws:

$$(A \cap B)' = A' \cup B'$$

and accomplish the proof by using the formal definition of equality. [Show that $(A \cap B)' \subset A' \cup B'$ and that $A' \cup B' \subset (A \cap B)'$.]

Solution Let $x \in (A \cap B)'$. Then

$$x \notin A \cap B \Rightarrow x \notin A \text{ or } x \notin B \Rightarrow x \in A' \text{ or } x \in B'$$
$$\Rightarrow x \in A' \cup B'$$
$$\Rightarrow (A \cap B)' \subset A' \cup B'$$

Let $x \in A' \cup B'$. Then

$$x \in A' \text{ or } x \in B'$$
$$\Rightarrow x \notin A \text{ or } x \notin B \Rightarrow x \notin A \cap B \Rightarrow x \in (A \cap B)'$$
$$\Rightarrow A' \cup B' \subset (A \cap B)'$$

Therefore $(A \cap B)' = A' \cup B'$

Proofs such as the one above would not be easily accomplished by yourself. There would be very little value in attempting to memorize the proof given above. This example is given to illustrate the general outline for such a proof. We will see that there are alternative methods for verifying algebraic set statements using diagrams.

Venn Diagrams Arbitrary sets can be conveniently represented by diagrams that have come to be known as Venn* diagrams. These are very similar to Euler diagrams employed in Chapter 2. We can use these diagrams to verify various set relationships. In the strictest sense, however, they are not acceptable as rigorous proofs because their use is regarded as merely an inductive procedure. Nevertheless, since the use of such diagrams is very convincing to our common sense, we will use them.

Where $n = $ the number of sets to be considered, the Venn diagrams are shown for cases $n = 1$, 2, and 3. It is well-known that the number 2^n represents the number of possible subregions within the universal set U.

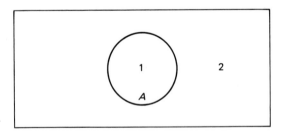

$n = 1$, *two subregions*

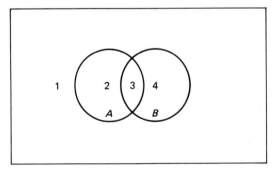

$n = 2$, *four subregions*

* John Venn authored a paper entitled "Boole's Logical System" in which these diagrams were used; the paper was published in 1876.

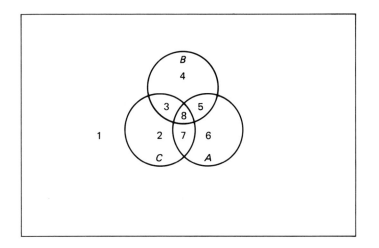

n = 3, *eight subregions*

It is possible that until 1974, no one believed that an aesthetically pleasing Venn diagram could be drawn for the case *n* = 4. However, in April of 1974, Carol Guadagni, a freshman at Nassau Community College, drew a felicitous diagram for this case containing 16 subregions.* It appears below.

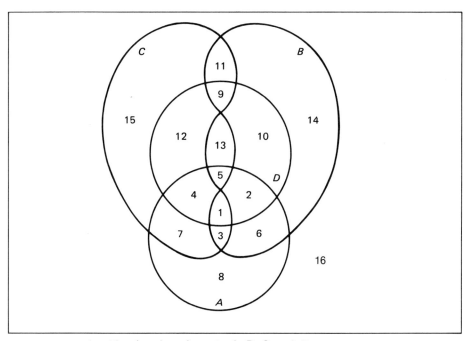

n = 4,   16 subregions for sets *A*, *B*, *C*, and *D*

* Rosenfeld, Robert, "A Beautiful Diagram in Set Theory," *The Matyc Journal* **8**, No. 1 (1974), p. 17.

Example 6

Prove, using a Venn diagram, that $(A \cap B)' = A' \cup B'$ (which was proved in Exmple 5).

Solution Venn diagrams of the two expressions have the same shading:

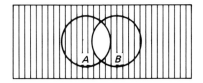

Shaded region is $(A \cap B)'$.

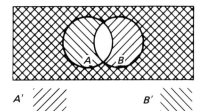

$A' \cap B'$ is the region having single or double cross-hatched shading.

Example 7

Prove, using a Venn diagram, that $A \cap (B \cup C) = (A \cap B) \cup (A \cup C)$. (Note that this is the first version of the Distributive law.)

Solution Venn diagrams of the two expressions have the same shading:

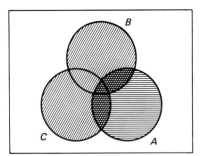

$A \cap (B \cup C)$ is the doubly cross-hatched region with the darkened boundary, where

$B \cup C \ ////$

$A \ \equiv$

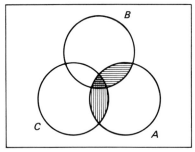

$(A \cap B) \cup (A \cap C)$ is the region having either single or double cross-hatching, where

$A \cap B \equiv$

$A \cap C \ ||||$

Example 8

Prove, using the theorems on page 65, that

$$A \cup (B \cap A') = A \cup B$$

Solution	$A \cup (B \cap A')$	Theorem 15
	$= (A \cup B) \cap (A \cup A')$	Theorem 7
	$= (A \cup B) \cap U$	Theorem 9
	$= A \cup B$	

Example 9

For the set diagram below, find an algebraic expression that represents the shaded portion.

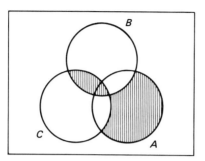

Solution Notice that the shaded portion represents the union of two regions: the overlapping of B and C, and all points in A that are not in $B \cup C$. Hence the solution is $(B \cap C) \cup [A - (B \cup C)]$.

Exercise 3.2 1. Given that $U = \{1, 2, 3, 4, 5, 6\}$, $A = \{1, 2,\}$, $B = \{6\}$, $C = \{2, 3, 6\}$, and $D = \{1, 4, 5\}$, find the following.

    a. $A \cup B$ b. $C \cup D$ c. $A \cap D$ d. $C \cap B$
    e. $C - A$ f. $A - C$ g. C' h. $A \cap D'$
    i. $C - (A \cup B)$ j. $(B \cup C) \cap (B \cup D)$

2. Draw a Venn diagram illustrating each of the following for sets A, B, and C within a universal set U.

    a. $A \cup (B \cup C)$ b. $A \cap (B \cap C)$ c. $A \cup (B \cap C)$
    d. $(A \cup B)'$ e. $A - (B \cup C)$ f. $U - A$
    g. $(B \cup C) - (A \cap C)$ h. $(A - B') \cap (C' \cup A')$

3. Given the sets

$A = \{x \mid x$ is a positive integer$\}$
$B = \{x \mid x$ is a positive even integer$\}$
$C = \{x \mid x$ is a positive integral multiple of 4$\}$
$D = \{x \mid x$ is a positive integral multiple of 5$\}$

list, when possible, at least ten elements of each of the following sets.

    a. $A \cap B'$ b. $B \cup B'$ c. $B \cap C$
    d. $B \cap D$ e. $C \cap D$ f. $B' \cap C \cap D$

4. Given the universal set

   $U=$ set of all customers who entered any of Ruby's department stores today

   and the sets

   $A=$ set of customers carrying Ruby's charge cards
   $B=$ set of customers carrying Imperial Express cards
   $C=$ set of customers carrying their own driver's licenses

   interpret (in words) each of the following sets.

   a. $A \cap (B \cap C)$ b. $(A \cup B \cup C)'$ c. $(A \cap C) \cup B$
   d. $(A \cap C) \cap B'$ e. $B \cap (A \cup C)'$ f. $A' \cup B' \cup C'$

5. Prove the following using the method of formal proof (Do not use diagrams; use the method of Example 5.)

   a. $(A \cup B)' = A' \cap B'$ *b. $A \cap (B \cup C) = (A \cap B) \cup (A \cap C)$

   Also verify each of the above using Venn diagrams.

6. Prove the following using Venn diagrams only.

   a. $A \cap (A \cup B) = A$
   b. $(A - B) \cup (B - A) = (A \cup B) - (A \cap B)$
   c. $A \cap (B - C) = B \cap (A - C) = A \cap B \cap C'$
   *d. $(A \cap B) \cap (C \cup D) = (A \cap B \cap C) \cup (A \cap B \cap D)$

   (Use Carol Guadagni's diagram on p. 67.)

7. Use the algebraic method of proof illustrated in Example 8 and prove the following:

   a. $(A \cap B) \cup (A \cap B') = A$
   b. $A \cap (B \cup C' \cup A') = (A \cap B) \cup (A \cap C')$
   c. $(A \cap B) \cap (C \cup D) = (A \cap B \cap C) \cup (A \cap B \cap D)$

8. For the Venn diagrams below, find a simple set-algebraic expression for the shaded region.

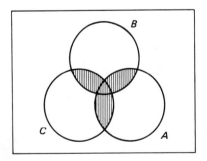

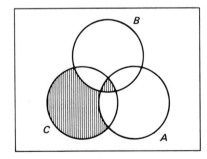

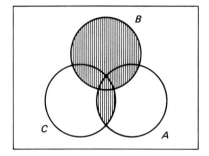

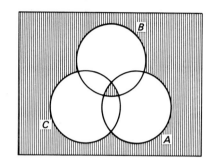

9. Let the universe of discussion be the set of all integers:

$$U = \{\ldots, -3, -2, -1, 0, 1, 2, 3, \ldots\}$$

Let A be the subset of all integral multiples of 3, B be all integral multiples of 2, and C be all integral multiples of 5. Express the following as the result of operations on the given sets by using symbols such as $A \cup B$, $A \cap C$, and $(A \cup B \cup C)'$, etc.

a. The set of all integral multiples of 6
b. The set of all integral multiples of 10
c. The set of all integral multiples of 15
d. The set of integers that are not even and are not multiples of 3
e. The set of integers that are not even, are not multiples of 3, and are not multiples of 5
f. The set of integral multiples of 5 that are odd
g. The set of all integral multiples of 30
h. The set of integers that are divisible by 5 but not divisible by 6

*10. Find the most general condition on the sets A and B so that

a. $A - B = B - A$ b. $A \cap B = A \cup B$ c. $A - B = A$
d. $A - B = B$ e. $A \cap B = A$
f. $A \cap B = B$ and $B \subset A$

*11. Simplify the set expression

$$[(A \cap B) \cup (A \cap D')] \cap (A' \cup D)$$

3.3 Supplementary Topics About Sets

How Much Parallelism is There Between the Properties of Sets and the Laws of Arithmetic? We have seen enough of set theory to be able to see that there is a close relationship between the algebra of sets and the laws of logic. If we permit p_x to represent an open statement involving the variable x and $\{p_x\}$ to represent the set of all elements of the universal set U that make p_x true, we can state four theorems that illustrate the connection between logic and sets.

Theorem 18	$\{(p \vee q)_x\} =$	$\{p_x\} \cup \{q_x\}$
Theorem 19	$\{(p \wedge q)_x\} =$	$\{p_x\} \cap \{q_x\}$
Theorem 20	$\{(p \rightarrow q)_x\} =$	$\{(\sim p)_x\} \cup \{q_x\}$
Theorem 21	$\{(\sim p)_x\} =$	$\{p_x\}'$

Theorem 18 says that the set of all elements x for which either p or q is true is the same as the union of the set of elements for which p is true with the set of elements for which q is true. The remaining theorems can easily be interpreted by a careful reading. Together these theorems constitute a unification of set theory and the logic of propositions. No doubt you have already noticed that every theorem concerning sets has a direct analog in logic. Once we have a way of converting open sentences that are implications into the disjunction of two open sentences we can use Theorem 21 to convert every statement in logic into an analogous one about sets. The parallelism between logic and sets is total.

This is not the case, however, between the properties of sets and the laws of arithmetic. There are five fundamental laws of arithmetic with which we are already familiar:

(i) $a + b = b + a$ (commutative law of addition)
(ii) $a \cdot b = b \cdot a$ (commutative law of multiplication)
(iii) $(a + b) + c = a + (b + c)$ (associative law of addition)
(iv) $(a \cdot b)c = a(b \cdot c)$ (associative law of multiplication)
(v) $a(b + c) = a \cdot b + a \cdot c$ (distributive law)

In set theory we have exactly parallel structures in which we can think of $+$ as being replaced by $\cup$ and $\cdot$ (multiplication) as being replaced by $\cap$. The parallel set structures are

(i) $A \cup B = B \cup A$
(ii) $A \cap B = B \cap A$
(iii) $(A \cup B) \cup C = A \cup (B \cup C)$
(iv) $(A \cap B) \cap C = A \cap (B \cap C)$
(v) $A \cap (B \cup C) = (A \cap B) \cup (A \cap C)$ (intersection "distributes over" union)

However, there is a point at which the parallel breaks down. In arithmetic it is not the case that addition "distributes over" multiplication, as the following illustration demonstrates:

$$2 + (5 \cdot 3) \neq (2 + 5) \cdot (2 + 3) \qquad \text{since} \qquad 17 \neq 35$$

But it is true in set theory that union distributes over intersection; thus we actually have two distributive laws in set theory, but only one in arithmetic:

$$A \cap (B \cup C) = (A \cap B) \cup (A \cap C) \qquad a(b+c) = a \cdot b + a \cdot c$$
$$A \cup (B \cap C) = (A \cup B) \cap (A \cup C) \qquad a + (b \cdot c) \neq (a+b)(a+c)$$

Example 1

If set subtraction is replaced by arithmetic subtraction, set intersection is replaced by multiplication, and union is replaced by addition, which of the following have analogously true arithmetic parallels?

a. $(A - B) - C = A - (B \cup C)$
b. $A - (B - C) = (A - B) \cup (A \cap C)$

Demonstrate, using Venn diagrams, that the statements are true in set theory.

Solution   a.   In arithmetic the parallel statement $(a - b) - c = a - (b + c)$ is true.

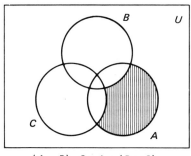

$(A - B) - C = A - (B \cup C)$

b.   In arithmetic the parallel statement $a - (b - c) = (a - b) + ac$ is generally false.

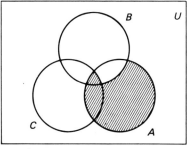

$A - (B - C) = (A - B) \cup (A \cap C)$

Power Sets Quite often it is useful to consider the set of all subsets that can be formed by choosing objects from a given set A. Such a set is called the *power set* of set A. Suppose for example, set A is given by

$$A = \{a, b, c, d, e\}$$

Then the subsets having one element are

$$\{a\}, \{b\}, \{c\}, \{d\}, \{e\}$$

Those of two elements are

$$\{a, b\}, \{a, c\}, \{a, d\}, \{a, e\}, \{b, c\}, \{b, d\}, \{b, e\}, \{c, d\}, \{c, e\}, \{d, e\}$$

Note that for each two-element subset that is chosen, there is a three-element subset of A remaining; hence there are just as many three-element subsets of A as there are two-element subsets. The three-element subsets are

$$\{c, d, e\}, \{b, d, e\}, \{b, c, e\}, \{b, c, d\}, \{a, d, e\}, \{a, c, e\},$$
$$\{a, c, d\}, \{a, b, e\}, \{a, b, d\}, \{a, b, c\}$$

Similarly there are five four-element subsets:

$$\{b, c, d, e\}, \{a, c, d, e\}, \{a, b, d, e\}, \{a, b, c, e\}, \{a, b, c, d\}$$

If we choose no objects from set A we obtain ϕ, the last subset of A. (Note that since $A \subset A$, the set A itself should also be included.) We see that if we count the number of subsets of r objects from a given set of five elements, we will obtain the same result as if we count the number of subsets of $5-r$ objects from the same set of five elements. This result is summarized in the following table.

Number of Subsets of r Elements Chosen from Five Elements

No. of elements in subset (r)	0	1	2	3	4	5
No. of subsets of r elements	1	5	10	10	5	1

Note that the total number of subsets $= N = 1 + 5 + 10 + 10 + 5 + 1 = 32$. It is either a coincidence or a remarkable fact that 32 is the fifth power of 2. At a later time we shall demonstrate that this is not a coincidence at all! We will be able to show that 2^e yields the number of subsets of a set of e elements. For the moment, however, we will accept the following theorem without proof:

> Theorem 22   Given a set A having e elements, there are 2^e possible subsets of set A. (Expressed slightly differently, the power set of set A has 2^e elements in it.)

Example 2

Given the set $B = \{1, 2, 3, 4, 5, 6\}$, find

a.   All subsets having two elements
b.   The number of subsets having four elements
c.   The total number of subsets of B using the theorem above

Solution a.   There are 15 subsets of two elements:

$$\{1, 2\}, \{1, 3\}, \{1, 4\}, \{1, 5\}, \{1, 6\}, \{2, 3\}, \{2, 4\}, \{2, 5\}, \{2, 6\}, \{3, 4\},$$
$$\{3, 5\}, \{3, 6\}, \{4, 5\}, \{4, 6\}, \{5, 6\}$$

b.   For each two-element subset chosen, there is a four-element subset remaining; hence, there are also 15 subsets of four elements that are possible.
c. $2^6 = 64$ subsets of a set of six elements.

Exercise 3.3 1.   Given the three set relationships

a. $A \cup (A \cap B) = A$ b. $A \cap (B - C) = B \cap (A - C)$
c. $(A - B) \cup (B - A) = (A \cup B) - (A \cap B)$

first demonstrate that the statements are true using Venn diagrams. Then making the following replacements

Replacing $\cup$ by addition $+$
Replacing $\cap$ by multiplication $\cdot$
Replacing set subtraction by arithmetic subtraction

determine which (if any) of the statements are analogously true in arithmetic.

2.   List all of the subsets of the set $\{a, b, c, d\}$. Using Theorem 22, see if your results are correct.

3.   In a set of seven elements, S_i is a subset having i elements, and $C(S_i)$ equals the number of different subsets having i elements. Which of the following are equal? Explain.

$C(S_0), C(S_1), C(S_2), C(S_3), C(S_4), C(S_5), C(S_6), C(S_7)$

List all the distinct subsets S_2. (*Hint:* There should be 21.)

3.4 Applications to Surveys

We will discuss sets whose elements can be directly counted. Although this might seem like a dull prospect for serious study, we can actually use counting procedures for sets in various interesting problems involving overlapping data. These notions will also be useful when we come to the subject of probability in a later chapter.

It will be helpful to denote the number of elements in a set A by the symbol $n(A)$, which is read "n of A." Thus $n(A) = 5$ means that set A has five elements in it. Now we consider the problem of finding a formula for the number of elements in the union of two given sets A and B. Suppose, for example, we survey all of the students in the class who are studying a foreign language and we ask the following three questions (separately):

(i)   Raise your hand if you're studying French.
       (10 studends raised their hands.)
(ii)   Raise your hand if you're studying Spanish.
       (17 students raised their hands.)
(iii) Raise your hand if you're studying a foreign language other than French or Spanish.
       (No student raised a hand.)

Now we ask ourselves, how many students are studying a foreign language? The "obvious" answer of $10 + 17 = 27$ is really not so obvious when you consider the possibility that some students may be studying both languages at once, in which case 27 is larger than the correct answer. Suppose we let

$A =$ set of students studying French and
$B =$ set of students studying Spanish

Assuming (and we don't know if this assumption is correct without asking the class a fourth question) that $A \cap B = \phi$, then it would follow that $n(A \cup B) = n(A) + n(B) = 10 + 17 = 27$.

Suppose it happens, however, that we ask one more question and receive the indicated response.

(iv)   Raise your hand if you're studying both French and Spanish.
       (Four students raised their hands.)

This information can be interpreted as $n(A \cap B) = 4$. Now if we attempt to find $n(A \cup B)$ by merely adding $n(A)$ and $n(B)$, we will be including the overlapping region $A \cap B$ twice. What we need to do therefore is to subtract $n(A \cap B)$ from the total of 27:

$$n(A \cup B) = n(A) + n(B) - n(A \cap B) = 10 + 17 - 4 = 23$$

Thus we have the following theorem

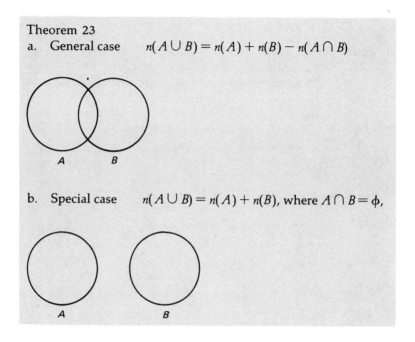

Theorem 23

a. General case $\quad n(A \cup B) = n(A) + n(B) - n(A \cap B)$

$\qquad\qquad\qquad\qquad A \qquad B$

b. Special case $\quad n(A \cup B) = n(A) + n(B)$, where $A \cap B = \phi$,

$\qquad\qquad\qquad\qquad A \qquad\qquad B$

Summarizing the data in the stated example yields

10 students are taking French.

17 students are taking Spanish.

Four students are taking both French and Spanish.

These data can be summarized nicely on the following diagram:

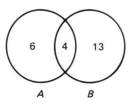

$\qquad A \qquad B$

Note that six students are studying only French, four students are studying both, and 13 students are studying only Spanish. The total $6 + 4 + 13 = 23$ agrees with the total using the formula given in the general case of the theorem above.

Example 3

Of 50 individuals surveyed, 20 own compact cars, 28 own station wagons, five own both compact cars and station wagons, and seven own neither of these two types of vehicles. Is the data set consistent or inconsistent?

Solution Let circle C represent the set of compact-car owners and S represent the set of station wagon owners. Here we shall fill in a Venn diagram in reverse order by first noting that the intersection of sets C and S is 5. It follows that the number of individuals owning compacts (but not station wagons) is $20 - 5 = 15$, and the number of individuals owning station wagons (but not compacts) is $28 - 5 = 23$. In this problem $n(U) = 50$.

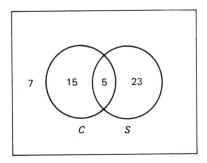

Since we have that $7 + 15 + 5 + 23 = 50$, the data are consistent. Note also that $n(A \cup B) = 20 + 28 - 5 = 43$, which, together with the fact that $n(A \cup B)' = 7$, strengthens our belief in Theorem 23.

Theorem 23, concerning the number of elements in the union of two sets, can be used, together with other theorems we have learned about sets, to extend our results to three sets having possible overlaps.

> **Theorem 24** Given any three sets A, B, and C, we have that
> $n(A \cup B \cup C) = n(A) + n(B) + n(C) - n(A \cap B) - n(A \cap C) - n(B \cap C) + n(A \cap B \cap C)$

Proof $n(A \cup B \cup) = n[(A \cup B) \cup C] = n(A \cup B) + n(C) - n[(A \cup B) \cap C]$
$= n(A) + n(B) - n(A \cap B) + n(C) - n[(A \cap C)$
$\qquad \cup (B \cap C)]$
$= n(A) + n(B) + n(C) - n(A \cap B) - n(A \cap C)$
$\qquad - n(B \cap C) + n(A \cap C \cap B \cap C)$
$= n(A) + n(B) + n(C) - n(A \cap B) - n(A \cap C)$
$\qquad - n(B \cap C) + n(A \cap B \cap C)$

This theorem can be explained by use of the following figure.

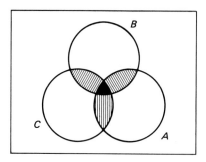

Obviously

$$n(A \cup B \cup C) \leq n(A) + n(B) + n(C)$$

If from the right side of this inequality we subtract the three cross-hatched areas above, we will have subtracted the two-circle overlappings. However the central, roughly triangular shape common to all three circles, corresponding to $A \cap B \cap C$, which was originally included three times in the total $n(A) + n(B) + n(C)$, will have been subtracted three times, and thus will not be included at all. We can correct for this by adding $n(A \cap B \cap C)$ back in. Thus we have that

$$
\begin{aligned}
n(A \cup B \cup C) = & \text{ (sum of elements in each of the three circles)} \\
& - \text{(sum of elements in each of the two-circle overlapping} \\
& \quad \text{areas)} \\
& + \text{(number of elements in the three-circle overlapping} \\
& \quad \text{triangular region)} \\
= & \; n(A) + n(B) + n(C) \\
& - n(A \cap B) - n(A \cap C) - n(B \cap C) \\
& + n(A \cap B \cap C)
\end{aligned}
$$

Example 4

A computer was programmed to scan the hospital records of all pulmonary patients currently in residence in hospitals located in a certain geographical area. 189 pulmonary patient records were counted, and within these

69 patients have cancer

73 patients have pneumonia

89 patients have emphysema

22 patients have cancer and emphysema

16 patients have pneumonia and emphysema

24 patients have pneumonia and cancer

 9 patients have all three ailments

10 patients have "other" lung ailments or an unrecorded diagnosis

The following questions are raised

a. Are the data consistent or is the computer program incorrect?
b. How many patients have cancer who do not have emphysema?
c. How many patients have cancer who do not have emphysema or pneumonia?
d. How many patients have emphysema and cancer but not pneumonia?

Solution Note first that $n(C \cap E \cap P) = 9$. This permits us to fill in the portions of the three two-area overlapped regions that are not in $C \cap E \cap P$. We can use the totals 69, 73, and 89 to deduce the number of patients having only one of the three ailments. The set diagram fills out nicely as follows:

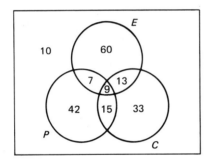

Now each question can easily be answered from the diagram.

a. $9 + 15 + 13 + 7 + 33 + 60 + 42 + 10 = 189$. Hence data are consistent.
b. 48 have cancer but not emphysema.
c. 33 have cancer but neither emphysema nor pneumonia.
d. 13 have emphysema and cancer but not pneumonia.

Example 5

In a door-to-door poll, 10 of 40 registered Democrats oppose abortion; 14 of 39 registered Republicans oppose abortion; and 4 of 11 registered independents oppose abortion. The poll-taker claims that these results prove that over 70% of the interviewed registered voters are in favor of abortions. Do the poll-taker's results justify the conclusion?

Solution Here the set diagram of three mutually overlapping regions may be unnecessarily confusing. A different diagram is possible in this problem because the Democrats, Republicans, and independents are mutually disjoint sets. The following diagram, with the oval center region indicating those who favor abortions, works well.

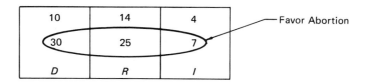

Since 62 favor abortions and 62/90 = 68.9%, the conclusion is not justified from the poll data.

Exercise 3.4 1. In a survey of science students it was found that 63 were studying physics, 39 were studying chemistry, and 12 were studying both physics and chemistry. How many students were studying at least one of these two sciences?

2. In a survey of social science majors

   90 are taking psychology
   101 are taking history
   92 are taking sociology
   39 are taking history and psychology
   54 are taking history and sociology
   20 are taking psychology and sociology

   Among 200 students interviewed who are social science majors, find the number of social science majors who are not taking any of the three courses. How many take only one of the three courses?

3. A survey of freshmen revealed that

   41% read *Playmacho* Magazine
   27% read *Snob's Digest*
   25% read *Scandal's Journal*
   7% read *Playmacho* and *Snob's*
   4% read *Playmacho* and *Scandal's*
   8% read *Snob's* and *Scandal's*
   2% read all three
   24% read none of these publications

   Show that the above data are consistent. What percent read *Playmacho* and *Snob's* but not *Scandal's*? What percent read *Snob's* who do not read *Playmacho*?

4. 410 housewives and 17 househusbands were interviewed in regard to their use of detergents A and B. The following facts were recorded:

7 househusbands used Brand A.

11 househusbands used Brand B.

3 househusbands used both A and B.

238 housewives used Brand A.

148 housewives used Brand B.

8 housewives used both A and B.

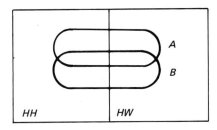

It was then reported that 393 housespouses used at least one of these two brands?

a. Is this figure correct?

b. How many housespouses used exactly one of these detergents?

c. How many housespouses used exactly two of these detergents?

5. Blood is classified as being Rh positive or Rh negative and as one of four types. If blood contains an A antigen, it is type A; if it has a B antigen, it is type B; if it has both A and B antigens, it is type AB; and if it has neither antigen, it is type O. Use a Venn diagram to illustrate these possibilities. How many different possibilities are there?

6. In a study of 14,600 people, only women or wage earners or parents of children under age 18 were included. The following data were obtained:

Women: 5918

Wage earners: 8222

Parents having children under 18: 7329

Female parents having children under 18: 2577

Wage earners having children under 18: 3402

Female wage earners: 2470

Female wage earners having children under 18: 1650

The data cannot be valid, and the study is suspect. Why?

*7. Find a formula for $n(A \cup B \cup C \cup D)$ and show that it is meaningful to interpret the result in light of Gaudagni's set diagram on page 67.

Basic Counting Techniques–
Indirect Methods

> "Only unsophisticated people think that in other parts of the universe, technologically advanced, alien beings may look like us. Sophisticated people believe that such life forms would not appear human, but the most sophisticated among us assume that their counting processes are the same as ours."
>
> R. W. Hamming

4.1   Introduction and Fundamental Counting Principle

Counting all of the elements of a set may or may not be an easy matter. It is trivial to count the elements in the set

$$\{3, 4, 5, \ldots, 12\}$$

but it is not trivial to be able to count the set of ways four telephone wires might be connected to four terminals. In this latter case a student might be able to come up with a way of directly counting all of the possible cases involved. However, in a more complicated case direct counting methods would be tedious at best and, at worst, nearly impossible. Therefore we would like to develop counting methods that work indirectly (by formula or mathematical procedure). While such procedures and formulas will be of great assistance to us in calculating probabilities, we will also find them interesting by themselves.

In this chapter we shall discuss two general types of counting situations: combinations and permutations. Combination formulas will help us to count the number of ways of making a *selection* of objects from a given set. Permutation formulas will enable us to count the number of ways of making an *arrangement* of objects from a given set.

Suppose, for example, we have a set of four individuals: Juan, Mary, David, and Tibor. We will abbreviate this set by the simple designation

$$\{J, M, D, T\}$$

We list the different sets (or, as we will sometimes say, selections) consisting of three of the four people in the original set:

$$\{J, M, D\}, \quad \{J, M, T\}, \quad \{J, D, T\}, \quad \{M, D, T\}$$

Each of the four sets is called a *combination.* Two combinations are the same if they contain the same objects, the order in which the objects were selected and the arrangement of the objects within the combination being immaterial.

Now let's enumerate the different linear *arrangements* of three individuals that can be chosen from the original four. (By "linear arrangements" we mean the ways of ordering the elements in a straight line.) There are 24 such arrangements:

JMD	JDM	MJD	MDJ	DJM	DMJ
JMT	JTM	MJT	MTJ	TJM	TMJ
JDT	JTD	DJT	DTJ	TJD	TDJ
MDT	MTD	DMT	DTM	TMD	TDM

Each of these arrangements is called a *permutation.* Note that we earlier listed four combinations JMD, JMT, JDT, and MDT. Each of these combinations gave rise to six distinct permutations, together giving us a total of 24 permutations. Thus there are 24 permutations of four objects taken three at a time. But there are four combinations of four objects taken three at a time.

There are also times when we want to count the elements of a set although it may not be immediately clear whether the elements of that set consitute a permutation or a combination.

Example 1

A rat enters a maze having two partitions, the first having three openings and the second having two openings. After the rat selects an opening through the first partition, it then selects an opening to pass through the second partition so it can exit from the maze. How many possible paths are there, assuming the rat can pass through an opening only once?

Solution Consider the following diagram.

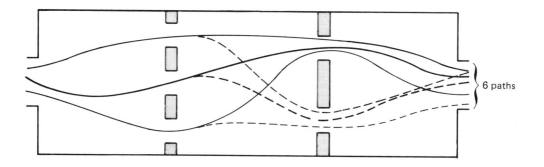

6 paths

Note that after choosing among the three openings in the first partition, the rat must then choose one of two openings in the second partition. This yields $3 \cdot 2 = 6$ possible paths.

The idea in the above problem, which can be extended to any number of partitions, suggests the following theorem, which we will not formally prove.

Theorem 1   (fundamental counting principle) If we perform a certain operation in m ways and if, after this operation has been performed, a second operation can be performed in n ways and if, after this operation has been performed, a third operation can be performed in p ways, etc., . . ., then the total number of ways the operations can be performed in the order named is $m \cdot n \cdot p \cdot$ . . . .

The rat's maze problem can be interpreted in light of Theorem 1 by illustrating with the use of a tree diagram.

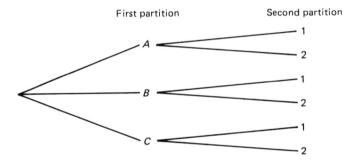

Here the number of possible paths corresponds to the number of final branch tips on the right side of the tree diagram. From each of the first three branches emanates two branches; hence there are $3 \cdot 2 = 6$ possible branches (paths) in all.

We can also clarify the problem of counting the number of permutations of three individuals chosen from the four we mentioned earlier:

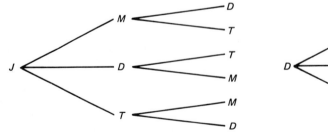
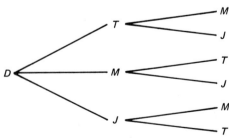

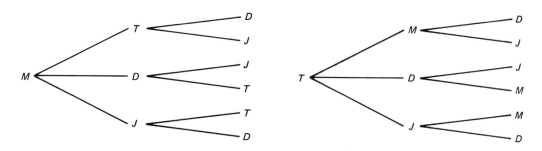

Note that there are four ways of selecting the first individual. Afterwards, there are three ways of selecting the second individual. Afterwards, there are two ways of selecting the third individual. Hence there are $4 \cdot 3 \cdot 2 = 24$ ways the operations can be performed, which we can interpret as 24 final branch tips on the tree diagram, each corresponding to one of 24 distinct linear permutations of four persons taken three at a time.

Example 2

From panels of seven persons representing labor, five representing management, and four representing the public, how many different three-person committees can be formed consisting of a representative from each of the three panels?

Solution Each number in the diagram below represents the number of ways of choosing a representative from each of the groups.

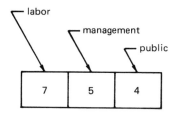

Hence, by the fundamental principle, the number of different committees is $7 \cdot 5 \cdot 4 = 140$.

Example 3

For the standard telephone dial (shown), how many different possible seven-symbol dialings are possible if each dialing consists of two letters followed by five digits. (Here we have to remember that AB2-5677 is not a different dialing from AC2-5677.)

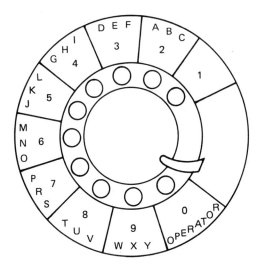

Solution   Notice that there are eight "letter holes" that could be chosen for each of the first two spins of the dial. For each of the last five spins of the dial, we could pick any one of 10 digits.

8	8	10	10	10	10	10

Thus we have $8 \cdot 8 \cdot 10 \cdot 10 \cdot 10 \cdot 10 \cdot 10 = 6{,}400{,}000$ possible dialings.

Example 4

Three dice are tossed, and each die is colored differently. In how many different ways may they fall?

Solution $6 \cdot 6 \cdot 6 = 216$ different ways.

Example 5

In how many different ways can five people be seated in a room containing seven chairs?

Solution   Here we might make the common error of trying to assign (or count) the number of people who can be chosen for the first chair, second chair, etc. Very quickly, however, we run out of people and we are stuck not knowing what to do with the last two chairs. Instead, if we reverse the point of view, we can count the number of chairs that can be assigned to each individual. Thus each number in the egg-slot diagram represents the number of chairs that could be chosen by each of the five people.

7	6	5	4	3

We find that $7 \cdot 6 \cdot 5 \cdot 4 \cdot 3 = 2520$ is the number of possible seating arrangements.

Exercise 4.1 1. There are five trains from New York to Philadelphia in the morning and three return trains in the afternoon. In how many ways can a daily round trip be made?

2. Consider the four distinct individuals: Karen, Joan, Cally, and Pedro.

    a. List all the combinations of two individuals chosen from the four;

    b. List all the permutations of two individuals chosen from the four.

3. Consider the four points pictured below. In how many ways can we draw a line connecting any two of the points? Is this a permutation or a combination problem?

$A \bullet$ $\bullet\, B$

$C \bullet$ $\bullet\, D$

4. List all the permutations of four letters chosen from the word "eats." How many of the spellings are meaningful?

5. In how many ways can a baseball coach arrange a batting order of nine players?

6. How many different blackjacks (an ace and a 10 or picture card) can be chosen from a standard deck of cards. (*Note:* Here we will consider the ace of diamonds and king of hearts a different blackjack from the ace of spades and the king of clubs.)

7. Nine horses are running in a race:

Affirmed	Secretariat	Lucky Lady
El Tigre	Man-O-War	Stempel
Red Fox	Alyzar	Ballantine

You can win big money (but don't bet on it!) if you win any of the following:

Daily double: pick two horses (first and second) in correct order

Exacta: pick 3 horses (first, second, and third) in correct order

Quinella: pick first and second horses (in any order).

How many possible outcomes are there for
a. Daily doubles   b. Exactas   c. Quinellas

8. A college instructor has five pairs of slacks, three sport coats, and four sweaters. How many different ensembles, each consisting of slacks, sport coat, and sweater, could he select? Draw a tree diagram.

9. From four married couples in how many ways can a pair of bridge partners consisting of a man and a woman be chosen if husband and wife are not to play together?

10. An automobile manufacturer has 10 different colors to choose from. In how many different ways can a three-tone automobile be colored, assuming that aesthetic monstrosities are just as permissible as tasteful combinations.

11. In how many ways can seven people line up for a group photograph?

12. Two flags are to be displayed vertically on the mast of a sailing vessel in order to convey a message to another vessel. If the two flags can be chosen from seven flags colored differently, how many different messages can be conveyed?

13. A breeder of hybrid corn is experimenting with four varieties of field corn. How many cross-pollinations must she perform to obtain every possible hybrid?

14. How many different four-digit street addresses may be formed from the digits 0, 1, 2, 3, 4, 5, 6, 7, 8, 9, assuming the first digit must be nonzero? (*Note:* Here repetitions are allowed.)

15. A car manufacturer advertises a model with four different colors for the top and a certain three of these colors for the body. How many different two-tone designs are possible? (*Note:* The answer is not 12.)

16. In how many ways can four students be seated in a row of eight seats?

17. How many different arrangements are possible for all of the letters of the word:
a. Campus   b. Sweet   c. Sneeze

18. What is the most important factor that would justify calling a "combination-lock" a permutation-lock? Suppose such a circular "combination-lock" had numbers 0, 1, 2, . . . , 45 on its dial, how many three-number "combinations" would be possible if the first

number would not be 0? If it takes 5 seconds to try each combination, how long will it take to try all possible combinations?

19. In how many ways can four men and three women be seated in a row of seven chairs if the end chairs are to be occupied by women?

20. A *monster* is defined to be the genetic offspring born to parents of different species. Given four different species S_1, S_2, S_3, S_4 and assuming that genetic engineering can accomplish it, how many distinguishable monsters can be created by a Frankenstein utilizing two parents from the four original species?

4.2   Linear Permutations and Factorial Notation

Our next objective is to develop formulas for combinations and permutations. We will start by defining the concept of a linear arrangement or permutation. Each of the parts of the following definition should be considered carefully.

Definition 1

(i)   A set of k distinct elements arranged in a line is called a linear *permutation* of the k elements.

(ii) Two linear permutations are *different* if at least one element in one is not in the other or if the same elements are in a different order.

(iii) The number of different permutations of r elements that can be formed from n distinct elements is denoted by $_nP_r$, where $r \leq n$.

At times we shall refer to $_nP_r$ as the number of permutations of n objects taken r at a time.

There is a short-hand notation that will often be useful when discussing permutations: factorial notation.

Definition 2 $0! = 1$, $1! = 1$, $2! = 2 \cdot 1$, $3! = 3 \cdot 2 \cdot 1$, $4! = 4 \cdot 3 \cdot 2 \cdot 1$, and in general $n! = n(n - 1)(n - 2)(n - 3) \cdots 3 \cdot 2 \cdot 1$, where the symbol $n!$ is read "n factorial."

Although it may seem rather arbitrary, we shall see later that $0! = 1$ is a meaningful and useful definition.

At the outset we consider the simple case of finding the number of permutations of n objects in sets of n items or, as we sometimes say, the number of permutations of n things taken n at a time. We will use a specific example.

Example 1

Suppose we wished to determine the number of ways four individuals may line up for a group photograph, assuming that we want all four individuals in the picture.

Solution We will use the individuals named in an earlier section: Juan, Mary, David, and Tibor. Note that JMDT is considered a different photographic arrangement (or a different permutation) from MDTJ even though the second picture contains the same individuals as the first. *The order is important.* To count all such permutations we point out that we have four choices for the first position in the photograph, then three choices for the second position in the photograph, then two choices for the third position, and finally one choice for the fourth position. By the fundamental counting principle we have

$$4! = 4 \cdot 3 \cdot 2 \cdot 1 = 24$$

different permutations. Notice that we have counted the permutations without actually listing all of the photographic arrangements.

Now we can generalize. If we begin with n distinct objects, we can easily compute the possible permutations of n of them. We have n choices for the first position on the line; to each of these there corresponds a "tree" in the diagram below (representing the case $n = 4$).

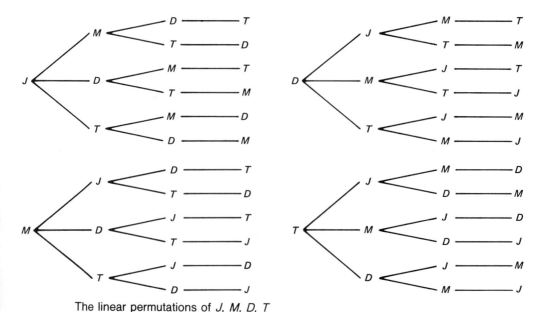

The linear permutations of *J, M, D, T*

After selecting the first object we have $(n - 1)$ choices left for the second position; thus for the first two positions there are $n(n - 1)$ possible choices. After the first two choices have been made, there are $(n - 2)$ choices for the third position; hence there are $n(n - 1)$ $(n - 2)$ possibilities for the first three objects. If this process is continued, we shall have only one choice remaining for the nth position. Thus n distinct objects can be arranged in $n(n - 1) (n - 2) \ldots (3) (2) (1)$ ways. We have provided a justification for the following theorem:

Theorem 2 $_nP_n = n!$

This says that the number of different permutations of n distinct objects taken n at a time is equal to n factorial.

Example 2.

Consider again the problem of photographing individuals in a line chosen from Juan, Mary, David, and Tibor. We could now raise the following question: in how many ways could two persons line up for a group photograph?

Solution By now it is clear that the first position could be occupied by any one of four individuals, the second position could be occupied by any one of three persons. Hence $_4P_2 = 4 \cdot 3 = 12$. This can be generalized in the following theorem:

Theorem 3 $_nP_r = \underbrace{n(n - 1) (n - 2) (n - 3) \ldots (n - r + 1)}_{r \text{ factors}}$

It is useful to note that, for example, $_7P_3 = 7 \cdot 6 \cdot 5 = 7!/4!$ since $4!$ cancels all the factors after the 5 in $7 \cdot 6 \cdot 5 \cdot 4 \cdot 3 \cdot 2 \cdot 1$. Thus we have an important alternate method of computing $_nP_r$ using factorial notation:

$$_nP_r = \frac{n!}{(n - r)!}$$

At this point we can see the reason for defining $\boxed{0! = 1}$. If, in the last formula, $r = n$, we would have that

$$_nP_n = \frac{n!}{0!}$$

which would be either meaningless or useless if we did not define $0! = 1$ so that $_nP_n = n!$

It is easy to derive the above formula for $_nP_r$ because we can multiply and divide the right side of

$$_nP_r = n(n-1)(n-2)\ldots(n-r+1)$$

by

$$(n-r)(n-r-1)(n-r-2)\ldots(3)(2)(1)$$

This will give us $n!$ in the numerator of

$$_nP_r = \frac{n(n-1)(n-2)\ldots(n-r+1)(n-r)(n-r-1)\ldots(3)(2)(1)}{(n-r)(n-r-1)\ldots(3)(2)(1)}$$

and thus

$$_nP_r = \frac{n!}{(n-r)!}$$

Example 3

In how many ways may four different books be arranged on a shelf?

Solution We want the number of linear arrangements of the four books:

$$_4P_4 = 4! = 4 \cdot 3 \cdot 2 \cdot 1 = 24.$$

Example 4

The telephone company is conducting an experiment regarding the time it takes to assemble a new telephone consisting of seven modular components that could be assembled in any order. If the telephone company is interested in the least time-consuming method of assembly and it wishes to test all possible assemblies, then how many different assemblies would it have to test?

Solution Here we want the number of permutations of seven objects taken seven at a time, or $_7P_7 = 7! = 5040.$

Example 5

Six color-coded wires are available for connection to terminals. In how many different ways may three of these wires be connected to three terminals?

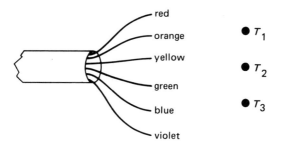

red
orange
yellow
green
blue
violet

$\bullet\, T_1$

$\bullet\, T_2$

$\bullet\, T_3$

Solution Note that the order of the connections to the terminals is important. Here we need $_6P_3 = 6 \cdot 5 \cdot 4 = 120$, which is the total number of ways we could connect three different wires (from six) to the three terminals.

Example 6

Show that if $_nP_r = n!/(n-r)!$, then it must follow that $_nP_0 = 1$.

Solution
$$_nP_0 = \frac{n!}{n!} = 1$$

Example 7

Simplify the fraction $n!/(n+2)!$

Solution Note that since $(n+2)! = (n+2)(n+1)(n)(n-1)\ldots(3)(2)(1)$, we can rewrite the problem and reduce it as follows:

$$\frac{n!}{(n+2)(n+1)(n!)} = \frac{1}{(n+2)(n+1)} = \frac{1}{n^2+3n+2}$$

Example 8

Show that

$$\frac{_nP_{n-1}}{_{n+1}P_n} = \frac{1}{n+1}$$

Solution
$$\frac{_nP_{n-1}}{_{n+1}P_n} = \frac{n!}{[n-(n-1)]!} \cdot \frac{1!}{(n+1)!} = \frac{1}{n+1}$$

Permutations with Repetitions Suppose we ask for the number of three-letter license plates that can be made using the letters A, B, C if repetitions are permitted (i.e., if plates such as AAC and BBB are possible). The first position can be filled in three ways, the second in three ways, and the third in three ways. Hence there are $3 \cdot 3 \cdot 3 = 3^3 = 27$ possible distinct license plates.

This concept is easily generalized. The number of different r permutations with repetitions of n distinct objects is given by

$$\underbrace{(n)\,(n)\,(n)\ldots(n)}_{r \text{ factors}} = n^r$$

Example 9

How many different three-letter Greek letter fraternity names are possible if letters may be used more than once? (*Note:* There are also 26 letters in the Greek alphabet.)

Solution $(26)^3 = 17{,}576$.

Permutations of n Objects not All Different Consider the number of permutations that could be made from the letters of the word *sneeze* using all of the letters without repetitions. This seems like a fairly difficult problem because three of the letters are identical. But let us suppose the answer to the problem is N, the number to be determined. Now we temporarily assume that the e's are distinguishable by using subscripts and indicating them by writing e_1, e_2, e_3. Now for each of the N different permutations, we could rearrange the e's in 3! ways. Therefore $(N)\,(3!)$ is the number of distinct permutations if we assume that the e's are distinguishable from each other. But this is the same as assuming that all the original letters of *sneeze* are distinguishable from each other. Thus

$$6! = (N)\,(3!) \text{ and } N = \frac{6!}{3!}$$

The same kind of reasoning can be used to prove the following:

> **Theorem 4**   The number of different n permutations from n objects, of which s are identical, t are identical, u are identical, ..., etc., is given by

$$N = \frac{n!}{s!\,t!\,u!\ldots}$$

Example 10

Using computer-generated musical tones, a UFO signal is to consist of 10 tones in a row. How many different 10-tone signals are possible consisting of three A flats, five G sharps, and two C naturals?

Solution The answer is the number of permutations of 10 tones of which a certain three are identical, another five are identical, and another two are identical. Therefore the result is

$$N = \frac{10!}{3! \; 5! \; 2!} = 2520$$

Example 11

How many distinguishable arrangements are there of all of the letters of the word "Mississippi"?

Solution

$$\frac{11!}{4! \; 4! \; 2!} = 34{,}650$$

Exercise 4.2 1. Compute each of the following.

a. 10!   b. $\dfrac{6! \; 4!}{3! \; 0!}$ c. $_8P_3$ d. $_8P_5$

2. Show by example that each of the following is *false* in general.

a. $(n!)^2 = (n^2)!$ b. $(2n)! = 2(n!)$
c. $(n + m)! = n! + m!$ d. $(nm)! = (n!) \, (m!)$

3. How many different baseball team positionings of nine are possible if 12 people are available and can play any of the nine positions?

4. Find the number of two-digit numbers that can be formed from the digits 1, 2, 3, 4, 5, 6, 7 if

a. Digits cannot be repeated.   b. Digits can be repeated.
c. Digits must be even.   d. Digits must be odd.
e. Units digit must be even and tens digit must be odd.

5. In how many ways can all of six people line up for a group photograph? Suppose two people insist on standing together?

6. How many codes consisting of four letters could be made from the letters of the word "groupie" if

a. No letter is repeated.   b. Letters may be repeated.

7. Find x if

a. $_8P_x = 336$ b. $_xP_2 = 20$ c. $_xP_x = 2 \, (x - 2)!$

8. In how many ways can we pick a first and second card from a 52-card deck, if the first card is selected, recorded, and then replaced before the second card is picked?

9. In how many ways can we pick a first and second card from a

52-card deck, if the first card is selected, recorded, but not replaced before the second card is picked?

10. In how many ways may we construct a five-digit number using only 1's or 2's or 3's as digits? Draw a tree diagram for illustrative purposes.

11. In how many ways can four different books be arranged on a shelf?

12. In how many ways can six books, four of which are math books, be arranged on a shelf if all the math books have to be next to one another?

13. How many different permutations are there for all of the letters of the words:

a. "Scram"   b. "Discomania"
c. "Lollapalooza"   d. "Screeeeeeek"

14. Five people get on a bus in which eight seats are vacant. In how many ways can they all be seated?

15. There are 10 true-false questions on a test. If you must answer every question, how many possible ways can all ten questions be answered?

16. How many different signals can be made by hoisting two yellow flags, four green flags, and three red flags on a ship's mast at the same time?

17. A four-tone audio signal consists of bleeps, bloops, blips, and blaps. How many four-tone signals are possible if tone repetitions are not permitted? Are permitted?

18. How many distinct five-digit numbers can be made using all of the digits 1, 2, 2, 2, 7 in any order?

19. In how many ways can we connect five color-coded wires to seven terminals if a terminal may not have more than one wire attached to it?

20. Simplify each formula:

a. $\dfrac{(n+3)!}{(n+2)!}$ b. $\dfrac{{}_nP_{n-2}}{{}_nP_{n-1}}$

21. Explain why 13! is divisible by 100.

22. Can $n!$ be larger than n^7? If so, find the smallest n such that $n^7 < n!$. Use a calculator to assist in your computations.

23. Construct a tree diagram for the number of permutations of {a, b, c, d} taken:

a. Two at a time   b. Three at a time   c. Four at a time

24. Margaret, Lui Chi, Billy, and Adele must all sit on a bench, but Billy, who is extremely neurotic, must sit to the right of Adele (not necessarily adjacent to her). How many acceptable seating

arrangements are there assuming we consider Billy's special requirements?

*25. Stirling's formula is given by

$$n! \sim \sqrt{2\pi}\ n^{n+(1/2)}e^{-n}$$

where the sign $\sim$ is used to indicate that the ratio of the two "sides" tends to unity as n becomes unboundedly large. This formula can be used to approximate numerically $n!$ for large n. Using a calculator, compute

a. Exact value of 13!
b. Approximate value of 13! using Stirling's formula

Show that the percentage error in (b) is less than 0.7% away from the true value. For your computations use $\sqrt{2\pi} =$ 2.506628275 and $e = 2.718281828$.

26. In the ancient Chinese *I Ching,* or *Book of Permutations,* there appear diagrams utilizing the two "principles": the male *yang* symbolized ▬▬▬▬ and the female *ying* symbolized ▬ ▬. One such diagram is the *sz'siang* or "four figures," which is the set of permutations of the two principles taken two at a time with repetitions.

Draw the permutations of these two principles taken three at a time with repetitions. These figures $\left(\text{for example, } \begin{matrix} ▬▬▬ \\ ▬ ▬ \\ ▬▬▬ \end{matrix}\right)$ are called the *pa-kua* (eight *kua*) or eight trigrams. They are over three thousand years old (from 1150 B.C.) and have been used extensively as symbols of much that is in Chinese philosophy.

There are also hexagrams in the *I Ching.* How many would you expect?

*27. Use the following BASIC language computer program to compute $n!$ for n equals 3, 7, and 12.

```
10  PRINT 'ENTER THE VALUE FOR N'
20  PRINT
30  INPUT N
40  A = 1
50  FOR I =1TO N
60  A = A*I
70  NEXT I
80  PRINT 'N FACTORIAL = '; A
90  END
```

*28. Write a BASIC program which can be used to compute $_nP_r$ and run the program by testing the computations of $_6P_2$, $_6P_4$, $_{52}P_5$, and $_7P_0$.

4.3 Combinations

At this point you may feel that many of the types of problems we have been solving are mechanical, dreary, pointless, arbitrary, or perhaps some *combination* of these four attributes. It is difficult to conceive of a problem such as "how many ways are there of choosing four books from eight different books?" as being useful in some practical field of endeavor. Also, it is not clear that knowing we can permute the letters of the word "sneeze in 120 distinguishable ways could be helpful in studying atomic physics or in determining actuarial results such as insurance rates. Nevertheless, permutations and combinations are extremely important tools of analysis in the study of applied probability. Being able to calculate the number of ways various events can occur is essential in the prediction of likelihoods, which is the subject of subsequent work in this text.

We have already mentioned that a combination is a unique selection (or subset) or r objects chosen from n given objects, without regard to order. Thus suppose we are given the four letters A, B, C, D and asked for the combinations of these four symbols taken two at a time. They are AB, BC, CD, AC, BD, and AD. We can observe graphically these six combinations by examining the following diagram:

At this stage, then, the following definition should make sense.

Definition 3   Given a set of n distinct elements.

i.   A unique subset of r elements $(r \leq n)$ is called a *combination of n objects taken r at a time.*
ii. Two combinations are *different* if at least one element in one is not in the other.
iii. The number of combinations of r elements that can be formed from n elements is denoted $_nC_r$, where $r \leq n$.

Our objective is to find a way of indirectly computing the number $_nC_r$ for given values of n and r without having to construct a tedious list of all possible combinations in a given example.

Example 1

Draw five points, no three of which lie on the same straight line, to represent the letters A, B, C, D, and E. Then list all possible distinct triangles that can be drawn connecting three of the five points. These triangles represent the number of combinations of five things taken three at a time.

Solution

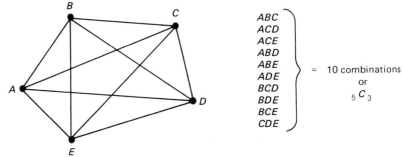

$$
\left.\begin{matrix} ABC \\ ACD \\ ACE \\ ABD \\ ABE \\ ADE \\ BCD \\ BDE \\ BCE \\ CDE \end{matrix}\right\} = \begin{matrix} 10 \text{ combinations} \\ \text{or} \\ {}_5C_3 \end{matrix}
$$

Example 2

Following up on Example 1, use a tree diagram to establish the relationship between the three quantities $_5C_3$, 3!, and $_5P_3$.

Solution Starting from the root of the tree, we have $_5C_3 = 10$ different initial branches. For each of these ten combinations there are 3! distinguishable permutations. Thus the number of branches is $_5C_3$ 3! $= 60$. This is the same as the number of permutations of five things taken three at a time which the large tree diagram below illustrates.

It is now not a difficult matter to prove the following theorem.

> **Theorem 5**   If there are n distinct objects, the number of ways of choosing combinations of r of them is given by
>
> $$_nC_r = \frac{_nP_r}{r!}, \text{ where } r \leq n.$$

We prove this by noting that each of the $_nC_r$ combinations can be permuted in $r!$ ways, which is the same number as the permutations of n objects taken r at a time. Hence $_nC_r\,(r!) = {}_nP_r$. Therefore $_nC_r = {}_nP_r/r!$

It is useful to recall that $_nP_0 = 1$ and that $_nP_n = n!$. We also defined $0! = 1$. It will therefore be consistent to observe that $_nC_0 = 1$ and

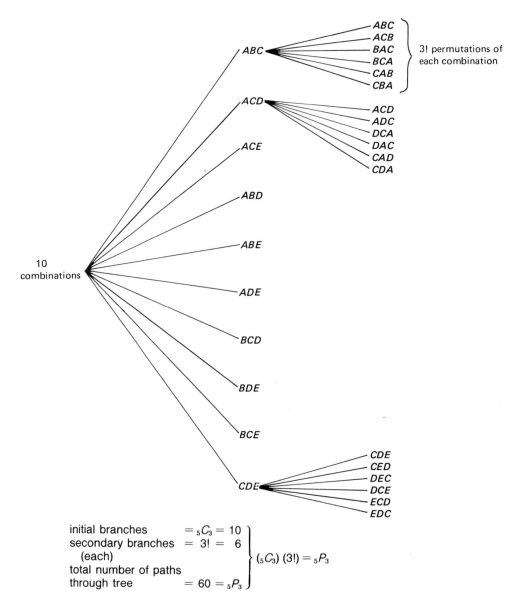

$$n C_n = 1.$$ We had an alternate expression for $_nP_r$, which allows us to write the following formula.

$$_nC_r = \frac{_nP_r}{r!} = \frac{n!}{r!\,(n-r)!}$$

The latter form will sometimes be preferred.

Example 3

Given five points, no three of which lie on the same straight line, how many distinct lines can be drawn connecting any two of them?

Solution This is just the number of ways of forming combinations of five things taken two at a time (see the following Figure) or

$$_5C_2 = {_5P_2}/2! = (5 \cdot 4)/(2 \cdot 1) = 10$$

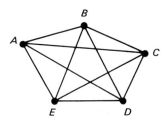

Example 4

Show that $_nC_r = {_nC_{n-r}}$.

Solution

$$\frac{n!}{r! \, (n-r)!} = \frac{n!}{(n-r)! \, [n-(n-r)]!}$$

Example 5

In how many ways can we select 30 stars from a constellation of 32 stars?

Solution Since $_{32}C_{30} = {_{32}C_2}$, we can use $_{32}C_2$. Thus we have $_{32}C_2 = 32 \cdot 31/2! = 496$.

Example 6

From a penny, a dime, and a nickel how many different sums of money can be formed?

Solution This is the number of combinations of three things taken one, two, and three at a time. Hence we have $_3C_3 + {_3C_2} + {_3C_1} = 7$ possible different sums of money (or combinations).

Example 7

In how many ways can nine books be equally distributed among three people?

Solution Here we use combinations together with the fundamental counting principle. There are $_9C_3$ ways of choosing three books for the first person, then there are $_6C_3$ ways of choosing three books for the second person, then there are $_3C_3 = 1$ way of choosing the remaining books for the third person. Therefore we obtain $(_9C_3)(_6C_3)(_3C_3) = 1680$ different equal-sized book distributions.

Example 8

In casino blackjack played with one standard deck of cards, there are 16 10-value cards and four aces. (10-value cards are either 10, J, Q, K of any suit). A blackjack consists of any ace and any 10-value card (two cards in all).

    a. How many blackjacks are possible?
    b. How many two-card hands are possible?

Solution a. By the fundamental counting principle, there are $16 \cdot 4 = 64$ possible blackjacks.
      b. There are $_{52}C_2 = 1326$ possible two-cards hands.

Example 9

Solve the same problem as the above using four decks.

Solution a. $(64)(16) = 1024$ possible blackjacks
      b. $_{208}C_2 = 21{,}528$ possible two-card hands
(The relative proportion of blackjacks is higher with one deck than with four.)

Example 10

How many different bridge hands of 13 cards may be dealt from a standard 52-card deck?

Solution $_{52}C_{13}$ is much too large to compute precisely on a 10-place calculator. However we can represent an approximate answer as $_{52}C_{13} \approx (6.35) \cdot 10^{11}$, which is 635,000,000,000. Bridge players will never run out of new situations.

Example 11

How many different poker hands are possible? (Here we distinguish between hands having different suits.)

Solution
$$_{52}C_5 = \frac{(52)(51)(50)(49)(48)}{5!} = 2{,}598{,}960 \text{ hands}$$

Example 12

A multiple life insurance policy is issued to a family of four individuals. The insurance company will have to pay benefits if any one or more of the four individuals dies. How many possible situations can arise in which the company will pay benefits, assuming the policy terminates 10 years after it is issued?

Solution There can be one, two, three, or four deaths, which can occur in a total of $_4C_1 + _4C_2 + _4C_3 + _4C_4 = 15$ ways.

Exercise 4.3   1.   Find the value of the following.

   a. $_8C_2$ b. $_8C_6$ c. $_{50}C_{48}$
   d. $_5C_1$ e. $_5C_0$ f. $_5C_5$

2. The winner of a contest can choose any five of eight prizes. In how many ways can the selections be made?

3. Four points A, B, C, and D form the vertices of a square. How many lines can be drawn connecting any two of the points? (Solve this problem indirectly as well as by actually diagramming the square.)

4. Four points A, B, C, and D form the vertices of a square. How many triangles can be formed? (One such triangle is shown.) Solve the problem indirectly as well as by using a diagram.

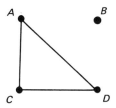

5. In how many ways can the Supreme Court give a majority decision? (There are nine justices on the Supreme Courts.)

6. Show that
$$_4C_0 + _4C_1 + _4C_2 + _4C_3 + _4C_4 = 16$$

7. The previous example is a generalization of the statement that
$$_nC_0 + _nC_1 + _nC_2 + \ldots + _nC_n = 2^n$$

Test the statement for the cases $n = 3$ and $n = 5$.

8. Explain why the following two problems are equivalent:

   a. Find the number of three-person committees that are possible when choosing from seven people.
   b. Find the number of four-person committees that are possible when choosing from seven people.

9. Six people are seated around a table and, during a champagne toast, each person clicks her/his glass with each other person. How many clicks will be produced?

10. List all the possible combinations of three people that could be chosen from: Toshiko, Jocelyn, Stacey, and Fritz.

11.   A Little League baseball team has 12 players available for a nine-member team.

    a.   How many different nine-member batting orders are possible?
    b.   How many different nine-member teams are possible?

12.   Explain why the term "combination lock" is a misnomer.

*13.   Using the formula following Theorem 5, prove the following result:

$$_{n+1}C_{r+1} = {_n}C_r + {_n}C_{r+1}$$

14.   Three cards are drawn from a standard 52-card deck. In how many ways could we draw three of a kind?

15.   In how many ways can six books be equally distributed among two people? Three people?

16.   How many different sums of money can be formed from a penny, a nickel, a dime, and a quarter?

17.   Using a calculator, estimate the value of $_{40}C_{10}$.

18.   How many six-star constellations are possible when we view 12 stars in a telescope?

19.   Consider the game of *sim* which utilizes a six-point cluster:

The game is based on the fact that if all possible lines determined by the six points are colored with two colors, then a monochromatic triangle must occur. In sim, two players each pick a color and alternately color one of the lines. The first to complete a monochromatic triangle loses the game.

    a.   How many different lines can be drawn?
    b.   Play the game of sim with another person.

**20.   Using your knowledge of combinations, permutations, and the fundamental counting principle, explain and justify each of the following computations.

Number of possible five-card hands drawn in poker		
Straight flush	$10(_4C_1) =$	40
Four of a kind	$(_{13}C_1)(_4C_4)(_{12}C_1)(_4C_1) =$	624
Full house	$(_{13}C_2)2(_4C_2)(_4C_3) =$	3,744
Flush (nonstraight)	$(_{13}C_5)(_4C_1) - 40 =$	5,108
Straight (nonflush)	$10(4^5) - 40 =$	10,208
Three of a kind	$(_{13}C_1)(_4C_3)(_{12}C_2)4^2 =$	54,912
Two pairs	$(_{13}C_2)(_4C_2)(_4C_2)44 =$	123,552
One pair	$(_{13}C_1)(_4C_2)(_{12}C_3)4^3 =$	1,098,240
No points	$a - $ (all of the above) $ =$	1,302,540
Any five cards	$a = {}_{52}C_5 =$	2,598,960

5

Discrete Probability
with Applications

> The physical world of civilized man also included such activities as throwing dice, playing cards, betting on horse races, playing roulette, and other forms of gambling. To understand and master these very phenomena, a new branch of mathematics, the theory of probability, was created. However, the theory now has depth and significance far beyond the sphere for which it was originally intended.
>
> Morris Kline

5.1 Equiprobable Sample Spaces and a Definition of Probability

Consider the following two problems:

(i)   Three balanced coins are flipped. What is the probability they will all come up heads?

(ii)   A medical researcher is attempting to measure the reliance she can place on a proposed treatment for a certain cancer. Without any treatment it is known that 50% of all afflicted persons die within 5 years. The proposed treatment is tried on three people and all of them recover (do not die within 5 years). What is the probability that the three individuals would have recovered anyway without the treatment?

It is remarkable that both of the above problems are essentially the same. We will soon see how we can compute an answer to either question (it turns out to be $\frac{1}{8}$). The point here is that there is a strong underlying link between such apparently frivolous questions involving coins, cards, and dice and quite serious problems involving life and death.

Probability theory began its actual development in the 17th century when certain questions arose involving the disreputable activity of gambling. Since then, mathematical theory and techniques concerning questions of likelihood and risk have expanded into a very rich and well-recognized subject. Probability and its very close partner, statistics, have been applied to a wide range of scientific and technological issues.

These include the theory of heat, astronomy, genetics, marketing research, educational research, voting pattern analysis, credit analysis,
game theory applied to hot or cold arts of warfare, stock market analysis
and arbitrage, diffusion theory, information theory, and the theory
of queues. Although we may not understand the details of the applications mentioned, knowing that they exist helps motivate us to want
to know more about this important subject. What we need to do first
is to formulate a clear idea concerning the meaning of the likelihood
or probability of some experiment or event.

We seek to achieve a meaningful way of numerically measuring
the likelihood of an event occurring within an experiment. For example,
concerning the experiment of flipping a coin, we might ask about the
probability of the event that the coin comes up heads. Here the words
"experiment" and "event" will remain formally undefined, as will be
the case with certain other key words. This means we are proceeding
intuitively: examples and discussions will be used to explain the concepts surrounding words that are difficult to define rigorously at an
elementary level.

Consider the following "experiments" and the various associated
"outcomes" that are possible.

(i)   A balanced coin is flipped, with possible outcomes of either a
       head or a tail.

(ii)   A standard deck of cards is well shuffled and one card is selected
       with 52 different outcomes possible.

(iii) A nickel is spun on its edge on a very smooth and level surface,
       with possible outcomes of either a head or a tail or the nickel
       remaining on its edge.

(iv)   A fair die is tossed onto a table, with possible outcomes of the
       die landing with any one of its six surfaces facing up.

We should note certain "key" words: "balanced coin," "well-shuffled
deck," and "fair die." These words help explain the concept of *equal
likelihood*. By a "balanced coin" we mean one whose head and tail are
equally likely to land on top. When we select a card from a "well-
shuffled" deck, we have no reason to expect that a particular card is
any more (or less) likely to be chosen than any other. When we say
a die is "fair" we mean the six possible outcomes (1, 2, 3, 4, 5, or 6)
are equally likely. Some of us will recognize, perhaps, the circularity
in explaining "equally likely" in terms of "likelihood;" however, we
hope the concept will become clear. Experiment (iii) above is a bit
different from the others: it turns out that the head and tail outcomes
are not equally likely. Stephen Willoughby of New York University
has observed that when you spin a nickel, a head is not as likely as

a tail because the rim edge of a nickel is more pronounced on the head and has a tendency to kick over the nickel a disproportionate number of times onto one of the sides.

We will use the term *sample space* to refer to the set of all possible outcomes that can occur as a result of an experiment. An event E is some subset of the sample space. In this section we will define probability for sample spaces having equally likely outcomes.

> **Definition 1**   Suppose we are given a sample space with n equally likely outcomes. Suppose, further, that an event E occurs in k of these outcomes, where $0 \le k \le n$. Then $P(E)$, the probability of event E, is given by
>
> $$P(E) = \frac{k}{n} = \frac{\text{number of outcomes favorable to } E}{\text{number of possible outcomes}}$$

Again, although we recognize the circularity in defining probability in terms of "equally likely" (which has a probabilistic notion already contained in it), we are relying on our intuition as to what is meant by this phrase. We will list some simple examples.

Example 1

A balanced coin is flipped. The letter E represents the event that the coin comes up heads. Find $P(E)$.

Solution Sample space {H, T} consists of two equally likely outcomes, with only one of them favorable to E. Hence. $P(E) = 1/2$.

Example 2

A fair die is tossed onto a table. $E =$ event the die comes up either 1 or 2. Find $P(E)$.

Solution The sample space consists of six equally likely outcomes, with two of them favorable to E. Hence $P(E) = 2/6 = 1/3$.

Example 3

A standard deck of cards is well shuffled, and one card is selected. $E =$ event the card chosen is a diamond. Find $P(E)$.

Solution
$$P(E) = \frac{13}{52} = \frac{1}{4}$$

Thus the probability of an event E is a number that we are denoting $P(E)$. This number $P(E)$ gives us an indication of how likely the event E is to occur. The greater the likelihood of E, the larger the value of the probability $P(E)$. The values of $P(E)$ for any event E will be in the range

$$0 \leq P(E) \leq 1$$

The extreme value $P(E) = 0$ corresponds to an event E that is an *impossibility*. The extreme value $P(E) = 1$ corresponds to an event E that is a *certainty*.

As we will see, ratios of likelihoods are preserved, so that an event that is in some sense twice as likely to occur as some other event should have twice the probability. Equally likely events have the same probability.

Fallacious Assignment of Likelihoods In each of the previous examples it is clear that the sample space consists of equally likely outcomes. We therefore have a very strong feeling about the correctness of our definition of probability. If a sample space does *not* consist of equally likely outcomes, hasty conclusions can sometimes be misleading. We can walk across the street blindfolded and either be struck by a car or not be struck by a car; this does *not* mean that we can compute the probability of being struck by writing

$$P(E) = \frac{1}{2}$$

since we have no reason to suppose that being struck and not being struck are equally likely.

We may feel we can assume that probability of conceiving a male child is 1/2, since common knowledge tells us there should be no difference in likelihood between conceiving a boy or a girl. In this case, however, "common knowledge" may not be correct. In the United States during 1960 there were 4,258,000 births, of which 2,180,000 were males. The ratio

$$\frac{2,180,000}{4,158,000} = .512 \text{ (rounded)};$$

moreover, this ratio has persisted for many many years.

Sometimes there are superstitions that lead people to incorrect conclusions about some sample spaces. Suppose a fair coin is flipped 10 times in a row and a very unusual sequence of events occurs: all 10 flips come up heads. The coin is to be flipped again, and we ask what is the probability the coin will come up heads. There are many people who would say that on the eleventh toss it is more likely that a head will appear because the coin is on a "streak of heads;" others might say that a tail is more likely because the coin is "due" for a tail. This kind of "gambler's mentality" assumes that since, in the long run, the number of heads should be approximately the same as the number of tails, the coin somehow has to make up for its bizarre past behavior. There is no doubt that in a very large sequence of flips, the ratio of heads to tosses will get closer to 1/2, but no matter how many heads have appeared during some sequence of tosses, the probability of a head on the next toss is still 1/2. Another way of expressing this is to say that "a coin has no memory."

During a lecture delivered at Marymount College in 1967, the mathematical historian Oystein Ore described an interesting fallacious sample space for tossing two dice that was considered valid by the ancient Romans. Using modern terminology the Roman viewpoint was as follows:

Fallacious sample space for two dice

Sum	2	3	4	5	6	7	8	9	10	11	12	Total
Outcomes listed	1–1	2–1	2–2 or 3–1	3–2 or 4–1	3–3 or 4–2 or 5–1	4–3 or 5–2 or 6–1	2–6 or 3–5 or 4–4	5–4 or 6–3	5–5 or 6–4	6–5	6–6	
Number of outcomes	1	1	2	2	3	3	3	2	2	1	1	21

The Romans thus computed the probability of obtaining a 7 as

$$P(\text{obtaining a total of } 7) = \frac{3}{21} = \frac{1}{7}$$

They also computed the probability of obtaining a 6 and found the result to be identical since

$$P(\text{obtaining a total of } 6) = \frac{3}{21} = \frac{1}{7}$$

They knew, however, from actual practice with dice that the total 7 came up more frequently than any other total including 6 or 8. This strange (or so it seemed to the Romans) excess of 7's was attributed to the mystical and "divine" powers enveloped in the number 7.

The blunder is seen when we realize that 4–3 must be considered as a separate case from 3–4. In fact there are six possible outcomes favorable to a total of 7; and there are only five possible outcomes favorable to a total of 6.

These kinds of errors in thinking are not restricted to the ancient Romans. There is a persistent story, possibly true, that the famous co-inventor of calculus, Gottfried Wilhelm Leibniz, believed that it was just as likely to throw an 11 with a pair of dice as it is to throw a 12. In fact, it is more likely that an 11 will occur because there are two ways of obtaining an 11 but only one way of obtaining a 12. Charles Sanders Peirce was correct when he said that "In no other branch of mathematics is it so easy for experts to blunder as in probability theory." No doubt we will make some of the same kinds of errors. However, by learning more about probability we can certainly hope to avoid them.

Example 4

A fair die is tossed on a table. Find the probability of each of the following events.

E_1 = event the die comes up 3
E_2 = event the die comes up 3 or 4
E_3 = event the die comes up 1 or 2 or 3 or 4 or 5 or 6
E_4 = event the die comes up 7

Solution As we have mentioned before, the sample space consists of six equally likely outcomes. Correct results are as follows.

$$P(E_1) = 1/6$$
$$P(E_2) = 2/6 = 1/3$$
$$P(E_3) = 6/6 = 1$$
$$P(E_4) = 0/6 = 0$$

Note that the probabilities range from 0 (an *impossibility*) to 1 (a *certainty*). If a computed probability comes out to be greater than 1, an error has been made and the problem needs to be looked at more carefully. Likewise, a probability should never come out negative.

Example 5

Two fair dice are tossed on a table. (Think of one die as having light dots and the other die as having dark ones.) Show that there is a sample space consisting of 36 equally likely outcomes to this experiment.

Solution We can use the following matrix array to describe all 36 of the outcomes, each of which is equally likely.

J = light die

	1–1	1–2	1–3	1–4	1–5	1–6
	2–1	2–2	2–3	2–4	2–5	2–6
I = dark die	3–1	3–2	3–3	3–4	3–5	3–6
	4–1	4–2	4–3	4–4	4–5	4–6
	5–1	5–2	5–3	5–4	5–5	5–6
	6–1	6–2	6–3	6–4	6–5	6–6

Note that the first number of each I–J pair represents the outcome of the dark die, and the second number (J) represents the outcome of the light die. There are 36 pairs in the above chart. If the dice are balanced, then there is no reason for supposing any outcome to be more likely than any other outcome. Thus the sample space consists of 36 equally likely outcomes.

We observe also that if we could not distinguish the dice (that is, if the darkness were identical), there would still be 36 equally likely outcomes. This is so since 3–6 and 6–3 represent two physically distinct situations, regardless of whether or not the dice are different. The 36 distinct outcomes can be pictured as follows.

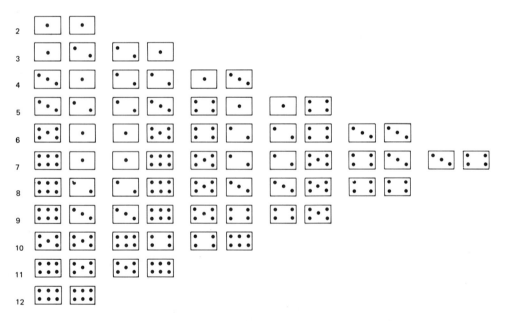

It is instructive to recall the fundamental principle of counting in light of the previous example. Since one of the dice can fall in any one of six ways, and the other die can also fall in six ways, then both dice can fall in a total of (6) (6) = 36 different physical positions. This result agrees with the outcomes diagrammed above.

Example 6

Two fair dice are thrown. Using the results obtained in the previous example, list the probabilities of each of the events given below. Also find the sum of each of the probabilities and interpret the result.

$$E_2 = \text{a 2 is thrown}$$
$$E_3 = \text{a 3 is thrown}$$
$$E_4 = \text{a 4 is thrown}$$
$$E_5 = \text{a 5 is thrown}$$
$$E_6 = \text{a 6 is thrown}$$
$$E_7 = \text{a 7 is thrown}$$
$$E_8 = \text{an 8 is thrown}$$
$$E_9 = \text{a 9 is thrown}$$
$$E_{10} = \text{a 10 is thrown}$$
$$E_{11} = \text{an 11 is thrown}$$
$$E_{12} = \text{a 12 is thrown}$$

Solution

$$P(E_2) = 1/36$$
$$P(E_3) = 2/36$$
$$P(E_4) = 3/36$$
$$P(E_5) = 4/36$$
$$P(E_6) = 5/36$$
$$P(E_7) = 6/36$$
$$P(E_8) = 5/36$$
$$P(E_9) = 4/36$$
$$P(E_{10}) = 3/36$$
$$P(E_{11}) = 2/36$$
$$P(E_{12}) = 1/36$$

Note that the sum of the probabilities is given by

$$\frac{1+2+3+4+5+6+5+4+3+2+1}{36} = \frac{36}{36} = 1$$

which indicates the *certainty* that the events listed above exhaust all of the possible outcomes.

Example 7

Two fair dice are thrown. Find the probabilities of the events specified.

$$A = \text{any identical pair is thrown}$$
$$B = \text{a 5 or a 7 is thrown}$$
$$C = \text{a 2 or 3 or 4 or 11 or 12 is thrown}$$

Solution The identical pairs are indicated on the diagram.

1–1	1–2	1–3	1–4	1–5	1–6
2–1	2–2	2–3	2–4	2–5	2–6
3–1	3–2	3–3	3–4	3–5	3–6
4–1	4–2	4–3	4–4	4–5	4–6
5–1	5–2	5–3	5–4	5–5	5–6
6–1	6–2	6–3	6–4	6–5	6–6

Thus

$$P(A) = 6/36 = 1/6$$
$$P(B) = 10/36 = 5/18$$
$$P(C) = 9/36 = 1/4$$

It is instructive to note that event B is more likely to occur than event C.

Example 8

Three balanced coins are flipped: a dime, a nickel, and a quarter. How many outcomes are there? List them.

Solution There are $(2)(2)(2) = 8$ distinct outcomes.

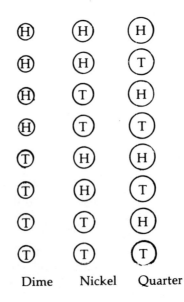

Dime   Nickel   Quarter

Example 9

Three balanced pennies are tossed. Find the probability of obtaining exactly two heads and one tail.

Solution Just as in the previous example, there are still eight physically distinct outcomes, of which those indicated are favorable to two heads and one tail.

HHH

HHT

HTH

HTT

THH

THT

TTH

TTT

Thus the probability is 3/8.

Example 10

One balanced penny is tossed three times. Find the probability of obtaining two heads and one tail.

Solution The problem is equivalent to the previous one, and thus the answer is still 3/8.

Exercise 5.1   1.   A balanced nickel and dime are both flipped. List the outcomes of the sample space. Find the probability of each of the following events.

      a. $E_1 =$ both coins are heads   b. $E_2 =$ both coins are tails
      c. $E_3 =$ both coins are different (neither both heads nor both tails)

    2.   A standard deck of cards is well shuffled, and one card is selected. Find the probability of each event.

      a.   The card is a spade.
      b.   The card is any picture (jack, queen, or king).
      c.   The card is an ace.
      d.   The card is either a diamond or a 7.

3. A fair die is tossed onto a table. Find the probability of each event.

   a. $E_1 =$ obtaining either a 1, 2, or 3
   b. $E_2 =$ obtaining a 1, 2, 3, 4, 5, or 6   c. $E_3 =$ obtaining a 7

4. Two fair dice are tossed onto a table. Find the probability that the dice will total the values given in each event listed:

   a. Totals of 2, 4, 6, 8, 10 or 12   b. Totals of 2, 7, or 11
   c. Any even total   d. Any total less than 9
   e. Any total between 3 and 10 inclusive

5. Explain the fallacies in the following.

   a. There's a 50% chance I'll need my umbrella because it will either rain or it will not rain.
   b. Your chances are about even when you bet on the competence of a lawyer. After all, lawyers are just like everyone else: some are good and some are lousy.

6. Five cards are selected at random from a well-shuffled deck. Show that the probability of selecting a royal flush is .000001539. (A royal flush consists of a ten, jack, queen, king, ace of the same suit.)

* 7. There are $_{52}C_2$ possible two-card selections in the game of "21" when one deck is in use; there are $_{208}C_2$ two-card selections when four decks are in use. Show that the probability of getting a blackjack (an ace and a ten or picture card) is higher in a one-deck game than in a four-deck game.

8. A ball is drawn at random from a bag containing four white balls and six red balls. Find the probability that the ball chosen is

   a. Red   b. White   c. Red or white   d. Purple

* 9. Two balls are chosen at random from a bag containing four white balls and six red balls (the first ball is not replaced before the second ball is selected). Find the probability that the balls chosen will both be red.

10. The sample spaces for each of the following problems have the same number of elements. Construct a model for each sample space and show that the answer to both questions is 1/8.

   a. Three balanced coins are tossed. What is the probability they will all come up heads?
   b. A medical researcher is attempting to measure the reliance she can place on a proposed treatment for a certain cancer. Without any treatment it is known that 50% of all afflicted

persons die within 5 years. The proposed treatment is tried on three people, and all of them recover (do not die within 5 years.) What is the probability that the three individuals would have recovered anyway without the treatment?

*11. Two aces and four ten-value cards (10, jack, queen, or king) are removed from a one-deck game of "21." Show that this drastically reduces the probability of obtaining a blackjack. (Compare to problem 7.)

*12. Two dice are tossed, but each die is "loaded" by having a small weight placed on the surface having six dots, thus increasing the probability of each die coming up a 1, which is the number on the face opposite the 6. Examine a pair of dice and explain why the probability of throwing a 7 with this pair of dice is smaller than with a balanced pair of dice.

*13. (Martin Gardner) Show that the probabilities for the totals 2, 3, 4, 5, 6, 7, 8, 9, 10, 11, 12 of the two non standard odds-preserving dice shown below are, respectively, 1/36, 2/36, 3/36, 4/36, 5/36, 6/36, 5/36, 4/36, 3/36. 2/36, 1/36. These are the same as the respective probabilities for the totals on a pair of standard dice. Demonstrate this.

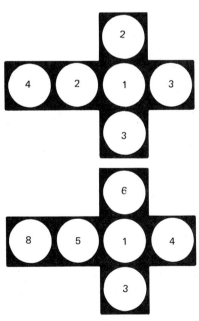

Odds-preserving dice.

5.2   Statistical or Empirical Probability

Many kinds of events, such as whether or not an individual of a certain age will live until age 65, whether a home in a particular area will be burglarized during the next year, whether a restaurant will be substantially damaged by fire during the next 5 years, etc., cannot be determined *a priori*. This means that without the benefit of past experience, it is difficult to estimate a probability for certain kinds of events. When a sample space consists of outcomes that are not equiprobable (such as 36 outcomes with dice), it may be impossible to obtain meaningful probabilities without statistical experience.

We consider such an event. Suppose we found that over a 5-year period 132 of 12,478 restaurants were destroyed by fire. We could use the number

$$\frac{132}{12,478} = 0.01058$$

as a probability *estimate* that a restaurant will be destroyed by fire during the next 5-year period. It may well be that in some cases such as this one, there is no other way of obtaining an accurate probability estimate, nor is there any way of improving that estimate until further data are gathered. This type of estimate is called a *relative frequency*, an *empirical, statistical,* or *a posteriori* (after the fact) measure of probability.

> Definition 2   If an experiment is performed n times, where n is large, and if k is the number of times a particular event occurs, then k/n is the *statistical probability estimate* of that event.

There are two important difficulties with this definition. The first is that we are not defining what we mean by large. Mathematicians are aware that in a random experiment the ratio k/n becomes stable in the long run, that is, approaches a limit. Our intuition certainly is not very helpful in deciding what is "large enough" in some particular case. We hasten to add, however, that such questions can be answered and are normally taken up in a course in statistics. The second difficulty with this definition is that people will often make too much of it: it may not be the case that we can use such empirical estimates to predict the relative frequency of future events. This is so because over a period of time, the "random experiment" is continuously changing. For example, it may be that (in the example of restaurants destroyed by fire) building materials are becoming more fireproof and that improved police protection is reducing the number of fires due to arson. Thus the definition is most useful when the "experiment" we are studying is the same one each time it is being performed.

Example 1

A tack is tossed on a table top 1000 times, and the following results are recorded:

A = Tack lies on its side = 749 times
B = Tack lies on its flat head = 251 times

Find the statistical probability estimates for events A and B.

Solution

$$P(A) = \frac{749}{1000} = .749$$

$$P(B) = \frac{251}{1000} = .251$$

Example 2

Imagine that the year is 1959. We observe from statistical data that of 6,800,531 persons of age 65 alive at the start of 1958, 6,584,614 survived to reach age 66. (Here by age 65 we mean age of nearest birthday.)

a. Compute the probability of survival of a person of age 65 during 1958 to age 66.
b. Suppose there were 6,900,432 persons of age 65 alive at the start of 1959. Use your answer to (a) to estimate the number who will survive to age 66.
c. Suppose there are 9,200,654 persons of age 65 alive at the start of 1977. Use the answer to (a) to estimate the number who will survive to age 66.
d. Explain why the survival estimate in (c) is not so good as the one computed in (b).

Solution a. $\dfrac{6,584,614}{6,800,531} = .9682499$

b. Since .9682499 is viewed as the relative frequency of survival to age 66 (for 65 year olds), we can obtain an estimate this way:

(.9682499) (6,900,432) = 6,681,343 persons of age 66 alive during 1959

c. Similarly, if there are 9,200,654 persons of age 65 alive during 1977, we can estimate the same way:

$$(.9682499)\ (9,200,654) = 8,908,532 \text{ of age 66 alive in 1978}$$

d. The survival estimate in (c) is not so good because we are using an old survivorship ratio (for 1958) to make a prediction concerning a very recent population segment. The population mix may have changed considerably from 1958 to 1978, medical care may have improved substantially, and the general well being of current 65 year olds may have changed and thus altered the survivorship ratio considerably. It would have been better had we used survivorship ratios of more recent years.

Example 3

A pair of unknown dice are tossed onto a table 36,000 times and the following results are recorded

2	3	4	5	6	7	8	9	10	11	12
811	1781	2797	4022	5498	6020	5505	4166	2790	1790	820

Find the empirical probability for each of the events named. Compare to the *a priori* probabilities for a pair of fair dice.

Solution In each case we divide the recorded number of occurrences by 36,000 to obtain relative frequency estimates.

	2	3	4	5	6	7	8	9	10	11	12
Unknown dice	.0225	.0495	.0777	.1117	.1527	.1672	.1529	.1157	.0775	.0497	.0228
Known fair dice	1/36 = .0278	2/36 = .0556	3/36 = .0833	4/36 = .1111	5/36 = .1389	6/36 = .1667	5/36 = .1389	4/36 = .1111	3/36 = .0833	2/36 = .0556	1/36 = .0278

Note the discrepancies between the empirical probabilities for the unknown dice and the *a priori* probabilities obtained from a pair of known fair dice. It would appear, for example, that the probability of a 6 or 8 is significantly higher than are the corresponding probabilities in the fair dice. It is difficult to judge whether or not the difference is significant, whether there is a measurable likelihood that the unknown dice are loaded in some way and the deviations are not a chance occurrence. This is a topic for statistics.

It is worth making some comparison between the *a priori* probability definition for equiprobable sample spaces and the statistical or empirical definition of probability. When a coin is "fair" and the sample space {H, T} has equally likely outcomes, then we define the probability of a head to be 1/2. This does not mean that there is a 1/2 probability of obtaining exactly 50 heads in 100 tosses. We are saying, however, that the *a priori* value of 1/2 is a limiting value and that the ratio of heads to tosses will more nearly approach the value of 1/2 as the number of tosses becomes unboundedly large. From the statistical point of view, therefore, it makes sense to define a probability utilizing the ratio k/n, where n is the number of times an experiment is actually performed and k is the number of outcomes favorable to some particular event. We have a strong feeling that an *a priori* probability exists for every experiment (but we may not be able to obtain it), so we estimate its value by making use of a statistical definition. In utilizing the statistical definition we may be sure that the larger n is, the more accurate is our estimate of the actual or *a priori* probability. This can easily be seen in the following experiment involving coin tossing. We have recorded the number of heads in n tosses of a coin, where n has increasing values, and computed the ratio k/n of heads to tosses.

$n =$ number of tosses	$k =$ number of heads	k/n
2	0	0
10	4	.4
20	8	.4
30	12	.4
40	18	.45
50	21	.42
100	45	.45
1000	516	.516
10000	5036	.5036

Note that as n becomes larger, the computed value of k/n more nearly equals 1/2. If the coin is indeed fair, then the difference between k/n and 1/2 will approach 0. What is quite remarkable about the results given in the table is that although k/n is approaching 1/2, the *difference* between the number of heads and the number of tails appears to be widening. If k is the number of heads in n tosses, then $n - k$ is the number of tails and $k - (n - k) = 2k - n =$ difference between the number of heads and the number of tails.

Listing the values obtained in tabular form, we have the following table

n (tosses)	k (heads)	$n-k$ (tails)	$2k-n$ (heads-tails)	k/n
2	0	2	-2	0
10	4	6	-2	.4
20	8	12	-4	.4
30	12	18	-6	.4
40	18	22	-4	.45
50	21	29	-8	.42
100	45	55	-10	.45
1000	516	484	-32	.516
10000	5036	4964	$+72$	.5036

It is possible to show, using more advanced work in probability, that $2k - n$ becomes unboundedly large, both in a positive and a negative sense. Moreover, this is happening while (simultaneously) k/n is approaching the limiting value of $1/2$. This is a remarkable phenomenon. One of its implications is that if two gamblers persist in playing a fair, even-money game ($p = 1/2$), ultimately one of the players will lose all of his money to the other player. It is simply not true that a player's bankroll will remain "about the same" as when he entered the game. Think about that for awhile.

Example 4

(Here we apply empirical probability to population estimation.) In a small pond there is an unknown number of fish above a certain size. An ecologist randomly selects 100 fish (above the minimum size), marks them each with a small tag, and returns them to the pond. One week later 75 fish are randomly recaptured. Of these, 12 have tags. Estimate the fish population x in the pond.

Solution Here we will assume that the relative frequency of tagged fish remains constant for 1 week. Thus the empirical probability that a randomly chosen fish is tagged is given by

$$p = \frac{100}{x}$$

where $x =$ total fish population. When a sample of 75 fish is removed 1 week later, we assume that the proportion p of tagged fish in the pond is the same as the proportion of tagged fish in the sample. Thus

$$\frac{100}{x} = \frac{12}{75}$$

and $12x = 7500$ or $x = 625$ fish.

The above method of solution neglects a number of factors that may be important, such as the following.

(i)   Some of the marked fish might die due to the trauma of the tagging process.

(ii) The marked fish may not be thoroughly mixed in with the un-marked fish in the lake.

(iii) The tagged sample of 75 fish may not be statistically large enough to provide reasonable accuracy.

The result of 625 fish must be interpreted in light of these weaknesses.

Exercise 5.2 1. Corporation CBA has 2340 employees. A record is kept of the number of employees who call in sick for each of the days of one particular week. These were the results:

Monday	162
Tuesday	48
Wednesday	39
Thursday	42
Friday	79

Using the definition of empirical probability, find the probability that a randomly chosen employee will call in sick on some subsequent Monday, Tuesday, Wednesday, Thursday, and Friday. Explain why we call each of the five results a probability estimate? Explain the limitations of using these results as predictors of future sick-call behavior.

2. An unknown coin is tossed n times for various values of n, and the number of heads is recorded. Here were the results:

n	No. of heads
10	5
20	12
30	21
40	26
50	34
100	67
1000	695

Explain why (or why not) you believe this coin is biased.

3. Ask 60 different people to pick one digit from the four digits 1, 2, 3, and 4. Record the results. Explain why this is not a random selection process and therefore why the outcomes are not necessarily equally likely.

4. Roll a pair of fair dice 72 times and record the results. Compare empirical probability estimates with *a priori* probabilities.

5. For a particular 100-year period, the following mortality statistics have been compiled for 100,000 children 10 years old at the beginning of the period.

Age	Number living	Age	Number living
10	100,000	60	57,914
20	92,624	70	38,579
30	85,397	80	14,471
40	78,101	90	842
50	69,816	100	3
		110	0

Using empirical probability estimates, find the probability that

a. A 10 year old will live to 50
b. A 10 year old will live to 80
c. A 20 year old will live to 30
d. A 40 year old will live to 70
e. A 70 year old will live to 80
f. A 30 year old will live to 100
*g. A 30 year old will die between ages 60 and 70

6. A large jar is filled with an unknown number (x) of white beans. A sample of 50 beans is randomly selected and each is marked with a red dot and then returned to the jar. The jar of beans is then thoroughly mixed. A second sample of 20 beans is removed, which is found to contain four beans with red dots. Estimate x.

5.3 Finite Probability Spaces and Mutually Exclusive Events

Suppose we are given a finite sample space $S = \{a_1, a_2, \ldots, a_n\}$ consisting of n distinct elementary outcomes that exhaust all of the ways in which a particular experiment can turn out. We refer to each elementary outcome a_i as a *point* in the sample space.

Definition 3   A *finite probability space* is any assignment of values $P(a_i)$ for each point a_i such that

(i) $P(a_i) \geq 0$ for each i
(ii) $P(a_1) + P(a_2) + \ldots + P(a_n) = 1$

Each value $P(a_i)$ is called the *probability* of point a_i.

An *event* A is any subset of a sample space $S = \{a_1, a_2, \ldots, a_n\}$. It could happen that $A = \phi$ (A is impossible), in which case $P(A) = 0$, or it could happen that $A = S$ (A is a certainty), in which case $P(A) = 1$.

An *equiprobable space* is one in which

$$P(a_1) = P(a_2) = \ldots = P(a_n) = \frac{1}{n}$$

so that it follows that $P(a_1) + \ldots + P(a_n) = n(1/n) = 1$. When we use the phrase "at random," we are referring to equiprobable spaces only.

Since we can view an event as a set of elementary outcomes of a sample space, we can form events using set notations and operations. The following will be used in this chapter:

(i) $A \cup B =$ event that occurs if and only if A occurs or event B occurs (or both occur)

(ii) $A \cap B =$ event that occurs if and only if A occurs and B occurs

(iii) $\overline{A}$ = event that occurs if and only if A does *not* occur ($\overline{A}$ is called the complement of event A)

If it should turn out that $A \cap B = \phi$, then it would be impossible for event A and event B to *both* occur. In this case we would have $P(A \cap B) = 0$ and would refer to A and B as *mutually exclusive* events.

It is possible to prove the following theorem based on Definition 3 of a finite probability space. We will omit the proof, which follows from the fact that the probability of an event is the sum of the probabilities of its points.

Theorem 1   For all events in a finite probability space S:

(i)   For each event A, $0 \leq P(A) \leq 1$
(ii) $P(S) = 1$
(iii) If events A and B are mutually exclusive, then
       $P(A \cup B) = P(A) + P(B)$
(iv) $P(\overline{A}) = 1 - P(A)$

Although we have mentioned it before, we will state a formal definition of mutually exclusive events.

Definition 4   Two events A and B of a finite sample space are said to be *mutually exclusive* if they have no elementary events in common. Expressed symbolically, this is equivalent to $A \cap B = \phi$.

Example 1

Consider the sample space $S = \{a_1, a_2, a_3, a_4, a_5, a_6\}$ for a fair die in which a_i is the elementary outcome of the die coming up with i dots showing after a random toss. Find the probability of each event specified below.

a. $A = \{a_2, a_5\}$ b. $B = \{a_1, a_3, a_6\}$ c. $A \cap B$
d. $A \cup B$ e. $\overline{A}$ f. $\overline{B}$

Solution Since the die is fair, this is an equiprobable sample space. We therefore assign $P(a_i) = 1/6$ for each i. Then we have

a. $P(a_2 \text{ or } a_5) = 2/6 = 1/3$
b. $P(a_1 \text{ or } a_3 \text{ or } a_6) = 3/6 = 1/2$
c. $A \cap B = \phi$ since A and B have no elementary outcomes in common. Hence $P(A \cap B) = 0$ and by definition A and B are mutually exclusive.
d.   Since A and B are mutually exclusive, $P(A \cup B) = P(A) + P(B) = 1/3 + 1/2 = 5/6$.
e. $P(\overline{A}) = 1 - P(A) = 1 - 1/3 = 2/3$
f. $P(\overline{B}) = 1 - P(B) = 1 - 1/2 = 1/2$

Example 2

Consider the *non*equiprobable sample space

$$S = \{a_1, a_2, a_3, a_4, a_5, a_6\}$$

for a die that is loaded in such a way that the opposite surfaces a_2 and a_5 are equally likely but are each twice as likely to occur as the four remaining outcomes a_1, a_3, a_4, and a_6, which are also equally likely themselves. Assign correct probabilities to the outcomes in the sample space. Then answer the same questions as in Example 1 above.

Solution Let $x = P(a_1)$. Then $P(a_1) = P(a_3) = P(a_4) = P(a_6) = x$ and $P(a_2) = P(a_5) = 2x$. Since we want a finite probability space, we require that

$$x + x + x + x + 2x + 2x = 1$$

Thus $8x = 1$. Finally $x = 1/8$. Thus we assign the following probabilities:

$$P(a_1) = 1/8, \; P(a_2) = 1/4, \; P(a_3) = 1/8,$$
$$P(a_4) = 1/8, \; P(a_5) = 1/4, \; P(a_6) = 1/8$$

a.   Since a_2 and a_5 are mutually exclusive, $P(a_2 \text{ or } a_5) = P(a_2) + P(a_5)$
    $= 1/4 + 1/4 = 1/2$

b. Similarly, $P(a_1 \text{ or } a_3 \text{ or } a_6) = 1/8 + 1/8 + 1/8 = 3/8$
c. $A = \{a_2, a_5\}$ and $B = \{a_1, a_3, a_6\}$ implies that A and B are mutually exclusive. Therefore $P(A \cap B) = 0$
d. $P(A \cup B) = P(A) + P(B) = 1/2 + 3/8 = 7/8$
e. $P(\overline{A}) = 1 - 1/2 = 1/2$
f. $P(\overline{B}) = 1 - 3/8 = 5/8$

Note that these results for the loaded die are quite different from those for the fair die in Example 1.

Example 3

Two unbalanced coins are tossed, each having a .6 probability of obtaining a head and a .4 probability of obtaining a tail. Consider the sample space $S = \{HH, HT, TH, TT\}$. Later on in this chapter we will be able to show that we should assign probabilities of 9/25, 6/25, 6/25, and 4/25 (respectively) to each of the elementary outcomes. Explain why this is more plausible than assigning 1/4 to each elementary outcome.

Solution First we note that since $9/25 + 6/25 + 6/25 + 4/25 = 1$, the given assignment constitutes a valid probability space. Assigning values of 1/4 to each outcome is incorrect, because it is certainly more likely that we would obtain HH than TT with a pair of such unbalanced coins.

Example 4

Two balanced coins are tossed. Find the probability of obtaining at least one head.

Solution The space consists of four equiprobable outcomes:

$$\{HH, HT, TH, TT\}$$

of which three are favorable to the specified event. Hence the probability is 3/4.

Alternate solution Let A = event of obtaining at least one head. Then $\overline{A}$ = event of obtaining no heads. Since there are $2 \cdot 2 = 4$ equally likely ways the coins may fall and only one of these is favorable to obtaining no heads, $P(\overline{A}) = 1/4$. Then $P(A) = 1 - P(\overline{A}) = 1 - 1/4 = 3/4$.

Exercise 5.3 1. Spin the arrow and observe in which region the arrow falls. Assign probabilities to each point in the sample space $S = \{a_1, a_2, a_3, a_4\}$.

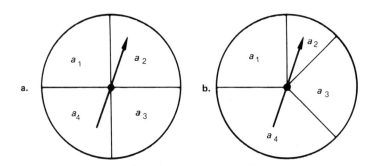

2. A coin is tossed four times. If the coin is balanced, there are 16 equally likely outcomes. List them. Find the probability of each of the following events:

   a. No heads
   b. Exactly one head
   c. Exactly three heads
   d. Exactly four heads

3. A "con artist" arranges the following game with a "sucker." Two fair dice are to be rolled and even money is wagered on the outcome. The con artist wins if a total of 4, 6, 7, or 8 is rolled. The sucker wins if 2, 3, 5, 9, 10, 11, or 12 is rolled. Find the probability of a win for the con artist.

4. The con artist in the above example plays the game 10 times but loses in six of the games! He concludes that either the dice are loaded or the sucker somehow managed to cheat when the dice were rolled. What's wrong with the con artist's conclusion?

5. If the probability that a married couple will have at least one child during their marriage is 7/9, what is the probability that the couple will have no children at all during the marriage?

6. A blue die, a red die, and a yellow die are tossed together. Find the probability of throwing a total of 18; a total of 16.

7. Compute the probability of each of the following events.

   a. *Not* drawing a king from a well shuffled deck of cards.
   b. Rolling a total of less than 5 in a single roll of a pair of balanced dice.
   c. Selecting a defective radio when one radio is randomly selected from a bin of 170 radios of which 10% are defective.
   d. Arriving at a traffic light when it is green if it stays green for 60 seconds, red for 40 seconds, and yellow for 5 seconds.
   e. Getting an even, positive number on a roulette wheel. There are 38 equally likely outcomes consisting of the numbers 1–36, 0, and 00.
   f. Randomly selecting one of the letters of the alphabet and getting one of the letters of the word "exobiology."

8. Three fair coins are tossed. List all of the possible outcomes.

    $A =$ no heads
    $B =$ exactly one head
    $C =$ exactly two heads
    $D =$ exactly three heads

    Find $P(A)$, $P(B)$, $P(C)$, $P(D)$, and $P(A \cup B \cup C \cup D)$.

9. If the letters E, E, E, N, Z, S are arranged on a line at random, find the probability that they will spell the word "sneeze."

10. One card is selected at random from the cards shown

    $\{A_s, 2_s, 3_h, 4_h, 5_h, 6_d, 7_c, 8_c, 9_c, 10_c, J_d, Q_d, K_h\}$

    The following events are defined:

    $A =$ picking a 2
    $B =$ picking a picture card
    $C =$ picking a club
    $D =$ picking a diamond

    a. Show that events A and C are mutually exclusive.
    b. Show that events B and D are not mutually exclusive.
    c. Find $P(A)$, $P(B)$, $P(C)$, $P(D)$, $P(A \cup C)$, and $P(B \cup D)$.

11. The following even-money game is arranged. Four balanced coins are tossed simultaneously. A chump wins if exactly two heads and two tails come up; a swindler wins for any other outcome. Find the probability of the chump's winning.

12. A die is loaded in such a way that the probability of throwing a 3 is 1/3, the probability of throwing a 5 is 1/3, and the remaining four possible outcomes are equally likely. Assign values to each outcome so that we have a valid finite probability space.

13. In Problem 12, find the probability of throwing

    a. 1 or 2 or 3   b. 4 or 5 or 6   c. 1 or 4 or 6

14. One die is loaded in such a way that 1, 3, 5 are each three times as likely as the outcomes 2, 4, 6. Assign correct probabilities so that a finite probability space is formed. Find the probability that when the die is thrown, the die will come up

    a. An odd number   b. An even number

15. Define mutually exclusive events A and B.

5.4 Using Combinations to Compute Probabilities

There are certain types of probability problems in which many of the indirect counting techniques, such as combinations, may be used to compute probabilities directly. This will be easily accomplished if the outcomes of an experiment are all equally likely. In this section we are considering problems that can be modeled by equiprobable sample spaces only and to which results from Chapter 4 may be applied.

Consider the following urn in which we have nine numbered balls, six of which are colored red, and three of which are colored black.

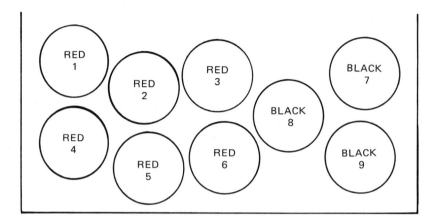

Three balls are selected at random (the balls are well mixed beforehand and the selector does not look into the urn as he picks) and in *succession* (each ball selected is not replaced). Find the probability that all three balls selected are red.

First we note that there are $_9C_3$ different ways of selecting three balls from nine. As long as the balls are well mixed and randomly selected, we have no reason to expect that any one of these

$$_9C_3 = \frac{9 \cdot 8 \cdot 7}{3 \cdot 2 \cdot 1} = 84$$

elementary outcomes is more likely than any other outcome. Thus the sample space S consists of 84 equally likely outcomes. Since there are $_6C_3$ ways of selecting three red balls from six red balls, we have

$$_6C_3 = 20 \text{ ways}$$

favorable to picking three red balls. Thus the probability is

$$\frac{_6C_3}{_9C_3} = \frac{20}{84} = \frac{5}{21}$$

In this problem the balls were numbered to emphasize that $R_1R_2R_3$ is a different selection from, say, $R_2R_3R_6$. But these two different selections should be counted separately even if the balls were not numbered. (If they were not numbered, they would still be physically distinct ball-triplets.) Thus the problem should be handled the same way mathematically whether or not the balls are numbered.

Example 1

Two items are chosen at random from a lot containing 20 items, of which seven are defective. Let A = event both items are defective and let B = event both items are nondefective. Find $P(A)$ and $P(B)$.

Solution The sample space is an equiprobable space of $_{20}C_2 = 190$ points. Event A can occur in $_7C_2 = 21$ ways; event B can occur in $_{13}C_2 = 78$ ways. Therefore

$$P(A) = 21/190$$
$$P(B) = 78/190$$

Example 2

Find the probability that 23 randomly selected persons celebrate distinct birthdays (that is, no two persons were born on the same day of the same month).

Solution Since there are 23 people and 365 distinct days, there are 365^{23} different ways (all equally likely) in which 23 people can have their birthdays.

Let us count the ways that 23 people can have *distinct* birthday celebrations. The first person can be born on any one of 365 days; the second person can be born on any one of 364 days; the third person can be born on any one of 363 days; etc. Hence there are $365 \cdot 364 \cdot 363 \cdot 362 \ldots 343$ ways the 23 people can have distinct birthdays. Thus the required probability is

$$\frac{365 \cdot 364 \cdot 363 \cdots 343}{365^{23}} = .493 < \frac{1}{2}$$

This shows that for 23 randomly selected individuals there is a better than even chance that at least two of them celebrate the same birthday. It turns out that if there were 50 people, there would be a 97% probability that at least two of them celebrate the same birthday!

Example 3

Two cards are drawn (without replacement) from a standard deck of 52 cards. Find the probability that they are *not* of the same suit.

Solution There are $_{52}C_2$ ways of selecting two cards from a deck or 1,326 equiprobable points in the sample space. There are

$_{13}C_2 = 78$ ways of drawing two diamonds

$_{13}C_2 = 78$ ways of drawing two clubs

$_{13}C_2 = 78$ ways of drawing two hearts

$_{13}C_2 = 78$ ways of drawing two spades

Thus there are (4) (78) = 312 ways of drawing two cards from the same suit. The probability of drawing two cards from the same suit is therefore 312/1326 = 4/17. Thus the probability that the two cards will not be of the same suit is $1 - 4/17 = 13/17$.

Example 4

On the first deal in a standard poker game, five cards are drawn at random and dealt to a player. Find the probability of obtaining four of a kind (four aces or four kings or four cards of any one rank) on the first deal. Recall that there are $_{52}C_5 = 2,598,960$ different five-card selections.

Solution There are 13 ways of choosing a rank; once the rank is chosen, there are then 48 ways of choosing the fifth card. Thus there are (13) (48) = 624 distinct four-of-a-kind situations. The probability is therefore 624/ 2,598,960 = .00024

Example 5

There are 100 tickets in a lottery, of which 10 are winners. A man holds three tickets. Find the probability that he will win with all three tickets.

Solution There are $_{10}C_3$ ways of winning out of a total of $_{100}C_3$ ways of selecting three tickets from 100. Thus the probability is

$$\frac{_{10}C_3}{_{100}C_3} = \frac{1}{990}$$

Example 6

A bag contains six white balls and nine black balls. If five balls are selected at random, find the probability that three will be black and two will be white.

Solution There are $_9C_3$ ways of selecting three black balls from nine and, then, $_6C_2$ ways of selecting two white balls from six. Thus there are a total of $(_9C_3) (_6C_2) = 1260$ outcomes favorable to three black and two white selections. Since there are $_{15}C_5$ ways of drawing five balls from 15, the required probability is

$$\frac{1260}{_{15}C_5} = \frac{60}{143}$$

Example 7

Suppose it is known that of 20 stars, five have planetary systems. Three stars are chosen at random from the 20. Find the probability that

a. None has a planetary system.
b. Exactly one has a planetary system.
c. At least one has a planetary system.

Solution There are $_{20}C_3 = 1140$ ways to choose three stars from 20.

a. There are 15 stars without planetary systems; hence there are $_{15}C_3$ ways to choose stars without planets. Thus the probability is $_{15}C_3/_{20}C_3 = 455/1140 = 91/228$.
b. There are five stars with planetary systems and $_{15}C_2$ ways to choose pairs of nonplanetary stars. Hence there are $5(_{15}C_2) = (5)(105) = 525$ ways to select three stars, exactly one of which has planets. Thus the probability is given by $525/1140$.
c. The event that at least one star has a planetary system is the complement of the event that none has a planetary system. Thus the probability is $1 - 91/228 = 137/228$.

Example 8

An ESP experimenter shuffles the following 10 cards:

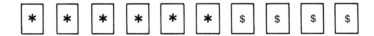

The experimenter draws three cards at random. All three cards have asterisks. A subject hidden behind a partition and blindfolded is told to identify the three cards drawn (the composition of the deck is known to the subject). The subject correctly identifies the three cards as asterisks. Find the probability that she would have been correct even if she did not have ESP.

Solution There are $_{10}C_3 = 120$ ways to select three cards from the 10 cards in the deck. There are $_6C_3$ ways to select three asterisked cards from six. Thus

$$\frac{_6C_3}{_{10}C_3} = \frac{20}{120} = \frac{1}{6}$$

is the required probability.

Alternate Since the cards are selected one after another, there are $10 \cdot 9 \cdot 8 = 720$
solution ways to select three cards in order and $6 \cdot 5 \cdot 4 = 120$ ways to select
three asterisked cards in order. Thus the required probability is $120/720 = 1/6$.

Exercise 5.4   1.   Consider the urn below from which four balls are drawn at random. There are seven red balls, five white balls, and three green balls in the urn. Find the probability that all four balls removed are red.

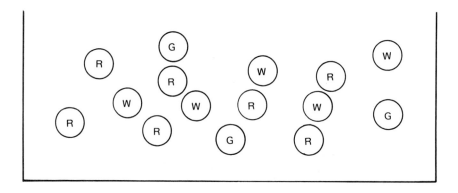

2.   Two radios are chosen at random from a lot containing 100 radios, 10 of which are defective.

A = event both are defective
B = event both are not defective
C = event one is defective and the other is not

Find $P(A)$, $P(B)$, $P(C)$, and $P(A \cup C)$. Does $P(A) + P(B) + P(C) = 1$?

3.   Find the probability that three randomly selected persons celebrate distinct birthdays (see birthday Example 2).

4.   Four cards are drawn from a standard deck. Find the probability that none is a diamond.

5.   Two cards are drawn from a standard deck. Find the probability of drawing a pair. Do the same for four decks.

6.   In five-card poker, suppose five cards are drawn from a well-shuffled deck. Explain why the given expression below represents the probability of drawing two pairs.

$$\frac{(_{13}C_2)\,(_4C_2)\,(_4C_2)\,(44)}{_{52}C_5} = .0475$$

* 7. In five-card poker, show that the probability of three of a kind is given by

$$\frac{54{,}912}{_{52}C_5}$$

8. At the present moment radiotelescopes are searching the stars in an attempt to "hear" an intelligent signal from a civilization sufficiently advanced to transmit a powerful radio signal. Suppose we assume that if a star is randomly chosen from our galaxy, then the probability of an intelligent signal coming from an associated planetary system is .0000000028. Show that if we conduct a careful search of 500,000,000 stars in our galaxy, then the probability that we will hear at least one intelligent signal is given by $1 - (.9999999972)^{500,000,000}$ or approximately 75%.

9. An ESP experimenter shuffles the following 15 cards:

Three cards are drawn at random. Find the probability that

   a. All have asterisks.
   b. Two have asterisks and one, a percent sign.
   c. None has a dollar sign.

*10. A woman holds three lottery tickets. 1000 tickets were sold, of which 10 are winning tickets. Find the probability that she will win with at least one of her tickets.

5.5 Events not Mutually Exclusive

In a previous section we defined events A and B to be mutually exclusive if $P(A \cap B) = 0$, which means that events A and B cannot both occur. In this case we showed that $P(A \cup B) = P(A) + P(B)$. The idea of two events being mutually exclusive can be extended to three events (A, B, and C) being *pairwise mutually exclusive* when

$$P(A \cap B) = P(B \cap C) = P(A \cap C) = 0$$

In this case it can be shown that $P(A \cup B \cup C) = P(A) + P(B) + P(C)$. The extension can be made to any finite number of events. When events are pairwise mutually exclusive, the probability of the union of all of them equals the arithmetic sum of the probabilities of the events taken individually.

In this section, we will investigate events that are not mutually exclusive. We will begin by analyzing a very simple example involving the following 13 random cards: A_s, 2_s, 3_h, 4_h, 5_h, 6_d, 7_c, 8_c, 9_c, 10_c, J_d, Q_d, and K_h. Suppose one card is drawn at random and the following events are defined:

A = event card drawn is a spade
B = event card drawn is a club

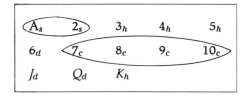

It is clear that we have 13 equiprobable points in the sample space, that there are two events favorable to A, and that there are four events favorable to B. If we now ask "what is the probability of the compound event $(A$ or $B)$?" we are really asking for $P(A \cup B)$. The circled points favorable to A (see diagram) do not overlap the region of points favorable to B. As we have said, events A and B are mutually exclusive. It is no surprise, therefore, that $P(A \cup B) = P(A) + P(B) = 2/13 + 4/13 = 6/13$.

However, now suppose the following non-mutually-exclusive events are defined:

C = event card drawn is a picture card
D = event card drawn is a diamond

In this case the events are not mutually exclusive because it is possible to draw a picture card that is a diamond; that is, it is possible for events C and D to both occur. Since there are four cards that are either pictures or diamonds, it is evident that

$$P(C \cup D) = \frac{4}{13}$$

However, we see that

$$P(C) + P(D) = \frac{3}{13} + \frac{3}{13} \neq \frac{4}{13}$$

The reason for this situation becomes clear when we examine the overlapping regions in the sample space in the following figure.

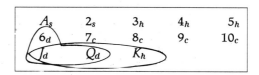

Although there are three events favorable to C and three events favorable to D, if we mistakenly add $3 + 3$ to count the events favorable to $C \cup D$, we note that two of the six outcomes (J_d and Q_d) are being counted *twice*. To correct for this in our probability statement we can write

$$P(C \cup D) = P(C) + P(D) - P(C \cap D)$$
$$= 3/13 + 3/13 - 2/13$$
$$= 4/13$$

It turns out that this result is true for any two events A and B and that, in all situations, $P(A \cup B) = P(A) + P(B) - P(A \cap B)$. This result is analogous to the theorem for overlapping sets:

$$n(A \cup B) = n(A) + n(B) - n(A \cap B)$$

Example 1

A card is drawn at random from a standard deck. The following events are defined:

A = event of drawing a red card (heart or diamond)
B = event of drawing an ace

Find $P(A)$, $P(B)$, $P(A \cap B)$, and $P(A \cup B)$.

Solution

$$P(A) = 13/52$$
$$P(B) = 4/52$$
$$P(A \cap B) = P(\text{red ace}) = 2/52$$
$$P(A \cup B) = P(\text{red card or an ace}) = P(A) + P(B) - P(A \cap B)$$
$$= 13/52 + 4/52 - 2/52$$
$$= 15/52$$

Example 2

A fair coin and a balanced die are both tossed.

A = event coin comes up a head
B = event die comes up 1, 2, 3, or 4

Find $P(A \cup B)$.

Solution By the fundamental counting principle, there are $(2) \cdot (6) = 12$ equiprobable outcomes. These are pictured below with regions corresponding to events A and B.

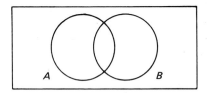

Thus the probabilities $P(A) = 6/12$ and $P(B) = 8/12$. The overlapping region, which would be counted twice in $P(A) + P(B)$, is $(A \cap B)$, where $P(A \cap B) = 4/12$. Hence $P(A \cup B) = 6/12 + 8/12 - 4/12 = 10/12 = 5/6$. Note that this result agrees with a direct count of 10 outcomes favorable to 1, 2, 3, or 4 on the die or a head on the coin. The results of these examples can be generalized in an important and useful theorem that is not difficult to prove.

Theorem 2   For any two events A and B, $P(A \cup B) = P(A) + P(B) - P(A \cap B)$.

Proof By using a Venn diagram of the type shown below it is easy to verify that

$$(i) \quad A \cup B = A \cup (B \cap \bar{A})$$

where these two events are mutually exclusive, and

$$(ii) \quad B = (B \cap A) \cup (B \cap \bar{A})$$

where these two events are mutually exclusive. Thus

$$P(A \cup B) = P[A \cup (B \cap \bar{A})] = P(A) + P(B \cap \bar{A})$$
$$P(B) = P[(B \cap A) \cup P(B \cap \bar{A})] = P(B \cap A) + P(B \cap \bar{A})$$

Subtracting the second from the first of the previous two equations, we have

$$P(A \cup B) - P(B) = P(A) - P(B \cap A)$$

which by rearranging and using the fact that $A \cap B = B \cap A$ yields the result

$$P(A \cup B) = P(A) + P(B) - P(A \cap B)$$

and the proof is complete. This theorem can be applied to problems in which the sample space consists of outcomes not necessarily equi-probable.

Example 3

From statistical experience, it might be known that a randomly cho-sen driver at a toll gate has probabilities:

$P(A)$ $\quad = P$(having a current driver's license) $= .97$
$P(B)$ $\quad = P$(having a current inspection sticker) $= .93$
$P(A \cap B)$ $\: = P$(having current license and inspection sticker) $= .91$

Find $P(A \cup B)$.

Solution Using Theorem 2, we have

$$P(A \cup B) = .97 + .93 - .91 = .99$$

Example 4

Two dice are thrown, and the following events are defined:

$A =$ event dice total 6
$B =$ event dice come up 3–2 in any order
$C =$ event dice come up 4–2 in any order

Find $P(A)$, $P(B)$, $P(A \cup B)$, $P(A \cup C)$.

Solution From previous results we know that $P(A) = 6/36 = 1/6$ and $P(B) = 2/36 = 1/18$; also $P(C) = 2/36 = 1/18$. Since A and B are mutually exclusive.

$$P(A \cup B) = P(A) + P(B) = \frac{1}{6} + \frac{1}{18} = \frac{2}{9}$$

However, since A and C are not mutually exclusive, we must use the fact that, in this case, $P(A \cap C) = 1/18$. We then have

$$P(A \cup C) = P(A) + P(C) - P(A \cap C)$$
$$= 1/6 + 1/18 - 1/18$$
$$= 1/6$$

Example 5

Margaret attends a singles' party at which 24% of males have college degrees, 47% do not make alimony-support payments, and 16% have college degrees and do not make alimony-support payments. Margaret selects a man at random. Find the probability that the man selected has no college degree and makes alimony-support payments.

Solution Let

A = event male selected has college degree

B = event male selected does not make alimony-support payments

Then we have that $P(A) = .24$, $P(B) = .47$, and $P(A \cap B) = .16$. The problem can be interpreted in the following way: We want $P(\bar{A} \cap \bar{B})$. But

$$P(\bar{A} \cap \bar{B}) = P(\overline{A \cup B}) = 1 - P(A \cup B)$$
$$= 1 - [P(A) + P(B) - P(A \cap B)]$$
$$= 1 - (.24 + .47 - .16)$$
$$= -.55 = .45 = 45\%$$

Exercise 5.5 1. Suppose we are given two events A and B such that $P(A) = .4$ and $P(B) = .5$. Find $P(A \cup B)$ given that

a. A and B are mutually exclusive
b. A and B are not mutually exclusive and $P(A \cap B) = .2$

2. Two balanced dice are tossed, one red and the other white.

A = event that the total is an odd number

B = event that the total is a prime number

Find $P(A)$, $P(B)$, $P(A \cup B)$. Are events A and B mutually exclusive?

3. Two fair coins are tossed.

A = event that both coins are heads

B = event that one coin is a head and the other is a tail

Find $P(A)$, $P(B)$, $P(A \cup B)$. Are events A and B mutually exclusive?

4. Events A, B, and C are all possible outcomes of an experiment; A, B, and C are pairwise mutually exclusive. Explain why the following probability assignments are impossible.

a. $P(A) = .5$, $P(B) = .2$, $P(C) = 0$
b. $P(A) = .5$, $P(B) = .4$, $P(C) = .2$
c. $P(A) = .6$, $P(B) = .4$, $P(C) = 0$, $P(A \cap B) = .1$
d. $P(A) = .8$, $P(B) = .5$, $P(C) = -.3$

5. Suppose that statistical experience shows that a randomly chosen reader of *Fortune* Magazine with probability .8 has a college degree, with probability .6, an income of over $25,000, and with probability .5 has both.

   a. What is the probability that a reader either has a college degree or has an income of over $25,000?
   b. What is the probability that a reader does not have an income of over $25,000?
   c. What is the probability that a reader fits into neither of the described categories?

6. At an airport, experience has shown that during rush hours there are generally a number of planes flying in holding patterns while waiting for permission to land. The probabilities associated with each number of planes waiting in holding patterns are as follows.

Planes in holding pattern	0–5	6	7	8	9	10 or more
Probability	0	.07	.12	.18	.25	.38

Find the probability that

   a. There are at least eight planes in holding patterns
   b. There are at most eight planes in holding patterns
   c. There are at least six planes in holding patterns
   d. There are less than six planes in holding patterns

7. Events A and B are mutually exclusive where $P(A) = .40$ and $P(B) = .45$. Find the following:

   a. $P(A \cup B)$ b. $P(A \cap B)$ c. $P(\bar{A} \cap \bar{B})$

5.6 Conditional Probability

Most of the probabilities previously encountered consist of a ratio relative to an entire sample space. However, there will be cases where we have certain additional information in a problem so that the relevant outcomes of an event will be limited to a proper subset of the sample space. This could change the probabilities involved.

It would be helpful if we examine a very simple example that will help to explain the concept involved and that will allow us to define a useful new symbol. Suppose a card is selected at random from the following sample space of seven cards:

$$\{A_h, 2_s, 3_s, 10_d, J_s, Q_s, K_h\}$$

Here we will define two events:

A = event card chosen is a spade
B = event card chosen is a picture card

It is certainly a simple matter to compute the probabilities:

$$P(A) = 4/7$$
$$P(B) = 3/7$$
$$P(A \cap B) = 2/7$$

But now let us solve a further problem

Example 1

Find $P(A$ given that B has already occurred).

Solution In effect what has now happened is that the original space has been cut down from seven points to three. Thus the probability $P(A$ given that B has occurred), denoted $P(A \mid B)$, is easily seen to be

$$P(A \mid B) = \frac{2}{3}$$

This value is exactly the same as the fraction $n(A \cap B)/n(B)$. Equivalently,

$$\frac{P(A \cap B)}{P(B)} = \frac{2/7}{3/7} = \frac{2}{3}$$

This example illustrates the logic and the usefulness of the following important definition.

Definition 5   Given two events A and B where $P(B) > 0$, the *conditional probability of A given that B has occurred* is given by

$$P(A \mid B) = \frac{P(A \cap B)}{P(B)}$$

Example 2

A recent poll of a sample of residents yielded the following information regarding adults over the age of 21.

	Married (R)	Separated (S)	Divorced (D)	Widowed (W)	Single (S)
Male (M)	120	10	20	5	50
Female (F)	140	20	40	10	70

A resident is selected at random. Find

a. $P(M \mid R)$ b. $P(R \mid M)$ c. $P(S \cup D \mid F)$ d. $P(S \cup D \mid M)$

e. $P(W \mid M)$ f. $P(W \mid F)$ g. $P(M \mid W)$ h. $P(F \mid \bar{D})$

i. Show that $P(M \mid R) = \dfrac{P(M \cap R)}{P(R)}$

Solution a. $P(M \mid R) = 120/260 = .46$ b. $P(R \mid M) = 120/205 = .59$

c. $P(S \cup D \mid F) = 60/280 = .21$ d. $P(S \cup D \mid M) = 30/205 = .15$

e. $P(W \mid M) = 5/205 = .02$ f. $P(W \mid F) = 10/280 = .04$

g. $P(M \mid W) = 5/15 = .33$ h. $P(F \mid \bar{D}) = 240/425 = .56$

i. $P(M \mid R) = \dfrac{120}{260} = \dfrac{P(M \cap R)}{P(R)} = \dfrac{120/475}{260/475} = \dfrac{120}{260}$

Example 3

Two cards are drawn in succession from a well-shuffled deck. The
following events are defined:

P1 = event first card is a picture (jack, queen, or king)
P2 = event second card is a picture
C1 = event first card is a club
C2 = event second card is a club

Find the following probabilities

a. That the first card is a club
b. That the second card is a club given that the first card is a picture
c. That the first card is a picture
d. That the second card is a picture given that the first card is a
   picture
e. That the second card is a picture given no information at all about
   the first card.

Solution a. $P(C1) = 13/52 = 1/4$

b. $P(C2 \mid P1) = 3/12 = 1/4$. Note that the probability of a club on
the second draw (knowing that the first is a picture) is the same

as the probability of a club on the first draw. In this case the probability is the same even though the sample space has been reduced.

c. $P(P1) = 12/52 = 3/13$

d. $P(P2 \mid P1) = 11/51$. Note that this result would be the same if we were to use the definition of conditional probability and obtain

$$P(P2 \mid P1) = \frac{P(P2 \cap P1)}{P(P1)} = \frac{{}_{12}C_2/{}_{52}C_2}{3/13} = \frac{(12)\,(11)}{(2)\,(1)}\,\frac{(2)\,(1)}{(52)\,(51)}\,\frac{13}{3} = \frac{11}{51}$$

e. The answer may not be obvious to many of us who realize that the probability of P2 is affected by what happens on the first draw. Event P2 can occur in two mutually exclusive ways.

P2 can occur by either $\qquad$ (P1 and P2) $\qquad$ or $\qquad$ ($\overline{P1}$ and P2) $\qquad$ mutually exclusive. Thus

we can write $P2 = (P1 \cap P2) \cup (\overline{P1} \cap P2)$, which can be verified by Venn diagrams. Thus

$$
\begin{aligned}
P(P2) &= P(P1 \cap P2) + P(\overline{P1} \cap P2) \\
&= P(P1)\,P(P2 \mid P1) + P(\overline{P1})P(P2 \mid \overline{P1}) \\
&= (12/52)\,(11/51) + (40/52)\,(12/51) \\
&= 612/2652 = 3/13
\end{aligned}
$$

which is the same as $P(P1)$. Thus if an unknown card is removed on the first draw, the probability of picking a particular card on the second draw is the same as we would obtain if it were the first draw. At first this may seem remarkable, but it is nevertheless correct!

Example 4

Suppose that 50% of all patients afflicted with a certain type of cancer will die within 5 years of diagnosis. Three of these cancer patients are chosen at random, and it turns out that these patients are neither related nor acquainted with each other in any way. The first patient dies within 5 years. Find the probability that all three will die within 5 years of diagnosis. Also, explain why the results might be different in actuality if the patients knew each other or were members of the same family.

Solution Let

D = event of death of a patient within 5 years of diagnosis

L = event patient will live at least 5 years after diagnosis

A = event all three die within 5 years of diagnosis

Mathematically this is the same as a coin being flipped three times, with $P(D) = P(L) = 1/2$. Prior to the death of the first patient, the sample space is

$$\{DDD,\ DDL,\ DLD,\ DLL,\ LDD,\ LDL,\ LLD,\ LLL\}$$

where each event is equally likely. Let $B =$ event first patient died. We want $P(A \mid B)$, or the probability of three deaths given that the first patient died. Note that $P(A \cap B) = 1/8$ and $P(B) = 1/2$. Then we have that

$$P(A \mid B) = \frac{P(A \cap B)}{P(B)} = \frac{1/8}{1/2} = \frac{1}{4}$$

This is the same as we would obtain if we limited the sample space to $\{DDD,\ DDL,\ DLD,\ DLL\}$ and obtained $P(A \mid B) = 1/4$ directly. We conclude that with three randomly chosen, unrelated persons afflicted with this type of cancer of whom the first dies, in 25% of all such cases all three will die within 5 years.

The remark that the patients are unrelated and unacquainted is deliberately made. If the first and second patients were married to each other, for example, the death of the first patient would very likely boost the probability of the death of the second patient to something above 1/2; this would mean our computed answer of 1/4 would be inaccurate. This problem assumes that the death of any one patient is independent of the death of any other. The distinction between independent and dependent events will be taken up in the next section.

Exercise 6.6 1. One card is drawn from a well-shuffled deck.

   $A =$ event the card is an ace
   $B =$ event the card is black (club or spade)

   Find

   a. $P(A)$ b. $P(B)$ c. $P(A \cap B)$
   d. $P(A \cup B)$ e. $P(A \mid B)$ f. $P(B \mid A)$

2. In a certain community, a village census revealed the following information:

	Children (C) (below age 13)	Teenagers (T) (ages 13–19)	Adults (A) (ages 20–65)	Senior citizens (S) (above age 65)
Male (M)	65	120	342	73
Female (F)	71	123	394	92

A village resident is selected at random; find

a. $P(M)$	b. $P(F)$	c. $P(A\mid M)$
d. $P(M\mid A)$	e. $P(T)$	f. $P(T\mid M)$
g. $P(A\cup S)$	h. $P(A\cup S\mid F)$	i. $P(A\cup S\mid M)$
j. $P(\overline{C\cup T})$	k. $P(C\cup T\cup A)$	l. $P(M\mid T\cup A\cup S)$

3. Two cards are drawn in succession from a well-shuffled deck. The following events are defined:

    $T1$ = event first card is a red 10
    $T2$ = event second card is a red 10
    $H1$ = event first card is a heart
    $H2$ = event second card is a heart

    Find the following.

a. $P(H1)$	b. $P(T1)$	c. $P(T2\mid T1)$
d. $P(T2)$	*e. $P(H2\mid T1)$	

4. A husband and wife have two children, of whom at least one is male. Find the probability that both are male. [Assume $P(M) = P(F) = 1/2$.]

5. A husband and wife have two children, the *youngest* being male. Find the probability that both are male. [Assume $P(M) = P(F) = 1/2$.]

6. Three dice are tossed (all three are balanced): one is red, another white, and the third is blue.

    A = event the red die comes up 6
    B = event the white die comes up 6
    C = event the blue die comes up 6

    Given that $P(A\cap B)=1/36$, $P(B\cap C)=1/36$, $P(A\cap C)=1/36$, and $P(A\cap B\cap C)=1/216$. Using the formula for the probability of the union of three nonmutually exclusive events

    $$P(A\cup B\cup C)= P(A)+ P(B)+ P(C) - P(A\cap B) - P(B\cap C) - P(A\cap C)+ P(A\cap B\cap C)$$

    find $P(A\cup B\cup C)$.

7. You are given that

    P(adult male smoker will have a heart attack before age 60) = 1/2 and P(adult male nonsmoker will have a heart attack before age 60) = 1/4

    Two unrelated adult males are chosen at random. Find the probability that at least one will have a heart attack before age 60 if
    a. Both are smokers   b. Both are nonsmokers

*8. Since $P(A \cap B) = P(B \cap A)$, it follows that $P(A)\, P(B \mid A) = P(B)\, P(A \mid B)$. Use this result to solve the following problem. At a certain toll gate it is found that

(i)   40% of the drivers are male

(ii)   20% of the male drivers are wearing seat belts

(iii) 35% of the female drivers are wearing seat belts.

A driver is selected at random and is wearing a seat belt. Find the probability that the driver is a man.

5.7   Independent and Dependent Events

In this section we will attempt to define and explain what is meant by independent events. We will begin by discussing the idea of one event A being independent of one other event B. This concept is of vital umportance to probability.

Suppose we have two well-defined events A and B and suppose first that we compute the probability of A *without knowing if event B has occurred or not;* call this result $P(A)$. Secondly, suppose that event B has occurred and we then compute the probability of A accordingly; call this result $P(A \mid B)$. If these two results are equal, that is, if $P(A \mid B) = P(A)$, then we agree to call the events A and B *independent.* If it should turn out that $P(A \mid B) \neq P(A)$, then we will say that events A and B are *dependent.*

Two simple examples should suffice to explain the concepts.

Example 1

One card is drawn from a well-shuffled deck and the following events are defined:

A = event that the card drawn is an ace

H = event that the card drawn is a heart

Solution First assume that we have no idea whether H has occurred and compute $P(A)$. Here we have that

$$P(A) = \frac{4}{52} = \frac{1}{13}$$

It is a simple matter to compute $P(H)$ since we have 13 hearts in a standard deck:

$$P(H) = \frac{13}{52} = \frac{1}{4}$$

Now we will use the definition of conditional probability in order to compute the probability P(drawing an ace given that we know the card drawn is a heart):

$$P(A \mid H) = \frac{P(A \cap H)}{P(H)} = \frac{1/52}{1/4} = \frac{1}{13} = P(A)$$

Notice that the fact that we know the card is a heart does nothing to alter the first computation $P(A) = 1/13$. Thus the probability of drawing an ace is *independent* of whether the card is a heart or not.

At first glance the next problem may seem the same as Example 1, but read carefully! Something different is involved.

Example 2

One card is drawn from a well-shuffled deck, and the following events are defined:

R = event that the card drawn is a red ace
H = event that the card drawn is a heart

Solution Similarly, we begin by computing $P(R)$ without knowing if event H has occurred. We obtain

$$P(R) = \frac{2}{52} = \frac{1}{26}$$

Now recall that $P(H) = 1/4$ from the previous example. Using conditional probability, we obtain

$$P(R \mid H) = \frac{P(R \cap H)}{P(H)} = \frac{1/52}{1/4} = \frac{1}{13} > P(R)$$

Knowing that the card is a heart has improved the probability of drawing a red ace. Thus the probability of drawing a red ace is *dependent* on the event that the card is a heart.

The results in the previous two examples lead naturally to the following definition of independence.

> **Definition 6**   We are given events A and B, with $P(A) \neq 0$ and $P(B) \neq 0$. Events A and B are said to be *independent* if $P(A \mid B) = P(A)$. If $P(A \mid B) \neq P(A)$, then events A and B are *dependent*.

It may seem strange that we are requiring nonzero probabilities for events A and B. It is essential, however, since if we use a conditional form such as $P(A \mid B)$, then the definition of conditional probability

$$P(A \mid B) = \frac{P(A \cap B)}{P(B)}$$

does not permit a zero in the denominator of the right-hand side of the equation. Likewise, an expression such as $P(B \mid A)$ does not permit the possibility that $P(A) = 0$.

If events A and B are independent, it follows that events B and A (expressed in reverse order) are also independent, for if $P(A \cap B) = P(B \cap A)$, then $P(B)P(A \mid B) = P(A)P(B \mid A)$. Substituting $P(A \mid B) = P(A)$ into the last equation, we have $P(B \mid A) = P(B)$. Thus, saying that events A and B are independent is equivalent to saying that events B and A are independent. The following theorem will be useful in many applications of probability. However, we hasten to emphasize its applicability only in cases in which events A and B are known to be independent.

Theorem 3   Given two events A and B, then $P(A \cap B) = P(A)P(B)$ if and only if A and B are independent.

Proof If A and B are independent, then

$$P(A) = P(A \mid B) = \frac{P(A \cap B)}{P(B)}$$

and thus

$$P(A \cap B) = P(A)P(B)$$

Conversely if

$$P(A \cap B) = P(A)P(B)$$

then

$$P(A \mid B) = \frac{P(A \cap B)}{P(B)} = \frac{P(A)P(B)}{P(B)} = P(A)$$

and thus A and B are independent.

Example 3

Two balanced coins are tossed, a dime and a nickel. Find the probability that both come up heads.

Solution Let

D = event dime comes up heads
N = event nickel comes up heads

Events D and N are independent since the nickel coming up heads has no effect on the probability that the dime will come up heads. Using the theorem we obtain

$$P(D \cap N) = P(D)P(N) = \left(\frac{1}{2}\right)\left(\frac{1}{2}\right) = \frac{1}{4}$$

which is the same as the result we would obtain by considering the four possible outcomes of this experiment TH, HT, TT, HH that are equally likely.

> The independence of two events does not imply that they are mutually exclusive and vice versa.

The statement above should be carefully considered because many students confuse the two concepts. In Example 3 above events D and N are *not* mutually exclusive since they can both occur, that is, $P(D \cap N) \neq 0$. Likewise, the mutual exclusivity of two events does not necessarily imply they are independent: a coin cannot come up both heads and tails at the same time. Still, the probability of a head is quite definitely affected by knowing that it came up tails.

In solving problems involving two events A and B it is useful to summarize two very important formulas.

> Formula 1 (for independent events) $P(A \cap B) = P(A)P(B)$
> Formula 2 (for dependent events) $P(A \cap B) = P(A)P(B|A)$

Suppose it should happen that we get confused and we are not immediately sure whether events are independent or not. In this case use Formula 2 because it is more general; that is, it reduces to Formula 1 in case events are independent.

Example 4

An urn is filled with five white balls and seven red balls. Two balls are removed at random, but the first ball is not replaced before the second ball is removed. Find the probability that both balls are white.

Solution Let

A = event first ball is white

B = event second ball is white

These two events are not independent because the fact the first ball is white will affect the probability of a white ball on the second draw. Thus we will use Formula 1.

$$P(A \cap B) = P(A) \, P(B \mid A) = \left(\frac{5}{12}\right)\left(\frac{4}{11}\right) = \frac{5}{33}$$

Alternate solution Analyze the problem in terms of the selection of two balls. There are $_{12}C_2 = 66$ ways of selecting two balls from 12, and there are $_5C_2$ ways of selecting two white balls from five white balls. Thus the probability is given by the quotient

$$\frac{_5C_2}{66} = \frac{10}{66} = \frac{5}{33}$$

It is useful to point out that when considering independent events A and B, it often happens that we are interested in $P(A \cap B)$. One way of approaching this problem is to construct the entire sample space and then count the number of outcomes favorable to $A \cap B$. However, when A and B are independent it is often easier to use Theorem 3 and compute $P(A)P(B)$. This will be illustrated in the following two examples.

Example 5

Given two unrelated throws with a fair die, find the probability of obtaining at least 3 on each throw.

Solution Rather than embark on a discussion of the 36 equally probable outcomes in the sample space, simply define two events.

A = event of at least 3 on the first throw

B = event of at least 3 on the second throw

$P(A) = 4/6 = 2/3$, $P(B) = 2/3$, and since A and B are independent, we have

$$P(A \cap B) = P(A)P(B) = \left(\frac{2}{3}\right)\left(\frac{2}{3}\right) = \frac{4}{9}$$

Example 6

Hospital records in New York State indicate that .514 of the births are male and .486 of the births are female. Consider two unrelated births and find the probabilities associated with each of the outcomes of the sample space

$$\{MM, \quad MF, \quad FM, \quad FF\}$$

Solution The outcomes in the sample space are not equiprobable. For the first outcome MM we want $P(M \cap M)$. Since the births are unrelated, they are independent and we have

$$P(M \cap M) = P(M)P(M) = (.514)(.514) = .264$$

Similarly we have

$$P(M \cap F) = P(M)P(F) = (.514)(.486) = .250$$
$$P(F \cap M) = P(F)P(M) = (.486)(.514) = .250$$
$$P(F \cap F) = P(F)P(F) = (.486)(.486) = .236$$

Notice that since the sum of these probabilities is 1, the four outcomes constitute a finite probability space.

The theorem we have been using for two independent events can be extended to any finite number of independent events (for example, three events are independent if the occurrence of any 1 or 2 of the events has no effect on the probability of the third). Thus

$$P[(A \cap B) \cap C] = P(A \cap B)P(C \mid A \cap B)$$
$$= P(A)P(B \mid A)P(C \mid A \cap B) = P(A)P(B)P(C)$$

Therefore we have the following theorem.

> **Theorem 4**   The probability of the intersection of a finite number of independent events equals the product of their respective probabilities.

Example 7

A consumer advocate estimated that 25% of the automobiles in the United States do not meet the minimum standards of the Clean Air Act. Five cars are chosen randomly by a research team. Find

a. The probability that all the cars meet the standards
b. The probability that at least one car does not meet the standards

Solution Assuming the events are independent, let

$$P(i\text{th car meets standards}) = P(E_i) = .75 \quad \text{for} \quad i = 1, 2, 3, 4, 5$$

Then

$$P(E_1 \cap E_2 \cap E_3 \cap E_4 \cap E_5) = (.75)\,(.75)\,(.75)\,(.75)\,(.75) = (.75)^5 = .24$$

represents the probability that all five cars meet the standards. The probability that at least one car does not meet standards is $1 - .24 = .76$.

Example 8

An employment agency knows from experience that 98% of those interviewed are ineligible for a certain job classification. Ten persons are interviewed. Find the probability that at least one person is eligible for the job.

Solution $P(\text{at least one eligible}) = 1 - P(\text{none eligible})$
$$= 1 - (.98)^{10} = 1 - .82 = .18 = 18\%$$

Sometimes it is useful to be able to show that two events are not independent. Here we can establish that $P(A \cap B) \neq P(A)P(B)$.

Example 9

In a survey of 1000 elderly people, individuals are grouped into smokers and nonsmokers and those having had prior heart attacks together with those who have had no prior heart attacks. The following data are assembled:

	Smokers (S)	Nonsmokers ($\bar{S}$)
Prior heart attacks (H)	540	190
No prior heart attacks ($\bar{H}$)	60	210

Show that events S and H are not independent.

Solution $$P(H) \quad = 730/1000 = .730$$
$$P(S) \quad = 600/1000 = .600$$
$$P(H \cap S) = 540/1000 = .540$$

but note that

$$P(H)P(S) = (.730)\,(.600) = .438 \neq .540$$

Alternate solution

$$P(H) = .730$$
$$P(H \mid S) = 540/600 = .900$$

For this sample the probability of a person's having had a heart attack is higher among smokers than among the persons in the entire sample. We hasten to point out that this does not mean we have established a causative link between smoking and heart ailments. The probabilistic evidence may suggest this causative link, but the above procedure alone does not prove causation.

Mathematical Dependence and Common Fallacies When it happens that $P(A \mid B) > P(A)$, it is sometimes tempting to conclude that event B "tends to cause" event A. It is well known, for example, that the conditional frequency of lung cancer is greater among heavy smokers than in the general population. Again, the conditional frequency of tooth decay among children is higher in areas where the fluorine content of the water is low. It might seem logical to conclude that heavy smoking causes cancer and that fluorine prevents cavities among children. These arguments bear further examination, however. When events A and B tend to go together, it may not mean that B "causes" A but rather that

(i) A causes B (the reverse situation) or
(ii) A and B are causally related to other factors but do not exert any direct influence on each other

Two examples should suffice to point out the fallacies involved.

An example of (i) is that it may be noticed that the conditional frequency of heart ailments is much higher among those taking nitroglycerine tablets. We cannot conclude, however, that taking nitroglycerine tablets causes heart ailments. An example of (ii) is that it may be observed that the conditional frequency of voting Republicans is higher among those people making more than $25,000 annually than among the general population. This does not prove that having a high income causes one to become a Republican. The data may reflect that as people get older they tend towards more conservative political views and higher salaries.

It turns out that more sophisticated statistical experiments can be used to establish causal relationships (such as that smoking tends to cause cancer). We are merely emphasizing that simple mathematical dependence is not sufficient to establish causation.

Exercise 5.7   1.   One card is drawn from a well-shuffled deck and the following events are defined:

A = event the card is a picture
B = event the card is a club

Find $P(A)$, $P(B)$, $P(A \cap B)$, and $P(A \mid B)$. Also show that A and B are independent events.

2. One card is drawn from a well-shuffled deck and the following events are defined:

C = event that the card drawn is a club
B = event that the card drawn is a black picture card

Find $P(B)$, $P(C)$, $P(B \cap C)$. Also show that events B and C are dependent events.

3. The probability that Simone will live to the year 2000 is 1/3. The probability that Fred will live to the year 2000 is 1/6. Fred and Simone do not know each other nor are they related. Find the probabilities that

   a. Fred and Simone will both be alive in the year 2000
   b. Simone will be alive and Fred will be dead in the year 2000
   c. Simone will be dead and Fred will be alive in the year 2000
   d. Both will be dead in the year 2000

4. An urn is filled with 10 white balls and five red balls. Two balls are removed without replacement. Find the probabilities.

   a. The first ball is red
   b. The second ball is red given that the first ball is red
   c. Both balls are red
   d. The second ball is red given that an unknown first ball is removed

5. Give examples of two events where both are

   a. Mutually exclusive and dependent
   b. Not mutually exclusive and dependent
   c. Mutually exclusive and independent
   d. Not mutually exclusive and independent

6. Find the probability of throwing two totals of 7 in a row with two tosses of a pair of balanced dice.

7. Given that P(male birth) = .514 and P(female birth) = .486, find the probability that

   a. Two unrelated births will both be male
   b. Two unrelated births will be a boy and a girl (in any order)
   c. Three unrelated births will be two boys and one girl (in any order)

8. An airplane tries to fly safely through three artillary barrages. The probability of a hit during any single barrage is 10%. Find

the probability that the plane will not be hit during any of the three barrages.

9. A medical manufacturer recently experimented with a new drug called *Lethicin,* which supposedly reduces blood fat, especially excess plasma cholesterol. The test results indicate that *Lethicin* is effective in 60% of the cases. Two patients are chosen at random. Find the probabilities

   a. *Lethicin* was totally ineffective in both cases
   b. *Lethicin* was effective in one case but not in the other
   c. *Lethicin* was effective in both cases

   (Assume independence.)

*10. The amazing Foudini has a show-stopper based on probability rather than his alleged powers of ESP. He selects seven people at random from the audience and claims that at least two of them were born in the same month. The trick works almost 90% of the time. Show why this is so by finding the probability that none of the seven people were born in the same month.

*11. The probability that a lie detector indicates the truth when a person is lying is .2; the probability that it indicates a lie when the person is telling the truth is .1.

   Two people are arrested as suspects. One is guilty; the other innocent. Each of them is asked two questions. If the lie detector indicates no lies, the suspect is released; both lies, the suspect is arrested; one lie, the suspect is detained. Assuming that the guilty person always lies and the innocent person always tells the truth, find the probability that

   a. The guilty person is released
   b. The innocent person is released
   c. The guilty person is arrested
   d. The innocent person is arrested
   e. The guilty person is detained
   f. The innocent person is detained

12. Two companies, A and B, are listed on the stock exchange. The probabilities that each will have a successful year are .4 and .2, respectively. If the success of each company is independent of the other, find the probability that

   a. Neither will be successful during the year
   b. Both will be successful during the year
   c. At least one will be successful during the year
   d. Exactly one will be successful during the year

*13. Players A and B are equally matched. Each time player A loses a game she becomes fatigued and discouraged and her probability of winning the next game decreases by .2; if she wins, however, then her elation overcomes her fatigue and the probability of her winning the next game increases by .1. In a three-game match find the probability that A wins at least two games.

*14. Two equilateral tetrahedrons (four-sided pyramidal solids), A and B, are tossed in a game of Egyptian craps. Each of the sides is numbered 1–4, but due to the curse of the sphinx, the following probabilities exist for each of the dice:

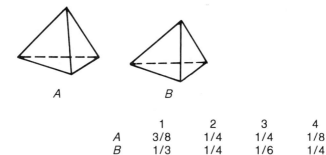

	1	2	3	4
A	3/8	1/4	1/4	1/8
B	1/3	1/4	1/6	1/4

Find the finite probability space for each of the totals 2, 3, 4, 5, 6, 7, and 8.

15. At a check-out counter experience has shown that one-fourth of all persons pay by check. Explain why the probability that at least one of 10 persons on a line will pay by check is given by

$$1 - \left(\frac{3}{4}\right)^{10} = .94$$

16. In a survey of 1000 corporate personnel, individuals are grouped into college graduates, non-college-graduates, those having incomes of at least $25,000, and those having incomes below $25,000. The following data were assembled.

	Incomes over $25,000 ($H$)	Incomes below $25,000 ($\bar{H}$)
College grads. (C)	140	670
Non-college grads. ($\bar{C}$)	30	160

Are the following events independent? (Prove your contention.)

a. H and C b. $\bar{H}$ and $\bar{C}$ c. $\bar{H}$ and C

17. A man has four keys, of which only one fits his lock. He tries each of them once. Find the probability that a key fits with exactly two tries.

*18. Two people play five-card poker. Both agree to take no additional cards. A is lucky and draws three deuces. Find the probability that B holds three of a kind also. Very hard: find the probability that B will win.

19. Ten men agree to play the macabre game of "suicide roulette." They agree beforehand to the following procedure: nine white balls and one black ball are placed in a hat and well mixed. The ten men will line up and each will remove a ball without replacing it in the hat; the moment a man removes the black ball he is instantly shot and the game is over. Assuming a man wants to live, where on the line should he stand in order to minimize his chance of being shot: first, last, or does it not matter?

20. Comment on the following fallacious arguments.

   a. There is a higher incidence of insomnia among those who use tranquilizers than among the general population. Therefore tranquilizers tend to cause insomnia.
   b. On rainy days it is observed that wind velocities are higher than on randomly chosen days. Thus rain tends to cause wind.

21. Of the patients on which a certain type of brain surgery is performed, 25% die during the operation. Of those who survive, 15% die from after effects. What is the over-all probability of a patient's dying from one of these two causes?

*22. An experimental psychologist ran 50 mice through a maze and recorded the following data:

   25   were male
   25   were previously trained
   20   turned left at the first forked path
   10   were previously trained males
    4   males turned left at the first forked path
   15   previously trained mice turned left at the first forked path
    3   previously trained males turned left at the first forked path

   One mouse is randomly selected from the 50 for learning experimentation. Find the probability that the mouse chosen was

   a. An untrained female who turned right
   b. An untrained male who turned left
   c. A female who turned right
   d. An untrained mouse who turned left

e. A trained mouse who turned right

f. A trained female who turned left.

*23. (Martin Gardner) The following game is played on the four "non-transitive" dice shown below. Player 1 picks one die from the set; then player 2 picks a die from the remaining three; both dice are tossed, and the high number wins.

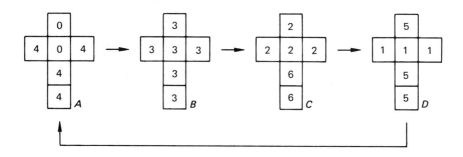

a. Show that the dice are nontransitive; that is, that

die A has a greater than 50% probability of beating B
die B " " " " " " " " C
die C " " " " " " " " D
die D " " " " " " " " A

*b. Show that in this the game probability is 2/3 in favor of the second picker being the winner.

24. You are given a system of mechanical or electrical components c_i that are connected in a chain:

If you know the probability $P(c_i)$ that device c_i will perform adequately for some specified period of time and if each component operates independently of all other components, then

$$R = P(c_1)\, P(c_2)\, P(c_3)\, \ldots\, P(c_n)$$

is a measure called the reliability R of the system, where if any one or more component(s) break(s) down, the system fails. Thus

$$P(\text{system failure}) = 1 - R$$

a. The separate component probabilities for adequate performance of a computer system are given below for a specified time of 1 year. Show that the probability of system failure during the year is approximately 25%.

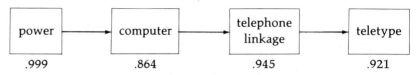

power	computer	telephone linkage	teletype
.999	.864	.945	.921

*b. Find the probability of system failure if there is a backup computer as shown.

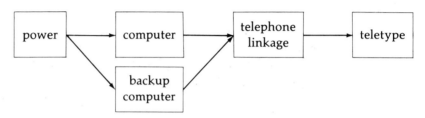

Assume the same component probabilities as in (a).

6

Special Topics in
Probability and the
Binomial Theorem

> Probability . . . can be applied to help reconcile man with a universe where uncertainty is rampant.
>
> Mark Kac

6.1   The Binomial Theorem and Pascal's Triangle

In probability and in many other areas of mathematical theory and application we often find it useful to be able to raise a binomial expression to some positive integral power. For example, if we wanted to compute $(a + b)^3$ by "brute force" we could tediously multiply three factors of $(a + b)$:

$$
\begin{aligned}
(a + b)^3 &= (a + b)(a + b)(a + b) \\
&= (a^2 + 2ab + b^2)(a + b) \\
&= a^3 + 3a^2b + 3ab^2 + b^3
\end{aligned}
$$

We would like to be able to write down an immediate answer to problems such as the one above without having to go through a laborious multiplication process. We will use combinations to explain a beautiful result called the *binomial theorem*. This theorem, together with a special array of numbers called *Pascal's triangle*, will enable us to do just that. Moreover, we will be able to apply these results to certain interesting questions in probability.

In the above problem of cubing $(a + b)$, suppose the three factors each had distinct subscripts. After a long multiplication process we would find that

$$
\begin{aligned}
(a_1 + b_1)(a_2 + b_2)(a_3 + b_3) &= a_1 a_2 a_3 \\
&+ \boxed{a_1 a_3 b_2 + a_2 a_3 b_1 + a_1 a_2 b_3} \\
&+ a_3 b_1 b_2 + a_1 b_2 b_3 + a_2 b_1 b_3 \\
&+ b_1 b_2 b_3
\end{aligned}
$$

Observe that each term of the answer consists of one and only one element from each of the three binomials, an a or a b. Observe that in three of the terms, those boxed, we have exactly two a's and one b. When the subscripts are omitted from these three terms we obtain

$$a_1 a_3 b_2 + a_2 a_3 b_1 + a_1 a_2 b_3 = aab + aab + aab = 3a^2 b$$

The coefficient 3 can be interpreted as the number of ways of selecting exactly two a's from the three that are available. Restating this, we have that there are $_3C_2 = 3$ ways of selecting exactly two a's from the set $\{a_1, a_2, a_3\}$.

Similarly, if we had to expand $(a + b)^5$, we would have terms

$$a^5, \ a^4 b, \ a^3 b^2, \ a^2 b^3, \ ab^4, \ b^5$$

where the coefficients have been omitted. Finding the coefficient of the $a^3 b^2$ term would be equivalent to asking, in how many ways can we select exactly three a's from the five that appear in the product

$$(a_1 + b_1)(a_2 + b_2)(a_3 + b_3)(a_4 + b_4)(a_5 + b_5)$$

The answer would be $_5C_3 = 10 =$ the coefficient of $a^3 b^2$ resulting when the subscripts are dropped.

The results for expanding $(a + b)^5$ are summarized in the table below.

Term	Coefficient
a^5	$1 = {_5C_5} =$ ways of selecting five a's from five available
$a^4 b$	$5 = {_5C_4} =$ ways of selecting four a's from five available
$a^3 b^2$	$10 = {_5C_3} =$ ways of selecting three a's from five available
$a^2 b^3$	$10 = {_5C_2} =$ ways of selecting two a's from five available
ab^4	$5 = {_5C_1} =$ ways of selecting one a from five available
b^5	$1 = {_5C_0} =$ ways of selecting no a's from five available

We have that

$$(a + b)^5 = a^5 + 5a^4 b + 10a^3 b^2 + 10a^2 b^3 + 5ab^4 + b^5$$

The above results can be generalized in the following theorem.

Theorem 1   The coefficient of $a^{n-r} b^r$ in the binomial expansion of $(a + b)^n$ is equal to $_nC_r$. (Here it is assumed that n and r are integers and $0 \leq r \leq n$.)

This result can be stated in another form, which has come to be known as the binomial theorem for positive integral exponents:

Theorem 2   (*binomial theorem*) Where n is a positive integer

$$(a+b)^n$$
$$= {}_nC_na^n + {}_nC_{n-1}a^{n-1}b + {}_nC_{n-2}a^{n-2}b^2 + \cdots$$
$$+ {}_nC_2a^2b^{n-2} + {}_nC_1ab^{n-1} + {}_nC_0b^n$$

Example 1

Expand $(x+y)^6$.

Solution The coefficients are given by

$${}_6C_6 = 1, \qquad {}_6C_5 = 6, \qquad {}_6C_4 = 15, \qquad {}_6C_3 = 20, \qquad {}_6C_2 = 15,$$
$${}_6C_1 = 6, \qquad \text{and } {}_6C_0 = 1$$

so the result can be written

$$x^6 + 6x^5y + 15x^4y^2 + 20x^3y^3 + 15x^2y^4 + 6xy^5 + y^6$$

Example 2

Find the coefficient of the a^6b^7 term in the expansion of $(a+b)^{13}$.

Solution
$${}_{13}C_6 = \frac{13!}{6!(13-6)!}$$
$$= \frac{13 \cdot 12 \cdot 11 \cdot 10 \cdot 9 \cdot 8 \cdot 7 \cdot 6 \cdot 5 \cdot 4 \cdot 3 \cdot 2 \cdot 1}{6 \cdot 5 \cdot 4 \cdot 3 \cdot 2 \cdot 1 \cdot 7 \cdot 6 \cdot 5 \cdot 4 \cdot 3 \cdot 2 \cdot 1} = 1716$$

Example 3

Suppose we expand $(a+b)^n$. Explain why it is true that the coefficients are symmetric; that is, that the coefficient of $a^{n-r}b^r$ is equal to the coefficient of a^rb^{n-r}.

Solution Coefficient of $a^{n-r}b^r = {}_nC_{n-r}$
Coefficient of $a^rb^{n-r} = {}_nC_r$

From results we had in Chapter 4 we know that ${}_nC_r = {}_nC_{n-r}$. Hence the coefficients are always symmetric in a binomial expansion of the given form.

Pascal's Triangle It is remarkable but nevertheless true that the Arabs knew how to compute binomial coefficients in the thirteenth century! It is not known clearly what methods they used for finding these coefficients when the exponents were large. Combinatorial methods came much later in the history of mathematical development. An alternative method was known to an Italian mathematician named Tartaglia (1547) using a triangular array of numbers. Despite the fact that this method was known 100 years before Pascal used it, the method has come to be known as *Pascal's triangle*. It involves a pattern in the coefficients of ascending powers of $(a + b)$.

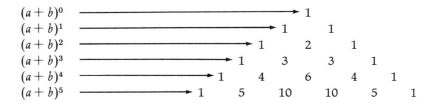

Notice that the left and right borders of the triangle are composed entirely of 1's. Every other entry of the triangle is the sum of the two numbers above it (to the left and to the right). It turns out that each horizontal line of numbers corresponds perfectly to the binomial coefficients of the associated binomial expansion.

It is not difficult to justify this procedure. For example, the entries in the triangle

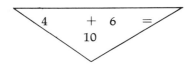

correspond to the combinatorial equality

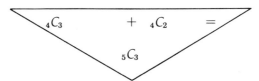

This result is generalized in the following theorem:

Theorem 3   (justification of Pascal's triangle)

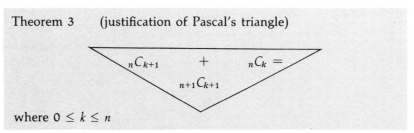

where $0 \leq k \leq n$

Proof (combinatorial argument) Since $_{n+1}C_{k+1}$ equals the number of ways of choosing $(k + 1)$ things from $(n + 1)$ things, we can argue combinatorially as follows: Paint one of the $(n + 1)$ things RED, so we can talk about it. When selecting the $(k + 1)$ things from the $(n + 1)$, you either (i) include the red one in $_nC_k$ ways, or you (ii) do not include the red one in $_nC_{k+1}$ ways. Thus

$$_{n+1}C_{k+1} = {_nC_k} + {_nC_{k+1}}$$

Alternate proof (algebraic argument) We want to show that

$$_nC_{k+1} + {_nC_k} = {_{n+1}C_{k+1}}$$

Working on the left side, we have that

$$\frac{n!}{(k+1)!(n-k-1)!} + \frac{n!}{k!(n-k)!}$$

$$= \frac{n!(n-k)}{(k+1)!(n-k-1)!(n-k)} + \frac{n!(k+1)}{k!(k+1)(n-k)!}$$

$$= \frac{n!(n-k) + n!(k+1)}{(k+1)!(n-k)!}$$

$$= \frac{n!(n-k+k+1)}{(k+1)!(n-k)!}$$

$$= \frac{n!(n+1)}{(k+1)!(n-k)!}$$

$$= \frac{(n+1)!}{(k+1)!(n-k)!}$$

$$= {_{n+1}C_{k+1}}$$

Example 4

Use Pascal's triangle to expand $(a + b)^7$.

Solution Continuing the triangle on the previous page, we have

$(a+b)^5$		1	5	10	10	5	1	
$(a+b)^6$	1	6	15	20	15	6	1	
$(a+b)^7$	1	7	21	35	35	21	7	1

or $(a + b)^7 = a^7 + 7a^6b + 21a^5b^2 + 35a^4b^3 + 35a^3b^4 + 21a^2b^5 + 7ab^6 + b^7$

Finally we observe that a consequence of the binomial theorem can be used to solve certain types of indirect counting problems. Suppose, for example, we wished to find the total number of subsets that can be formed from the set $\{a_1, a_2, a_3, a_4, a_5\}$. This problem can be solved directly either by listing all of the subsets (a horrible prospect) or else by computing

$$_5C_5 + {}_5C_4 + {}_5C_3 + {}_5C_2 + {}_5C_1 + {}_5C_0$$

which is also fairly tedious. However, we notice that the terms of the above expression are the binomial coefficients of the expansion of $(a + b)^5$. If we let $a = b = 1$ in the binomial equality

$$(a + b)^5 = {}_5C_5a^5 + {}_5C_4a^4b + {}_5C_3a^3b^2 + {}_5C_2a^2b^3 + {}_5C_1ab^4 + {}_5C_0b^5,$$

we will have the very nice result that

$$2^5 = {}_5C_5 + {}_5C_4 + {}_5C_3 + {}_5C_2 + {}_5C_1 + {}_5C_0 = 32$$

Thus there are 32 subsets that can be made from five distinct elements (including the empty set).

Theorem 4 $_nC_n + {}_nC_{n-1} + {}_nC_{n-2} + \cdots + {}_nC_0 = 2^n$

Corollary Given n distinct objects, it is possible to form 2^n different subsets (including the empty set).

Exercise 6.1 1. Use the binomial theorem to expand $(a + b)^4$.
2. Use Pascal's triangle to expand $(a + b)^4$.
3. Use the binomial theorem to find the coefficient of a^3b^6 in the expansion of $(a + b)^9$.
4. Use Pascal's triangle to find the coefficient of a^3b^6 in the expansion of $(a + b)^9$. What other term will have the same coefficient?
5. In how many ways can we select

   a. Four objects from four distinct objects?
   b. Three objects from four distinct objects?
   c. Two objects from four distinct objects?
   d. One object from four distinct objects?
   e. Zero objects from four distinct objects?

   Show that the sum of answers (a)–(e) is equal to 2^4.

6. How many distinct subsets can be formed from the elements of the set

$$\{A, B, C, D, E, F, G\}?$$

*7. Prove that

$$5^n = 4^n{}_nC_n + 4^{n-1}{}_nC_{n-1} + \cdots + 4^2{}_nC_2 + 4^1{}_nC_1 + 1$$

*8. Use the binomial theorem to expand $(x - 2y)^4$. (*Hint:* Let $a = x$ and $b = -2y$.)

6.2 Bernoulli Trials and Applied Problems

Consider a sequence of identical experiments in which:

(i) Each experiment can have only one of two outcomes, S (success) or F (failure)

(ii) Each experiment is independent of the others

Such experiments are called *Bernoulli** trials.* The following are examples:

(a) A number of throws of a pair of dice such that on each throw you win in one prescribed situation and lose in any other

(b) Guessing all of the answers to a multiple-choice examination in which each problem has four possible answers

(c) A constant percentage of tin cans produced by a certain manufacturing machine are dented during production. One hundred tin cans are produced and the rest are recorded.

It is important to realize that $P(S)$ is the same for each experiment, which is equivalent to saying that the experiment must be performed under the same conditions each time.

Since there are only two outcomes to each experiment, it follows that

$$P(S) + P(F) = 1$$
$$P(S) = 1 - P(F) = P(\overline{F})$$

Suppose we list the possible outcomes for two Bernoulli trials using "egg-slot" diagrams. Alongside each diagram we have computed the probabilities of each alternative. We let $P(S) = p$ and $P(F) = q$.

---

* James Bernoulli (1654–1705) in his work *Ars Conjectandi,* the first significant book on probability, originated the ideas we are discussing in this section.

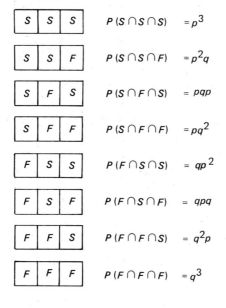

| S | S | | $P(S \cap S) = p^2$ |

| S | F | | $P(S \cap F) = pq$ |

| F | S | | $P(F \cap S) = qp$ |

| F | F | | $P(F \cap F) = q^2$ |

and we note that $(p + q)^2 = p^2 + pq + qp + q^2$. Similarly for *three* Bernoulli trials we have the following situation:

| S | S | S | $P(S \cap S \cap S)$ | $= p^3$ |

| S | S | F | $P(S \cap S \cap F)$ | $= p^2 q$ |

| S | F | S | $P(S \cap F \cap S)$ | $= pqp$ |

| S | F | F | $P(S \cap F \cap F)$ | $= pq^2$ |

| F | S | S | $P(F \cap S \cap S)$ | $= qp^2$ |

| F | S | F | $P(F \cap S \cap F)$ | $= qpq$ |

| F | F | S | $P(F \cap F \cap S)$ | $= q^2 p$ |

| F | F | F | $P(F \cap F \cap F)$ | $= q^3$ |

and $(p + q)^3 =$ sum of above probabilities $= p^3 + 3p^2q + 3pq^2 + q^3$.

In general if there n trials, the sum of the probabilities of all the different outcomes is $(p + q)^n$, and $(p + q)^n = 1$.

Now we examine a long sequence of Bernoulli trials of length n in which there are k S's and $(n - k)$ F's. Of course there are many such sequences, but a typical one might look like the following:

| S | F | F | S | F | S | S | S | | F | S | S | F | S |

n slots containing k S's and $(n - k)$ F's.

Here n slots contain k S's and $(n-k)$ F's. The probability of this particular sequence occurring is $p^k q^{n-k}$. Suppose now we ask what is the probability of obtaining k S's and $(n-k)$ F's in n trials in any order? Here we need to count the number of possible sequences of length n having k S's and $(n-k)$ F's. This is equivalent to asking for the number of ways we can distribute k S's among the n slots; this is the same as finding the number of k-slot combinations that can be selected from the n slots available, or

$$_nC_k = \frac{n!}{k!(n-k)!}$$

[The right side of the above equation can also be interpreted as the number of distinguishable arrangements of n objects of which k are identical and of which $(n-k)$ are identical.] Thus the probability of exactly k successes in n trials is given by

$$P(\text{exactly } k \text{ } S\text{'s in } n \text{ trials}) = {_nC_k} p^k q^{n-k}$$

We will represent the probability of exactly k successes in n Bernoulli trials by the expression $P(k, n, p)$, so that

$$P(k, n, p) = {_nC_k} p^k q^{n-k}$$

where p = probability of success for each trial, q = probability of failure for each trial, and $p + q = 1$.

Example 1

Find the probability of obtaining exactly two 6's in five throws of a fair die.

Solution Here $p = 1/6$ and thus $q = 1 - 1/6 = 5/6$. Also $n = 5$ and $k = 2$. Therefore

$$P(2, 5, 1/6) = {_5C_2}\left(\frac{1}{6}\right)^2\left(\frac{5}{6}\right)^3 = \frac{5 \cdot 4}{2 \cdot 1}\frac{1}{6^2}\frac{5^3}{6^3} = \frac{1250}{7776}$$

$$= .1608 \text{ or about } 16\%$$

Example 2

Find the probability of obtaining at least two 6's in five throws of a fair die.

Solution Here we want the probability of at least two 6's in five throws or, expressed differently, exactly two 6's or exactly three 6's or exactly four 6's or exactly five 6's. We want the probability of the union of four mutually exclusive events. In this case we can add the four separate probabilities, obtaining

$$
\begin{aligned}
P(\text{exactly two 6's}) &= P(2, 5, 1/6) = .1608 \\
P(\text{exactly three 6's}) &= P(3, 5, 1/6) = .0322 \\
P(\text{exactly four 6's}) &= P(4, 5, 1/6) = .0032 \\
P(\text{exactly five 6's}) &= P(5, 5, 1/6) = \underline{.0001} \\
&\qquad\qquad\qquad\qquad \text{sum} = .1963
\end{aligned}
$$

Alternate solution Realize that

$$
\begin{aligned}
P(\text{at least two 6's}) &= 1 - P(\text{less than two 6's}) \\
&= 1 - P(\text{no 6's or exactly one 6}) \\
&= 1 - [(5/6)^6 + P(1, 5, 1/6)] \\
&= 1 - (.4019 + .4019) \\
&= .1962
\end{aligned}
$$

where the slight discrepancy is due to rounding errors.

It is quite important to recognize the independence of a set of repeated Bernoulli trials. Actually the mathematics would be quite different if the trials were dependent. This distinction will become even clearer if we examine two examples which, on the surface, appear to be similar. Actually they are somewhat different.

Example 3

Of the marbles manufactured by a toy company 20% are red and 80% are white. Five marbles are selected at random from a production bin containing a large unknown number of marbles. Find the probability that at least one is red.

Solution

$$
\begin{aligned}
P(\text{at least one red}) &= 1 - P(\text{none are red}) \\
&= 1 - (4/5)\,(4/5)\,(4/5)\,(4/5)\,(4/5) \\
&= .6723
\end{aligned}
$$

Notice that each term in the product is identical to each other term. The probability that the second marble selected is red is unaffected by the color of the marble for the first choice. The same is true for the third marble selection, the fourth, etc. The trials are independent.

Example 4

Two red balls and eight white balls are mixed in an urn. Five balls are selected at random. Find the probability that at least one ball selected is red.

Solution Here the outcome of each trial is definitely affected by the previous trials. These are not independent trials and thus Bernoulli's formula cannot be applied. It is possible, however, for us to solve this problem. When two events A_1 and A_2 are dependent, we know that

$$P(A_1 \cap A_2) = P(A_1) P(A_2 | A_1)$$

This formula can be extended to any finite number of events. Without too much trouble you should be able to show that

$$P(A_1 \cap A_2 \cap A_3 \cap A_4 \cap A_5)$$
$$= P(A_1) P(A_2 | A_1) P(A_3 | A_1 \cap A_2) P(A_4 | A_1 \cap A_2 \cap A_3)$$
$$P(A_5 | A_1 \cap A_2 \cap A_3 \cap A_4)$$

so that

$$P(\text{at least one red ball}) = 1 - P(\text{none are red})$$
$$= 1 - (8/10)(7/9)(6/8)(5/7)(4/6)$$
$$= .7778$$

Observe that this result has a value somewhat higher than the result of Example 3. Although Examples 3 and 4 are conceptually the same, the difference is due to the fact that, in Example 3, the marble is selected from a very large population, and the probability that the second marble is white does not change appreciably from 4/5 after the first one is selected. On the other hand, in Example 4 we have a small population of known size, and the trials are dependent.

Example 5

In Nigeria approximately 1 in 10 are affected by sickle cell anemia (actually have the disease or are recessive carriers). In a random sample of 20 people find the probability that at least two are affected by sickle cell anemia.

Solution
$$P(\text{at least 2}) = 1 - P(\text{less than 2})$$
$$= 1 - [P(\text{none}) + P(\text{exactly 1})]$$
$$= 1 - [P(0, 20, 1/10) + P(1, 20, 1/10)]$$
$$= 1 - [_{20}C_0 (.1)^0 (.9)^{20} + _{20}C_1 (.1)^1 (.9)^{19}]$$
$$= 1 - (.1216 + .2702)$$
$$= 1 - .3918$$
$$= .6082 \text{ or about } 61\%$$

Example 6

A tire manufacturer applies a vigorous endurance test to its standard line of tires and finds that one in five tires breaks down. Four new chemical additives A_1, A_2, A_3, A_4 are mixed in the rubber of the standard line of tires. Different sample sizes of the new tires are then given the same endurance test. Interpret the following results:

Tires with	Number of tires tested	Number of breakdowns
A_1	10	1
A_2	15	2
A_3	25	3
A_4	50	6

Solution The question here is whether or not the chemical additives are effective in preventing tire breakdowns. If a chemical additive were absolutely ineffective, we would still expect one in five tire breakdowns. The fact that of 10 tires with A_1 additive only one tire broke down is an indication (but not an incontrovertible proof) that A_1 is somewhat effective in preventing breakdowns. If the additives had not been included in the tires, then the probabilities of the resulting breakdowns for the various sample sizes would be as follows.

One breakdown for 10 tires	$P(1, 10, 1/5) = .2684$
Two breakdowns for 15 tires	$P(2, 15, 1/5) = .2309$
Three breakdowns for 25 tires	$P(3, 25, 1/5) = .1358$
Six breakdowns for 50 tires	$P(6, 50, 1/5) = .0554$

Note that two breakdowns in 15 would be a rarer event than one breakdown in 10 if no additives had been included in the tires. Thus there is stronger evidence for the effectiveness of additive A_2 over the available evidence for the effectiveness of additive A_1. Examining all of the results, we see that we have the strongest evidence for the effectiveness of additive A_4 because without using the additives six breakdowns in 50 tires tested would be a rarer event than the results of the other three samples tested.

Example 7

Suppose it is known that one out of six insomniacs is relieved by a placebo. A patent-medicine manufacturer claims that *Sleeperex* tablets will relieve insomniacs 70% of the time. The FDA decides to accept the manufacturer's claim if *Sleeperex* tablets relieve at least five out of seven insomniacs.

a. What are the manufacturer's chances of having its claim accepted, even if in fact *Sleeperex* tablets are no better than placebos?
b. What are the manufacturer's chances of having its claim rejected, when in fact its claim is true?

Solution to part a We assume that *Sleeperex* tablets behave like placebos, that is, have no medicinal effect. The FDA would want this probability to be small to avoid having people ingest ineffective patent medicines. If we assume $p = 1/6$, then the manufacturer's claim will be accepted anyway if five, six, or seven insomniacs are relieved. Thus $P(5, 7, 1/6) + P(6, 7, 1/6) + P(7, 7, 1/6) = .0020$, which is small. The FDA can feel well protected by its test.

Solution to part b Here we assume that *Sleeperex* tablets can relieve 70% of all insomniacs, but question what is the probability that the tablets will fail the FDA's test anyway? Here $p = .7$ and we need to find $P(\text{zero or one or two or three or four insomniacs are relieved})$. This is given by $P(0, 7, .7) + P(1, 7, .7) + P(2, 7, .7) + P(3, 7, .7) + P(4, 7, .7) = .3529 = 35\%$. Since 35% is rather high, the manufacturer may well feel the FDA's test is too strict. On the other hand, if the manufacturer really believes the claim is correct, there is a 65% chance that *Sleeperex* tablets will pass the test.

Exercise 6.2

1. Using the formula $P(k, n, p) = {}_nC_k \, p^k q^{n-k}$, compute (by hand) each of the following probabilities.

   a. $P(2, 5, 1/2)$ b. $P(2, 5, 1/6)$ c. $P(1, 5, 1/4)$
   d. $P(0, 5, 1/4)$ e. $P(5, 5, 1/4)$ f. $P(4, 5, 1/4)$

2. Using Table on page (507), compute each of the following probabilities.

   a. $P(6, 14, .4)$
   b. $P(6, 14, .6)$ [*Hint:* Use the fact that $P(k, n, p) = P(n - k, n, q)$.]
   c. $P(3, 10, .2)$ d. $P(9, 13, 1/2)$ e. $P(5, 10, .9)$

3. Find the probability of rolling exactly three 5's in ten rolls of one fair die.

4. Find the probability of rolling at least three 5's in ten rolls of one fair die.

5. Find the probability of rolling no 5's in ten rolls of a fair die.

6. Assuming the probability of each male birth is 1/2 (and births within the same family are mathematically independent), find the following probabilities.

   a. That a family with two children consists of exactly one boy and one girl
   b. That a family with six children consists of exactly three boys and three girls

    c. That a family of two children consists of at least one boy

    d. That a family of six children consists of at least three boys

7. A baseball player has a .300 batting average. Find the probability that, in five times at bat, she will have

a. At least one hit	b. At least two hits
c. At least three hits	d. At least four hits
e. Five hits	f. No hits

8. The American Medical Association recently experimented with a new drug called *Lethicin,* which reduced blood fat (especially excess plasma cholesterol). The results indicated that *Lethicin* was effective in 60% of a very large number of patients. Twelve patients were selected at random to participate in a case study. Find the probability that

    a. *Lethicin* was totally ineffective

    b. *Lethicin* was effective in at most half of the cases

    c. *Lethicin* was effective for at least eight of the cases

9. A manufacturing machine produces 25% defective items. Find the probability that a sample of size 20 will contain at most two defective items.

10. An engineering consultant claims that he has a device which, when added to the machine described above, will reduce the percentage of defectives to 10%. The manufacturer offers to accept the consultant's claim if at most two defective items appear in a sample test of 20 items.

    a. What are the consultant's chances of having his claim accepted, even if the added device has no effect whatsoever?

    b. What are the consultant's chances of having his claim rejected when in fact its claim (of 10%) is true?

*11. An ESP deck of 25 cards consists of 20 cards marked with a triangle and five cards marked with a star.

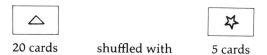

    20 cards   shuffled with   5 cards

A test game is played in the following way: a psychologist shuffles the 25 cards and draws one card; she asks the participant (who is behind a screen) to identify the card selected; the card is then replaced in the deck, and the deck is shuffled again for a repeat test. Three participants P_1, P_2, and P_3 are tested various numbers of times. These are the results:

Participant	Number of test games	Number of times star is correctly identified	Number of times triangle is correctly identified
P_1	10	1	5
P_2	15	2	9
P_3	20	3	11

Which participant presents the strongest evidence in favor of alleged ESP powers? Are the participants apparently better at identifying stars than triangles or is it the reverse?

12. A fair coin is tossed

   a. Twice   b. Three times   c. Four times

   Find the probabilities of obtaining exactly two heads in each of these three situations.

13. Of the voting citizens of Typical City, 60% are opposed to a candidate named Slippery Sam; the remaining voting citizens support his candidacy. Eight people are polled. Find the probability that a majority of the eight will support Slippery Sam. What do you conclude from your analysis?

*14. How many times must a pair of fair dice be tossed in order for you to be 90% certain that a total of 7 appears at least once?

*15. The mean (average) fertility span for a woman is four days per 28-day cycle.† There are a number of factors, some of which are not completely understood, which impede conception for a fertile woman who may want to become pregnant. The ratio $4/28 = 1/7$ may therefore be regarded as an approximation of probability p that a woman (not utilizing birth control) will conceive from coition occurring on a randomly chosen day of the cycle. Thus

$$p \approx \frac{1}{7}$$

Find the approximate probability that a woman who desires conception will become pregnant as a result of coition which occurs on each of five randomly chosen days of a 28-day cycle.

*16. In an urn there are n balls, of which k are red and $n - k$ are white. In a random process, r balls are selected without replace-

† Four days in 28 is common. However, there are normal variations from one cycle to another and considerable variances between different individuals.

ment. Show that the probability p of selecting at least one red ball is given by

$$p = 1 - \left(\frac{n-k}{n} \frac{n-k-1}{n-1} \frac{n-k-2}{n-2} \cdots \frac{n-k-r+1}{n-r+1} \right)$$

**17. Various scientific projects are under way which assume that technically advanced civilizations may exist on the planets of some of the stars in our galaxy. Moreover, it is believed probable by some scientists that a significant number of these civilizations have existed long enough and are advanced enough to transmit radio signals that we are capable of receiving and recognizing as "intelligent" radio sources. Dr. Carl Sagan, Professor of Astronomy and Director of the Laboratory for Planetary Studies at Cornell University, is quoted as saying that "if there are a million technical civilizations in a galaxy of some 200 billion stars, we must turn our receivers to 200,000 stars before we have a fair statistical chance of detecting a single extraterrestrial message." Making the following assumptions, find the probability of detecting at least one alien radio signal if we aim our radiotelescopes at 200,000 stars:

(i)   We assume we are able to receive and recognize signals from each of the 1,000,000 presumed civilizations.

(ii) We assume we are able to check each of the 200,000 stars in our sample drawn from the 200,000,000,000 stars of the galaxy.

In order to solve this problem, use the formula contained in Problem 16 and a computer program to perform the calculations.

*18. Prove the formula

$$P(k, n, p) = P(n - k, n, q)$$

where $p + q = 1$.

19. Brown, Jones, and Smith shoot at a target in alphabetical order, with probabilities of .3, .6, and 1.0, respectively (Smith never misses). Which of the three women has the best chance of being the *first* woman to hit the target on her first shot (find all probabilities involved)?

20. Players A and B are equally matched. Each time player A loses a game he becomes fatigued and discouraged and his probability of winning the next game decreases by .2; if he wins, however, then his elation overcomes his fatigue, and the probability of his winning the next game increases by .1. In a three-game match find the probability that A wins at least two games.

*21. A target for darts is to consist of a bull's eye and two concentric rings with associated scoring 5, 2, 1. Let the radius of the bull's eye be 1 in. Determine the radius of each of the other rings so that if a dart is thrown at a random point on the target it is five times more likely to hit the outer ring than the bull's eye and twice as likely to hit the inner ring than the bull's eye.

22. (This problem is due to Prof. H. D. Brunk of the University of Missouri.) One of the problems that contributed to the early growth of the theory of probability in the seventeenth century was posed to Pascal by a French nobleman fond of gambling, the Chevalier de Mère. He had found experimentally that the probability of obtaining at least one 6 in four throws of a die is larger than the probability of obtaining at least one double 6 in 24 throws of two dice, a result that seemed to him unreasonable. Find these two probabilities.

6.3 Bayes' Formula and Its Applications to Medical Diagnosis

In this section we will discuss Bayes' formula for the calculation of certain conditional probabilities, given a prior probability and some observed "after-the-fact" data. It turns out that Bayes' formula can be very useful for applications in which the associated sample space of outcomes can be divided or "partitioned" into two or more mutually exclusive events. This concept will become clear after we have considered several examples.

The first example is a simple one that explains the basic idea behind the general formula. The example has two parts. Our real interest in this problem is in the solution to its second part.

Example 1

Suppose we have two urns *A* and *B* as indicated below, which contain the red and white balls shown.

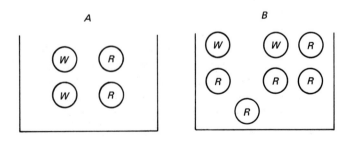

An urn is selected at random and then a ball is picked at random from that urn.

a. Find the probability that the ball selected is red.
b. Find the probability that the ball came from urn B given the fact that the ball is red.

Solution a. Let

$R =$ event the ball drawn is red
$A =$ event the urn A is chosen
$B =$ event the urn B is chosen

Note that event R can happen in one of two mutually exclusive ways: either the ball chosen is red and is picked from urn A or the ball chosen is red and is picked from urn B. Thus event R can be represented as

$$R = (R \cap A) \cup (R \cap B)$$

This formula, previously justified with Venn diagrams (in Chapter 3 on sets), represents a *partition* of the sample space S into the two mutually exclusive spaces A and B. The partitioning of S into A and B becomes clear by using the set diagram that follows.

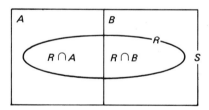

Here $S = A \cup B$ and $A \cap B = \phi$. Since A and B are mutually exclusive, it follows that the two compound events $(R \cap A)$ and $(R \cap B)$ are also mutually exclusive. Thus

$$P(R) = P[(R \cap A) \cup (R \cap B)] = P(R \cap A) + P(R \cap B)$$
$$= P(A)P(R \mid A) + P(B) P(R \mid B)$$

in which we have utilized formulas for the probability of the intersection of two events. Thus we can compute $P(R)$ using

$$P(R) = P(A) P(R \mid A) + P(B) P(R \mid B)$$
$$= (1/2) (2/4) + (1/2) (5/7) = 17/28$$

b. Since $P(R \cap B) = P(B \cap R)$, it follows that $P(R)\ P(B\,|\,R) = P(B)$ $P(R\,|\,B)$

and then we have

$$P(B\,|\,R) = \frac{P(B)\ P(R\,|\,B)}{P(R)} = \frac{P(B)\ P(R\,|\,B)}{P(A)\ P(R\,|\,A) + P(B)\ P(R\,|\,B)}$$

which is an elementary form of Bayes' formula. Using the prior result in the denominator, we have that

$$P(B\,|\,R) = \frac{(1/2)\ (5/7)}{17/28} = \frac{10}{17}$$

This is consistent with our intuition that it is more likely that the ball originated from urn B since urn B contains a higher proportion of red balls than urn A. We can extract what is important from Example 1 and summarize it by stating the essential concepts in the form of a definition and two theorems.

Definition 1   Given events A and B of a sample space S in which

(i) $A \neq \phi,\ B \neq \phi$
(ii) $A \cup B = S$
(iii) $A \cap B = \phi$

then A and B form a *partition* of S.

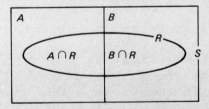

Theorem 5   Given that A and B form a partition of a sample space S, for any event R in S, $P(R) = P(A)\ P(R\,|\,A) + P(B)$ $P(R\,|\,B)$.

Theorem 6   (simplified version of Bayes' formula). Given a sample space S partitioned into events A and B, if R is an event in S, then

$$P(B \mid R) = \frac{P(B)\, P(R \mid B)}{P(A)\, P(R \mid A) + P(B)\, P(R \mid B)}$$

Example 2

At a department store an analysis is being done of people who cash personal checks to make purchases. A good credit risk is defined as a check-casher who has not bounced a check at the store over the past 5 years. The following facts are known:

(i)   Of all check-cashers 90% are good credit risks.
(ii)   Two-thirds of the good credit risks have New York State drivers licenses.
(iii)   One-quarter of the bad credit risks have New York State drivers licenses.

Find the probability that a check-casher with a drivers license is a good credit risk.

Solution Let

G = event a check casher is a good credit risk
$\bar{G}$ = event a check casher is a bad credit risk
D = event a check casher has a driver's license

Note that the sample space consists of all check-cashers S and this sample space is partitioned by events G and $\bar{G}$.

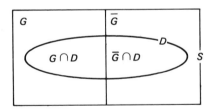

We are given that $P(G) = .9$ [whence it follows that $P(\bar{G}) = .1$], $P(D \mid G) = 2/3$, and $P(D \mid \bar{G}) = 1/4$. Using Bayes' formula simplified we have

$$P(G \mid D) = \frac{P(G)\, P(D \mid G)}{P(G)\, P(D \mid \bar{G}) + P(G)\, P(D \mid G)} = \frac{(9/10)\, (2/3)}{(1/10)\, (1/4) + (9/10)\, (2/3)}$$

$$= 24/25 = 96\%$$

These two examples illustrate a simple form of Bayes' formula. What this formula accomplishes is to find the probability of one of the "event-sections" of the partition of the sample space when a known outcome limits the number of elements in the sample space to some reduced subset. Reducing the number of elements in S to some subset has the effect of improving the probability estimate that a particular event-section will occur.

In the simplified form of Bayes' formula, S is split into two mutually exclusive event-sections. There is no reason to limit the situation to two sections; in actual practice it is often useful to extend Bayes' formula to any finite number of sections for the purpose of constructing a partition. The method of derivation of the formula is the same as that for two sections, which we saw in Example 1. All we need to have is a sample space S that is partitioned into n pairwise mutually exclusive event-sections $A_1, A_2, A_3, \ldots, A_n$

in which $A_i \cap A_j = \phi$ for all $i \neq j$ and $A_1 \cup A_2 \cup A_3 \cup \ldots \cup A_n = S$. Then if we want the probability of one particular event-section given that the sample space S is reduced to some subset R [which we call $P(A_j \mid R)$], then Bayes' general formula is

$$P(A_j \mid R) = \frac{P(A_j \cap R)}{P(R)}$$

which is usually written out completely for calculation purposes as

$$P(A_j \mid R) = \frac{P(A_j)\, P(R \mid A_j)}{P(A_1)\, P(R \mid A_1) + P(A_2)\, P(R \mid A_2) + \cdots + P(A_n)\, P(R \mid A_n)}$$

Bayes' formula has been successfully used for diagnostic purposes in medicine. We will examine a highly idealized example in order to see how this is accomplished.

Example 3

Suppose it happens that a medical research institute maintains careful records of all the patients it tests and examines. A patient enters the institute with one notable symptom: a 20% body-weight loss over the past 6 months.

Solution The examining physician considers five possibilities:

D_1 = cancer
D_2 = diabetes
D_3 = hyperthyroidism
D_4 = anorexia nervosa
D_5 = none of the above

It is known from careful record-keeping of all entering patients that the above five situations occur with the following frequencies:

$$P(D_1) = .13$$
$$P(D_2) = .25$$
$$P(D_3) = .20$$
$$P(D_4) = .02$$
$$P(D_5) = .40$$

Thus, ignoring symptomology, the physician estimates the probability that an entering patient has cancer is 13/100. The additional knowledge that a patient has a certain symptom such as

$$S = 20\% \text{ body-weight loss during 6 months prior to}$$
$$\text{first examination by the institute}$$

obviously increases the probability that the patient has cancer. But by how much? What we are interested in is $P(D_1|S)$. In order to compute this the institute would have to know, from past records, the relative likelihoods of this particular symptom among those in the classes D_1, D_2, D_3, D_4, and D_5. Suppose they are known to be

$$P(S|D_1) = .80$$
$$P(S|D_2) = .20$$
$$P(S|D_3) = .30$$
$$P(S|D_4) = .95$$
$$P(S|D_5) = .02$$

Then it is possible to compute an improved probability estimate that the patient has cancer given his symptom. This can be done because we have effectively reduced the number of elements in the sample space by limiting discussion only to patients having this particular symptom.

D_1	D_2	D_3	D_4	D_5	
$D_1 \cap S$	$D_2 \cap S$	$D_3 \cap S$	$D_4 \cap S$	$D_5 \cap S$	sample space

Then using Bayes' formula, we have

$$P(D_1 \mid S) = \frac{P(D_1)\,P(S \mid D_1)}{P(D_1)\,P(S \mid D_1) + P(D_2)\,P(S \mid D_2) + \cdots + P(D_5)\,P(S \mid D_5)}$$

$$= \frac{(.13)\,(.80)}{(.13)\,(.80) + (.02)\,(.95) + (.25)\,(.20) + (.20)\,(.30) + (.40)\,(.02)}$$

$$= 43\%$$

which is considerably higher than $P(D_1) = 13\%$. What has happened is that the additional knowledge of one particular symptom has altered the probabilistic measure of this individual's having cancer. The other conditional probabilities can be similarly computed and are the following:

$$P(D_2|S) = 21\% \text{ (diabetes)}$$
$$P(D_3|S) = 25\% \text{ (hyperthyroidism)}$$
$$P(D_4|S) = 8\% \text{ (anorexia nervosa)}$$
$$P(D_5|S) = 3\% \text{ (none of the above)}$$

Notice that we can now present a ranked set of diagnoses. From the most likely to the least likely we have:

Cancer (43%)
Hyperthyroidism (25%)
Diabetes (21%)
Anorexia nervosa (8%)
None of the above (3%)

This ranking is a considerably different ranking from the one that reflects the relative frequencies of those treated at the institute.

In Example 3 we have merely considered *one* symptom to produce a diagnostic ranking. Other factors such as blood pressure, blood analysis, urine analysis, etc., should certainly be considered in a Bayesian diagnostic system. If each of n symptoms (or tests) can be reduced to a dichotomous yes-no situation (either the patient has or does not have the symptom), then there are 2^n different sets of symptom complexes that must be considered and analyzed and for which statistical data must be amassed. If 10 symptoms are considered, then $2^n = 1024$ represents the number of distinct symptom combinations that must be analyzed. Such procedures have actually been utilized and tested. Comparisons have been made against the diagnoses of trained internists and subsequent follow-up studies. This mathematical approach to symptomology was accomplished with the aid of electronic computers that have the capacity to store and maintain detailed records and that are also used to perform the lengthy calculations required. The results were highly favorable. At this very moment, people are working to construct diagnostic models that are more accurate than 80% of all trained diagnosticians!

Bayes' formula assumes that $D_1, \ldots, D_5$ are pairwise mutually exclusive, which means that our simple example avoids the overcomplicating possibility that a patient could have more than one of the ailments $D_1, \ldots, D_5$. If multiple diseases occur often enough, our probability estimates using the basic Bayes' model would be distorted. One problem that an applied mathematician would be interested in is how to alter the basic Bayes' model to permit events that are not necessarily mutually exclusive.

Certainly the above example and discussion points to some of the dramatically humane contributions of mathematics to the betterment of humanity.

Exercise 6.3   1.   Two urns A and B shown below contain red and white marbles. An urn is selected at random and then one ball is selected at random from that urn.

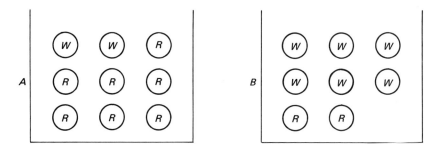

a.   Find the probability that the ball selected is white.
b.   Find the probability that the ball came from urn B given that the ball selected was white.

2.   Two fair dice are tossed.

a.   Find the probability that the total is 7.
b.   Find the probability of throwing 5 and 2 given that the total was 7.

3.   At Police Precinct No. 65 the records show the following facts:

(i)   90% of all persons arrested by the police have prior criminal records.

(ii)   20% of all persons arrested having prior criminal records have been found to be carrying illegal weapons at the time of their arrest.

(iii)   3% of those arrested having no prior criminal record have been found to be carrying illegal weapons.

A person is arrested and is found to be carrying an illegal weapon. Find the probability that he has a prior criminal record.

4. The city of Goldmine has 400,000 males and 600,000 females. Medical records of the population prove that 15% of the men are smokers while only 10% of the females are smokers. A person is chosen at random and is found to be a smoker. Find the probability that the person chosen is female.

5. The Protection Insurance Company classifies its policy-holders according to the scheme given in the table below:

Policy-holder	% of policy-holders	Probability of an accident-free year
Married persons of age 21 or over	46%	.99
Unmarried persons of age 21 or over	30%	.96
Married persons under age 21	10%	.88
Unmarried persons under age 21	14%	.75

If Jo Speedy buys a policy and subsequently has an accident before the end of the 1-year period of the policy, what is the probability that she is unmarried and under the age of 21?

6. The probability that a lie detector indicates the truth when a person is lying is .3; the probability that it indicates a lie when a person is telling the truth is .1.

Two suspects, A and B, are arrested at the scene of a crime. One is guilty and the other is innocent. Each of them is asked one incriminating question. If the lie detector indicates no lie, the suspect is released. If the lie detector indicates lie, the suspect is arrested. Assuming the guilty suspect will always lie and the innocent one will always tell the truth, find the probability that

a. The guilty suspect is released
b. The innocent suspect is released
c. The guilty suspect is arrested
d. The innocent suspect is arrested

7. Electronic radios are produced by two factories, A and B, but factory A produces three times as many radios as factory B in any given time. A radio is checked and found to be defective.

a. Find the probability that the radio came from factory A given no additional information.
b. Find the probability that the radio came from factory A given the additional facts that 2% of the radios made at factory A are defective and 10% of the radios made at factory B are defective.

8. An obstetrician is using a certain pregnancy test. He finds that if the woman is pregnant, the test gives a positive result 96% of the time and if she is not pregnant, the test gives a positive result 4% of the time. In addition, 85% of the women he tests turn out to be pregnant. A woman enters the office, is tested, and the test shows positive. Find the probability that the woman is pregnant.

9. A neurologist working in a hospital handles patients that fall into several categories. She kept careful records over a period of years of the types of patients who have been referred to her by other doctors who work at the hospital. From her experience she found that the following percentages of referrals turned out to have the following ailments:

A: 12% turned out to have brain tumors
B: 10% turned out to have psychosomatic ailments
C: 8% turned out to have cervical spine problems
D: 5% turned out to have migraines
E: 3% turned out to have optical problems
F: 2% turned out to have sinusitis
G: 60% turned out to have something other than the above categories

In each of the above categories, patients complained of severe headaches at the initial examination in the following percentages of the cases:

A: 80% had severe headaches
B: 20% "   "   "
C: 40% "   "   "
D: 100% "   "   "
E: 5% "   "   "
F: 50% "   "   "
G: 10% "   "   "

A patient with severe headaches is referred to the neurologist. With no other symptoms or medical information available to the neurologist concerning this patient, find the probability that the patient will fall into each of the categories. Give a ranked initial diagnosis.

10.   Explain the assumptions under which the analysis in Problem 9 is correct.

6.4 Mathematical Expectation

If a fair coin is tossed 1000 times, we expect there will be roughly 500 heads. It turns out that the probability of exactly 500 heads in 1000 tosses is quite small. When we say, therefore, that we expect roughly 500 heads in 1000 tosses, we really mean that the ratio of actual heads to tosses is close to 1/2. Moreover, we have a strong intuition that for 10,000 tosses, the ratio of heads to tosses will be closer to 1/2 than the ratio of heads in 1000 tosses.

Suppose we have a sequence of n Bernoulli trials in which an event S (success) has an associated probability $p = P(S)$. Then we consider p to be an estimate of the proportion of times that event S actually occurs. If $n(S)$ represents the number of times event S actually occurs in n trials, then for large n we expect that

$$\frac{n(S)}{n} \approx p$$

In more advanced work, there is a theorem called the law of large numbers. The statement and proof of this theorem is inappropriate at this level; however, it is a consequence of this theorem that

$$\frac{n(S)}{n} \to p$$

where the arrow (which is read "approaches") is used to mean that the fraction $n(S)/n$ becomes arbitrarily close to the value p for n sufficiently large.

Let's take a simple example. If a pair of fair dice are rolled n times, then we expect that the actual proportion of 7's rolled will approach the value $p = 1/6$, or

$$\frac{n(7's)}{n} \to \frac{1}{6}$$

In one dozen rolls we expect that there will be two 7's. But variations from the number 2 in any particular set of 12 rolls may be considerable. In actual repetitions of dozens of rolls we might see results such as shown below.

Eight Experiments Consisting of 12 Rolls of Dice

Number of rolls	Number of 7's in each dozen
12	0
12	3
12	2
12	3
12	2
12	4
12	1
12	2

In most of the experiments two 7's did not occur, but two 7's occurs more frequently than any other number of 7's. We would see that this pattern persists for a larger number of repetitions. Also note that in 96 rolls there are a total of seventeen 7's and

$$\frac{17}{96} = .1771 \approx \frac{1}{6}$$

In 96 rolls we would have expected $(96)(1/6)$ = sixteen 7's.

> **Definition 2**   If p is the probability of the occurrence of an event in a single Bernoulli trial, then the *expected number of occurrences* of that event in n trials is np.

Example 1

Suppose the probability that an adult male of age 38 does not survive an additional year is 0.00173. Suppose there are 50,000 males 38 years old. Find the expected number that will not survive an additional year.

Solution $np = (50,000)(0.00173) = 86.5$

Suppose we have an experiment in which there are k mutually exclusive and exhaustive outcomes $A_1, A_2, \ldots, A_k$. Sometimes it happens that each possible outcome has associated with it a particular numerical result (sometimes called a "value"). Suppose each outcome has the associated values $V_1, V_2, \ldots, V_k$. Moreover let $p_1 = P(A_1)$, $p_2 = P(A_2)$, etc.

Definition 3   Under the conditions described above, the *expected value* of the experiment is defined to be $E = p_1 V_1 + \cdots + p_k V_k$.

Example 2

A fair coin is tossed four times. The possible numbers of heads that can occur with their respective probabilities are as follows.

No. of heads	0	1	2	3	4
p_i	1/16	4/16	6/16	4/16	1/16

Using 0, 1, 2, 3, 4 as values, find the expected value of this experiment.

Solution $E = (1/16)\,(0) + (4/16)\,(1) + (6/16)\,(2) + (4/16)\,(3) + (1/16)\,(4) = 2$

Notice that $E = 2 = np$. It turns out that for any binomial distribution the expected number of times any event will occur equals the expected value, or $E = np$.

The definition of expected value is particularly useful in analyzing various gambling games, where E may be thought of as the value of the game to the player.

> If $E > 0$, the game is favorable to the player.
> If $E < 0$, the game is unfavorable to the player.
> If $E = 0$, the game is fair.

Example 3

A player tosses a fair die. If 1 occurs, she receives \$12; if 2 occurs, she receives \$6; but if 3 or 4 or 5 or 6 occur, she gets \$0.

a. Find the expected value E of the game.
b. How much money should she pay to play the game so that the game is fair?

Solution a. $E = (1/6)\,(\$12) + (1/6)(\$6) + (1/6)\,(0) + (1/6)\,(0) + (1/6)\,(0) + (1/6)\,(0) = \$3$

b. If the player pays \$$b$ to play, then each outcome is reduced by \$$b$. For the game to be fair we thus want $E = 0$ and therefore

$$0 = (1/6)(12 - b) + (1/6)(6 - b) + (1/6)(-b) + (1/6)(-b)$$
$$+ (1/6)(-b) + (1/6)(-b) = 3 - b$$

Hence $b = \$3$ makes the game fair.

Example 4

Suppose the probability that a 60-year-old man will survive to age 65 is .8. He bets $\$b$ that he will die prior to reaching age 65. If he does die prior to age 65, he "wins" and his beneficiaries receive $\$1000$. If he lives to age 65, he loses $\$b$. Find b so the game is fair.

Solution Probability of surviving $= p = .8$
Probability of not surviving $= 1 - p = .2$

We want the game to be fair, so we want $E = 0$. Thus

$$E = (.8)(-b) + (.2)(\$1000) = 0$$
$$.8b = 200$$
$$b = \$250$$

In actual practice, the precise insurance premium would be more than $250. This extra amount would include the insurance company's expenses, profit, commission to the salespersons, and a small amount called "reserves" held by the company to offset the possibility that the actual survivorship ratio might fall below .8.

Example 5

A carton contains eight radios, of which three are defective. Four are chosen at random without replacement. What is the expected number of defective radios in the sample of four?

Solution The sample can contain 0, 1, 2, or 3 defectives.

$$P(\text{no defectives}) = \frac{(_3C_0)(_5C_4)}{_8C_4} = \left(\frac{5}{8}\right)\left(\frac{4}{7}\right)\left(\frac{3}{6}\right)\left(\frac{2}{5}\right) = \frac{1}{14}$$

$$P(\text{one defective}) = \frac{(_3C_1)(_5C_3)}{_8C_4} = \frac{3}{7}$$

$$P(\text{two defectives}) = \frac{(_3C_2)(_5C_2)}{_8C_4} = \frac{3}{7}$$

$$P(\text{three defectives}) = \frac{(_3C_3)(_5C_1)}{_8C_4} = 1/14$$

Thus

$$E = (1/14) (0) + (3/7) (1) + (3/7) (2) + (1/14) (3) = 21/14 = 1.5$$

which we can interpret to mean that if this experiment were repeated a number of times, there would be an average of 1.5 defectives in the samples of four chosen.

Example 6

A carton contains nine radios, of which one is defective. Find the expected number of radios that must be tested in order to locate the defective radio.

Solution The defective radio may be located in any one of nine positions, with probability 1/9 that it is in any particular position. If the defective radio is in the kth position, then k radios will have been checked. Thus

$$E = (1/9) (1) + (1/9) (2) + (1/9) (3) + \cdots + (1/9) (9) = 45/9 = 5$$

This means that, on the average, five radios will have to be checked in order to locate the defective radio.

Exercise 6.4 1. Find the expected number of

  a. Heads in 500 tosses of a fair coin
  b. 7's in 216 tosses of a pair of fair dice
  c. 6's in 216 tosses of a pair of fair dice

2. Find the expected number of girls in a family with six children (assume sex distribution to be equally probable). What is the probability that the expected number of girls does occur?

3. The probability that a male of age 18 will not survive one additional year is 0.00058. At Macabre University there are 2,000 18-year-old male freshmen. Find the expected number that can be expected to live to be sophomores.

4. Adam Smith said that "lotteries are the greatest single device ever invented by the ingenuity of man to separate a fool from his money." A fool buys one ticket (costing $1) in a lottery having:

1	winning ticket with a $250,000 prize
2	winning tickets each having a $50,000 prize
10	winning tickets each having a $10,000 prize
100	winning tickets each having a $1,000 prize
2,000	winning tickets each having a $100 prize
987,887	losing tickets
1,000,000	total number of tickets

Find the fool's expected value of this game. How much profit is made by the operator of the lottery if all 1,000,000 tickets are sold?

5. A dealer offers to pay a player $5 if a 10, jack, queen, or king is drawn from a well-shuffled deck and $10 for an ace. The player must pay the dealer $4 for any other card that is drawn. Find the expected value for the player.

6. Suppose the probability that a 35-year-old female will survive to age 40 is .98. She bets b that she will die prior to reaching age 40. If she does die prior to age 40, she "wins" and her beneficiaries collect $10,000. If she lives to age 40, she loses b. Find b so the game is exactly fair.

7. Jones and Smith figure the probability that the White Sox beat the Orioles to be 5/7. Jones will win $20 if White Sox win. What should Smith win (in case the Orioles win) for the wager between Jones and Smith to be fair?

8. A witness to a crime believes she can identify a picture of an assailant. The police have 20 photographs of different suspects. If one of the photographs actually is the assailant, find the expected number of photographs the witness will have to examine in order to identify the assailant. (See Example 6.)

9. An urn contains 12 balls, of which two are red and 10 are white. Four balls are selected without replacement. Find the expected number of red balls selected.

*10. A box contains 10 transistors, of which two are defective. A transistor is selected from the box, tested, and the process is repeated until *both* defectives are identified. Find the expected number of transistors to be chosen.

6.5 Casino Roulette, Craps, and Remarks on Gambling Games

In this section we are not attempting to teach you to gamble, nor are we attempting to express an opinion, either pro or con, on its social and moral implications. Rather, the analysis of a few casino gambling games constitutes a clear application of the theory of mathematical expectation that was developed in the previous section. In the process of analyzing two popular games (roulette and casino craps) we will also see why gambling is a poor "investment" for the player and why these two particular games reap tremendous profits for casino operators. This particular kind of analysis is timely because gambling is now legal in some form in more than half the states.

American Roulette The American roulette wheel has slots for 38 numbers (1, 2, 3, . . . , 34, 35, 36, 0, 00). Every slot is colored, red alternating with black, except for the two "house" numbers 0 and 00, which are green.

The dealer spins the wheel counterclockwise and flips the ball on a circular track so that it travels clockwise. The ball eventually slows down and stops between two metal partitions of the wheel indicating the winning number and color.

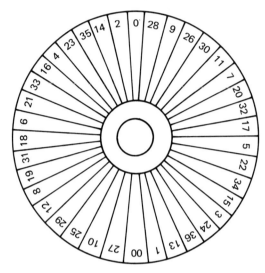

American roulette wheel

A bet can be placed on the table shown for any of the bets marked *A, B, C, D, E, F, G, H, I, J,* and *K.*

Typical american roulette layout

The payoffs for each of the bets are indicated in the following table.

	Bets on	House pays
A	Single number	35 to 1
B	Two numbers	17 to 1
C	Three numbers	11 to 1
D	Square bet (Four numbers)	8 to 1
E	Five numbers	6 to 1
F	Six numbers	5 to 1
G	Column	2 to 1
H	Dozens	2 to 1
I	Color (red or black)	1 to 1
J	Odd or even	1 to 1
K	High or low	1 to 1

For example, suppose a player places $1 on bet D (square bet) shown in the illustration. The player will win $8 if any of the four numbers 32, 33, 35, or 36 comes out. He will lose his $1 bet if any other number comes out. Of the 38 wheel slots there are thus

Four ways he can win $8	and	34 ways he can lose $1

The mathematical expectation E (or "house percentage" in gambling parlance) can be computed using the formula

$$E = \text{(Probability of winning) (amount won)} - \text{(probability of losing) (amount lost)}$$

In the example above,

$$E = (4/38)(\$8) - (34/38)(\$1) = -2/38 = -\$0.0526316$$

or about 5¢ lost on every dollar played. In any gambling game the advantage or disadvantage is determined by the sign of E.

If $E < 0$, the game is disadvantageous to the player.
If $E = 0$, the game is fair
If $E > 0$, the game is advantageous to the player

In the above example the value of $E = -.053$ can be interpreted as the average amount the player will lose for every dollar placed on that particular bet. If the game were played 100 times (at $1 bet per play), the average expected loss would be ($100) (.0526316) = $5.26. Great caution must be exercised in the interpretation of this result since it is an average and deviations from this figure can be considerable, as we shall see. It might be better to say that if a large number of individuals were each to play the above game 100 times, then the numerical average of the wins and losses among them would be about $5.26 (in the direction of a *loss*).

Example 1

Find the expectation E of the color bet (I) in the game of roulette if a $1 bet is placed on the color red.

Solution There are 18 red numbers, 18 black numbers, and two "house numbers" 0 and 00 colored green.

$$P(\text{win}) = 18/38$$
$$P(\text{loss}) = 20/38$$
$$E = (18/38)\ (\$1) - (20/38)\ (\$1) = -2/38 = -.0526316$$

or about 5.26% disadvantage to the player.

Example 2

A serious gambler plays the color red 50 times in one evening at $20 per bet. Find his theoretical expected loss.

Solution He has placed a total of ($20) (50) = $1000 in bets. His expected losses, therefore, are ($1000) (.0526) = $53 (approximately).

Example 3

Find the expectation for the five-number bet (E) for a $1 wager.

Solution

$$P(\text{win}) = \frac{5}{38} \qquad P(\text{loss}) = \frac{33}{38}$$

For a $1 bet, if the player wins, he wins $6. If the player loses he loses $1. Thus

$$E = \left(\frac{5}{38}\right)(\$6) - \left(\frac{33}{38}\right)(\$1) = \frac{3}{38} = -.0789474$$

or about a 7.89% disadvantage to the player. Clearly this is a worse bet for the player than either the color bet or the square bet.

Table Craps In this game two dice are tossed onto a table on which there are a number of different betting propositions. You may bet with the shooter or against the shooter or you may make any number of additional side bets in which it is irrelevant whether the shooter wins or loses.

Craps

(i) Pass line. You're betting with the dice, and the payoff is even money. You win on a natural 7 or 11 on the first roll, lose on "craps" 2, 3, or 12 on the first roll. Any other number on the first roll is the shooter's "point." You win if the point is thrown again, unless a 7 is thrown first, in which case you lose.

(ii) Don't pass line. Same as above, except that you're betting against the dice, and everything is reversed. You lose on a natural 7 or 11 on the first roll, you win on a "craps" 2 or 3. (When 12 is rolled it's a "stand-off": nobody wins.) You lose after the first roll if the shooter rolls 7 before making his point.

(iii) Come. The simplest explanation of come bets is that you're betting with the dice exactly as on the pass line, except that come bets are made any time after the first roll. You win on naturals 7 or 11, you lose on craps 2, 3, and 12. Any number that comes up is the "come point." The bet is shifted to that number in the space above. You win if your come point shows before a 7; otherwise you lose.

(iv) Don't come. The play is again reversed. You are betting on the second roll, but your bet is treated as if it were the first roll. You're betting against the dice exactly as on the don't pass line. You lose on naturals 7 or 11, you win on craps 2 or 3. (When 12 is rolled it's a stand-off: nobody wins.) If a 4, 5, 6, 8, 9, or 10 comes up on the second roll, you lose if the shooter makes that point on any subsequent rolls; you win if a 7 is rolled before the number shows again.

(v) The odds. Once a point is made (either a shooter's point on the first roll or a come point on a succeeding roll), you can get odds with the dice or give the odds against the dice. You get 2–1 on 10 and 4, 3–2 on 5 and 9, 6–5 on 8 and 6. You lay the same odds when you bet against the point. The payoff is made on whether or not the point shows before the 7.

(vi) Place bets. You may make a place bet on the numbers 4, 5, 6, 8, 9, or 10. The number you place must be made by the shooter before a 7 is thrown. The payoff is as follows: 9–5 on 4 or 10; 7–5 on 5 or 9; 7–6 on 6 or 8. Place bets may be removed at any time before a roll.

(vii) Field. You can bet on any roll that one of the following numbers comes up: 2, 3, 4, 9, 10, 11, or 12. If it does, you get even money, or 2–1 on 2, and 2–1 on 12. If 5, 6, 7, or 8 comes up, you lose.

(viii) Big 6 or 8. You win even money if 6 or 8 shows before a 7 is rolled.

(ix) Any 7. You bet that the next roll is a 7, and you collect 5 for 1.

(x) Any craps. You bet that the next roll is a 2, 3, or 12, and you collect 8 for 1.

(xi) Hard ways. You win if the exact combination you bet shows up. You lose if the same total number is rolled any other way except the hard way, or if a 7 comes up.

The table on which the game is played is shown below together with the various betting propositions.

The most commonly played bet is the pass line bet (*i*) which is an even-money bet; you are betting *with* the shooter (either yourself or any other). On the first roll you win if a natural (a 7 or 11) comes up, and you lose on "craps" (2, 3, or 12). Any other number on the first roll is the shooter's point. To win now, the point must be thrown again before a 7 in order to win. If a 7 is thrown before the point, you lose.

Example 4

Analyze the pass line bet for a $1 wager and determine the expectation.

Solution We will solve this problem by first finding the probability that a player will win. There are eight mutually exclusive winning situations.

W_7 = 7 on the first roll
W_{11} = 11 on the first roll
W_4 = winning by establishing a point of 4 and then making that point
W_5 = " " " " " " 5 " " " " "
W_6 = " " " " " " 6 " " " " "
W_7 = " " " " " " 7 " " " " "
W_8 = " " " " " " 8 " " " " "
W_9 = " " " " " " 9 " " " " "
W_{10} = " " " " " " 10 " " " " "

The first two are easy to compute:

$$P(W_7) = 6/36 = 1/6$$
$$P(W_{11}) = 2/36 = 1/18$$

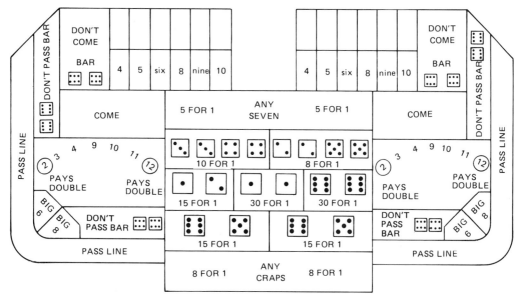

Casino layout for dice

The others are a bit more difficult. W_4, for example, is really a compound event: that we throw a 4 on the first throw and then that we throw a 4 before throwing a 7. Consider the case of establishing the point 4 on the first throw and then making that point on the second throw. In this case, since the two throws are independent,

$$P(W_4) = P(4 \text{ on first throw and winning on second throw})$$
$$= (3/36)P(\text{winning on the second throw})$$

Observe that there are six cases in which we can lose on the second throw (4–3, 3–4, 5–2, 2–5, 6–1, 1–6) and three cases in which we can win (3–1, 1–3, 2–2). The remaining 27 cases can be ignored because they are ties. Thus

$$P(W_4) = \left(\frac{3}{36}\right) P(\text{winning on second throw}) = \left(\frac{3}{36}\right)\left(\frac{3}{3+6}\right) = \frac{1}{36}$$

We observe that if, say, an 8 is rolled on the second throw, nothing happens. The shooter merely rolls again to try and make a 4 on the third throw. Thus it is also true that

$$P(W_4) = (3/36)P(\text{winning on } n\text{th throw}) = 1/36 \text{ for } n \geq 2$$

All of the other point situations are handled in the same way and are shown below.

$P(W_5) = (4/36)[4/(4 + 6)] = 2/45$
$P(W_6) = (5/36)[5/5 + 6)] = 25/396$
$P(W_8) = (5/36)[5/(5 + 6)] = 25/396$
$P(W_9) = (4/36)[4/(4 + 6)] = 2/45$
$P(W_{10}) = (3/36)[3/(3 + 6)] = 1/36$

Since these winning situations are mutually exclusive, we find that

$P(\text{win on pass line}) =$
$$P(W_7) + P(W_{11}) + P(W_4) + P(W_5) + P(W_6)$$
$$+ P(W_8) + P(W_9) + P(W_{10}) = 244/495$$
$P(\text{loss on pass line}) = 1 - 244/495 = 251/495$

The expectation is thus

$$E = (244/495)\ (\$1) - (251/495)\ (\$1) = -0.0141414$$

or about 1.41% disadvantage to the player.

Remarks on Gambling Games

Martingale betting schemes

There are various individuals who attempt various "doubling-up" betting schemes that they claim are "sure things." One such system can be easily described. Bet $5 on the color red in roulette. If you lose, bet $10 on red again. If you lose this second time also (you've lost a total of $15 so far), bet $20. If you win on the third bet, note that you're ahead $5. If you lose on the third bet, then wager $40 on the next bet, etc. Individuals who play this scheme feel that it is virtually impossible to have a string of successive losses that might bring them over the betting limit. This is false.

Consider the case of betting on red in the game of roulette. In this situation $P(\text{win}) = 18/38$ and $P(\text{loss}) = 20/38$. A person using a doubling-up scheme might feel that it is impossible to have eight losses in a row. Using a result from advanced probability theory it is possible to show that (for a roulette color bet) the probability of at least eight losses in a row in n spins of the wheel is given by

$$p = 1 - (1.0172644)\ (1.0028616)^{-n}$$

where n is large. Examine the results for various values of n.

If $n = 100$, $p = .24$
If $n = 1,000$, $p = .94$
If $n = 10,000$, $p = .99$

Thus for 100 successive color bets in roulette, there is a 24% probability of a losing streak of at least eight losses in a row. Thus the longer such doubling-up systems are continued, the greater will be the probability of disaster! If such a streak occurs, as described, the player would lose

$$\$5 + \$10 + \$20 + \$40 + \$80 + \$160 + \$320 + \$640 = \$1275$$

If such a streak did not occur in 100 trials, the net profit would be much smaller by comparison and would be more than offset by the results of a disastrous streak. Betting schemes can never make a negative expectation into a positive expectation.

Variability in games of chance or what will happen in the long run

We have seen that in a sequence of n Bernoulli trials, each having a probability of success p associated with it, there is an expected number of successes $E = np$. In statistics it is shown that a good measure of the variability in the number of successes is the standard deviation given by the formula

$$\sigma = \sqrt{npq}$$

where $q = 1 - p$. This number (which depends on n) tells us how much variation there is due to chance in the number of successes obtained in n trials when the probability of success in an individual trial is p. For the binomial distribution it turns out that approximately two-thirds of the time the actual number of successes S in n trials falls within the range

$$E - \sqrt{npq} \leq S \leq E + \sqrt{npq}$$

Thus in 1000 tosses of a fair coin we might expect to have 500 heads, but since the standard derivation $\sigma = \sqrt{1000(1/2)(1/2)} \approx 16$, the actual number of heads would fall in the range

$$500 - 16 \leq S \leq 500 + 16$$

or

$$484 \leq S \leq 515$$

in two-thirds of the cases in which this experiment would be performed. Note that as n increases, the variability increases.

If we translate the above results into a gambling game in which a player wins \$1 when the coin comes up heads and loses \$1 when it comes up tails, we observe some interesting facts. It is not difficult to show that a player's running bankroll B = total wins − total losses will be in the range

$$-2\sqrt{npq} \le B \le 2\sqrt{npq}$$

in two-thirds of the cases in which the gambling experiment is repeated. A graph of B as a function of n follows.

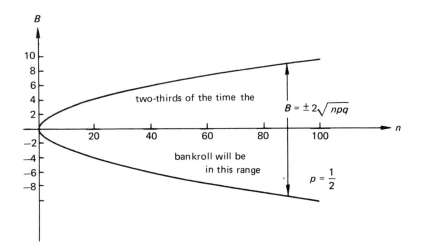

The above graph shows that even in a fair game, the total amount won minus the total amount lost could become unboundedly large (both in a positive and a negative sense if you were to play without stopping. Moreover if the experiment were repeated a number of times, in two-thirds of the cases the total bankroll B will lie within a very wide range. It turns out that even in a fair game between two players each having a finite initial stake, it is virtually a certainty that one of the players will be wiped out for n sufficiently large.

What would happen in an unfair game? In a gambling game between a player and an opponent (perhaps a casino) suppose we have the following information given:

i.   For each \$1 bet by the player, the player will win y dollars in every winning situation.

ii. p = probability of winning

iii. $q = 1 - p$ = probability of losing

iv. n = the number of times the game is played

v. B = running bankroll (assumed to have the initial value 0)

It turns out that there is a probability of 2/3 that the player's running bankroll will be in the range

$$ypn - qn - (y+1)\sqrt{npq} \le B \le ypn - qn + (y+1)\sqrt{npq}$$

In the case of betting on a color in roulette ($p = 18/38$) we have the following computed ranges for the bankroll B:

n	bankroll B
0	0
100	between -15 and $+5$
200	between -26 and $+4$
300	between -33 and $+2$
400	between -41 and -1
500	between -49 and -4
1000	between -84 and -21

These results are graphed below.

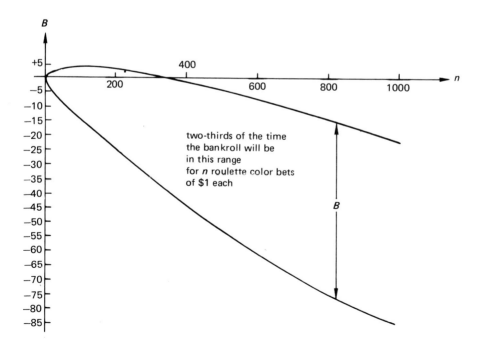

two-thirds of the time
the bankroll will be
in this range
for n roulette color bets
of $1 each

It is not difficult to see that as n increases without bound, the range for B becomes *negatively* infinite.

Other illustrations are given below.

1000 plays at level bets of $1

Bet	Expectation	68% chance the winnings will be
Roulette color	−5.3%	Between −$ 85 and −$ 21
Roulette number	−5.3%	Between −$235 and $129
Craps pass line	−1.4%	Between −$ 46 and $ 18

The conclusion is inescapable. When the expectation is negative (unfavorable to the player), a large value of n increases the probability of a large variation down and away from the mathematical expectation. If you couple this to two other unfavorable facts:

(i)   The casino has maximum betting limits and
(ii) The player has far less money than the casino

we see that the prospect is very dim for a player who continues to bet for a long period of time. A persistent player will, with an inexorably increasing probability, be wiped out by one of the ever-widening deviations in the negative direction.

Some people still insist that a player could "break the bank." However, probability theory as well as the unrealized dreams of many who have attempted it demonstrates that such events are extremely rare. The slim possibility of making a fortune is much more than offset by the virtual certainty of total ruin.

Striking when the table is hot

A "hot" dice table is an expression that is used to describe a table in which the players are winning many more times than they are losing. People get very excited when this happens, and they bet even greater amounts of money! The hope is that the "trend" will continue. It may or it may not. In any binomial game with independent trials, there is no way to predict future outcomes from previous ones. The dice have no memory, and therefore these two cubical objects do not "intend" to continue with nor compensate for previous statistical variations, whether unusual or not.

Exercise 6.5   1.   For the following bets in roulette, find the probability of a win (see p. 199).

A Single number
B Two numbers
C Three numbers
F Six numbers
G Column
H Dozens
J Odd or even
K High or low

2. Find the expectations for each of the betting situations in Problem 1.

3. In European roulette there is only one house number, 0. (The American wheels have two house numbers, 0 and 0-0.) Find the expectations on a European wheel for bets *A, B, C, D, F, G, H, I, J,* and *K.*

4. A gambler plays roulette 200 times by wagering $50 on single-number bets. Find her expected loss in dollars.

5. A gambler plays roulette 200 times by wagering $50 on five-number bets. Find her expected loss in dollars.

6. Use the result of Example 4 to answer this question. A gambler plays table craps 200 times by wagering $50 on pass line bets. Find his expected loss in dollars.

7. In table craps, find the expectation for a $1 wager on any craps.

8. In table craps, find the expectation for a $1 wager on field.

9. In table craps, find the expectation for a $1 wager on big 6 or 8.

*10. In table craps, find the expectation for a $1 wager on don't pass line.

**11. In table craps suppose you bet $1 on pass line. If a point is established, many casinos will permit an odds bet (also $1), which is an additional wager that the shooter will make the point. Show that this effectively reduces the expectation of pass line, where you always take the odds bet when possible, to $E = -.848$.

12. The following formula gives the probability of a run of at least 10 heads in a row in n tosses of a fair coin. For large n

$$p = 1 - (1.003937)(1.0004908)^{-n}$$

Find the probability of a run of at least 10 heads in a row in 100, 1000, or 10,000 throws of a fair coin. Use a calculator to perform the computations.

*13. Write a BASIC language program that will simulate the color bet for roulette. Allow the player to have a $250 stake with which to martingale if she loses with the following progression: $5, $10, $20, $40, $80. Allow the computer to record a running account of the player's bankroll and order the program to stop at any time the bankroll is less than or equal to 0, and record n (the number of times the game was played).

14. Find the expectation in the numbers racket. Numbers "policy slips" numbered 1, 2, 3, 4, . . . , 10,000 are sold at 50¢ each. There are four winners, who each win $500.

> "Only 50¢ wins you $500 ! ! !"

15. In downtown Las Vegas there is the following game of chuck-a-luck: Three dice are tossed inside a basket and it costs $5 to play.

    i.   If no 6 appears on the face of any die, you lose.
    ii. If one 6 appears on the face of only one die, you win $5 (and you get your bet returned to you).
    iii. If two 6's appear on the faces of only two dice, you win $10 (and you get your bet returned to you).
    iv. If three 6's appear on the faces of all the dice, you win $15 (and you get your bet returned to you).

    Find the mathematical expectation.

16. Experiment with the following game graph. Flip a coin. If it comes up heads, put an upward mark (shown below) on a graph; if it comes up tails, put a downward mark on the graph. Attach each mark to the previous one so that you have a running count of wins minus losses. Your graph might look like the following:

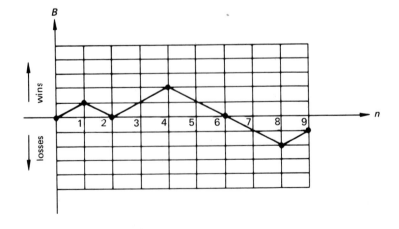

17. Construct a simple game as follows. Your stake is five pennies and your opponent's stake is five pennies. A coin is flipped. If heads, you win 1¢ from your opponent. If tails, your opponent wins 1¢ from you. Continue playing this game and demonstrate that it does not take too long for one of you to be wiped out.

Linear Equations and Inequalities

> The straightness of a straight line requires consideration.
>
> > Alfred North Whitehead
>
> Descartes's great contribution to geometry was the invention of co-ordinate geometry. . . . What was original in him was the use of co-ordinates, i.e., the determination of the position of a point in a plane by its distance from two fixed lines. He did not himself discover all the power of this method, but he did enough to make further progress easy.
>
> > Bertrand Russell

7.1   Linear Equations and Their Graphs

In this chapter we shall learn how to graph linear equations and linear inequalities. We shall determine various specific points and sets of points on our graphs. These ideas are being studied (or reviewed) because they are essential to the subject of linear programming, which will be taken up in subsequent chapters.

We are probably all familiar with a *rectangular coordinate* system, in which two real lines are placed at right angles to one another in such a way that the zero points coincide. Traditionally the horizontal real line is referred to as the *x axis* and the vertical real line is called the *y axis*. Sometimes we will use the same scale on both axes. However, as we will see in future applications, it is sometimes advantageous to choose different scales. The usual convention is to choose positive directions as upward or to the right of the center point (called the *origin*) and negative directions downward or to the left.

Many useful and interesting mathematical relationships can be represented as ordered pairs of real numbers (x, y). Also, each and every pair of real numbers (x, y) can be pictorially represented as a point on the rectangular coordinate system. For example, the pair $(2, -3)$ is the point located

(i)   2 units to the right of the y axis and

(ii)   3 units below the x axis

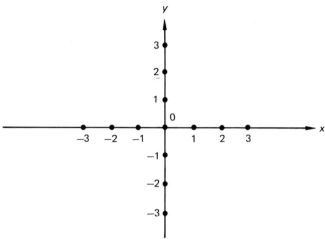

Rectangular coordinate system

Rectangular coordinate system

Note that in every ordered pair of numbers, we agree that the first number of the pair is an *x-coordinate* and the second number in the pair is a *y-coordinate.* The first and second numbers of a pair are also referred to as the *abscissa* and the *ordinate,* respectively.

Example 1

Draw a rectangular coordinate system and locate the points corresponding to the ordered pairs: (5, 2), (2, 5), (−3, 0), (−2, 1), (−2, −3), (0, −2), (3, −1), (4, 0), (0, 0).

Solution

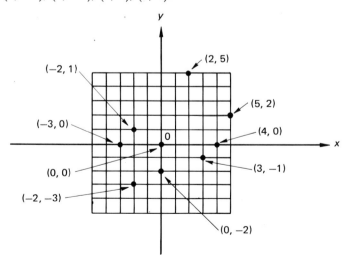

Note that the origin has coordinates (0, 0).

Example 2

Find the ordered pairs corresponding to the points shown on the rectangular coordinate system shown.

Solution

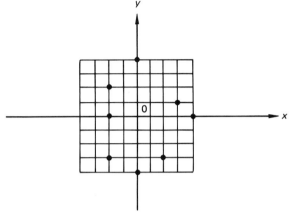

On the y axis we have the point $(0, 4)$. Proceeding clockwise, we have $(3, 1)$, $(4, 0)$, $(2, -3)$, $(0, -4)$, $(-2, -3)$, $(-2, 0)$, and $(-2, 2)$.

Examples such as the previous ones demonstrate that there is a one-to-one correspondence between pairs of real numbers and points in the plane. Essentially this means that

(i)   For each pair of real numbers (x, y) there corresponds a unique point

(ii) For each point in the plane, there corresponds a unique number pair (x, y)

Many kinds of algebraic relationships can be described by an equation involving x and y. Some of these relationships are rather simple, and others are quite complicated. Here are a few examples:

$$y = 3x - 2$$
$$xy = 1$$
$$x^2 + y^3 = 64$$
$$2x + y = x^{1/4}y^{1/2}$$

The first two are fairly simple, but the last two are much more difficult. Each of them, however, is satisfied by a set of ordered pairs of real numbers. If we selected a particular algebraic relationship and if we determined a representative set of ordered pairs (x, y) that satisfied that relationship, we could graph the set of ordered pairs on a rectangular coordinate system. This graph would enable us to "see" the relationship between x and y in a pictorial sense. We will develop a way to do this for linear equations.

We begin by saying that a linear equation is an algebraic relationship between two variables (say x and y), which when graphed on a rectangular coordinate system, yields a straight line. But this is not saying very much. It does not tell us, for example, how to recognize a linear equation when we see one. Moreover it does not tell us how to graph an equation.

Before algebraically characterizing all linear equations in x and y we will look at a few examples of them. In each of these examples, unless otherwise noted, we will assume that the variable x can be any real number.

Example 3

Graph the equation $y = 3x$.

Solution Since x is free to take on any and all real values, we will arbitrarily choose the x values: $-3, -2, -1, 0, 1, 2, 3$. For each of these seven numbers, we will find the corresponding y value, and summarize the results in a table. Note that, for example, if $x = -3$, then we have that $y = 3\,(-3) = -9$. Now we view each of the ordered pairs (x, y) in the table as *points* on our rectangular grid. The points appear to lie on the same straight line.

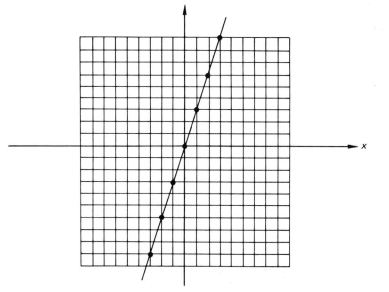

x	,	y
-3		-9
-2		-6
-1		-3
0		0
1		3
2		6
3		9

Notice that between adjacent ordered pairs we have a 1-unit difference in the x coordinates and 3-unit differences in the corresponding y coordinates. Our intuition tells us that in fact the points do lie on the same straight line.

Now we will examine a linear equation having a slightly more complicated form.

Example 4

Graph the equation $y = \dfrac{1}{2}x - 2$.

Solution In choosing arbitrary x values, for convenience we will select even integers so that the expression $(1/2)x - 2$ will be an integer. We choose: $-4, -2, 0, 2, 4,$ and 6.

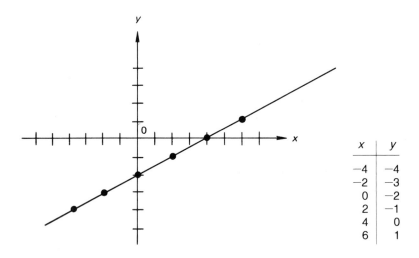

x	y
-4	-4
-2	-3
0	-2
2	-1
4	0
6	1

Again, notice that between the adjacent ordered pairs we have selected, there is a constant 2-unit difference in the x coordinates, and a correspondingly constant (in this case, 1-unit) difference in the respective y coordinates. For the moment, we assume that they all lie on the same straight line and that all

(i)   Points on the line satisfy the equation

(ii) Pairs satisfying the equation correspond to points on the line

We will see that if an equation is an equation of a straight line, then for every pair of points satisfying the equation the ratio of the difference in the y coordinates to the difference in the x coordinates will be the same.

A straight-line graph can be quite useful. For a given value x_1 we may want to find the corresponding y value satisfying the equation. One way we can do this, of course, is to substitute x_1 into the equation and calculate y_1. However, if the straight line is a correct representation of our equation, then we can merely erect a line perpendicular to the x axis at x_1 and note the ordinate of the point of intersection with the line.

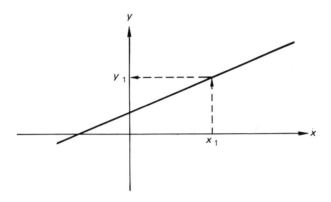

This enables us to visualize, with a reasonable degree of accuracy, the y values corresponding to various x values.

In order to be able to develop general equations for straight lines we will need to formulate a measure of the steepness of a line. We want this measure to be small (close to 0) for lines having a small inclination such as in the following figure:

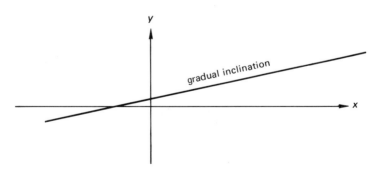

And we want this measure to be relatively large (in absolute value) for lines having a large inclination.

We could use an angular measure (for example, the degree measure from any horizontal line counterclockwise to the straight line); however, it is more convenient to use a measure called *slope* designated by the letter m. The slope m of a line measures the ratio of the difference

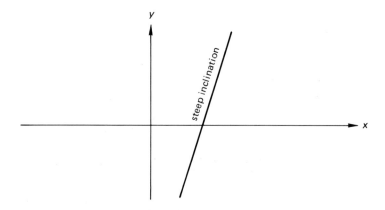

of the ordinates of two points on the line to the difference of the abscissas of the two points. Sometimes this is expressed by writing:

$$\text{slope} = m = \frac{\text{difference between } y \text{ coordinates}}{\text{difference between } x \text{ coordinates}} = \frac{\text{rise}}{\text{run}}$$

To make this clear, we will be more precise in our terminology by stating a complete definition.

Definition 1   Given two distinct points $P(x_1, y_1)$ and $Q(x_2, y_2)$, the *slope m* of the line L containing these two points is given by

$$m = \frac{y_2 - y_1}{x_2 - x_1}$$

where $x_1 \neq x_2$. If it turns out that $y_2 \neq y_1$ and $x_2 = x_1$, m is undefined because we have a zero in the denominator, and the line L is *vertical*. If it happens that $y_2 = y_1$ and $x_2 = x_1$, then P and Q are identical and do not determine a unique straight line, so it would be meaningless to discuss the slope.

We can observe the reason for the above measure m by examining a few concrete illustrations. We will compute (and illustrate with a graph) the slope of the lines through

(i)   The points (1, 2) and (7, 3)

(ii)   The points (−1, −2) and (1, 6)

(iii)   The points (−1, 5) and (2, 1)

(iv)   The points (−1, 2) and (4, 2)

Diagrams for these four cases are given below together with the associated computations for the slope.

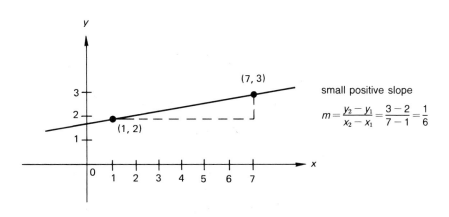

small positive slope

$$m = \frac{y_2 - y_1}{x_2 - x_1} = \frac{3 - 2}{7 - 1} = \frac{1}{6}$$

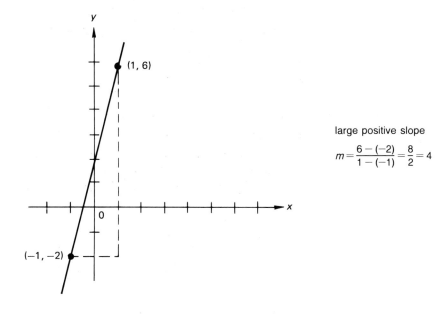

large positive slope

$$m = \frac{6 - (-2)}{1 - (-1)} = \frac{8}{2} = 4$$

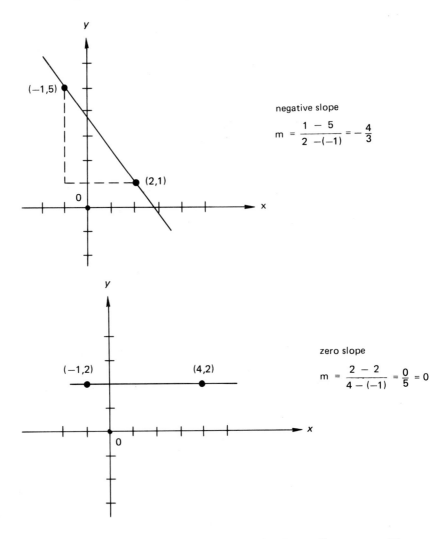

We can make several observations about the above illustrations: Viewing each line from left to right

(i)   Gradual rising inclinations have small positive slopes
(ii)   Steep rising inclinations have large positive slopes
(iii) Falling inclinations have negative slopes
(iv)   Horizontal (or level) inclinations have zero slopes

Thus the measure we have introduced is related very nicely to our preconceived notions about steepness. Moreover the sign of a particular slope measurement tells us whether the line is rising ($m > 0$), falling ($m < 0$), or horizontal ($m = 0$).

It is useful to note that when we are given two points (x_1, y_1) and (x_2, y_2) the order of subtraction is not important as long as we perform the subtraction in the same order for both numerator and denominator. This is easily seen because

$$\frac{y_2 - y_1}{x_2 - x_1} = \frac{y_1 - y_2}{x_1 - x_2}$$

It may be, in some cases, that we have more than two points that we know are on the same line. In these situations we will have several different ways of computing the slope. We want to be sure that the measure we have developed will yield the same value m for different pairs of points. Our intuition tells us that if the inclination is the same, then the slopes should be identical. We will prove this using a simple idea from geometry.

Theorem 1   Given four distinct points P, Q, P', Q', which all lie on the same straight line, the slope of line segment $\overline{PQ}$ is equal to the slope of line segment $\overline{P'Q'}$.

Proof The rise and run for segment $\overline{PQ}$ are shown as a and b, respectively, on the diagram. Similarly the rise and run for $\overline{P'Q'}$ are shown as c and d, respectively.

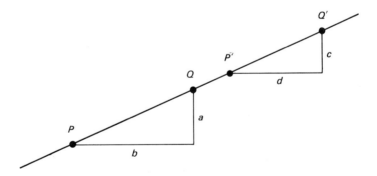

Then we have

$$\text{slope of } PQ = a/b$$
$$\text{slope of } \overline{P'Q'} = c/d$$

The two triangles shown are *similar* (corresponding angles are equal). For similar triangles, corresponding sides are in proportion. Therefore

$$\frac{c}{a} = \frac{d}{b}$$

This implies that $ad = bc$. Dividing both sides by db, we have

$$\frac{ad}{db} - \frac{bc}{db}$$
$$a/b = c/d$$

The slopes are equal.

For vertical lines, we should emphasize that slopes are undefined. But we will need a way of representing vertical lines by using an equation. Suppose, for example, we wish to represent the vertical line passing through the point (a, b). How should we do this? First we note that all points on a vertical line through (a, b) have the same x coordinates, namely $x = a$, while the y coordinates take on all real values. We will therefore represent the vertical line through (a, b) by the simple equation $x = a$, with the tacit understanding that y can take on all real values.

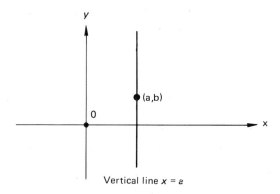

Vertical line $x = a$

We now wish to formulate an algebraic characterization of all nonvertical straight lines. The following theorem will assist us in accomplishing this. This is a very important theorem and it should be studied carefully.

Theorem 2   Consider a line L with slope m passing through the point $(0, b)$. The equation described by this line is given by the formula

$$y = mx + b$$

Proof Take an arbitrary point (x, y) on line L, where $(x, y) \neq (0, b)$. Then by the definition of slope

$$m = \frac{y_2 - y_1}{x_2 - x_1} = \frac{y - b}{x - 0}$$

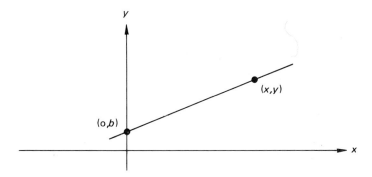

Then

$$y - b = mx$$
$$y = mx + b$$

It is also easy to show that any equation of the form $y = mx + b$ must have slope m and pass through the point $(0, b)$. Thus our proof is complete.

As a convention, when a line passes through the point $(0, b)$ (which is on the y axis), the number b is called the y *intercept*. Equations written in the form $y = mx + b$ are said to be in the *slope-intercept* form.

In the next section we will look at various other forms for equations of straight lines.

Example 5

Given that there is a linear equation describing the relationship between temperature x measured in centigrade, and temperature y measured in Fahrenheit degrees, find the slope-intercept form for it.

Solution Since 0° centigrade corresponds to 32° Fahrenheit and 100° centigrade corresponds to 212° Fahrenheit, we can interpret the equation of the line as passing through the two points

$$(0, 32) \text{ and } (100, 212)$$

Note that the y intercept is $b = 32$ and the slope

$$m = \frac{212 - 32}{100 - 0} = \frac{180}{100} = \frac{9}{5}$$

Thus the relationship is given by

$$y = \frac{9}{5}x + 32$$

Example 6

Use the answer to Example 5 to find the Fahrenheit temperature equivalent to a centigrade temperature of 20°.

Solution Since x is in centigrade, let $x = 20$ and then

$$y = \frac{9}{5}(20) + 32 = 36 + 32 = 68° \text{ Fahrenheit}$$

Example 7

Jake's Towing Service charges a flat fee of \$20 for the hookup to a disabled car and a variable fee of \$1.50 per mile for the trip. Write an equation for the cost y of a trip of x miles. Graph the equation. Find the cost of a trip of 60 miles.

Solution Construct a simple table:

x (miles)	y (cost)
0	\$20
1	21.50
2	23.00
3	24.50
4	26.00

Notice that the point (0, 20) yields the y intercept $b = 20$, and the slope is given by

$$m = \frac{21.50 - 20}{1 - 0} = 1.50$$

Thus the cost equation is $y = 1.50x + \$20$. To read the graph more

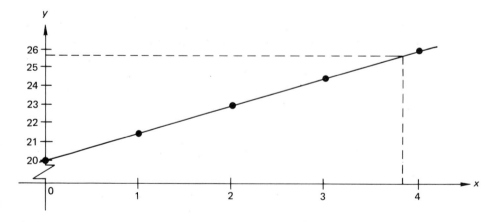

easily we choose a different scale on the x-axis from the scale on the y-axis.

A trip of 60 miles would cost $y = 1.50\ (60) + 20 = 110.00$.

Example 8

From the graph given in Example 8 *estimate* the cost of a trip of 3.8 miles.

Solution Estimating the position of $x = 3.8$ on the graph (see dotted line above), we see that y is approximately \$25.60. This is quite close to the exact value $y = 1.50\ (3.8) + 20 = \$25.70$.

Exercise 7.1   1. Construct a table and graph each of the following straight-line equations.

   a. $y = 5x - 7$
   b. $y = x$
   c. $y = (1/2)x + 3$
   d. $y = (-1/2)x + 3$
   e. $y = 3$
   f. $x = -6$

2. Complete the table and construct scales suitable to make a graph of the equation

$$y = 100x - 30$$

x	y
0	
1	
2	
3	

3. A linear graph has 2 units of rise for every 1 unit of run, and passes through the origin (0, 0). State and graph the equation.

4. A linear graph has 1 unit of rise for every 3 units of run, and passes through the origin (0, 0). State and graph the equation.

5. Show that the equation $5y = x + 10$ can be written in $y = mx + b$ form. Using the y intercept b together with the slope m, graph the equation.

6. State the equations of lines with

   a.   Slope 5 and y intercept 6
   b.   Slope $-1/4$, passing through the point (5, 8)
   c.   An inclination of 45° and passing through (0, 0)

7. The values in the table below reveal a linear relationship between
    y and x. State this relationship and complete the table.

y	130	90	50	10		
x	-2	0	2	4	6	8

8. It is difficult to demonstrate graphically whether the point (2893)
    lies on the graph of $y = 502x - 117$. Prove that in fact it does
    not. Is it slightly above the line or slightly below it?

9. Draw 5 different lines having the equation $y = mx + 3$.

10. Find the slopes of the lines through P and Q. Illustrate graphically.

    a. $P = (-1, 6)$ and $Q = (-2, -3)$
    b. $P = (7, 3)$ and $Q = (-2, 2)$
    c. $P = (-1, 4)$ and $Q = (5, -6)$
    d. $P = (6, 2)$ and $Q = (-7, 2)$
    e. $P = (2, 6)$ and $Q = (2, -7)$ (Watch out!)

11. A line L passes through the points $(1, -1)$ and $(5, 11)$ and has a
    y intercept of $b = -4$. Find the equation of the line.

12. Five lines are shown below. Which have positive slopes? negative
    slopes? zero slopes? undefined slopes?

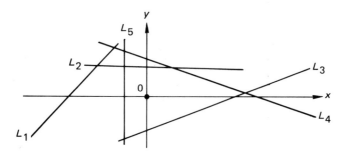

13. Using the graph on page 229, estimate y when $x = 1955$.

14. The number of students at Westchester Community College is
    given by the formula

$$y = 200x + 5000$$

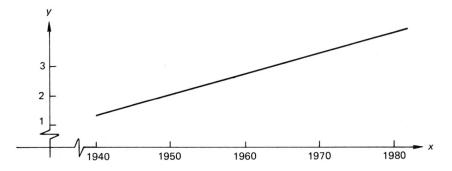

where x is in years, and $x = 0$ corresponds to the year 1960. Calculate the following.

   a. y when $x = 0$
   b. y when $x = 1$
   c.   The number of students during 1970
   d.   The number of students during 1980
   e.   The year there will be 10,000 students

*15.   Ace Moving Vans bases the total charge to the customer on the following:

   (i) $80 flat initial fee
   (ii) $.50 per mile of traveling distance
   (iii) $45 per hour of loading and unloading time

Answer the following questions.

   a.   Find the total cost C of a trip involving x mi of traveling and 6 hr of loading and unloading.
   b.   If $C = \$400$ and the loading and unloading time is 6 hr, find x.
   c.   Express the total cost C of a trip involving x mi of traveling and y h of loading and unloading.
   d.   Construct a graph to illustrate some different ways this particular cost $C = \$400$ can arise for various values of x and y.

7.2 Graphing and Solving Basic Linear Systems

It should be clear from the examples given in the previous section that linear equations are sometimes useful in describing certain practical situations. For reasons that will be apparent later, it is also useful to be able to find out if two linear graphs have any point or points in common. If they *do,* we often want to be able to find their coordinates. This is what we mean by solving a linear system in the variables x and y.

We already discussed the slope-intercept form for a straight line:

$$y = mx + b$$

slope-intercept form

and we found that if a line has slope m and passes through the point $(0, b)$, then the equation of the line can be written in the above form. Conversely, if an equation has the above form, we can show that it must have slope m and pass through the point $(0, b)$. In this sense the above form characterizes the straight line.

It can be shown that various other forms also characterize straight lines. These forms will also be useful to us when we attempt to graph and solve linear systems. These forms are given below, and we should remind ourselves that these are only for nonvertical lines.

(i)   A straight line with slope m passing through the point (x_1, y_1) can be represented by the equation

$$y - y_1 = m(x - x_1)$$

point-slope form

(ii)   A straight line can be represented by the equation

$$Ax + By + C = 0$$

linear form

where A, B, and C are constants and $B \neq 0$.

(iii)   A straight line passing through the distinct points (x_1, y_1) and (x_2, y_2) where $x_1 \neq x_2$ can be represented by the equation

$$y = y_1 + \frac{y_2 - y_1}{x_2 - x_1}(x - x_1)$$

two-point form

Example 1

Show that all of the above forms are equivalent to the slope-intercept form $y = mx + b$.

Solution Form (i)

$$y - y_1 = m(x - x_1)$$

can be rewritten in the form

$$y = mx + y_1 - mx_1$$

which is now in slope-intercept form with $b = y_1 - mx_1$.

Form (ii)

$$Ax + By + C = 0$$

with $B \neq 0$, can be rewritten in the form

$$y = -\frac{A}{B}x - \frac{C}{B}$$

which is in slope-intercept form with $m = -A/B$ and $b = -C/B$.

Form (iii) can be written

$$y - y_1 = \frac{y_2 - y_1}{x_2 - x_1}(x - x_1)$$

which is now in the form of (i).

It is also possible to convert the equation $y = mx + b$ into any one of the other forms. Thus all of the forms are equivalent.

Example 2

Justify form (i) by showing that if a line has slope m and passes through (x_1, y_1), then it can be written $y - y_1 = m(x - x_1)$.

Solution Take an arbitrary point on the line $(x, y) \neq (x_1, y_1)$.

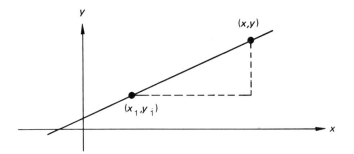

Then by the definition of slope we have that

$$m = \frac{y - y_1}{x - x_1}$$

$$y - y_1 = m(x - x_1)$$

Example 3

Given the line having slope 2/3 and passing through the point (2, −2)

   a.   Construct a graph from the given information.
   b.   Estimate the y intercept from the graph.
   c.   Find the exact value of the y intercept.

Solution Since the slope $m = \dfrac{2}{3}$,

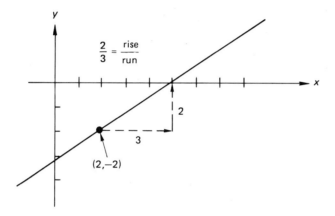

From the graph we see that $b \approx -3.2$. In order to find the exact value of b we need to find the equation of the straight line. Using the point-slope formula we have that

$$y - (-2) = \frac{2}{3}(x - 2)$$

which we will convert into slope-intercept form in order to see the value for b.

$$y = (2/3)x - 4/3 - 2$$
$$y = (2/3)x - 10/3$$

$b = -\dfrac{10}{3}$ is the exact y intercept.

Example 4

Graph the line representing the equation $3x - 2y - 12 = 0$ by finding the two points where the line intersects the respective axes.

Solution First observe that since the equation is in linear form, we know the equation represents a straight line. The slope is defined and nonzero, so the line must intersect the x axis at some point and the y axis at some other point. We know that the point where the line intersects the x axis has a y coordinate of 0, hence set $y = 0$ and obtain

$$3x - 12 = 0 \qquad \text{or} \qquad x = 4$$

so that (4, 0) locates the x intercept. Similarly by setting $x = 0$ in the equation of the line we have

$$-2y - 12 = 0 \qquad \text{or} \qquad y = -6$$

yielding (0, −6) for the point where the line intersects the y axis. The graph is shown below.

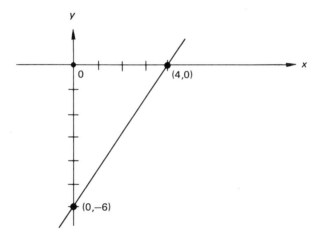

Example 5

Find the equation of the line passing through the points (1, 3) and (6, 8)

Solution Calculating the slope, we have that

$$m = \frac{8 - 3}{6 - 1} = 1$$

and by picking one of the two given points, say (1, 3), and using the point-slope formula, we have that

$$y - 3 = 1(x - 1) \qquad \text{or} \qquad y = x + 2$$

Alternate Using the two-point formula, we have
Solution

$$y = 3 + \frac{8-3}{6-1}(x-1)$$

which yields the same result $y = x + 2$.

Example 6

Graph the two lines $x + y = 2$ and $x + y = 5$. Explain why it is not possible for any point to lie on *both* lines.

Solution Using the method given in Example 4, we have $x + y = 2$ with intercept points $(2, 0)$ and $(0, 2)$ and $x + y = 5$ with intercept points $(5, 0)$ and $(0, 5)$.

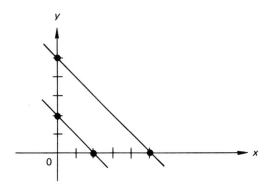

It appears that the two lines are parallel and do not intersect. However, it might be possible that the two lines intersect at some distant point. Suppose they did intersect. Then that point would satisfy each of the two linear equations. In this case the sum $x + y$ would equal both 2 and 5. But this is impossible. Hence the two lines cannot possibly intersect.

Of course the example we just solved happens to consist of two very simple equations. If the equations were in different forms, it might have been more difficult to see whether the two equations could be satisfied simultaneously by a common point. It would be useful to have criteria for determining when the equations representing two lines have (i) no common point, (ii) one common point, (iii) an infinite number of common points. These three situations are referred to, respectively, by the terms *parallel, intersecting,* and *coincident.* The following criteria are helpful in identifying which of the three situations is correct in a given situation:

Two lines are *coincident* if and only if their equations are equivalent.
Two distinct lines are *parallel* if and only if their slopes are equal.

Two distinct nonvertical lines *intersect* if and only if their slopes are unequal.

Examples of each of these situations are shown below.

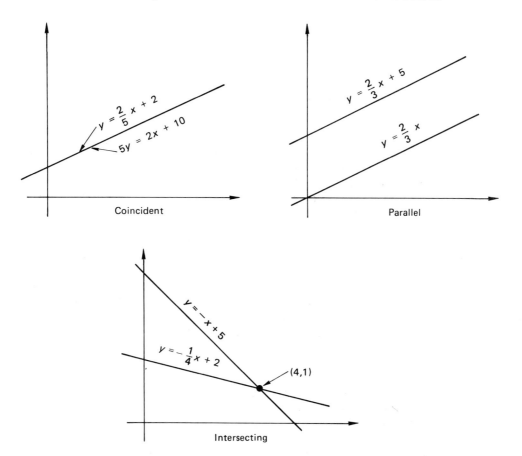

Coincident

Parallel

Intersecting

Terms useful to us in this and later chapters are summarized below. For the moment we will use them when discussing linear equations in x and y.

graph of two lines	coincident	parallel	intersecting
two equations	dependent	inconsistent	consistent

Example 7

What can be said about each of the following pairs of linear equations?

a. $2x - 5y + 7 = 0$ and $3x - 6y + 8 = 0$
b. $2x - 5y + 7 = 0$ and $4x - 10y + 14 = 0$
c. $2x - 5y + 7 = 0$ and $2x - 5y + 8 = 0$

Solution a.   The slopes are unequal, thus the graphs intersect and the equations are consistent.

b.   The equations are equivalent since we can obtain the second equation by multiplying both sides of the first equation by 2. Thus the graphs are coincident and the equations are dependent.

c.   The equations are distinct and have equal slopes. Thus the graphs are parallel and the equations are inconsistent.

Example 8

Find the point of intersection of the two equations:

$$4x + 3y = 12$$
$$-2x + 3y = 3$$

Solution (graphical method) Alternately letting $x = 0$ and then $y = 0$ in the above equations, we obtain the intercepts:

First line   (0, 4) and (3, 0)
Second line   (0, 1) and (−3/2, 0)

From these two pairs of points we produce the figure below.

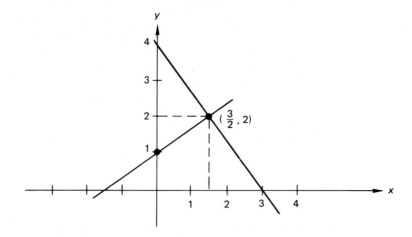

Note that the only point satisfying both equations is the intersection point (3/2, 2). Of course we were lucky. This method often yields results that are only approximate.

Alternate (addition or subtraction method) Since the terms involving y are identi-
Solution cal in both equations, we can subtract corresponding sides of both
equations, obtaining

$$4x + 3y = 12$$
$$\underline{-2x + 3y = 3}$$
$$6x = 9 \text{ or } x = \frac{9}{6} = \frac{3}{2}$$

Substituting this result into one of the equations, we have

$$4(3/2) + 3y = 12$$
$$6 + 3y = 12$$
$$3y = 6$$
$$y = 2$$

$x = 3/2$ and $y = 2$ simultaneously satisfy both equations, and thus
$(3/2, 2)$ is the intersection point.

Alternate (substitution method) Solving for y in the first equation, we have that
Solution

$$y = \frac{12 - 4x}{3}$$

Substituting this result into the second equation, we obtain

$$-2x + 3\left(\frac{12 - 4x}{3}\right) = 3$$

$$-2x + 12 - 4x = 3$$

$$-6x = -9$$

$$x = \frac{3}{2}$$

Similarly, if this value is now substituted in one of the equations (say,
the second one), we have

$$-2\left(\frac{3}{2}\right) + 3y = 3$$

$$3y = 6$$

$$y = 2$$

Example 9

A woman wants her annual income from two investments to be $1400 annually. One investment earns 5%, and the other earns 7%.

a. Using a linear equation and a graph, show how the amounts invested in each can be made in many different ways.
b. If the amounts invested in each must be equal, how much money does she need to maintain the $1400 income? Illustrate graphically.

Solution Let

x = amount invested at 5%
y = amount invested at 7%

Since we require that the total return must be $1400, we have that

$$0.05x + 0.07y = \$1400$$

or, written more easily,

$$5x + 7y = \$140,000$$

This equation is satisfied by an infinite number of number pairs (x, y), all of which must satisfy the given requirements. Some of these are listed below together with an illustrative graph.

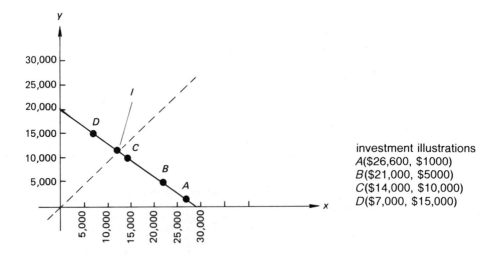

investment illustrations
A($26,600, $1000)
B($21,000, $5000)
C($14,000, $10,000)
D($7,000, $15,000)

If the amounts invested must be equal, then $y = x$ (shown above as a dotted line on the graph). Using the substitution method, we have

$$5x + 7y = \$140,000$$
$$y = x$$

or

$$5x + 7x = \$140,000$$
$$12x = \$140,000$$
$$x = \$11,666.67$$

which are the x and y coordinates of the intersection point I. Thus $11,666.67 must be invested at each rate in order to have (i) equal amounts invested at each rate, and (ii) a total yield of $1400 annually.

Example 10

In economic theory it is well known that both the *demand* (the number of items consumers will purchase) and the *supply* (the number of items available to be sold) for an item depend on the price x.

As x increases, supply increases and demand decreases. As x decreases, supply decreases and demand increases. As a result of this, free-market fluctuations tend to stabilize near an ideal point called the *market price*, which is the point where supply = demand.

Suppose we are given the supply and demand data below. Find the market price for automobiles manufactured annually in the United States. Illustrate with a graph.

Supply

x = average price per car	$2500	3000	3500	4000	4500	5000	5500	6000
y = number of cars available to be sold (in millions)	20	30	40	50	60	70	80	90

Demand

x = average price per car	$2535	3055	3575	4095	4615	5135
y' = number of cars the public will buy (in millions)	46	38	30	22	14	6

Solution Using the point-slope formula for each case, we obtain the following results.

$$y = \text{number cars available} = 20 + \frac{30 - 20}{3000 - 2500}(x - 2500)$$

or

$$y = \left(\frac{1}{50}\right)x - 30$$

$$y' = \text{number of cars public will buy} = 46 + \frac{38 - 46}{3055 - 2535}(x - 2535)$$

or

$$y' = \left(-\frac{1}{65}\right)x + 85$$

To find the market price, set supply = demand and solve for x:

$$(1/50)x - 30 = (-1/65)x + 85$$
$$x = \$3250$$

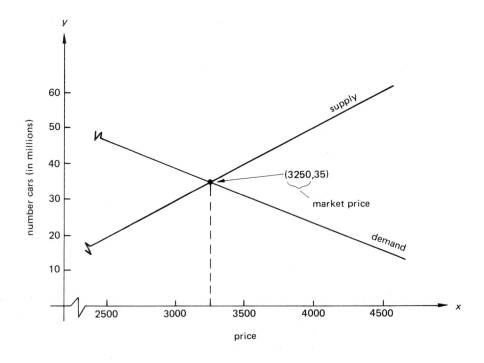

Graphing supply and demand lines* on the same set of axes, we have the illustrative graph shown.

Example 11

Solve the linear system

$$5x - 7y = 34$$
$$4x + 3y = 10$$

Solution Multiplying both sides of the first equation by 4 and both sides of the second equation by 5, we have

$$20x - 28y = 136$$
$$\underline{20x + 15y = 50} \text{ and subtracting corresponding sides}$$
$$-43y = 86$$
$$y = -2$$

Substituting into the first equation, we have

$$5x - 7(-2) = 34$$
$$5x = 34 - 14$$
$$5x = 20$$
$$x = 4$$

and the system is solved. The point $(4, -2)$ is the intersection point of the two lines.

Example 12

(hedge betting) Prior to a Giants vs Jets game, a mathematician with $100 to wager finds two football bettors, one who wants to bet on the Giants, and the other who wants to bet on the Jets. Both bettors see the Giants as the favorite, but offer different odds:

Odds

Bettor A G:J is 7:6   (A bets on Jets to win.)
Bettor B G:J is 3:2   (B bets on Giants to win.)

Thus for every $7 bet with A, the mathematician could win $6 if the Giants win, and for every $2 bet with B, the mathematician will win $3 if the Jets win. How could the mathematician apportion her $100 into two bets that, when combined together, will guarantee her a maximum positive return independent of the outcome of the game?

---

* With more realistic data, the graphs would be curves rather than straight lines; we have utilized a simple data set for our model.

Solution Let

$$x = \text{amount wagered with } A,$$
$$100 - x = \text{amount wagered with } B$$

If the Giants win, then the mathematician will win 6/7 of every dollar wagered with A and will lose all of her dollars wagered with B. Thus her return R is given by

$$R = \frac{6}{7}x - (100 - x)$$

If the Jets win, then the mathematician will win 3/2 times every dollar wagered with B and will lose all of her dollars wagered with A. Thus her return R is given by

$$R = \frac{3}{2}(100 - x) - x$$

When both of the equations are solved simultaneously we obtain $x = \$57.37$ and $R = +\$6.56$ as the solution to both. Thus a maximum guaranteed profit of \$6.56 will occur, regardless of the outcome of the game. It is informative to examine the graphs of the lines, which have the simplified equations:

$$R = (13/7)x - 100$$
$$R = 150 - (5/2)x$$

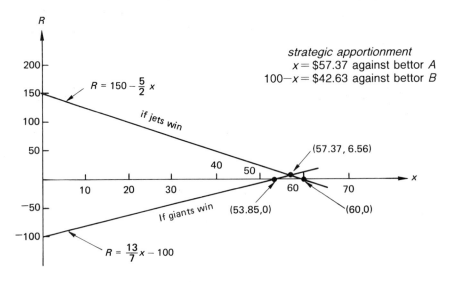

The above strategic apportionment will yield 6.56% of each dollar wagered. The x intercepts reveal that if the mathematician wagers between 53.85 and 60 with bettor A and the remainder of her money with bettor B, then the apportionment must guarantee a profit. The maximum guaranteed profit, however, will occur when $x = 57.37$.

This example merely illustrates how a linear system can be used as a model to map the effects of hedge betting in certain situations involving unequal payoff odds. The student is cautioned against attempting to utilize the technique for "sure" profit. Unequal payoff odds rarely exist in practice. Sports betting is often illegal, and even if it were legal, the technique rests on the rather naive assumption that the loser (of the two bettors A and B) will always make good on a losing wager.

The author is indebted to Professor Jean-Claude Derderian, of Staten Island Community College, whose article "Maximin Hedges" provided the theoretical basis for the above problem. The curious student will find the article in the May, 1978 issue of the *Mathematics Magazine* (**51**, No. 3, pp. 188–192).

Exercise 7.2   1.   Show that each of the following equations describe the identical straight line:

     a. $y + 5 = (-1/2)(x - 3)$
     b. $y = (-1/2x) - 7/2$
     c. $x + 2y + 7 = 0$

    2.   Find the equation of each line.

     a.   Having slope 1/4 and passing through the point $(3, -6)$.
     b.   Passing through the points $(2, 3)$ and $(-2, 9)$.

    3.   Graph the two straight lines shown by finding the intercepts.

$$x + y = 1$$
$$3x - 8y = -30$$

Estimate the position of the intersection point and then find the exact position of the intersection point by using an algebraic method.

    4.   Given the line having slope 3/4 and passing through the point $(7, -1)$.

     a.   Construct a graph from the given information.
     b.   Estimate the x and y intercepts from the graph.
     c.   Find the x and y intercepts exactly.

    5.   Explain why there are an infinite number of points simultaneously satisfying the equations $4x - 2y = 10$ and $y = 2x - 5$.

6. Explain why there is no intersection point for the graphs of the straight lines $2x + 4y = 12$ and $y = (-1/2)x + 4$.

7. Solve the system shown by

   a. Graphical methods
   b. Addition or subtraction
   c. Substitution

$$x + 7y = -11$$
$$3x - 8y = \;\;\; 25$$

8. An investor has $12,000 invested in two types of bonds yielding 7.5% and 9%, respectively. Her annual income from the bonds is $960. How much has she invested in each of the two types of bonds?

9. The variables x and y satisfy a linear relationship indicated in the table shown. Find and graph the equation describing this relationship.

x	2	5	8	11
y	−4	0	4	8

10. The thermometers shown indicate the freezing and boiling points of water for the three temperature scales (i) Fahrenheit, (ii) Celsius (centigrade), and (iii) Kelvin. Find linear formulas that will convert

    a. Centigrade degrees into Fahrenheit degrees
    b. Fahrenheit degrees into centigrade degrees
    c. Fahrenheit degrees into Kelvin degrees
    d. Kelvin degrees into centigrade degrees

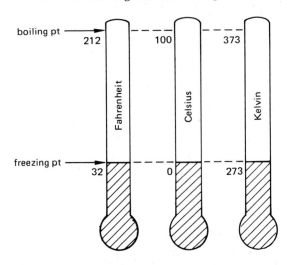

11. Find and graph the three intersection points of the lines described by

$$2x + 3y = 24$$
$$x = \quad 3 \text{ (vertical line)}$$
$$y = \quad 4 \text{ (horizontal line)}$$

12. Find and graph the three intersection points of the lines described by

$$5x - 4y + 3 = \quad 0$$
$$3x + 2y = 29$$
$$x - 3y + 5 = \quad 0$$

13. In order to provide a retail drug used to relieve emphysema and to ensure that he will have a sufficient supply of the drug on hand, a pharmacist must use 54 units of *Direne* and 86 units of *Seren*. However, the pharmacist can order commercial compound I, which contains 6 units of *Direne* and 4 units of *Seren*, and commercial compound II, which contains 1 unit of *Direne* and 9 units of *Seren*. How much of each type of commercial compound must be used to produce the correct proportion of drugs required?

14. Supply and demand data for the average number y of TV sets manufactured in the United States are shown below. Find the market price.

Supply

Average price x	$50	100	150	200	250	300
No. supplied (in millions)	1	2	3	4	5	6

Demand

Average price	$25	100	175	250	325
No. demanded (in millions)	5	4	3	2	1

Illustrate the data and the solution with a graph.

*15. Show that the equations in the system

$$Ax + By + C = 0$$
$$Dx + Ey + F = 0 \ (D, E, F \neq 0)$$

are inconsistent if and only if

$$\frac{A}{D} = \frac{B}{E} \neq \frac{C}{F}$$

(*Hint:* Write the equations in slope-intercept form.)

*16.   Prior to an exhibition game between the Yankees and the Dodgers, it is known that the Yankees are the favorite. A bookie offers the following payoff odds:

Y:D is 8:5 if you bet on the Dodgers ($5 will win you $8)
Y:D is 8:4 if you bet on the Yankees ($8 will win you $4)

Show that hedge betting cannot guarantee a positive profit for a bettor attempting to apportion $100 by splitting it into two bets, one in favor of the Yankees, and one in favor of the Dodgers. Illustrate the outcomes with two linear equations and their graphs. Find the guaranteed minimum loss for the hedge bettor.

7.3   Linear Inequalities in One Variable

Suppose we wanted to find all the real numbers x, which, when doubled, would be less than 8. If we use the symbol $<$ to represent "less than," we can write the previous statement as

$$2x < 8$$

which is a very simple example of a linear inequality in one variable. Although we may see, intuitively, that $x < 4$ satisfies the inequality and that any number greater than or equal to 4 fails to satisfy the inequality, our intuition might well fail us when we examine the problem

$$-3x + 16 < -12$$

Thus we will have to know certain properties of inequality relations that will allow us to rewrite them as simpler equivalent inequalities (inequalities having the same solution set).

There are four important inequality symbols that we will use:

$a < b$ a is less than b
$a \leq b$ a is less than or equal to b
$a > b$ a is greater than b
$a \geq b$ a is greater than or equal to b

Sometimes we may write "a is not less than b" by using a slash to negate a given inequality:

$$a \not< b$$

Since the statement "a is not less than b" is equivalent to "a is greater than or equal to b," it is so that $a \not< b$ and $a \geq b$ represent identical inequalities.

It turns out that there are many kinds of inequalities, some of which are very complicated and of not much use at this level. We will therefore restrict ourselves to a discussion of linear inequalities in one variable, which we will define as any inequality that can be written in the form

$$Ax + B < C$$

where $A \neq 0$ and where the inequality symbol may be any one of the four symbols listed above.

It is useful to recognize a pictorial representation of the real numbers, a *real number line*

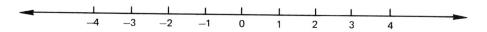

on which the negative reals are to the left of a center point 0 and on which the positive reals are to the right of 0. Thus when we say that a is a real number, exactly one of the following holds:

(i) $a < 0$ (a is negative)

(ii) $a = 0$ (a equals 0)

(iii) $a > 0$ (a is positive)

Much more can be said about the set of real numbers and its various subsets. Although it is inadequate to define real numbers in terms of a number line, it is sufficient for our purposes to think of them that way since we are mainly interested in defining and exploiting an "ordering" relationship that can be applied to inequalities. These inequalities can be represented as subsets of the real number line.

We want to define an ordering relationship that will accomplish the following goal in a straightforward way: If a "is to the left of" b on the number line, then $a < b$. We also would like this relationship to be defined in an algebraic way since in complicated inequalities it may not be easy to think exclusively in terms of various quantities being "to the left of" (or "to the right of") various other quantities. The following definition is simple and is consistent with the usual notions concerning order.

Definition 2 a is less than b, or $a < b$, if $b - a > 0$. Thus

$2 < 8$	since	$8 - 2 > 0$
$-9 < -6$	since	$(-6) - (-9) = +3 > 0$
$-17 < 0$	since	$(0) - (-17) = 17 > 0$
$5 \not< 5$	since	$5 - 5 \not> 0$

Also we agree that $b > a$ is equivalent to $a < b$ and we understand the statement $a \le b$ to mean that $b - a \ge 0$. Thus we agree that 3 $\le$ 6 and 3 $\le$ 3 are both true.

Example 1

On a real number line, illustrate all of the numbers x for which it is true that $x \ge -3$.

Solution Here we want all numbers located at or to the right of -3.

This picture is consistent with our definition since $x \ge -3$ is equivalent to $-3 \le x$, which will be satisfied if and only if $x + 3 \ge 0$. All of the real numbers x that correspond to points at or to the right of -3 satisfy this latter inequality. Moreover no points to the left of -3 satisfy the inequality.

Example 2

Illustrate graphically all of the numbers x for which it is true that $x < 2$.

Solution Since $x = 2$ does not satisfy the given "strict" inequality, we must omit the point corresponding to 2 on our graph. This will be denoted by a small open circle.

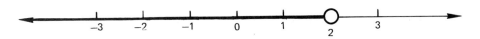

There are many properties of inequalities that can be derived from the given definition. We will list only the four of them that will be useful to us in subsequent work. In all a, b, c are real numbers.

Theorem 3	If $a < b$, then for all real c, $a + c < b + c$.
Theorem 4	If $a < b$, then for all real $c > 0$, $ac < bc$.
Theorem 5	If $a < b$, then for all real $c < 0$, $ac > bc$.
Theorem 6	If $a < b$ and $b < c$, then $a < c$.

We will prove only one of these, for illustrative purposes. The interpretation of these theorems is, however, quite important. We need to know what they mean and how they can be used.

Interpretation   **Theorem 3**   Addition (or subtraction) of the same number to (or from) each side of an inequality produces an equivalent inequality in the same sense.

Theorem 4   Multiplication (or division) by the same positive number on both sides of an inequality produces an equivalent inequality in the same sense.

Theorem 5   Multiplication (or division) by the same negative number on both sides of an inequality produces an equivalent inequality in the reverse sense.

Theorem 6   Inequalities are transitive (a relation R is transitive if $a\ R\ b$ and $b\ R\ c$ implies $a\ R\ c$).

It is important that we do not confuse Theorems 4 and 5. For example, $-3 < 8$ and $4 > 0$ imply that $(-3)\,(4) < (8)\,(4)$. However, $-3 < 8$ and $-4 < 0$ imply that $(-3)\,(-4) > (8)\,(-4)$, in which the inequality is reversed.

Equivalent inequalities can be constructed by multiplication by a negative number or a positive number provided the inequality symbol is oriented in the correct sense. Thus the following inequalities are equivalent:

$$-x \geq -2$$
$$-2x \geq -4$$
$$x \leq \ \ 2$$

Example 3

Find a simple inequality equivalent to

$$2x + 6 < -7$$

Solution

$$2x + 6 - 6 < -7 - 6$$
$$2x < -13$$

Now if we multiply both sides by $\dfrac{1}{2}$ (or divide both sides by 2), we have

$$x < -\dfrac{13}{2}$$

Example 4

Prove Theorem 5 above, that if $a < b$ and $c < 0$, then $ac > bc$.

Solution If $a < b$, then $b - a$ is positive and $a - b$ is negative; since c is also negative it follows that

$$c(a - b) = ca - cb = ac - bc$$

is positive, from which it follows that $ac > bc$.

Example 5

From inequalities $-x < -y$ and $2y < z + y$ find an inequality relation between x and z.

Solution $-x < -y$ implies $x > y$ and $2y < z + y$ implies $y < z$. By using the transitive property (Theorem 6), $x < z$.

Example 6

Find a simple inequality equivalent to

$$-6 - 4x \geq 30$$

Solution Adding $+6$ to both sides, we have $-4x \geq 36$. Dividing both sides by -4, we have $x \leq -9$.

Example 7

Where A is positive, show that every inequality of the form $Ax + B < C$ is equivalent to $x < \dfrac{C - B}{A}$

Solution
$$Ax + B < C$$

implies

$$Ax < C - B$$

and if $A > 0$, then

$$x < \frac{C - B}{A}$$

The steps are reversible; therefore the inequalities are equivalent.

Finally we observe that all of the above (definition, theorems, and examples) would be handled in the same way if strict inequality symbols $<$ are replaced with compound inequality symbols $\leq$ and vice versa.

Exercise 7.3 1. Graph each of the following sets on a separate real number line.

    a. All x such that $x < -3$ d. All x such that $x \geq 10$

    b. All x such that $x \geq -9$ e. $\{x \mid x < 5\} \cap \{x \mid x \geq -2\}$

    c. All x such that $x < 4$ f. $\{x \mid x \geq 4\} \cup \{x \mid x < -3\}$

  2. Solve each of the following linear inequalities.

    a. $2x + 1 \leq 17$

    b. $3x - 5 > 13$

    c. $-3 - 5x > 12$

    d. $\dfrac{4 - x}{-7} \leq -1$

    e. $\dfrac{2x - 3}{7} + \dfrac{x + 2}{2} < 5$

  3. The inequality $(2x + 10)/-11 > -2$ is satisfied by all $x < 4$ but is also satisfied by $x = 5$. Why?

  4. Are any of the following statements true for *all* real a, b, c, d? (Hint: try various numbers for a, b, c, d)

    a. $a < b \Rightarrow ac < bc$

    b. $a < b \Rightarrow a^2 < b^2$

    c. $a < b \Rightarrow 1/a > 1/b$

    d. $a < b$ and $c < d \Rightarrow ac < bd$

    For those of the above that are false, can you specify any conditions on a, b, c, d whereby the statememt is true?

  5. Show that the inequality $2/x < 8$ can be represented as the union of two sets defined by linear inequalities.

  6. Show that $2x^2 - x - 3 < 0$ can be represented by the nonempty intersection of two sets defined by linear inequalities.

  7. Prove Theorems 3, 4, and 5.

7.4 Graphing Linear Inequalities in Two Variables

Suppose a plant manager can manufacture no more than 70,000 cars annually. For political reasons suppose she must deliver at most four times as many cars to England as she does to France. But in order to benefit from reduced tariff rates, suppose she must deliver at least 15,000 cars to England and at least 12,000 cars to France. How can this plant manager mathematically describe all of the distribution possibilities to England and France?

In the above described situation notice the words "no more than," "at most," and "at least." It turns out that a very neat description of the above situation can be made using a certain set of linear inequalities in two variables, with one variable representing the number of cars delivered to England and the other variable representing the number of cars delivered to France. Further, a graphical representation of these inequalities will make all of the manager's options clear.

First we examine a very simple example (later we will return to the plant manager's problem).

Suppose we wanted to determine all points in the plane satisfied by the inequality

$$3x + y - 4 < 0$$

This inequality can be rewritten in an equivalent but more revealing form:

$$y < -3x + 4$$

Now all points (x, y) on lines of the form $y = -3x + b$ will satisfy the relation

$$y = -3x + b < -3x + 4$$

if and only if $b < 4$. This means that lines of the form $y = -3x + b$ having a y intercept of less than 4 must lie below the line $y = -3x + 4$.

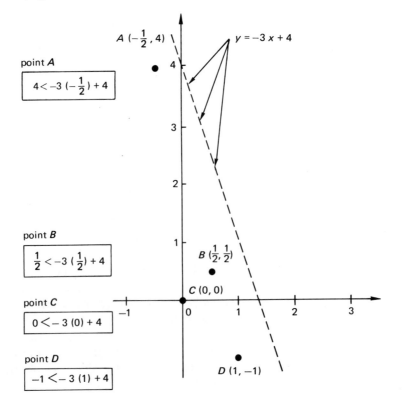

point A

$$4 < -3 \left(-\frac{1}{2}\right) + 4$$

point B

$$\frac{1}{2} < -3 \left(\frac{1}{2}\right) + 4$$

point C

$$0 < -3 \,(0) + 4$$

point D

$$-1 < -3 \,(1) + 4$$

$A \left(-\frac{1}{2}, 4\right)$

$y = -3x + 4$

$B \left(\frac{1}{2}, \frac{1}{2}\right)$

$C \,(0, 0)$

$D \,(1, -1)$

Now for *any* point (x, y) that lies below the line $y = -3x + 4$ we can always find an equation of the form $y = -3x + b$, in which b must be less than 4. It follows that all points (x, y) below the line will have coordinates that satisfy $y < -3x + 4$.

See page 252 for an illustration of the situation. In it several sample points that satisfy the inequality are indicated.

All points that lie below the line $y = -3x + 4$ must satisfy the inequality $y < -3x + 4$ or (equivalently) $3x + y - 4 < 0$. The set of points described by the given inequality is therefore a half-plane lying below the boundary line $y = -3x + 4$. This is indicated by the shaded region of the following graph.

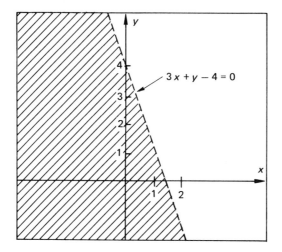

This helps to clarify our thinking concerning the following important result.

> **Theorem 7**   The points (x, y) that satisfy the inequality $Ax + By + C < 0$ lie in a half-plane on one side of the graph of $Ax + By + C = 0$.

We observe that as the theorem is stated, the boundary points of the half-plane (satisfying $Ax + By + C = 0$) are not included because the inequality sign used is $<$. If the inequality sign was $\leq$, then the boundary points would be included in the region described as a half-plane. If the theorem holds for $<$ symbols, then it must also hold for $>$ symbols; this is true because we can multiply both sides of $Ax + By + C < 0$ by -1, obtaining the form $-Ax - By - C > 0$, which is covered by the theorem. Which "side" of the boundary line is involved will of course depend on the particular combination of constants and inequality symbols involved.

Example 1

Graph the set of points satisfying the linear inequality

$$2x + 7y - 28 \leq 0$$

Solution First we graph the boundary line $2x + 7y - 28 = 0$. In this case the points on the boundary line also satisfy the inequality and should be included in our set. (If $\leq$ had been $<$, we would have excluded the boundary points.) Note that the intercepts of the line are $(0, 4)$ and $(14, 0)$.

Now we'll test a few points and see which one(s) satisfy the inequality. The points (arbitrarily selected) $(2, 2)$ and $(8, -2)$ clearly lie below the line; the points $(2, 6)$ and $(10, 4)$ lie above the line in the following figure.

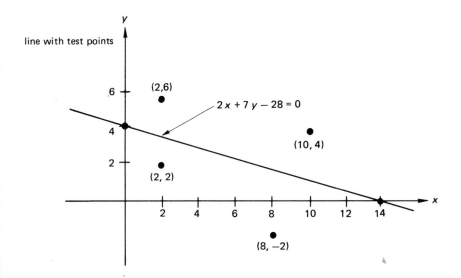

Substituting these test points into the given inequality, we obtain

$$
\begin{array}{llll}
2(2) & + 7(2) & - 28 & \leq & 0 & \text{for the point } (2, 2) \\
2(8) & + 7(-2) & - 28 & \leq & 0 & \text{for the point } (8, -2) \\
2(2) & + 7(6) & - 28 & \not\leq & 0 & \text{for the point } (2, 6) \\
2(10) & + 7(4) & - 28 & \not\leq & 0 & \text{for the point } (10, 4)
\end{array}
$$

In this case the two points below the line satisfied the inequality while the two points above the line did not. Our graph therefore consists of all points below the line as shown.

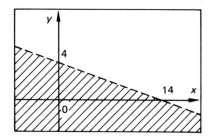

Of course we really did not have to do all this work. One point would have sufficed. This, the test-point method, is summarized below. Although this method utilizes the selection of one test point only, we nevertheless recommend that the student use at least two points to provide a partial check on the calculations. It follows from the theorem that if a test point satisfies the inequality, then *all* points on the same side of the line as the test point also satisfy the inequality. On the other hand, if a test point does not satisfy the inequality, then all points on the opposite side of the line will satisfy the inequality.

Test-point method for graphing linear inequalities

(i)   Replace the inequality sign with an equal sign and graph the resulting boundary line.

(ii)   Select a point (x_1, y_1) that is clearly on one side of the boundary line.

(iii) If (x_1, y_1) satisfied the inequality, then all points on the same side of the boundary satisfy the inequality; if (x_1, y_1) fails to satisfy the inequality, then all points on the opposite side of the boundary line satisfy the inequality.

Example 2

Using the test-point method, graph the region defined by the inequality $x - 3y + 12 < 0$.

Solution First sketch a graph of the boundary shown as a dotted line on our graph. If we are able to select $(0, 0)$ as a test point, it is very easy to make the substitution. Clearly $(0, 0)$ lies below the line and

$$0 - 3(0) + 12 \nless 0$$

Hence the region is all points above the line as shown.

It is a common error for students to think that if an inequality has a $<$ sign in it, then the region will automatically lie below the line.

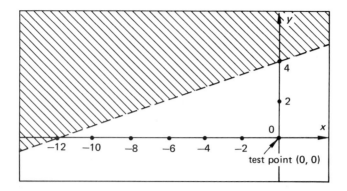

This is not the case! The previous example disproves this belief. If you carefully check with a test point, you can be sure your results are correct.

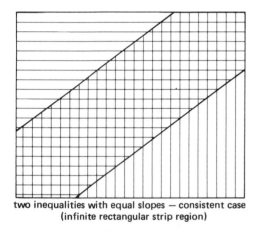

two inequalities with equal slopes — consistent case
(infinite rectangular strip region)

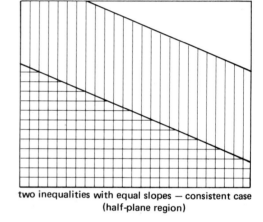

two inequalities with equal slopes — consistent case
(half-plane region)

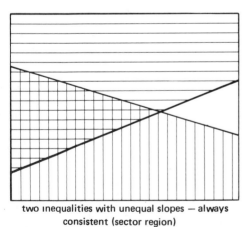

two inequalities with unequal slopes — always
consistent (sector region)

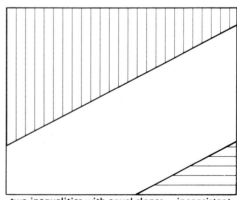

two inequalities with equal slopes — inconsistent
case (empty region)

In many practical problems we will have systems of linear inequalities, where we will want to identify the set of points that simultaneously satisfy two or more linear inequalities. Various regions of the plane will be described by two overlapping sets of points.

Two linear inequalities having boundaries with unequal slopes will always yield a sector of the plane as a solution. For two boundaries having equal slopes, several configurations are possible; in one of these situations, the overlapping set is empty.

Example 3

Show that the following system of linear inequalities is not satisfied by any point in the plane: $x + 3y > 6$ and $2x + 6y < 5$.

Solution First we observe that the boundary equations

$$x + 3y = 6 \quad \text{and} \quad 2x + 6y = 5$$

both have the same slope, namely, $-1/3$. Thus it is possible for the system to be inconsistent. The graph reveals that the two inequalities are indeed inconsistent. (See diagram below.)

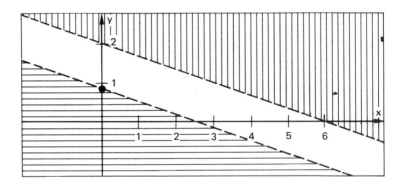

Example 4

Find the region defined by the linear system of inequalities: $x - 2y + 2 \leq 0$ and $2x + 5y - 50 \geq 0$.

Solution First we note the equations of the boundaries and their respective intercepts:

$$x - 2y + 2 = 0 \qquad \text{has intercepts } (0, 1) \text{ and } (-2, 0)$$
$$2x + 5y - 50 = 0 \qquad \text{has intercepts } (0, 10) \text{ and } (25, 0)$$

For convenience we choose a different scale for each axis. The intersection point for both boundaries is found to be (10,6). A test point needs to be selected: clearly (0, 0) is below both boundaries. The results of the test point (0, 0) are

$$0 - 2(0) + 2 \not\leq 0 \qquad \text{test fails}$$
$$2(0) + 5(0) - 50 \not\geq 0 \qquad \text{test fails}$$

Thus we have the region indicated by the doubly cross-hatched portion of the diagram.

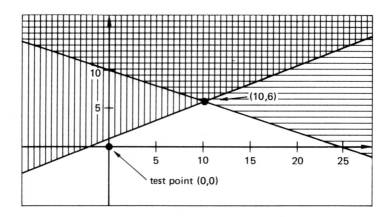

In the above example we had two linear inequalities with boundaries having unequal slopes. In such cases it is possible to show the system is always consistent and must yield an infinite sector of the plane.

With three linear inequalities having boundaries with unequal slopes the situation is not as simple. In fact, sometimes such systems are not consistent. When they are consistent, however, there are four different types of geometric configurations that are possible. We will give a typical example of one of these configurations.

Example 5

Graph the region defined by the three linear inequalities:

$$A: \quad y < x$$
$$B: \quad 2x + 3y < 20$$
$$C: \quad x - 6y + 5 < 0$$

Solution The intersection of boundaries A and B is found by solving the system $y = x$ and $2x + 3y = 20$. By substitution we see that $2x + 3x = 20$ or $x = 4$. Thus $(4, 4)$ is the intersection of boundaries A and B.

Similarly we find that boundaries A and C also intersect. Solving y

$= x$ and $x - 6y + 5 = 0$, we find that $(1, 1)$ is the intersection point.

Also, for B and C we find that $(7, 2)$ simultaneously satisfies both $2x + 3y = 20$ and $x - 6y + 5 = 0$.

The graph of the boundaries is shown below.

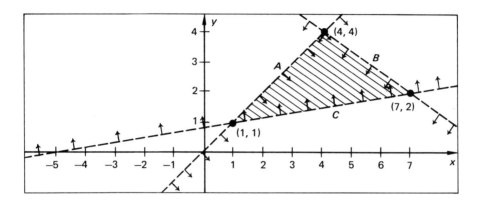

Note that we cannot use the test point $(0, 0)$ for the inequality $y < x$ since the origin lies *on* its boundary. Testing, we find that test point $(1, 0)$ works for A, test point $(0, 0)$ works for B, and test point $(0, 0)$ fails for C. Hence we have the sides of the boundaries indicated by the small arrows. The intersection of the three half-planes is the shaded triangular region, which satisfies all of the inequalities.

Of course we can have any finite number of inequalities; the regions defined by them do not have to be bounded regions. Consider the following example.

Example 6

Find the region defined by the linear system of inequalities:

$$2x - y + 10 \leq 0$$
$$x + 3y - 9 \geq 0$$
$$x + y \geq 7$$
$$x \geq 0$$
$$y \geq 0$$

Solution The boundaries and their intersection points are shown on the graph below. Also note that the test point $(0, 0)$ fails for the first three inequalities. The last two inequalities $x \geq 0$ and $y \geq 0$ indicate that we are restricted to the first quadrant only. The region is not bounded.

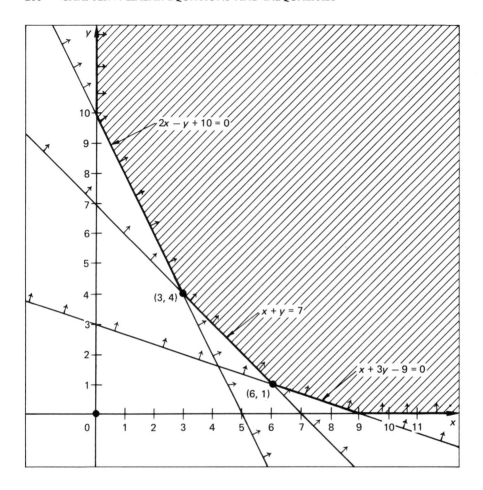

Now we are ready to tackle the problem first presented in this section, the plant manager.

Example 7

A plant manager can manufacture no more than 70,000 cars annually. For political reasons she must deliver at most four times as many cars to England as she does to France. To receive tariff discount rates, she must deliver at least 15,000 cars to England and at least 12,000 cars to France. Mathematically describe all of the plant manager's distribution options given the constraints stated.

Solution Let E = number of cars delivered to England, and F = number of cars delivered to France. The information we have can be stated mathematically as follows:

"at most four times as many cars to E as to F" translates as $E \leq 4F$
the manufacturing limitation translates as $E + F \leq 70,000$
"at least 15,000 cars to E" translates as $E \geq 15,000$
"at least 12,000 cars to F" translates as $F \geq 12,000$

Graphs of the four half-planes are indicated by small arrows on the respective boundaries:

$$E = 4F$$
$$E + F = 70,000$$
$$E = 15,000$$
$$F = 12,000$$

The shaded quadrilateral indicates the plant manager's options for distribution.

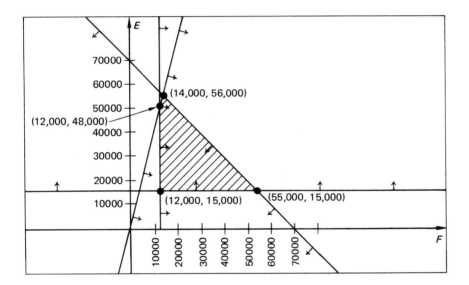

Exercise 7.4 1. Find and graph the regions defined by each of the following linear systems of inequalities:

a. $x + y \leq 5$
    $x \geq 0$
    $y \geq 0$

b. $x + y \leq 7$
    $x \geq 2$
    $y \geq 1$

c. $y < x$
    $x < 4$
    $y > 0$

d. $2x + 3y < 1$
    $x - y > 3$

e. $x \geq 2$
    $x \leq 8$
    $y \geq 3$
    $y \leq 7$

f. $2x + y \geq 5$
    $x \geq 1$
    $y \geq 1$

g. $6x + y \geq 11$ i. $y \leq (1/2)x$
    $2x + y \geq 9$ $y \leq 2x - 3$
    $3x + 5y \geq 24$ $y \geq 0$
    $y \geq 0$ j. $3y \leq x + 21$
    $x \geq 0$ $3y - 2x \leq 6$
h. $y \leq 2x + 1$ $x + 2y \leq -6$
    $y \leq 9$ $y \geq 2x - 5$
    $y \geq 5$

2. Explain why the following systems are inconsistent:

a. $x - y \geq 6$
    $x - 5 < y$
b. $6x + y < 11$
    $2x + y > 9$
    $3x + 5y < 24$

3. Translate the following statements into inequalities.
    a. On a used car lot there is at least one station wagon.
    b. There are at most 15 sedans.
    c. There is a total of less than 18 station wagons and sedans.
    d. There are at least many sedans as station wagons.

4. Graph each of the above inequalities in Problem 3 above. Explain why the solution set consists of a set of discrete points. Find all of the points satisfying all four conditions.

5. For each of the figures shown, find a set of inequalities that defines the shaded region.

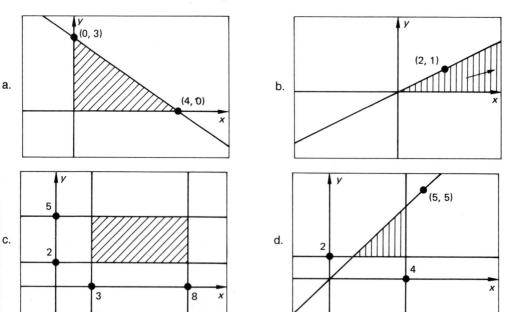

e.
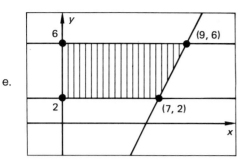

f.
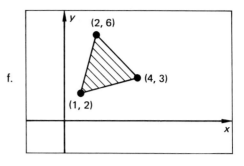

*6. Demonstrate that for three linear inequalities, no two of which have boundaries with equal slopes, that the resulting solution set consists of exactly one of the following:

i.   A closed triangular region
ii. An infinite sector
iii. A truncated infinite sector
iv. A single point
v.   The empty set

*7. A corporation will manufacture x units of product A and y units of product B. Each A unit requires 6 units of material, 4 units of labor, and 2 units of machinery. Each B unit requires 6 units of material, 2 units of labor, and 6 units of machinery. The total units available are 600 for materials, 360 for labor, and 420 for machinery. Describe the manufacturer's options using inequalities and their graphs.

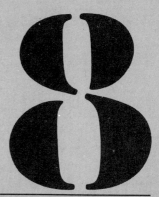

A First Look at Linear Programming

> It took over two thousand years for great mathematicians to hit upon the simple but sophisticated idea underlying the graphical representation of numerical data.
>
> Eric Temple Bell

8.1   Optimizing Linear Functions on Polygonal Convex Sets

Linear programming is essentially a method for dealing with a number of variables simultaneously and determining the best possible solution of a given linear problem within certain required linear limitations (or constraints). It can be applied to a wide range of problems involving management decisions, industrial transportation and distribution, manufacturing processes, product design, and many other business applications. Actually linear programming is a recently developed mathematical technique. Developed by John von Neumann, George Dantzig and a few other mathematicians, one of its first dramatic applications was the Berlin air lift by the United States Air Force.

Before we introduce any new terminology or state the general problem to which linear programming is addressed, let us examine a simple algebraic example that can be solved using careful reasoning together with the results of the previous chapter.

Example 1

Given the system of linear inequalities

$$-x + 5y - 18 \leq 0$$
$$5x - 2y - 25 \leq 0$$
$$-x - 2y + 5 \leq 0$$
$$-2x + y \leq 0$$

find the point (x, y) in the plane that maximizes the value of z in the expression $z = 3x + 4y + 2$ and that simultaneously satisfies the given system of inequalities.

Solution First observe that each of the four inequalities is a half-plane. Taken together, the intersection of the four half-planes consists of a region called a convex polygon. (This term will be explained later.) This figure is shown below.

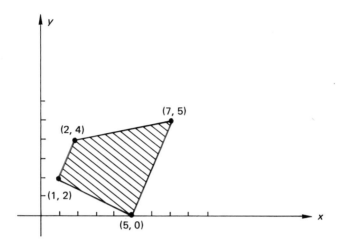

What we want to find is the point (or points) within or on the boundary of the region shown that will produce the maximum value of z in the formula

$$z = 3x + 4y + 2$$

We can find the optimal point in the region using geometric considerations.

Since the function $z = 3x + 4y + 2$ has three variables, the graph of such a function cannot lie wholly within the x–y plane. However, suppose we assign various arbitrary values to z and graph the resulting straight lines on the same graph as the region defined by the inequalities. This will give us a better idea of which point(s) in the polygon will maximize z. We choose $z = 2, 10, 18, 26, 34, 42$, and 50. These values give rise to straight lines, which we will designate A, B, C, D, E, F, G. They are listed below.

$z = 2$	line A:	$3x + 4y + 2 = 2$
$z = 10$	line B:	$3x + 4y + 2 = 10$
$z = 18$	line C:	$3x + 4y + 2 = 18$
$z = 26$	line D:	$3x + 4y + 2 = 26$
$z = 34$	line E:	$3x + 4y + 2 = 34$
$z = 42$	line F:	$3x + 4y + 2 = 42$
$z = 50$	line G:	$3x + 4y + 2 = 50$

Each of these lines has a slope of $-3/4$ and is graphed on the coordinate system shown.

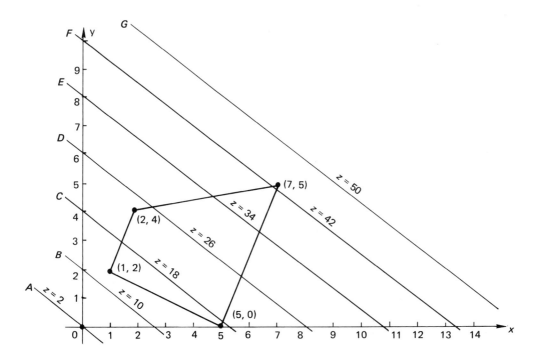

Note that in order to maximize z, we need to find the line with slope $-3/4$ that is the greatest distance from the origin but that passes through a point satisfying the inequalities. In this case, the z values increase for lines farther away from the origin. Thus the maximum value for z will occur at the vertex $(7, 5)$ of the polygon. This *maximum* value of z is seen to be

$$z = 3(7) + 4(5) + 2 = 43$$

We observe that the minimum value for z will also occur at one of the vertices of the polygon, namely, at the point $(1, 2)$, which is the point on the region closest to the origin.

$$z = 3(1) + 4(2) + 2 = 13$$

Two-dimensional interpretation

Note that different z values give rise to parallel lines in the plane. Sliding these lines in one direction normal (perpendicular) to the lines corresponds to increasing z, and in the other direction corresponds to decreasing z. To maximize the z value over the polygonal region, clearly you should simply slide the line in the increasing z direction until the final point where the line still touches the region. It is clear that it must be touching at least one vertex at that moment.

Three-dimensional interpretation

We observe that each of the lettered lines have equally spaced z values, equally spaced y intercepts, and equally spaced x intercepts. In the function

$$z = 3x + 4y + 2$$

if y is held constant and x is permitted to vary by equally spaced values, then the resulting z values will be equally spaced. Likewise if x is held constant and y is permitted to vary by equally spaced values, then the resulting z values will be equally spaced. It is not surprising, therefore, that if we add a z axis to our coordinate system, the graph of $z = 3x + 4y + 2$ will be a plane. In this case the plane lies entirely above the polygon defined by the given inequalities.

We do not expect the student to be able to draw such planes on a three-dimensional coordinate system. For illustrative purposes, however, we will draw the graph for Example 1. We must visualize three mutually perpendicular axes x, y, and z. It is necessary to draw such a graph in perspective. See the Figure on Page 270. Note the z values at each of the vertices of the polygon:

vertex	z value
(1, 2)	13
(2, 4)	24
(7, 5)	43
(5, 0)	17

From the diagram it is clear that extreme values of z must occur at vertices since the z function is a plane.

In any linear programming problem we restrict our discussions to z functions (or, as they are called, *objective* functions) of the linear type:

$$z = Ax + By + C$$

in which A, B, and C are constants and x and y are variables. In an x–y–z coordinate system of the type shown, such objective functions are graphed as planes.

We also restrict our discussions to certain types of systems of constraints (the conditions given by inequalities).

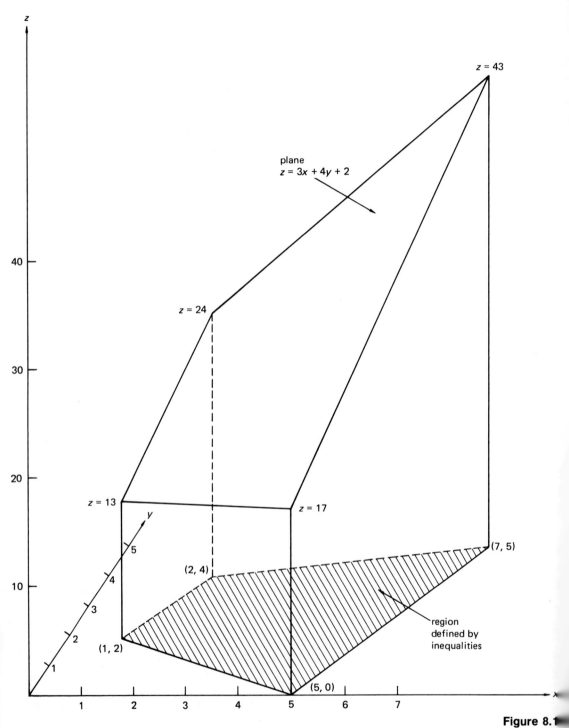

Figure 8.1

> **Definition 1**   A set of points S in the x–y plane is called a *convex set* if for any two points P and Q in S, the set of all points on the line segment $\overline{PQ}$ is in S.

A few examples are shown.

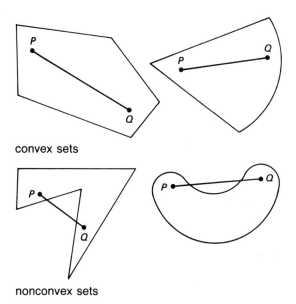

convex sets

nonconvex sets

We also observe that half-planes defined by inequalities of the form

$$ax + by \leq c \qquad (\text{or } ax + by \geq c)$$

are convex sets. We shall accept the following theorem without proof.

> **Theorem 1**   The intersection of any number of convex sets is convex.

It follows that a system of linear inequalities of the form

$$a_1x + b_1y \leq c_1$$
$$a_2x + b_2y \leq c_2$$
$$\cdots\cdots\cdots\cdots$$
$$a_nx + b_ny \leq c_n$$

is a convex set. Such systems are called *polygonal convex sets* and are the type to which our linear programming problems will be restricted.

In the many cases that such sets are bounded we will refer to them as *convex polygons*. Although we have not formally proved that objective functions of the form $z = Ax + By + C$ are planes when graphed on an x–y–z coordinate system, Example 1 certainly makes this claim reasonable. Thus the basic problem of linear programming may be formulated as follows: Given a set of feasible points in the x–y plane defined by a system of inequalities (a polygonal convex set), find the point(s) that maximize the value of the objective function and find the point(s) that minimize the objective function. In the discussion that follows it will be helpful to refer to the following four diagrams.

First we examine Figure (a). Notice that the base region of feasible points (shaded) is a bounded polyhedral convex set (convex polygon). Note that the maximum value of a linear objective function occurs at one of the vertices of the polygon. The minimum value also occurs at a vertex. This is a very common type of situation.

Now we look at Figure (b). Note that it can happen that the minimum value of a linear objective function could occur at two adjacent vertices. In this case the solution to the minimization of $z = Ax + By + C$ would consist of all the points on the line segment joining the two vertices. In the figure shown, the maximum occurs at one of the other vertices.

Figure (c) illustrates what would happen if the objective function was nonlinear, that is, not of the form $z = Ax + By + C$. Then the graph of the objective function might not be a plane but could be curved as shown. In cases such as this, the maximum or the minimum

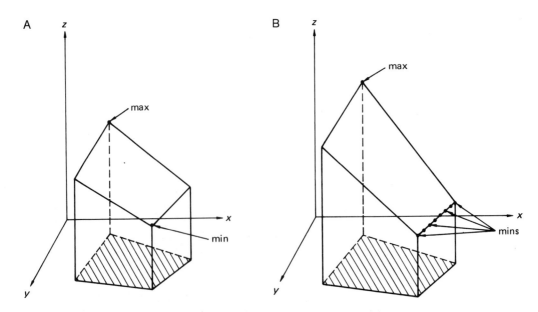

C

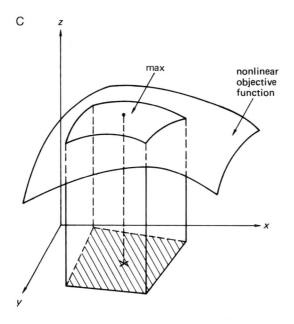

D

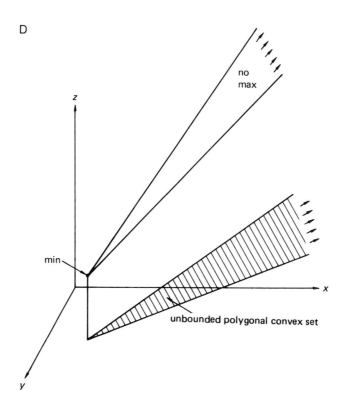

may occur at an interior point of the convex polygon and not at a vertex. For this reason we will not consider such cases. We will only consider problems in which the objective function is linear of the form $z = Ax + By + C$.

Figure (d) illustrates a situation in which the set of feasible points is an unbounded polygonal convex set. Such cases actually do occur, and we fully intend to deal with them. When the polygonal set is unbounded, the function may not attain either a maximum or a minimum value. However, if it does attain an extreme value, then it must occur at a vertex of the polygonal set.

It is now possible to state the main theorem regarding the kinds of linear programming problems we are considering.

> **Theorem 2** A linear objective function $z = Ax + By + C$ defined over a bounded polygonal convex set S takes on its maximum value at a vertex of S and its minimum value at a vertex of S.

If a linear objective function is defined on an *unbounded* polygonal convex set, then z may or may not actually take on a maximum or a minimum value.

The three-dimensional graphs were used to illustrate various possibilities and to help strengthen our belief in the theorem by means of a geometric discussion. It is not necessary to draw such graphs. We need only draw the feasible region defined by the inequalities in the x–y plane. Then we compute the z values of the objective function at the vertices. If the region is a convex polygon, then the vertex yielding the largest z value maximizes the objective function over the entire region, and the smallest z value minimizes the objective function over the entire region.

Example 2

Find the maximum and minimum of the objective function $z = x - 3y + 5$ over the convex polygon defined by the constraints

$$x + y \leq 4$$
$$-2x - y \leq 2$$
$$x - y \leq 2$$
$$y \leq 3$$

Solution To obtain the vertices of the convex polygon S, graph S as shown in the diagram. The points A, B, C, and D are the vertices of S. The coordinates of each point should be obtained by finding the intersection of the appropriate pair of boundary lines.

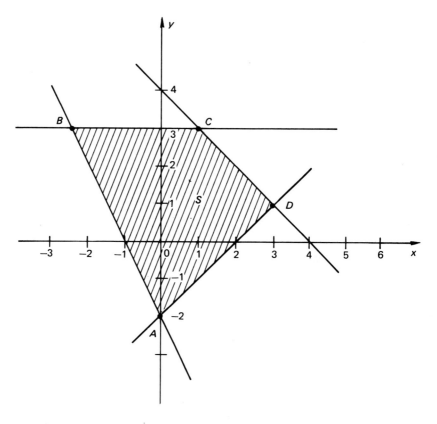

$A = (0, -2)$ is the solution of
$$-2x - y = 2$$
$$x - y = 2$$
$B = (-5/2, 3)$ is the solution of
$$-2x - y = 2$$
$$y = 3$$
$C = (1, 3)$ is the solution of
$$x + y = 4$$
$$y = 3$$
$D = (3, 1)$ is the solution of
$$x + y = 4$$
$$x - y = 2$$

Now we compute the value of z at each vertex.

At A, $z = 0 - 3(-2) + 5 = 11$
At B, $z = -5/2 - 3(3) + 5 = -6.5$
At C, $z = 1 - 3(3) + 5 = -3$
At D, $z = 3 - 3(1) + 5 = 5$

Thus the maximum value of z over the set S is 11 and occurs at A, and the minimum is -6.5 and occurs at B.

Theorem 2, together with Example 2, gives us a clear-cut procedure for finding the maximum and the minimum value of a linear function defined over a bounded polygonal convex set.

(i)	Find all the vertices of the polygon.
(ii)	Compute the value of z at each of these points.
(iii)	The smallest of these z values is the minimum, and the largest of these z values is the maximum, of z over the entire convex polygon.

Sometimes we will have to be careful about making hasty conclusions if the polygonal convex set is unbounded. As we have said before, in some cases we may not have a maximum or minimum value of z. Such a case will be illustrated in the following example.

Example 3

Show that the function $z = -x + 2y$ takes on a maximum value ·t no minimum value over the polygonal set defined by the constraints

$$2x + 3y \leq 6$$
$$y - x \leq 4$$
$$y \leq 2$$

Solution First we draw the polygonal convex set and compute the vertices. These turn out to be $A(0, 2)$ and $B(-2, 2)$. We observe that the family of parallel lines determined by the objective function $z = -x + 2y$ will intersect the polygonal set for every negative value of z. Consequently, z will not take on a minimum value. This is occurring because this particular convex set is *unbounded*.

But z will take on a maximum value since z cannot assume all positive values on the polygonal set. At the vertex $A(0, 2)$, $z = 4$; and at the vertex $B(-2, 2)$, $z = 6$. Thus the maximum value of the objective function $z = -x + 2y$ is 6, which occurs at vertex B.

Exercise 8.1 1. Given the convex polygon S shown in the diagram and the objective function $z = -x + y + 5$. Draw the set S on your own graph paper. Using z values of -6, -4, -2, 0, 2, 4, 6, 8, graph the respective lines that arise using $z = -x + y + 5$ for each z value

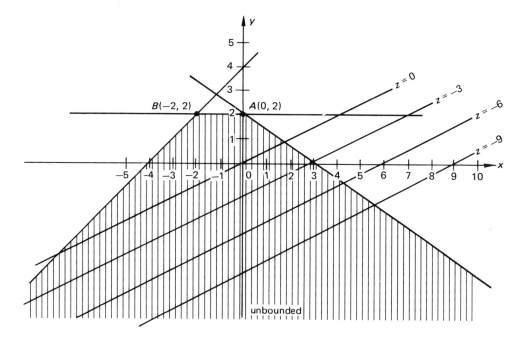

given. Which z value is a maximum on the set S? Where does it occur? Which z value is a minimum? Where does it occur?

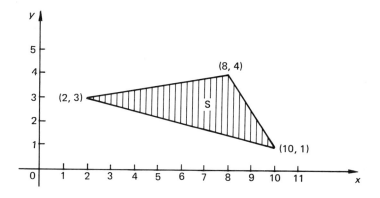

2. Using the objective function $z = x + y$, show that a different vertex maximizes z on the convex polygon given in Problem 1.

3. Find the maximum and minimum values of z, where $z = 2x - 3y + 8$ over the convex polygon defined by the constraints

$$x + 2y \le 4$$
$$x - y \ge 0$$
$$y \ge -1$$
$$x \le 4$$

4. Find the maximum and minimum values of z, where $z = x + 2y + 7$ over the convex polygon defined by the constraints

$$\begin{aligned} x + \ y &\le 9 \\ 3x - 2y &\le 6 \\ y - \ x &\le 3 \\ x &\ge 0 \\ y &\ge 0 \end{aligned}$$

5. Graph the unbounded polygonal set defined by the inequalities, given

$$\begin{aligned} y + 2x &\ge \ 4 \\ y - \ x &\ge \ 0 \\ x &\ge -1 \end{aligned}$$

6. Using the polygonal set given in Problem 5, show that the objective function $z = 3x - 6y + 4$ attains a minimum value but does not attain a maximum value.

7. Show that the objective function $z = -x + 2y$ takes on neither a maximum value nor a minimum value over the polygonal set defined by the constraints

$$\begin{aligned} 3y + 2x &\le 6 \\ y - \ x &\ge 0 \\ y &\le 3 \end{aligned}$$

8. Given the objective function $z = 3x + 2y + 5$ and the convex polygon defined by the constraints

$$\begin{aligned} y - \ x &\le \ 2 \\ 5y + 2x &\le 31 \\ 2y + 3x &\le 30 \\ 5y + \ x &\ge 10 \end{aligned}$$

a. Graph the convex polygon S.
b. Show that the minimum value of z occurs at one vertex.
c. Show that the maximum value of z occurs at two vertices and hence on the line segment joining these two vertices.

9. Using a suitable scale on the x and y axes, graph the unbounded polygonal convex set defined by

$$\begin{aligned} y + 3x &\ge 50 \\ y + \ x &\ge 30 \\ 4y + \ x &\ge 60 \\ x &\ge \ 0 \\ y &\ge \ 0 \end{aligned}$$

Find the minimum value of the objective function $z = 2x + 3y + 10$ defined over this set. Explain why it does not attain a maximum value.

*10.   Using an x-y-z coordinate system, draw a three-dimensional graph that illustrates Problem 8.

*11.   Given any convex polygon and an objective function $z = Ax + By + C$ in which the constants A and B are not both 0, explain geometrically why it is not possible for z to attain an extreme value at two nonadjacent vertices of the polygon.

8.2 Applications of Linear Programming in Two Variables

Of the many applications of linear programming that can be considered, we shall examine a number in various areas. Although some of these may seem a little artificial, they are really warmups for more significant problems. The author hopes that the student will examine each of these examples carefully. A thorough analysis of each example will be of help in solving the exercises at the end of this section.

Example 1

A metal parts manufacturer makes sprockets and gizmos. His manufacturing machines are in operation 75 hr per week. In order to produce a sprocket it is required that 3 hr of work be done on machine A and 1 hr of work on machine B. To produce a gizmo requires 6 hr of work on machine A and 7 hr on machine B. The manufacturer can earn \$5 profit on each sprocket and \$11 profit on each gizmo. How many of each type of part should be produced each week in order to maximize the manufacturer's profit?

Solution First we let

$x =$ number of sprockets produced per week
$y =$ number of gizmos produced per week

The manufacturing time on each machine can then be summarized on the following table:

	machine A	machine B
Sprockets	$3x$	x
Gizmos	$6y$	$7y$

Since no more than 75 h per week can be spent using either machine A or machine B, we have the two constraints

$$3x + 6y \leq 75$$
$$x + 7y \leq 75$$

Since the number of sprockets and gizmos produced must be non-negative, we have the additional constraints

$$x \geq 0$$
$$y \geq 0$$

Profit $\doteq P = 5x + 11y$ is the objective function to be maximized. The constraints thus consist of four inequalities that form a convex polygon. The optimal solution must therefore be at a vertex.

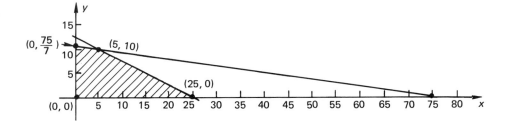

At each vertex, we now compute the profit.

vertex	profit $= P = 5x + 11y$	
(0, 0)	0	
(0, 75/7)	$117.86	
(5, 10)	$135.00	maximum
(25, 0)	$125.00	

Example 2

Using the same convex polygon as in Example 1, show that the optimal solution would have been radically different if the profit function had been $P = 5x + 9y$.

Solution In this case the profit computations would be as follows.

vertex	profit $= P = 5x + 9y$	
(0, 0)	0	
(0, 75/7)	$ 96.43	
(5, 10)	$115.00	
(25, 0)	$125.00	maximum

In this situation the profit margin on gizmos is just small enough to warrant that they not be manufactured at all. Producing 25 sprockets would therefore yield maximum profit.

Example 3

(A shipping problem) A kitchen appliance manufacturer has an inventory of 600 automatic dishwashers at warehouse I and 600 at warehouse II. The department stores Moxy's, Sarai's and Gimma's order 400, 300, and 500 of these dishwashers, respectively. The costs of shipping one dishwasher to each of these department store outlets from warehouses I and II are as follows:

	To Moxy's (400)	To Sarai's (300)	To Gimma's (500)
from I per unit	$40	$10	$80
from II per unit	$60	$10	$10

How can the orders be filled if it is important to minimize shipping costs?

Solution Let

$x = $ number of dishwashers sent from I to Moxy's
$y = $ number of dishwashers sent from I to Sarai's

Note that there are 600 dishwashers located at I and 600 dishwashers located at II. The following table summarizes all the constraints, where each quantity must be non-negative.

	To Moxy's (400)	To Sarai's (300)	To Gimma's (500)
from I	x	y	$600 - (x + y)$
from II	$400 - x$	$300 - y$	$500 - (600 - x - y)$

Thus we have six inequalities simplified as follows:

$$600 - x - y \geq 0$$
$$400 - x \geq 0$$
$$300 - y \geq 0$$
$$x + y - 100 \geq 0$$
$$x \geq 0$$
$$y \geq 0$$

The shipping costs $= C = 40x + 10y + 80(600 - x - y)$
$$+ 60(400 - x) + 10(300 - y) + 10(x + y - 100)$$
$$= -90x - 70y + 74{,}000$$

which will be used as our objective function. In order to complete the solution, we draw the polygonal region defined by the constraints. Note that the scale chosen must be suitable to the numbers involved. (In some problems it may be necessary to use a scale on the y axis different from the scale chosen for the x axis. This is perfectly acceptable.)

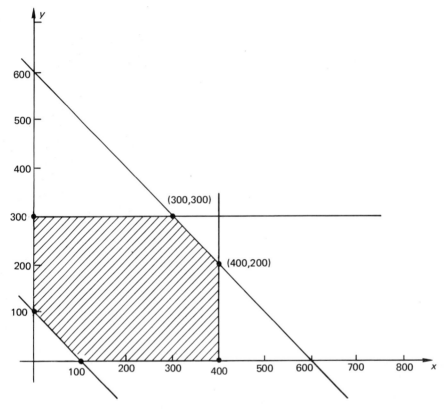

At each vertex of the convex polygon, the total shipping cost C is computed.

Vertex	Shipping cost $= C = -90x - 70y + 74,000$	
(0, 100)	$67,000	
(0, 300)	$53,000	
(300, 300)	$26,000	
(400, 200)	$24,000	minimum
(400, 0)	$38,000	
(100, 0)	$65,000	

The solution to the problem is that the dishwashers should be distributed according to the following format.

	To Moxy's	To Sarai's	To Gimma's
from I	400	200	0
from II	0	100	500

Example 4

A drug manufacturer must decide on the percentages, by weights, of three vitamins (vitamin B-1, vitamin B-6, and vitamin C) to be included in a special multivitamin tablet. There must be at least 15% of vitamin B-1. For proper vitamin regulation there must be at least 30% but not more than 50% of vitamin B-6. To provide sufficient variety, the percentage of vitamin C should not exceed the sum of the percentages of vitamins B-1 and B-6. The costs of vitamins B-1, B-6, and C in cents per milligram are .0017, .0021, and .0015, respectively.

a. Find the percentages of vitamins, by weight, that there should be of types B-1, B-6, and C in a 100-mg multivitamin tablet.
b. Find the precise percentages that would minimize the cost per 100-mg tablet.

Solution a. Let

$$x = \text{number of mg of B-1}$$
$$y = \text{number of mg of B-6}$$
$$100 - (x + y) = \text{number of mg of C}$$

Reading the problem as it is given, we have the inequalities

$$x \geq 15$$
$$y \geq 30$$
$$y \leq 50$$
$$100 - (x + y) \leq x + y$$

When we graph the polygonal region, it appears as if there is something wrong with our solution.

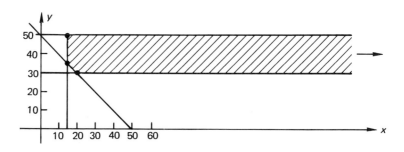

Note that the region is unbounded. This cannot be since it is clear that x cannot be excessively large (certainly it cannot exceed 100 mg). First observe that there is no minimum value of vitamin C. There is, however, a maximum value of vitamin B-6 given by $y \leq 50$. The sum of x and y cannot exceed 100 mg. This yields a maximum value for x given by $x \leq 50$. This latter inequality should therefore be added to our list of constraints, and a complete diagram (bounded) is given below.

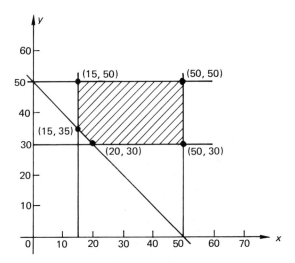

Any point in the above region is a feasible solution to the constraints.

b.   In order to minimize the costs, we evaluate the total cost at each vertex:

x, B-1	y, B-6	C	Total cost 100 mg	
15	35	50	.174¢	
15	50	35	.183¢	
50	50	0	.190¢	
50	30	20	.178¢	
20	30	50	.172¢	minimum

vertices

Example 5

(A problem yielding management options) A company owns two mines: Mine A produces 1 ton of high-grade ore, 3 tons of medium-grade ore, and 2 tons of low-grade ore each day; mine B produces 3 tons of high-grade ore, 2 tons of medium-grade ore, and 1 ton of low-grade ore each day. The company needs 90 tons of high-grade ore, 130 tons of medium-grade ore, and 70 tons of low-grade ore. How many days should each mine be operated if it costs $300 per day to operate mine A, and $200 per day to operate mine B?

Solution The following table summarizes all of the given information:

	mine A	mine B	production requirements
high grade	1	3	90
medium grade	3	2	130
low grade	2	1	70

Now let

$x =$ the number of days mine A is open
$y =$ the number of days mine B is open

Then we have the following system of constraints:

$$\begin{aligned}
x + 3y &\geq 90 \\
3x + 2y &\geq 130 \\
2x + y &\geq 70 \\
x &\geq 0 \\
y &\geq 0
\end{aligned}$$

In this case the set of feasible solutions is an unbounded polygonal convex set. The vertices are indicated on the following diagram.

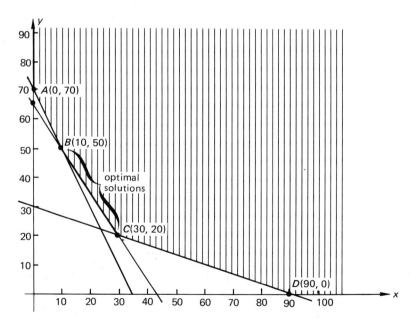

In this case we have an unusual outcome when we compute the total costs. The objective function for total costs is $C = 300x + 200y$.

Vertex	Total cost C	
A(0, 70)	$14,000	
B(10, 50)	$13,000	minimum
C(30, 20)	$13,000	minimum
D(90, 0)	$27,000	

This has occurred because the objective function $C = \$300x + \$200y$ gives rise to lines that are parallel to the constraint $3x + 2y = 130$. This means that any point on the line segment $\overline{BC}$ would yield the same minimal cost of $13,000. To see this, notice that the point (20, 35) is on the line $3x + 2y = 130$; at this point the cost $C = \$300(20) + \$200(35) = \$13,000$. This will also occur for an arbitrarily chosen point on line segment $\overline{BC}$. Thus the company management has many options. It can thus permit other considerations to dictate which point to choose and still maintain a minimum operational cost of $13,000 and satisfy all of the production requirements.

Exercise 8.2   1.   A dog breeder decides to raise a total of 100 shepherds, poodles, and Irish setters, with not more than 20 poodles included. Her breeding facilities require her to raise at least as many setters as shepherds and at most 60 setters. She anticipates profits of $40 per shepherd, $50 per poodle, and $30 per setter. How many of each type of dog should she breed in order to obtain the largest possible profit, and what is this profit?

2.   A nutritionist in an elementary school wishes to serve hot food lunches that provide the necessary protein and carbohydrates for the children. Foods A and B contain the following amounts of proteins and carbohydrates per pound of food:

	A	B
protein	3 units	5 units
carbohydrates	4 units	6 units

At least 180 units of protein and at least 220 units of carbohydrates must be provided. If the costs of A and B are $1.50 and $.70 per pound, respectively, how many pounds of each food should be ordered to meet minimum diet requirements while also reducing the total cost of the foods purchased to a minimum?

3. A local radio station is faced with a situation requiring linear programming. It is found that during the day, two types of programs draw different numbers of listeners:

    Program I: 20 min of rock music and 8 min of advertising draws
                 7000 listeners
    Program II: 50 min of pop music and 3 min of advertising draws
                 20,000 listeners

    The advertising agency insists that each day there must be at least 40 min devoted to advertising, but the radio station cannot have more than 440 min of air time devoted to music. How many times each day should each program be aired in order to maximize the number of listeners?

4. In Problem 3 how would the results be changed if program I drew 9000 listeners instead of 7000?

5. An appliance distributor must supply 1000 appliances to a large department store. If he must ship at least 200 television sets for a profit of $20 per set, at least 100 washing machines for a profit of $10 per machine, and *at most* 400 clothes dryers for a profit of $30 per dryer, how should he arrange his order for maximum profit?

6. An airline company can fly DC-9's and 747's on trips to San Francisco each day. The fuel, labor, and maintenance costs per trip, the crew needed for each trip, and the average profit per trip are indicated in the table.

	DC-9's	747's	Total available
fuel, labor, and maintenance costs per trip	$40,000	$100,000	$500,000
crew needed per trip	7	20	90
profit per trip	$3,700	$10,000	

The last column indicates that the number of trips per day is constrained by the daily cash available and the number of crew members who are available each day. Find the daily numbers of trips on the two types of aircraft to maximize profit.

7. A garment manufacturer has an inventory of 100 racks of dresses at warehouse I and 160 racks of the same dress at warehouse II. Retailers *A, B,* and *C* order 60, 80, and 120 racks of these dresses. The costs, in dollars, of transporting one rack to each of the retailers from I and from II are as follows:

	To *A*	To *B*	To *C*
from I	$3	$2	$4
from II	$4	$2	$2

How should the orders be filled if the garment manufacturer wishes to minimize the transportation costs?

8. A manufacturer has on hand 36, 60, and 21 units of raw materials *A, B,* and *C,* respectively. The manufacturer produces two products that require the following number of units of each ingredient:

	Raw materials		
	A	*B*	*C*
Product I	1	3	1
Product II	2	2	1

Product I sells for $40 and product II for $30. How many of each product should be made if the manufacturer wishes to maximize his gross income?

9. Answer Problem 8, but assume product I sells for $30 and product II sells for $20. Show that there is more than one optimal solution in this situation.

10. The management of a large movie house in New York City has agreed to schedule movie reruns for 75 days of a summer season. He is assured a profit of $1800 for each daily showing of Claws, $1000 for each daily showing of Annie Gal, and $1400 for each daily showing of Cosmic Wars. Because so many people have seen Claws, he considers it unwise to schedule more than 30 days of Claws. Because of other competing science fiction movies, he considers it unwise to schedule more than 35 days of Cosmic Wars. An agreement with the film distributor requires that he schedule at least 15 days of Annie Gal. In order to maximize the management's profit, how many days of each movie should be scheduled?

8.3   Linear Programming on Bounded Polyhedral Convex Sets

In the previous section the bounded polygonal convex sets (which arise from limitations, or constraints) were two-dimensional. Each of the inequalities involved two variables, generally labeled x and y. It can happen in many situations that the constraints involved give rise to inequalities involving three or more variables. Although the situation is somewhat more complicated, the methods previously described can be generalized to higher dimensions.

In this section we will illustrate problems involving constraints having three variables. We will attempt to optimize a function of the form $w = Ax + By + Cz + D$ subject to a system of constraints of the form:

$$a_1x + b_1y + c_1z \le d_1$$
$$a_2x + b_2y + c_2z \le d_2$$
$$\cdots\cdots\cdots\cdots\cdots$$
$$a_nx + b_ny + c_nz \le d_n$$

If the inequality sign is replaced with an equal sign, then the boundary points of each inequality consist of a plane. Each inequality therefore consists of all points lying on one side (and on the boundary) of a plane. Instead of the polygonal region we had in the two-dimensional situation, we will have a polyhedral convex set. If the sytem is bounded, the constraints will form a polyhedron rather than a polygon.

The vertices of the polyhedron are not always easy to obtain. Each vertex will arise from the intersection of three of the planes, but not all such intersection points will be vertices, that is, not all of the intersection points will simultaneously satisfy all of the inequalities. Unless a student is unusually skilled at making three-dimensional drawings, the following algebraic procedure will have to be followed in order to find the correct vertices:

PROCEDURE

(i)   List every combination possible consisting of three bounding planes chosen from the n inequalities. [There will be $_nC_3$ of them.]

(ii)   Find the intersection point common to each triplet of planes.

(iii)   Test each intersection point in the inequalities to be sure all of the inequalities are satisfied.

(iv)   The intersection points that satisfy all of the inequalities are the vertices of the polyhedral convex set to be tested.

If the polyhedral set is bounded, then the maximum value of the objective function must occur at one (or more) of the vertices. The same is true for the minimum value of the objective function $w = Ax + By + Cz + D$.

Geometric For an objective function of the form $w = Ax + By + Cz + D$, various
Interpretation w values give rise to parallel planes in three dimensions. Sliding these planes in one direction normal (perpendicular) to the planes corresponds to increasing w, and in the other direction, corresponds to decreasing w. To maximize the w value over a bounded polyhedral set, we merely slide the plane in the increasing w direction until the final point where the plane still touches the polyhedron. It is clear that the plane must be touching at least one vertex at that moment. This is similar to the figure on Page 268.

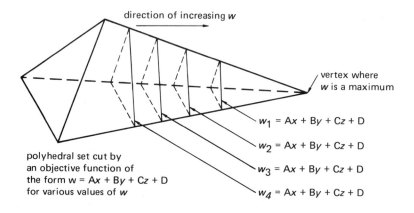

direction of increasing w

vertex where w is a maximum

$w_1 = Ax + By + Cz + D$

$w_2 = Ax + By + Cz + D$

polyhedral set cut by
an objective function of
the form $w = Ax + By + Cz + D$
for various values of w

$w_3 = Ax + By + Cz + D$

$w_4 = Ax + By + Cz + D$

Example 1

Find the maximum and the minimum values of $w = 3x + 6y - 2z + 7$ on the bounded polyhedral convex set given by the constraints

(i) $x \geq 0$ (ii) $x \leq 1$ (iii) $y \geq 0$ (iv) $y - z \leq 0$ (v) $x + y + z \leq 2$

Solution Since any three boundary planes may determine an intersection point, we have $_5C_3 = 10$ systems of equations to consider. Each of the combinations is listed below; note that some of them are inconsistent.

(1)–(2)–(3)
$\left. \begin{array}{l} x = 0 \\ x = 1 \\ y = 0 \end{array} \right\}$ no solution

(1)–(2)–(4)
$\left. \begin{array}{l} x = 0 \\ x = 1 \\ y - z = 0 \end{array} \right\}$ no solution

(1)–(2)–(5)
$\left. \begin{array}{l} x = 0 \\ x = 1 \\ x + y + z = 2 \end{array} \right\}$ no solution

$(1)-(3)-(4)$
$x = 0$
$y = 0$ $(0, 0, 0)$
$y - z = 0$

$(1)-(3)-(5)$
$x = 0$
$y = 0$ $(0, 0, 2)$
$x + y + z = 2$

$(1)-(4)-(5)$
$x = 0$
$y - z = 0$ $(0, 1, 1)$
$x + y + z = 2$

$(2)-(3)-(4)$
$x = 1$
$y = 0$ $(1, 0, 0)$
$y - z = 0$

$(2)-(3)-(5)$
$x = 1$
$y = 0$ $(1, 0, 1)$
$x + y + z = 2$

$(2)-(4)-(5)$
$x = 1$
$y - z = 0$ $(1, 1/2, 1/2)$
$x + y + z = 2$

$(3)-(4)-(5)$
$y = 0$
$y - z = 0$ $(2, 0, 0)$
$x + y + z = 2$

Notice that we have seven vertices, to which we give letter labels: $A(0, 0, 0)$, $B(0, 0, 2)$, $C(0, 1, 1)$, $D(1, 0, 0)$, $E(1, 0, 1)$, $F(1, 1/2, 1/2)$, $G(2, 0, 0)$. It is important to note that all but one of these points satisfied each of the five inequalities defining the constraints. The point $G(2, 0, 0)$ violates the second inequality, which requires that $x \leq 1$. The remaining six intersection points are the vertices of the bounded polyhedral convex set. A diagram follows.

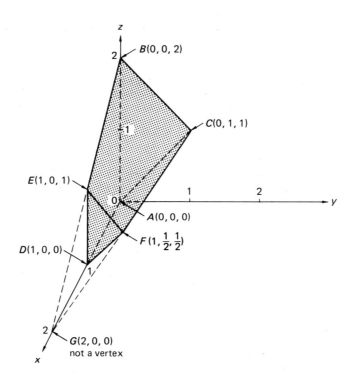

Now we compute the objective function values at each vertex.

VERTEX	$w = 3x + 6y - 2z + 7$	
$A(0, 0, 0)$	$w = 7$	
$B(0, 0, 2)$	$w = 3$	minimum
$C(0, 1, 1)$	$w = 11$	
$D(1, 0, 0)$	$w = 10$	
$E(1, 0, 1)$	$w = 8$	
$F(1, 1/2, 1/2)$	$w = 12$	maximum

Example 2

A mining company owns three coal mines A, B, and C, which each produce high- and low-grade coal according to the production schedule below.

	Tons of coal per day	
	High grade	Low grade
Mine A	6	4
Mine B	4	8
Mine C	8	4

The company can sell up to 960 tons of high-grade ore and up to 720 tons of low-grade ore. The net profit per day of operation is $3000 at mine A, $1500 at mine B, and $4500 at mine C. How many days should each mine be operating in order to maximize profits?

Solution Let

x = number of days operating mine A
y = number of days operating mine B
z = number of days operating mine C

Then we have the following constraints:

$$6x + 4y + 8z \leq 960$$
$$4x + 8y + 4z \leq 720$$
$$x \geq 0$$
$$y \geq 0$$
$$z \geq 0$$

The objective function to be maximized is given by

$$\text{profit} = P = 3000x + 1500y + 4500z$$

Our problem now is to determine the polyhedral set over which this function is defined. Then we must find the vertices. Using the method described in the previous example, we have the resulting diagram shown in the following figure. Note the vertices of the bounded polyhedron and the intercepts of the boundary planes for the first two inequalities. Now we compute the net profit P at each vertex.

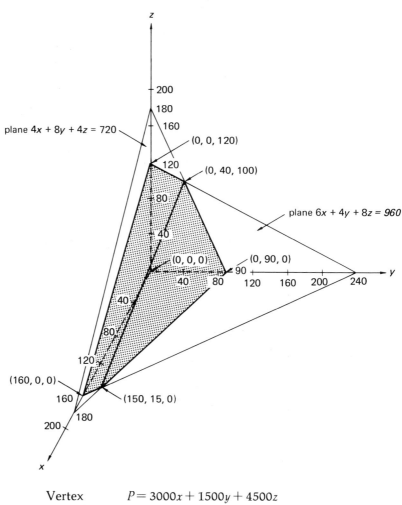

Vertex	$P = 3000x + 1500y + 4500z$	
(0, 0, 0)	0	minimum
(0, 90, 0)	$136,500	
(150, 15, 0)	$472,500	
(160, 0, 0)	$480,000	
(0, 40, 100)	$510,000	
(0, 0, 120)	$540,000	maximum

Exercise 8.3 1. Find the maximum and the minimum of the function

$$w = 6x + 5y + 6z + 30$$

subject to the polyhedron given by

$$4x + 10y + 2z \leq 2280$$
$$4x + 2y + 8z \leq 1520$$
$$x \geq 0$$
$$y \geq 0$$
$$z \geq 0$$

2. Find the maximum and the minimum of the function

$$w = 2x - 3y + 10z$$

subject to the polyhedron having six vertices given by

$$x + y + z \leq 6$$
$$x + 2y + 2z \leq 8$$
$$y - z \leq 0$$
$$y \geq 0$$
$$x \geq 0$$

3. A mining company owns three coal mines A, B, and C, which each produce high- and low-grade coal according to the production schedule below:

	Tons of coal per day	
	High grade	Low grade
Mine A	4	8
Mine B	2	6
Mine C	6	4

The company can sell up to 800 tons of high-grade ore and up to 1200 tons of low-grade ore. The net profit per day of operation is $2000 at mine A, $1200 at mine B, and $1600 at mine C. How many days should each mine be operating in order to maximize profits?

Matrix Algebra

> The ramifications of the theory of matrices are numerous.
>
> Morris Kline

9.1 Basic Definitions and Operations

In a previous chapter we discussed mathematical probability, which permits the determination of useful information from various models involving risk and chance occurrences. In this chapter we will study the algebra of certain numerical arrays called matrices and related matrix (singular) models; these topics are characteristic spin-offs of the subject known as *linear algebra.*

The underlying ideas about matrices, which go as far back as Cauchy, were actually crystallized and refined as recently as 1850, when Arthur Cayley published a remarkable series of articles on the subject. Some of the matrix applications at the end of this chapter were discovered (invented?) in the 1940s and are examples of contemporary mathematics.

The structure and implications of matrix algebra are in some respects quite different from ordinary algebra. After examining basic matrix properties, we will study some of the wide-ranging applications in business and the social sciences. We will also dispel some of the mystery surrounding the subject of cryptography. Since we can apply matrices to the analysis of large and unwieldy data sets, we will include an occasional BASIC language computer problem. As it turns out, computers would not always be easily programmed were it not for matrix concepts. An informed computer specialist is very grateful to matrices: they were discovered at just the right time!

At the outset we will present some of the basic definitions and operations involving matrices.

Definition 1   A *matrix* is a rectangular array of real numbers called *entries,* denoted by

$$
A = \begin{bmatrix} a_{11} & a_{12} & \ldots & a_{1n} \\ a_{21} & a_{22} & \ldots & a_{2n} \\ \vdots & \vdots & & \vdots \\ a_{m1} & a_{m2} & \ldots & a_{mn} \end{bmatrix}
$$

Notice that the array has m rows of n entries each; at times we will abbreviate and indicate the above general matrix by writing

$$A = (a_{ij})_{m,n}$$

where a_{ij} is the entry (or component) in the ith row and jth column of a matrix having m rows and n columns (or an $m \times n$ matrix). We will use capital letters to denote matrices and lower-case letters to denote entries and real numbers. The matrix

$$B = \begin{bmatrix} 1 & 3 & 5 \\ 2 & 0 & -7 \end{bmatrix}$$

has two rows and three columns and is said to have dimensions 2×3. Entries in the matrix are as follows:

$$\begin{array}{lll} b_{11} = 1 & b_{12} = 3 & b_{13} = 5 \\ b_{12} = 2 & b_{22} = 0 & b_{23} = -7 \end{array}$$

A matrix such as

$$C = \begin{bmatrix} 1 & 0 & 0 \\ 1 & 1 & 0 \\ 0 & -1 & 5 \end{bmatrix}$$

is of dimensions 3×3. A matrix with the same number of columns as rows [that is, of the form $(c_{ij})_{m,m}$] is a *square matrix.*
   The matrix

$$\begin{bmatrix} 0 & 0 \\ 0 & 0 \\ 0 & 0 \end{bmatrix}$$

is called a zero matrix of dimensions 3×2 and is often simply written as **0.**

Example 1

Give the dimensions of each of the following matrices and, in each case, state the requested entry.

$$A = \begin{bmatrix} 1 & 5 \\ 0 & -2 \end{bmatrix} \qquad a_{12} = ?$$

$$B = \begin{bmatrix} 5 & 3 & 4 & 2 \\ 1 & 2 & 3 & 7 \\ 0 & 0 & 1 & 1 \end{bmatrix} \qquad b_{21} = ?$$

$$C = \begin{bmatrix} 4 & 0 & 0 & 0 \\ 0 & 3 & 0 & 0 \\ 0 & 0 & 2 & 0 \\ 0 & 0 & 0 & 1 \end{bmatrix} \qquad c_{33} = ?$$

$$D = [\,0 \quad 5 \quad -7 \quad 3\,] \qquad d_{14} = ?$$

$$E = \begin{bmatrix} 0 \\ -7 \\ 5 \\ 3 \end{bmatrix} \qquad e_{11} = ?$$

Solution

matrix	dimensions	element requested
A	2×2	$a_{12} = 5$
B	3×4	$b_{21} = 1$
C	4×4	$c_{33} = 2$
D	1×4	$d_{14} = 3$
E	4×1	$e_{11} = 0$

We might mention that a matrix having only one row (such as D) or one column (such as E) is sometimes referred to, respectively, as a *row matrix* or *column matrix*.

Example 2

Summarize the following data in the form of a 5×3 matrix. A manufacturing company supplies parts for an electronics conglomerate. Factory A produces 150 transistors, 300 capacitors, and 900 resistors; factory B produces 1000 capacitors, 1500 resistors, 200 variable poten-tiometers, and 500 antenna coils; factory C produces 500 transistors, 200 resistors, 400 variable potentiometers, and 100 antenna coils.

Solution

	Factory A	Factory B	Factory C
Transistors	150	0	500
Capacitors	300	1000	0
Resistors	900	1500	200
Variable potentiometers	0	200	400
Antenna coils	0	0	100

This array may be represented simply as the matrix

$$D = \begin{bmatrix} 150 & 0 & 500 \\ 300 & 1000 & 0 \\ 900 & 1500 & 200 \\ 0 & 200 & 400 \\ 0 & 0 & 100 \end{bmatrix}$$

.hich is of dimensions 5×3.

Definition 2 (Equality of matrices)   Two matrices A and B are said to be *equal*, and we write $A = B$, if (i) the dimensions of A and B are identical and (ii) their corresponding entries are equal, if $a_{ij} = _{ij}$ for all i and j.

Thus if

$$\begin{bmatrix} 1 & 2 & 0 \\ 5 & -3 & 4 \end{bmatrix} = \begin{bmatrix} 1 & x & y \\ 5 & -3 & z \end{bmatrix}$$

then it must follow that $x = 2$, $y = 0$, and $z = 4$. Note that for equality of two matrices to exist, each of the corresponding dimensions must be the same. Thus

$$\begin{bmatrix} 0 & 0 & 0 \\ 0 & 0 & 0 \end{bmatrix} \neq \begin{bmatrix} 0 & 0 \\ 0 & 0 \\ 0 & 0 \end{bmatrix}$$

Definition 3 (Addition of matrices)   Given two matrices having the same dimensions, $A = (a_{ij})_{m,n}$ and $B = (b_{ij})_{m,n}$, the sum $A + B$ is the matrix given by $A + B = (a_{ij} + b_{ij})_{m,n}$.

Matrices having identical dimensions are said to be *conformable for addition*. Thus matrices

$$A = \begin{bmatrix} 1 & 3 & 2 \\ 0 & 1 & -5 \end{bmatrix} \qquad B = \begin{bmatrix} 0 & 1 & 2 \\ 3 & 4 & 5 \end{bmatrix}$$

are conformable for addition and

$$A + B = \begin{bmatrix} 1 & 4 & 4 \\ 3 & 5 & -1 \end{bmatrix}$$

Just as it is true that for every real number a we can always find a number $(-a)$ with the property that $a + (-a) = 0$, so it is also true that we can find *additive inverses* for matrices. It is not difficult to show that if $A = (a_{ij})_{m,n}$ then the additive inverse is $(-a_{ij})_{m,n}$, where the $-a_{ij}s'$ are merely the negatives of the corresponding real entries of the matrix $A = (a_{ij})_{m,n}$. Moreover, it is easy to prove that an additive inverse is unique for each matrix A. We will represent an additive inverse of A with the symbol $(-A)$, so that it follows that

$$A + (-A) = 0$$

The additive inverse permits us to define subtraction of matrices in a very elementary way:

> **Definition 4 (Subtraction of matrices)**   Given two matrices having the same dimensions, $A = (a_{ij})_{m,n}$ and $B = (b_{ij})_{m,n}$, $A - B = C$, where $A = C + B$.

It follows that $A - B = (a_{ij} - b_{ij})_{m,n}$; we can subtract matrices by subtracting corresponding entries. Thus

$$\begin{bmatrix} 1 & 3 & 2 \\ 0 & 1 & -5 \end{bmatrix} - \begin{bmatrix} 0 & 1 & 2 \\ 3 & 4 & 5 \end{bmatrix} = \begin{bmatrix} 1 & 2 & 0 \\ -3 & -3 & -10 \end{bmatrix}$$

and it is easy to verify that

$$\begin{bmatrix} 1 & 3 & 2 \\ 0 & 1 & -5 \end{bmatrix} = \begin{bmatrix} 1 & 2 & 0 \\ -3 & -3 & -10 \end{bmatrix} + \begin{bmatrix} 0 & 1 & 2 \\ 3 & 4 & 5 \end{bmatrix}$$

Next let us suppose we want to define meaningfully the multiplication of a matrix by a real number, called a *scalar*. If we refer to the problem involving electronics parts (Example 2), it might happen, for example, that 10% of all the manufactured parts are inoperable. We could, then, represent all of the *operable* parts manufactured by each factory as a product of a scalar .90 times the matrix D:

$$(.90)D = .90 \begin{bmatrix} 150 & 0 & 500 \\ 300 & 1000 & 0 \\ 900 & 1500 & 200 \\ 0 & 200 & 400 \\ 0 & 0 & 100 \end{bmatrix} = \begin{bmatrix} 135 & 0 & 450 \\ 270 & 900 & 0 \\ 810 & 1350 & 180 \\ 0 & 180 & 360 \\ 0 & 0 & 90 \end{bmatrix}$$

The following definition therefore seems appropriate.

> **Definition 5 (Multiplication of a matrix by a scalar)**   Given $A = (a_{ij})_{m,n}$, let c be a real number (called a scalar). Then the scalar multiplication of c and A is the matrix cA (or Ac) given by

$$cA = (ca_{ij})_{m,n}$$

The definition merely states that each and every element of the matrix A is multiplied by the scalar c.

We can now attach a meaning to expressions such as $3A + 4B$: triple each of the entries of matrix A, quadruple each of the entries of matrix B, and then add the two resulting matrices. Expressions such as $7A - 10B$ can be interpreted to mean $7A + (-10)B$ without any inconsistencies.

Example 3

Given the matrices

$$A = \begin{bmatrix} 1 & -3 \\ 0 & 4 \\ 1 & 2 \end{bmatrix}, B = \begin{bmatrix} 1 & 0 \\ 0 & -1 \\ 0 & 0 \end{bmatrix}, \text{ and } C = \begin{bmatrix} 5 & 4 \\ 3 & -2 \end{bmatrix}$$

find, whenever possible, the resulting matrix for each of the following.

a. $A + B$
b. $3A + 2B$
c. $A - 5B$
d. $-C$
e. $B + (-C)$

Solution

a. $A + B = \begin{bmatrix} 1 & -3 \\ 0 & 4 \\ 1 & 2 \end{bmatrix} + \begin{bmatrix} 1 & 0 \\ 0 & -1 \\ 0 & 0 \end{bmatrix} = \begin{bmatrix} 2 & -3 \\ 0 & 3 \\ 1 & 2 \end{bmatrix}$

b. $3A + 2B = 3\begin{bmatrix} 1 & -3 \\ 0 & 4 \\ 1 & 2 \end{bmatrix} + 2\begin{bmatrix} 1 & 0 \\ 0 & -1 \\ 0 & 0 \end{bmatrix}$

$= \begin{bmatrix} 3 & -9 \\ 0 & 12 \\ 3 & 6 \end{bmatrix} + \begin{bmatrix} 2 & 0 \\ 0 & -2 \\ 0 & 0 \end{bmatrix} = \begin{bmatrix} 5 & -9 \\ 0 & 10 \\ 3 & 6 \end{bmatrix}$

c. $A - 5B = A + (-5B) = \begin{bmatrix} 1 & -3 \\ 0 & 4 \\ 1 & 2 \end{bmatrix} + \begin{bmatrix} -5 & 0 \\ 0 & 5 \\ 0 & 0 \end{bmatrix} = \begin{bmatrix} -4 & -3 \\ 0 & 9 \\ 1 & 2 \end{bmatrix}$

d. $-C = \begin{bmatrix} -5 & -4 \\ -3 & 2 \end{bmatrix}$

e. Since B and $(-C)$ have different dimensions, they are not conformable for addition.

Example 4

Given that for every matrix A there exists a zero matrix $\mathbf{0}$ with the property that $A + \mathbf{0} = \mathbf{0} + A = A$, prove that the zero matrix is unique.

Solution Suppose otherwise; that is, that there exists a zero element $\mathbf{0}^*$ such that for every A, $A + \mathbf{0}^* = \mathbf{0}^* + A = A$, and $\mathbf{0} \neq \mathbf{0}^*$. Then we have that $\mathbf{0} + A = \mathbf{0}^* + A$. Adding $(-A)$ to both sides, we have

$$\mathbf{0} + A + (-A) = \mathbf{0}^* + A + (-A)$$
$$\mathbf{0} + \mathbf{0} = \mathbf{0}^* + \mathbf{0}$$
$$\mathbf{0} = \mathbf{0}^*$$

which is a contradiction. Hence it must be true that $\mathbf{0} = \mathbf{0}^*$ and the zero element is unique.

Exercise 9.1 1. Give the dimensions for each of the following matrices and, in each case, state the component(s) requested.

a. $A = \begin{bmatrix} 5 \\ -2 \\ 4 \end{bmatrix}$ $a_{21} = ?$

b. $B = \begin{bmatrix} 5 & 4 & 0 \\ -2 & 1 & 7 \\ 6 & 3 & 9 \end{bmatrix}$ $b_{32} = ?, \ b_{23} = ?$

c. $C = \begin{bmatrix} 4 & 3 & 7 & 9 \\ 1 & 2 & -2 & 4 \end{bmatrix}$ $c_{14} = ?, \ c_{22} = ?$

d. $D = \begin{bmatrix} 1 & 3 & 5 \\ 4 & 2 & 7 \\ 1 & 0 & 0 \\ 0 & 0 & 1 \end{bmatrix}$ $d_{42} = ?, \ d_{41} = ?$

2. Find x, y, and z so that

$$\begin{bmatrix} 1 & x \\ y & 5 \end{bmatrix} + \begin{bmatrix} z & y \\ 2 & 4 \end{bmatrix} = \begin{bmatrix} 5 & 4 \\ 8 & 9 \end{bmatrix}$$

3. Given the matrices

$$A = \begin{bmatrix} 3 & 5 & -7 \\ 2 & -6 & 9 \end{bmatrix}, B = \begin{bmatrix} 4 & 1 & 2 \\ -3 & 6 & 5 \end{bmatrix},$$

$$C = \begin{bmatrix} 1 & 4 & 3 \\ -1 & 3 & 8 \end{bmatrix}, D = \begin{bmatrix} 2 & 9 \\ -1 & -7 \end{bmatrix}$$

find if possible, the resulting matrix for the following expressions.

a. $A + (B + C)$ b. $(A + B) + C$
c. $A - (B + C)$ d. $(A - B) - C$
e. $2A + B - 3C$ f. $(3A + B) + D$
g. $6B - 3C$ h. $3(2B - C)$

4. Find the unknown matrix X, where A, B, and C are the matrices of Problem 3.

$$(A + 3X) - B = C$$

5. Summarize the following description in the form of a matrix of dimensions 2×3.

   In 1971 airline A made 100,000 airplane flights from cities in the United States, 10,000 flights from cities in Europe, and no flights from cities in Africa. In that same year, airline B made 4000 flights from cities within the United States, 50,000 flights from cities in Europe, and 2000 flights from cities in Africa.

6. Referring to Problem 5, suppose that during 1972 the number of takeoffs from all geographical areas increased by 20% compared to 1971, and suppose further that during 1973 all takeoffs decreased by 10% compared to 1971. Represent as a matrix expression all of the takeoffs during the combined years of 1971, 1972, and 1973 from points in the United States, Europe, and Africa for the two airline companies. Combine the resulting matrices into a single matrix.

7. Solve for x (and check) in the matrix equation:

$$x \begin{bmatrix} x & 2x \\ y & y^2 \end{bmatrix} = \begin{bmatrix} 4 & 8 \\ 10 & 50 \end{bmatrix}$$

8. Given that for each matrix A there exists an additive inverse $(-A)$ such that $A + (-A) = (-A) + A = \mathbf{0}$, prove that for each A, the matrix $(-A)$ is unique. (*Hint:* See Example 4.)

9. Given that matrices A, B, and C have the same dimensions, prove that if $A + C = B + C$, then $A = B$.

10. Prove that the alternate definition of matrix subtraction

$$A - B = A + (-1)B$$

is equivalent to Definition 4.

9.2 Properties of Matrix Addition and Multiplication by a Scalar

With just the small number of new notations and definitions so far developed, we are able to make some general statements that are always true for matrices and scalars. We can regard these statements as theorems capable of being proved. It turns out that these properties also hold for other kinds of mathematical entities besides matrices: those named *linear spaces*. Any system in which the scalars satisfy the same familiar properties as those of real numbers (called "field" properties) and in which these theorems hold true is called a linear space. Although your instructor may wish to describe other "linear systems," in this section we will focus only on "linear combinations" of matrices and real number scalars when using or referring to these theorems.

Theorem 1 Given any matrices A, B, and C, each of dimensions $m \times n$, and given that c and d are any real numbers (scalars), then

(i) $A + B$ is a matrix

(ii) $A + B = B + A$ (addition is commutative)

(iii) $A + (B + C) = (A + B) + C$ (addition is associative)

(iv) There is a unique matrix $\mathbf{0}$ of dimensions $m \times n$ such that $A + \mathbf{0} = A$ for all matrices A

(v)   For each matrix A there is a unique matrix $(-A)$ such that $A + (-A) = \mathbf{0}$

(vi) There is a unique scalar 1 such that $(1)A = A$ for every matrix A

(vii) $(cd)A = c(dA)$

(viii) $c(A + B) = cA + cB$

(ix) $(c + d)A = cA + dA$

Example 1

Prove Theorem 1 (ii).

Solution
$$(a_{ij})_{m,n} + (b_{ij})_{m,n} = (a_{ij} + b_{ij})_{m,n} = (b_{ij} + a_{ij})_{m,n}$$
$$= (b_{ij})_{m,n} + (a_{ij})_{m,n}$$

Therefore $A + B = B + A$.

Example 2

Prove Theorem 1 (vii).

Solution
$$(cd)A = (cd)\,(a_{ij})_{m,n} = (cda_{ij})_{m,n}$$
$$c(dA) = c(da_{ij})_{m,n} = (cda_{ij})_{m,n}$$

The theorem is proved.

Exercise 9.2   1.   Prove Theorem 1 (iii).

2.   Prove Theorems 1 (viii) and 1 (ix).

3.   Go to the library and find a book covering the subject of abstract (or "modern") algebra. Look up and list the "field" properties.

4.   Go to the library and find a book covering the subject of linear algebra. Find an example (other than matrices) of a mathematical structure that satisfies the properties of a linear space.

5.   Explain why it is true that for all matrices A

$$6A + 12A = 18A$$

9.3   Matrix Multiplication and Powers of a Matrix

In this section we show that it is possible to define the product of one matrix by another matrix. We will also show that this "new kind" of multiplication has certain properties that are similar to other kinds of algebraic operations; however, it turns out that for most of us this matrix multiplication will seem strange and novel. In some respects matrix multiplication does not "behave very nicely" at all. What is quite remarkable, nevertheless, is that we can actually use it! We will motivate our discussion of matrix multiplication by considering a descriptive example.

Example 1

The American Can Company produces four types of tin cans: fruit-juice, coffee, tuna-fish, and beer. The cans are manufactured using three basic materials: sheet metal, solder, and paper. The materials schedule in units of material for one can of each type is given in the array:

	Sheet metal	Solder	Paper	
Fruit-juice can	25	3	2	units of material per can
Coffee can	30	4	0	
Tuna-fish can	5	1	1	
Beer can	6	1	0	

The American Can Company has two plants that we are considering. One is located in New York, and the other is located in Pittsburgh. The costs in dollars for each unit of each material are different in each of the two locations and are given in the schedule:

	New York	Pittsburgh	
Sheet metal	0.01	0.007	cost in $ per unit of material
Solder	0.003	0.002	
Paper	0.001	0.001	

Find the total materials' cost for each type of tin can in each of the two locations.

Solution First we simplify the above data by writing them in the form of two matrices side by side. We consider first the cost of one fruit-juice can made in the New York plant; the relevant data appear in bold type.

$$
\begin{bmatrix} \mathbf{25} & \mathbf{3} & \mathbf{2} \\ 30 & 4 & 0 \\ 5 & 1 & 1 \\ 6 & 1 & 0 \end{bmatrix}
\begin{bmatrix} \mathbf{0.01} & 0.007 \\ \mathbf{0.003} & 0.002 \\ \mathbf{0.001} & 0.001 \end{bmatrix}
$$

Then the materials cost for producing a fruit-juice can made in New York is given by $(25)(0.01) + (3)(0.003) + (2)(0.001) = \$.261$. Notice that we have formed a special type of product from a row of the left matrix with a column of the right matrix. The entries of the row chosen in the left matrix correspond to the number of units of materials for the type of can produced; the entries of the column chosen in the right matrix corresponds to the materials costs in that plant location. Thus since there are four rows in the left matrix and two columns in the right matrix, we have eight possible cost combinations. The results are summarized below in the form of a matrix. Another of the resulting entries is illustrated in bold type.

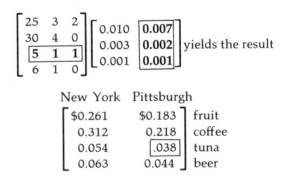

$$
\begin{bmatrix} 25 & 3 & 2 \\ 30 & 4 & 0 \\ \boxed{5} & \boxed{1} & \boxed{1} \\ 6 & 1 & 0 \end{bmatrix}
\begin{bmatrix} 0.010 & \boxed{0.007} \\ 0.003 & \boxed{0.002} \\ 0.001 & \boxed{0.001} \end{bmatrix}
$$ yields the result

New York   Pittsburgh
$$
\begin{bmatrix} \$0.261 & \$0.183 \\ 0.312 & 0.218 \\ 0.054 & \boxed{.038} \\ 0.063 & 0.044 \end{bmatrix}
\begin{matrix} \text{fruit} \\ \text{coffee} \\ \text{tuna} \\ \text{beer} \end{matrix}
$$

third row of left matrix

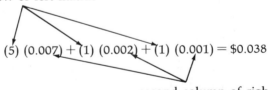

$(5)(0.007) + (1)(0.002) + (1)(0.001) = \$0.038$

second column of right matrix

Notice that the entry 0.038 of the result is located in the third row and second column. We used the third row of the left matrix and the second column of the right matrix to obtain 0.038. All of the other entries of the result are found in a similar fashion.

The above example suggests a way of defining the product of two matrices.

> **Definition 6 (The product of two matrices)**   Given $A = (a_{ij})_{m,n}$ and $B = (a_{ij})_{n,p}$, the matrix product $AB = C = (c_{ij})_{m,p}$, where the ijth entry of C is given by $c_{ij} = a_{i1}b_{1j} + a_{i2}b_{2j} + \cdots + a_{in}b_{nj}$.

Note that the entry c_{ij} in the resulting product matrix C is the result of multiplying the ith row of the left matrix by the jth column of the right matrix. These are indicated below in bold type.

$$
\begin{bmatrix}
a_{11} & a_{12} & a_{13} & \cdots & a_{1n} \\
\vdots & \vdots & \vdots & \cdots & \vdots \\
\mathbf{a_{i1}} & \mathbf{a_{i2}} & \mathbf{a_{i3}} & \cdots & \mathbf{a_{in}} \\
\vdots & \vdots & \vdots & & \vdots \\
a_{m1} & a_{m2} & a_{m3} & \cdots & a_{mn}
\end{bmatrix}
\begin{bmatrix}
b_{11} & \cdots & \mathbf{b_{1j}} & \cdots & b_{1p} \\
b_{21} & \cdots & \mathbf{b_{2j}} & \cdots & b_{2p} \\
b_{31} & \cdots & \mathbf{b_{3j}} & \cdots & b_{3p} \\
\vdots & \cdots & \vdots & \cdots & \vdots \\
b_{n1} & \cdots & \mathbf{b_{nj}} & \cdots & b_{np}
\end{bmatrix}
=
\begin{bmatrix}
c_{11} & \cdots & c_{1j} & \cdots & c_{1p} \\
\vdots & & \vdots & & \vdots \\
c_{i1} & \cdots & \boxed{c_{ij}} & \cdots & c_{ip} \\
\vdots & & \vdots & & \vdots \\
c_{m1} & \cdots & c_{mj} & \cdots & c_{mp}
\end{bmatrix}
$$

It is useful to emphasize that for a product AB to be formulated according to the above definition, we must have that the

$$(\text{number of columns of } A) = (\text{number of rows of } B)$$

We can crystallize things even further by noting that

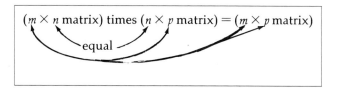

$(m \times n \text{ matrix}) \text{ times } (n \times p \text{ matrix}) = (m \times p \text{ matrix})$

equal

Example 2

Compute the product AB, where

$$A = \begin{bmatrix} 1 & 0 & -3 \\ 2 & 1 & 4 \end{bmatrix} \text{ and } B = \begin{bmatrix} 1 & 1 \\ 0 & 2 \\ -5 & 6 \end{bmatrix}$$

Solution Note that in finding AB we have a problem of the form

$$(2 \times 3)\ (3 \times 2) = (2 \times 2)$$

$$\begin{bmatrix} 9 & 2 & 3 \\ 0 & 1 & 4 \end{bmatrix} \begin{bmatrix} 1 & 1 \\ 0 & 7 \\ -5 & 6 \end{bmatrix}$$

$$= \begin{bmatrix} 9(1) + 2(0) + 5(-5) & 9(1) + 2(7) + 3(6) \\ 0(1) + 1(1) + 4(-5) & 0(1) + 1(7) + 4(6) \end{bmatrix} = \begin{bmatrix} -16 & 41 \\ -19 & 31 \end{bmatrix}$$

Notice that the shape of the product matrix is different from either of the two matrices A and B.

Example 3

For the same matrices A and B (in Example 2) compute BA

Solution

$$\begin{bmatrix} 1 & 1 \\ 0 & 7 \\ -5 & 6 \end{bmatrix} \begin{bmatrix} 9 & 2 & 3 \\ 0 & 1 & 4 \end{bmatrix} = \begin{bmatrix} 9 & 3 & 7 \\ 0 & 7 & 28 \\ -45 & -4 & 9 \end{bmatrix}$$

Note that $AB \neq BA$ and that, in general, matrix multiplication is *not commutative*. That is, even when both AB and BA are defined, it is not generally true that $AB = BA$.

Example 4

Find the indicated matrix products.

a. $\begin{bmatrix} 1 & 2 \\ 3 & 4 \end{bmatrix} \begin{bmatrix} -1 & 0 \\ 0 & 1 \end{bmatrix} =$

b. $\begin{bmatrix} -1 & 0 \\ 0 & 1 \end{bmatrix} \begin{bmatrix} 1 & 2 \\ 3 & 4 \end{bmatrix} =$

Solution a. $\begin{bmatrix} 1 & 2 \\ 3 & 4 \end{bmatrix} \begin{bmatrix} -1 & 0 \\ 0 & 1 \end{bmatrix} = \begin{bmatrix} -1 & 2 \\ -3 & 4 \end{bmatrix}$

b. $\begin{bmatrix} -1 & 0 \\ 0 & 1 \end{bmatrix} \begin{bmatrix} 1 & 2 \\ 3 & 4 \end{bmatrix} = \begin{bmatrix} -1 & -2 \\ 3 & 4 \end{bmatrix}$

Example 5

What can be said about the product AB, where

$$A = \begin{bmatrix} 1 & 3 & 2 \\ 0 & 1 & 5 \end{bmatrix} \qquad B = \begin{bmatrix} 4 & 2 \\ -1 & 0 \end{bmatrix}$$

Solution If the number of columns of A equaled the number of rows of B, we could find the product. However, we have matrices (2×3) and (2×2), which do not permit multiplication according to the definition.

We would like to have a multiplicative identity matrix I such that for all "appropriate" matrices A it would be true that

$$AI = IA = A$$

Notice, however, that if $A = (a_{ij})_{m,n}$ and $I = (d_{ij})_{p,q}$ and we want $(m \times n)(p \times q) = (p \times q)(m \times n) = (p \times q)$, then it must follow that $p = n$, $q = m$, $q = n$, and $p = m$. Therefore

$$p = q = m = n$$

Thus by appropriate matrices A and I, we mean *square matrices*.

Example 6

Demonstrate that

$$I = \begin{bmatrix} 1 & 0 \\ 0 & 1 \end{bmatrix}$$

is an identity matrix for any 2×2 matrix.

Solution
$$\begin{bmatrix} a & b \\ c & d \end{bmatrix} \begin{bmatrix} 1 & 0 \\ 0 & 1 \end{bmatrix} = \begin{bmatrix} 1 & 0 \\ 0 & 1 \end{bmatrix} \begin{bmatrix} a & b \\ c & d \end{bmatrix} = \begin{bmatrix} a & b \\ c & d \end{bmatrix}$$

It turns out that the above example can be extended to any square matrix A. All we have to do is place 1's along the main diagonal and place 0's elsewhere to formulate an identity matrix. Thus

$$\begin{bmatrix} a & b & c \\ d & e & f \\ g & h & i \end{bmatrix} \begin{bmatrix} 1 & 0 & 0 \\ 0 & 1 & 0 \\ 0 & 0 & 1 \end{bmatrix} = \begin{bmatrix} 1 & 0 & 0 \\ 0 & 1 & 0 \\ 0 & 0 & 1 \end{bmatrix} \begin{bmatrix} a & b & c \\ d & e & f \\ g & h & i \end{bmatrix} = \begin{bmatrix} a & b & c \\ d & e & f \\ g & h & i \end{bmatrix}$$

and we see that

$$I_{3 \times 3} = \begin{bmatrix} 1 & 0 & 0 \\ 0 & 1 & 0 \\ 0 & 0 & 1 \end{bmatrix}$$

Theorem 2 For any square matrix $A_{n \times n}$, there exists a unique identity matrix $I_{n \times n}$, where $AI = IA = A$ and

$$I = \begin{bmatrix} 1 & 0 & \cdots & 0 & 0 \\ 0 & 1 & \cdots & 0 & 0 \\ \vdots & \vdots & \ddots & \vdots & \vdots \\ 0 & 0 & \cdots & 1 & 0 \\ 0 & 0 & \cdots & 0 & 1 \end{bmatrix}$$

We will omit the proof of this theorem. Later in this chapter, however, we will prove the uniqueness of the identity matrix I.

There are also two additional properties of matrices that are useful and can be proved. Although we will omit both proofs, we will make the results plausible when we examine some examples.

> **Theorem 3**   Given any matrices A, B, and C that are conformable for the operations indicated, the following relations hold:
>
> (i) $A(BC) = (AB)C$ associativity
> (ii) $\left.\begin{array}{c} A(B+C) = AB + AC \\ \text{and} \\ (A+B)C = AC + BC \end{array}\right\}$ distributivity

At a later point in the chapter it will be useful to have a meaningful definition for powers of a square matrix.

> **Definition 7 (powers of a matrix)**   For all square matrices A, we define
>
> $$A^n = \underbrace{(A)\,(A)\,(A)\ldots(A)}_{n \text{ matrices } A}$$
>
> for all integers $n \geq 1$, and we will define $A^0 = I$.

Example 7

For matrices

$$A = \begin{bmatrix} 1 & 3 \\ 2 & -1 \end{bmatrix}, \quad B = \begin{bmatrix} 2 & 1 \\ 5 & 3 \end{bmatrix}, \quad C = \begin{bmatrix} 2 & 4 \\ 1 & 0 \end{bmatrix}$$

verify the associative and distributive properties:

a. $A(BC) = (AB)C$
b. $A(B+C) = AB + AC$

Solution a. $\begin{bmatrix} 1 & 3 \\ 2 & -1 \end{bmatrix} \left(\begin{bmatrix} 2 & 1 \\ 5 & 3 \end{bmatrix} \begin{bmatrix} 2 & 4 \\ 1 & 0 \end{bmatrix} \right) \overset{?}{=} \left(\begin{bmatrix} 1 & 3 \\ 2 & -1 \end{bmatrix} \begin{bmatrix} 2 & 1 \\ 5 & 3 \end{bmatrix} \right) \begin{bmatrix} 2 & 4 \\ 1 & 0 \end{bmatrix}$

$\begin{bmatrix} 1 & 3 \\ 2 & -1 \end{bmatrix} \begin{bmatrix} 5 & 8 \\ 13 & 20 \end{bmatrix} \overset{?}{=} \begin{bmatrix} 17 & 10 \\ -1 & -1 \end{bmatrix} \begin{bmatrix} 2 & 4 \\ 1 & 0 \end{bmatrix}$

$\begin{bmatrix} 44 & 68 \\ -3 & -4 \end{bmatrix} = \begin{bmatrix} 44 & 68 \\ -3 & -4 \end{bmatrix}$

b. $\begin{bmatrix} 1 & 3 \\ 2 & -1 \end{bmatrix} \left(\begin{bmatrix} 2 & 1 \\ 5 & 3 \end{bmatrix} + \begin{bmatrix} 2 & 4 \\ 1 & 0 \end{bmatrix} \right) \overset{?}{=} \begin{bmatrix} 1 & 3 \\ 2 & -1 \end{bmatrix} \begin{bmatrix} 2 & 1 \\ 5 & 3 \end{bmatrix}$

$$+ \begin{bmatrix} 1 & 3 \\ 2 & -1 \end{bmatrix} \begin{bmatrix} 2 & 4 \\ 1 & 0 \end{bmatrix}$$

$$\begin{bmatrix} 1 & 3 \\ 2 & -1 \end{bmatrix} \begin{bmatrix} 4 & 5 \\ 6 & 3 \end{bmatrix} \overset{?}{=} \begin{bmatrix} 17 & 10 \\ -1 & -1 \end{bmatrix} + \begin{bmatrix} 5 & 4 \\ 3 & 8 \end{bmatrix}$$

$$\begin{bmatrix} 22 & 14 \\ 2 & 7 \end{bmatrix} = \begin{bmatrix} 22 & 14 \\ 2 & 7 \end{bmatrix}$$

Example 8

Under what circumstances is it true that

$$(A + B)^2 = A^2 + 2AB + B^2$$

Solution First note that A and B must be square matrices in order for powers to be appropriate. Using the distributive property twice, we have

$$(A + B)^2 = (A + B)\,(A + B) = (A + B)A + (A + B)B$$
$$= A^2 + BA + AB + B^2$$

Since $BA + AB = 2AB$ only when $AB = BA$, the statement is true only when A and B commute under multiplication.

Example 9

For the matrix

$$A = \begin{bmatrix} 0 & 1 & 1 \\ 0 & 0 & 1 \\ 0 & 0 & 0 \end{bmatrix} \qquad \text{find } A^2 \text{ and } A^n, \text{ where } n \geq 3.$$

Solution

$$A^2 = (A)\,(A) = \begin{bmatrix} 0 & 1 & 1 \\ 0 & 0 & 1 \\ 0 & 0 & 0 \end{bmatrix} \begin{bmatrix} 0 & 1 & 1 \\ 0 & 0 & 1 \\ 0 & 0 & 0 \end{bmatrix} = \begin{bmatrix} 0 & 0 & 1 \\ 0 & 0 & 0 \\ 0 & 0 & 0 \end{bmatrix}$$

$$A^3 = (A)\,(A)\,(A) = A(A^2) = \begin{bmatrix} 0 & 1 & 1 \\ 0 & 0 & 1 \\ 0 & 0 & 0 \end{bmatrix} \begin{bmatrix} 0 & 0 & 1 \\ 0 & 0 & 0 \\ 0 & 0 & 0 \end{bmatrix} = \begin{bmatrix} 0 & 0 & 0 \\ 0 & 0 & 0 \\ 0 & 0 & 0 \end{bmatrix}$$

and $A^n = 0$ for all $n \geq 3$.

Exercise 9.3   1.   Show that $AB = BA$ but $CD \neq DC$, where

$$A = \begin{bmatrix} 6 & 1 \\ 5 & 1 \end{bmatrix}, \quad B = \begin{bmatrix} 2 & -2 \\ -10 & 12 \end{bmatrix}, \quad C = \begin{bmatrix} 1 & 2 \\ 3 & 4 \end{bmatrix}, \quad D = \begin{bmatrix} 1 & 0 \\ 5 & 2 \end{bmatrix}$$

2.   Find the matrix product AB, where

$$A = \begin{bmatrix} 1 & 0 & -2 & 4 \\ 0 & 1 & 0 & 1 \end{bmatrix} \quad \text{and} \quad B = \begin{bmatrix} 3 \\ 1 \\ 2 \\ 5 \end{bmatrix}.$$

Also explain why it is not possible to find the product BA.

3.   Find $AB + AC$ using only *one* matrix multiplication, where

$$A = \begin{bmatrix} 1 & 2 \\ 0 & -1 \end{bmatrix}, \quad B = \begin{bmatrix} 7 & 3 \\ 2 & 1 \end{bmatrix}, \quad C = \begin{bmatrix} 1 & 5 \\ -1 & 6 \end{bmatrix}$$

4.   Verify the associative property $A(BC) = (AB)C$ using the matrices of Example 1.

5.   Given matrices A_{mxn}, B_{pxq}, and C_{rxs}, under what conditions on m, n, p, q, r, s is the associative property of multiplication meaningful? Do the same for the distributive property.

6.   Given

$$A = \begin{bmatrix} 1 & 2 & 3 \\ 0 & 1 & -3 \end{bmatrix}, \quad B = \begin{bmatrix} 1 & 5 \\ -2 & 3 \end{bmatrix}, \quad C = \begin{bmatrix} 1 & 0 \\ -1 & 5 \end{bmatrix}, \quad I = \begin{bmatrix} 1 & 0 \\ 0 & 1 \end{bmatrix}$$

Find the indicated matrices:

a. BA	b. CI	c. IC	d. B^2
e. B^3	f. $(B-C)(B+C)$		g. $B^2 - C^2$
h. I^n, where $n \geq 1$	i. $CB + C$		j. $C(B+I)$

7.   Show that

$$\begin{bmatrix} 0 & a & b \\ 0 & 0 & c \\ 0 & 0 & 0 \end{bmatrix}^n = 0$$

for all $n \geq 3$.

8.   In solving the following problem, formulate two matrices and compute the matrix product.

A company wishes to purchase the following items: 150 units of A, 30 units of B, 1 unit of C, and 4 units of D. There are five distributors who sell all these items. Below is each distributor's price list, per unit item in the order in which the items are listed above.

Distributor 1: $25, $12, $28, $0.35
Distributor 2: $23, $15, $30, $0.25
Distributor 3: $27, $13, $29, $0.15
Distributor 4: $30, $11, $32, $0.20
Distributor 5: $21, $19, $33, $0.30

At which distributor will the company's bill be a minimum?

9. Express the system of equations in matrix notation.

$$2x + 3y + 4z = 5$$
$$x - y - 2z = 3$$
$$x + y + z = 1$$

10. Given that $AB = BA$, prove that $(A - B)(A + B) = A^2 - B^2$.

11. Explain why the following matrix "factoring" is generally invalid.

$$2A^2 + 7AB + 6B^2 = (A + 2B)(2A + 3B)$$

12. Prove each of the following:

a. $A^3A^2 = A^2A^3$ for any matrix that is square
b. $A^3 + 2BA^2 + A^2 = A^2(A + 2B + I)$, where A and B are square and commute.

13. Prove the left distributive property for all 2×2 matrices.

14. Find (by experimenting) three 2×2 matrices A, B, and C such that $B \neq C$ and $AB = AC$.

*15. Use the following BASIC language computer program to multiply the two matrices A and B in the order AB, where

$$A = \begin{bmatrix} 5 & 6 & 9 \\ 3 & 8 & -7 \end{bmatrix} \quad \text{and} \quad B = \begin{bmatrix} -7 & 4 & 6 & 7 \\ 1 & 0 & 5 & 9 \\ 2 & 2 & 2 & 8 \end{bmatrix}.$$

```
10   DIM A(2,3),B(3,4),C(2,4)
20   PRINT 'THE PRODUCT OF AB = C WHERE '
30   PRINT
40   MAT READ A,B
50   MAT C =A*B
60   PRINT 'MATRIX C = '
70   PRINT
80   MAT PRINT C:
90   DATA 5,6,9,3,8,-7,-7,4,6,7,1,0,5,9,2,2,2,8
100  END
     RUN
```

Before the BASIC matrix operations can be used in a program, each matrix used in the program must be declared in a DIM statement as

it is in line 10 above. For example DIM A(2,3) reserves storage for a
2×3 matrix named A. The DATA statement 90 contains entries of
the matrices A and B named in line 10, and (on most systems) the
data should be listed row by row for each matrix. Certain differences
exist for various computer systems: some require double quotation
marks for print statements; others enter matrix data column by column;
and on some systems the colon at the end of line 80 above should
be a semicolon or perhaps should be omitted entirely. Most systems
have the following commands in common:

MAT READ A	Read matrix A
MAT PRINT B	Print matrix B
MAT C = ZER	C equals zero matrix
MAT D = IDN	D equals identity matrix
MAT E = F + G	Add two matrices
MAT H = J − K	Subtract two matrices
MAT L = M∗N	Matrix multiplication
MAT R = (S)∗T	Multiply matrix T by scalar S
MAT U = INV(W)	Multiplicative inverse of matrix W
MAT X = TRN(Y)	Transpose of matrix Y

*16.   Use the BASIC language program for computing A^2, A^3, A^4, A^5,
where

$$A = \begin{bmatrix} 0 & 1 & 2 & 3 \\ 0 & 0 & 1 & 2 \\ 0 & 0 & 0 & 1 \\ 0 & 0 & 0 & 0 \end{bmatrix}$$

Since we cannot compute powers of a matrix directly, we must use
some kind of recursion (or "looping") process involving successive
multiplication to produce AA, AAA, $AAAA$, $AAAAA$. The following
program will achieve this.

```
 10   DIM A(4,4),X(4,4),Y(4,4)
 20   PRINT ' 2ND, 3RD, 4TH, AND 5TH POWERS OF MATRIX A '
 30   PRINT
 40   MAT READ A
 50   M = 2
 60   MAT X = MAT A
 70   FOR N = 1 TO 4
 80   MAT Y = X∗A
 90   PRINT 'MATRIX A TO THE POWER ';M; 'IS'
100   PRINT
110   PRINT MAT Y:
120   MAT X = MAT Y
130   M = M + 1
140   NEXT N
150   DATA 0,1,2,3,0,0,1,2,0,0,0,1,0,0,0,0
160   END
      RUN
```

9.4 The Inverse of a Matrix

Suppose we were given a matrix A and we wished to find another matrix A^{-1} with the property that $AA^{-1} = A^{-1}A = I$. This may or may not be possible for a given matrix A. The existence of matrix inverses is a very important abstract property of matrices and will ultimately lead to a very powerful method for solving applications involving linear systems of equations. In studying this section the student will have to be patient because the applications cannot be presented until the concept and properties of inverses are well understood.

> **Definition 8**   Given a square matrix A_{nxn}, if there is a matrix A^{-1} such that $AA^{-1} = A^{-1}A = I$, then we call A^{-1} the *inverse of A;* in this case we call A a *nonsingular* matrix.

We remark that when A^{-1} fails to exist for a given A, we call A a *singular* matrix.

Example 1

Find A^{-1} where

$$A = \begin{bmatrix} 1 & 3 \\ 0 & 1 \end{bmatrix}$$

and show that $AA^{-1} = A^{-1}A = I$

Solution We want

$$A^{-1} = \begin{bmatrix} a & b \\ c & d \end{bmatrix}$$

where

$$AA^{-1} = \begin{bmatrix} 1 & 0 \\ 0 & 1 \end{bmatrix}$$

Hence

$$\begin{bmatrix} 1 & 3 \\ 0 & 1 \end{bmatrix} \begin{bmatrix} a & b \\ c & d \end{bmatrix} = \begin{bmatrix} 1 & 0 \\ 0 & 1 \end{bmatrix}$$

means that the following equations must hold:

$$a + 3c = 1$$
$$c = 0$$
$$b + 3d = 0$$
$$d = 1$$

This system yields the unique solution $a = 1$, $b = -3$, $c = 0$, and $d = 1$. Thus

$$A^{-1} = \begin{bmatrix} 1 & -3 \\ 0 & 1 \end{bmatrix}$$

and we can check this by observing that

$$\begin{bmatrix} 1 & 3 \\ 0 & 1 \end{bmatrix} \begin{bmatrix} 1 & -3 \\ 0 & 1 \end{bmatrix} = \begin{bmatrix} 1 & 0 \\ 0 & 1 \end{bmatrix}$$

and it is also true that

$$\begin{bmatrix} 1 & -3 \\ 0 & 1 \end{bmatrix} \begin{bmatrix} 1 & 3 \\ 0 & 1 \end{bmatrix} = \begin{bmatrix} 1 & 0 \\ 0 & 1 \end{bmatrix}$$

The previous example might lead us to conjecture that if we can simply find a "right inverse" A^{-1} such that $AA^{-1} = I$, then (i) it must always be possible to find a "left inverse" A_*^{-1} such that $A_*^{-1}A = I$, and (ii) it must be true that $A_*^{-1} = A^{-1}$. It turns out that both assertions are correct. The proof of (i) is beyond the scope of the material presented here; however (ii) will be proved later.

It is instructive to note, however, that some matrices do not have inverses, as the following example will demonstrate.

Example 2

Show that the matrix

$$A = \begin{bmatrix} 2 & 4 \\ 1 & 2 \end{bmatrix}$$

is singular (that is, A^{-1} does not exist).

Solution We would want

$$\begin{bmatrix} 2 & 4 \\ 1 & 2 \end{bmatrix} \begin{bmatrix} a & b \\ c & d \end{bmatrix} = \begin{bmatrix} 1 & 0 \\ 0 & 1 \end{bmatrix}$$

but this leads to the following system of equations:

$$\left. \begin{array}{r} 2a + 4c = 1 \\ a + 2c = 0 \\ 2b + 4d = 0 \\ b + 2d = 1 \end{array} \right\} \text{ or } \left\{ \begin{array}{l} a + 2c = 1/2 \\ a + 2c = 0 \\ b + 2d = 0 \\ b + 2d = 1 \end{array} \right.$$

The latter system is clearly not solvable for any simultaneous values of a, b, c, and d. Hence, A^{-1} cannot be found for the given matrix A.

It will be useful to have a method for finding inverses of nonsingular 2×2 matrices. At a later point we will discuss a general method for finding inverses of all nonsingular matrices. Although a method for generating inverses of 2×2 matrices is quite restricted in scope, the examples the method can provide will serve as prototypes for the general theory of matrices to be developed.

Theorem 4 (Finding the inverse of a nonsingular 2×2 matrix)

$$\begin{bmatrix} a & b \\ c & d \end{bmatrix}^{-1} = \frac{1}{ad - bc} \begin{bmatrix} d & -b \\ -c & a \end{bmatrix}$$

whenever $ad - bc \neq 0$

Proof Note that $1/(ad - bc)$ is a scalar, and then

$$\begin{bmatrix} a & b \\ c & d \end{bmatrix} \left(\frac{1}{ad - bc} \right) \begin{bmatrix} d & -b \\ -c & a \end{bmatrix} = \frac{1}{ad - bc} \begin{bmatrix} a & b \\ c & d \end{bmatrix} \begin{bmatrix} d & -b \\ -c & a \end{bmatrix}$$

$$= \frac{1}{ad - bc} \begin{bmatrix} ad - bc & 0 \\ 0 & ad - bc \end{bmatrix} = \begin{bmatrix} 1 & 0 \\ 0 & 1 \end{bmatrix}$$

whenever $ad - bc \neq 0$

Theorem 4 gives us a quite efficient method for obtaining a quick 2×2 inverse. It turns out that $ad - bc = 0$ is a characterization of all singular 2×2 matrices. Now we will see how we can use the theorem.

Example 3

Find A^{-1}, where

$$A = \begin{bmatrix} 5 & -1 \\ 3 & 2 \end{bmatrix}$$

Solution To find A^{-1} make the following adjustments on A:

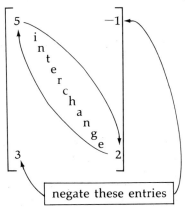

and multiply by the scalar

$$\frac{1}{(5)(2) - (3)(-1)}.$$

negate these entries

Thus $A^{-1} = \dfrac{1}{13} \begin{bmatrix} 2 & 1 \\ -3 & 5 \end{bmatrix}$

Since $AA^{-1} = A^{-1}A$, we have

$$\frac{1}{13} \begin{bmatrix} 2 & 1 \\ -3 & 5 \end{bmatrix} \begin{bmatrix} 5 & -1 \\ 3 & 2 \end{bmatrix} = \frac{1}{13} \begin{bmatrix} 13 & 0 \\ 0 & 13 \end{bmatrix} = \begin{bmatrix} 1 & 0 \\ 0 & 1 \end{bmatrix}$$

We can use matrix inverses to solve matrix equations and certain types of linear systems of equations. When we solve the algebraic equation $ax = b$ (where $a \neq 0$), we can multiply both sides by the reciprocal $1/a$ and obtain $(1/a)(ax) = (1/a)(b)$. Then we have that $x = b/a$. In a similar fashion if we had a matrix equation of the type

$$AX = B$$

(where A is nonsingular and where A and X are conformable for multiplication), then we could solve for the unknown matrix X and use A^{-1} in the fashion

$$A^{-1}(AX) = A^{-1}B$$
$$(A^{-1}A)X = A^{-1}B$$
$$IX = A^{-1}B$$
$$X = A^{-1}B$$

Example 4

Solve the matrix equation

$$\underset{A}{\begin{bmatrix} 2 & -3 \\ 3 & -1 \end{bmatrix}} \underset{X}{\begin{bmatrix} x \\ y \end{bmatrix}} = \underset{B}{\begin{bmatrix} 4 \\ 13 \end{bmatrix}}$$

Solution

$$A^{-1} = \frac{1}{7} \begin{bmatrix} -1 & 3 \\ -3 & 2 \end{bmatrix}$$

To find matrix X we can premultiply both sides by A^{-1}, to obtain

$$\frac{1}{7} \begin{bmatrix} -1 & 3 \\ -3 & 2 \end{bmatrix} \begin{bmatrix} 2 & -3 \\ 3 & -1 \end{bmatrix} \begin{bmatrix} x \\ y \end{bmatrix} = \frac{1}{7} \begin{bmatrix} -1 & 3 \\ -3 & 2 \end{bmatrix} \begin{bmatrix} 4 \\ 13 \end{bmatrix}$$

$$\frac{1}{7} \begin{bmatrix} 7 & 0 \\ 0 & 7 \end{bmatrix} \begin{bmatrix} x \\ y \end{bmatrix} = \frac{1}{7} \begin{bmatrix} 35 \\ 14 \end{bmatrix}$$

$$\begin{bmatrix} 1 & 0 \\ 0 & 1 \end{bmatrix} \begin{bmatrix} x \\ y \end{bmatrix} = \begin{bmatrix} 5 \\ 2 \end{bmatrix}$$

$$\begin{bmatrix} x \\ y \end{bmatrix} = \begin{bmatrix} 5 \\ 2 \end{bmatrix}$$

Check:

$$\begin{bmatrix} 2 & -3 \\ 3 & -1 \end{bmatrix} \begin{bmatrix} 5 \\ 2 \end{bmatrix} = \begin{bmatrix} 4 \\ 13 \end{bmatrix}$$

In the previous example, notice that the operations on the left side of the equation (when properly executed) will always yield the unknown matrix X so if A^{-1} is computed carefully, we can immediately say that if $AX = B$, then $X = A^{-1}B$. This can be applied to the solution of linear systems of equations.

Example 5

Solve the following 2×2 system of equations:

$$3x + 7y = 13$$
$$6x - 3y = 9$$

Solution Rewriting the system in matrix form, we have

$$\begin{bmatrix} 3 & 7 \\ 6 & -3 \end{bmatrix} \begin{bmatrix} x \\ y \end{bmatrix} = \begin{bmatrix} 13 \\ 9 \end{bmatrix}$$

and then

$$\begin{bmatrix} x \\ y \end{bmatrix} = \begin{bmatrix} 3 & 7 \\ 6 & -3 \end{bmatrix}^{-1} \begin{bmatrix} 13 \\ 9 \end{bmatrix}$$

$$= -\frac{1}{51} \begin{bmatrix} -3 & -7 \\ -6 & 3 \end{bmatrix} \begin{bmatrix} 13 \\ 9 \end{bmatrix} = -\frac{1}{51} \begin{bmatrix} -102 \\ -51 \end{bmatrix} = \begin{bmatrix} 2 \\ 1 \end{bmatrix}$$

Therefore $x = 2$ and $y = 1$. These can be checked easily.

Exercise 9.4   1.   Using the methods of Example 1, show that the following matrices are singular (inverses do not exist).

a. $A = \begin{bmatrix} -8 & -6 \\ 4 & 3 \end{bmatrix}$

b. $B = \begin{bmatrix} 1 & 1 & -2 \\ 0 & 3 & 8 \\ 0 & 0 & 0 \end{bmatrix}$

2.   Find A^{-1}, where $A = \begin{bmatrix} 5 & 2 \\ 0 & -1 \end{bmatrix}$

using two methods:

a.   The method of Example 1   b.   Theorem 4

3. Solve for the unknown matrix X, where

$$X = \begin{bmatrix} x_1 \\ x_2 \end{bmatrix}$$

in the equation

$$\begin{bmatrix} 3 & -2 \\ 1 & 4 \end{bmatrix} \begin{bmatrix} x_1 \\ x_2 \end{bmatrix} = \begin{bmatrix} 0 \\ 14 \end{bmatrix}$$

by using the inverse of the square matrix.

4. Rewrite the linear system

$$\begin{aligned} 4x - 5y &= 10 \\ x + y &= 7 \end{aligned}$$

in matrix form and solve by finding the inverse of the matrix of coefficients.

5. Given the following 3×3 linear system:

$$\begin{aligned} 2x + 3y - z &= 7 \\ x + 2y + z &= 8 \\ -x - y + 3z &= 6 \end{aligned}$$

a. Rewrite the system in matrix form.
b. Solve for x, y, and z utilizing the fact that

$$\begin{bmatrix} 2 & 3 & -1 \\ 1 & 2 & 1 \\ -1 & -1 & 3 \end{bmatrix}^{-1} = \begin{bmatrix} 7 & -8 & 5 \\ -4 & 5 & -3 \\ 1 & -1 & 1 \end{bmatrix}$$

6. Show that $AB = 0$, where

$$A = \begin{bmatrix} 4 & 1 \\ 8 & 2 \end{bmatrix} \qquad B = \begin{bmatrix} -1 & 4 \\ 4 & -16 \end{bmatrix}$$

*7. Use the following BASIC language computer program to find A^{-1}, where

$$A = \begin{bmatrix} 2 & 3 & -1 \\ 1 & 2 & 1 \\ -1 & -1 & 3 \end{bmatrix}$$

```
10   DIM A(3,3),X(3,3),Y(3,3)
20   PRINT 'PROGRAM FOR FINDING AND CHECKING A 3X3
     INVERSE '
30   PRINT
40   MAT READ A
50   MAT X = INV(A)
60   PRINT 'INVERSE OF A IS '
70   PRINT
80   MAT PRINT X:
90   PRINT
100  MAT Y = A*X
110  PRINT 'THE PRODUCT OF A WITH ITS INVERSE IS '
120  PRINT
130  MAT PRINT Y:
140  DATA 2,3,−1,1,2,1,−1,−1,3
150  END
     RUN
```

*8.   Make adjustments in the above program and find A^{-1}, where

$$A = \begin{bmatrix} 1 & 1 & -1 & 1 \\ -1 & 1 & 1 & 1 \\ 3 & -2 & -4 & -1 \\ 1 & 2 & -1 & -1 \end{bmatrix}$$

9.5 Proving Theorems About Matrices

Although we have thus far looked at a method for finding 2×2 matrix inverses, we are able to prove some useful and interesting theorems valid for all square matrices of dimensions $n \times n$. It is remarkable perhaps that we can prove them, without getting involved in the cumbersome details of entry notations, using abstract properties only. You may find Theorems 8 and 9 particularly surprising. Nevertheless, they are true.

Theorem 5.   If A is nonsingular and $AA = A$, then $A = I$.

Proof $AA^{-1} = I$

let $A = AA$

$$(AA)A^{-1} = I$$
$$A(AA^{-1}) = I$$
$$AI = I$$
$$A = I$$

The proof is complete.

Theorem 6   If A^{-1} and A_*^{-1} are, respectively, right and left inverses of matrix A, then $A^{-1} = A_*^{-1}$.

Proof By hypothesis we have that $AA^{-1} = I$ and $A_*^{-1}A = I$. It follows that

$$A^{-1} = IA^{-1} = (A_*^{-1}A)A^{-1} = A_*^{-1}(AA^{-1}) = A_*^{-1}I = A_*^{-1}$$

Thus $A^{-1} = A_*^{-1}$

Theorem 7   If A is nonsingular, A^{-1} is unique.

Proof Suppose the contrary; that is, that A_*^{-1} is also an inverse of A but $A_*^{-1} \neq A^{-1}$. Then since

$$AA^{-1} = I \text{ and } AA_*^{-1} = I$$
$$\text{we have} \quad AA^{-1} = AA_*^{-1}$$
$$\text{Then} \quad A^{-1}(AA^{-1}) = A^{-1}(AA_*^{-1})$$
$$\text{implies} \quad (A^{-1}A)A^{-1} = (A^{-1}A)A_*^{-1}$$
$$\text{and} \quad IA^{-1} = IA_*^{-1}$$
$$\text{or} \quad A^{-1} = A_*^{-1}$$

which is a contradiction. Thus the original assumption was impossible and A^{-1} is unique.

Theorem 8   If A and B are nonsingular, then AB is nonsingular and $(AB)^{-1} = B^{-1}A^{-1}$.

Proof $(AB)(B^{-1}A^{-1}) = A(BB^{-1})A^{-1} = AIA^{-1} = AA^{-1} = I$ and hence $B^{-1}A^{-1}$ must be the inverse of AB. Thus $(AB)^{-1} = B^{-1}A^{-1}$.

Theorem 9   If A and B are square matrices and $AB = \mathbf{0}$, then either $A = \mathbf{0}$ or $B = \mathbf{0}$, or *both* A and B are singular.

Proof (i)   If A is nonsingular and $AB = \mathbf{0}$, then

$$A^{-1}(AB) = (A^{-1}A)B = IB = B = \mathbf{0}$$

(In a similar fashion if B is nonsingular, then $A = \mathbf{0}$.)

(ii)   Suppose the contrary; that is, that $AB = \mathbf{0}$, $A \neq \mathbf{0}$, $B \neq \mathbf{0}$, and only A is singular. Then B^{-1} exists and

$$(AB)B^{-1} = (\mathbf{0})B^{-1}$$
$$A(BB^{-1}) = \mathbf{0}$$
$$AI = \mathbf{0}$$
$$A = \mathbf{0}$$

But we were given that $A \neq \mathbf{0}$. This is a contradiction, hence it must be *false* that only A is singular. Thus when two matrices (nonzero) satisfy $AB = \mathbf{0}$, they must *both* be singular.

Exercise 9.5 1. Given that A and B are nonsingular, prove each of the following:

a. If $AXA^{-1} = B$, then $X = A^{-1}BA$
b. $(A^{-1})^{-1} = A$
c. $A(A^{-1} + B) - (B^{-1}A^{-1})^{-1} = I$

2. Prove that if A, B, and C are nonsingular, then ABC is nonsingular and $(ABC)^{-1} = C^{-1}B^{-1}A^{-1}$.

*3. Show that the matrix transformation

$$\begin{bmatrix} \cos\theta & -\sin\theta \\ \sin\theta & \cos\theta \end{bmatrix} \begin{bmatrix} x \\ y \end{bmatrix} = \begin{bmatrix} x' \\ y' \end{bmatrix}$$

represents a counter-clockwise rotation in a plane through angle θ of the point (x,y) to the new point (x',y').

4. Prove that all nonsingular 2×2 matrices are commutative with their inverses.

9.6 A General Method for Finding Matrix Inverses

In the last section we saw that we could find the inverse of the matrix of coefficients of the linear 2×2 system of equations

$$ax + by = e$$
$$cx + dy = f$$

where $ad - bc \neq 0$. We also discovered that we could premultiply the matrix $\begin{bmatrix} e \\ f \end{bmatrix}$

by

$$\begin{bmatrix} a & b \\ c & d \end{bmatrix}^{-1}$$

and obtain the matrix

$$\begin{bmatrix} x \\ y \end{bmatrix}$$

Thus the inverse of the coefficient matrix was useful in finding solutions to the linear system.

Our objective now is to be able to find inverses of nonsingular square matrices of arbitrary dimensions $n \times n$. If we could accomplish this, then in principle we could solve any consistent system of n equations in n unknowns for which the solution is unique.

Suppose we wanted to find the inverse of the matrix A, where

$$A = \begin{bmatrix} 4 & 7 \\ 1 & 2 \end{bmatrix}$$

First we reexamine a basic method for finding A^{-1}. If A^{-1} does exist, then for some values of x_1, x_2, x_3, x_4,

$$\begin{bmatrix} 4 & 7 \\ 1 & 2 \end{bmatrix} \begin{bmatrix} x_1 & x_3 \\ x_2 & x_4 \end{bmatrix} = \begin{bmatrix} 1 & 0 \\ 0 & 1 \end{bmatrix}$$

$$A^{-1} = \begin{bmatrix} x_1 & x_3 \\ x_2 & x_4 \end{bmatrix}$$

The matrix equation above is equivalent to the following pair of linear systems, each having two equations and two unknowns:

System One
(i) $4x_1 + 7x_2 = 1$
     $x_1 + 2x_2 = 0$

System Two
(ii) $4x_3 + 7x_4 = 0$
      $x_3 + 2x_4 = 1$

In Chapter 7 we became familiar with a method for solving systems such as these. Sometimes it is called the method of elementary row operations. Using such methods we can multiply both sides of an equation by a convenient nonzero number; we can add the left and right sides of two of the equations; we can interchange one of the top equations in either pair with the corresponding bottom equation. Notice, however, that the coefficients of the unknowns in systems (i) and (ii) are identical. Therefore we can make use of elementary row operation techniques at the same time in both systems. We can accomplish this by combining both systems of equations in a single, abbreviated "augmented matrix" form:

$$\begin{bmatrix} 4 & 7 & | & 1 & 0 \\ 1 & 2 & | & 0 & 1 \end{bmatrix}$$

Multiplying the entire top row by a nonzero scalar would be equivalent to multiplying the first equations (in both systems) by that scalar; interchanging two rows would be equivalent to interchanging the order of the equations; adding one row to another would be equivalent to adding the respective sides of both systems. And, at each step in the process, we would create an equivalent pair of systems having the same solutions as the original form of the system. Let's see how this would work in actual practice by performing a sequence of operations on the rows of the augmented matrix.

$$\left[\begin{array}{cc|cc} 4 & 7 & 1 & 0 \\ 1 & 2 & 0 & 1 \end{array}\right]$$ add top row to (-4) times bottom row

$$\left[\begin{array}{cc|cc} 4 & 7 & 1 & 0 \\ 0 & -1 & 1 & -4 \end{array}\right]$$ add 7 times bottom row to top row

$$\left[\begin{array}{cc|cc} 4 & 0 & 8 & -28 \\ 0 & -7 & 7 & -28 \end{array}\right]$$ multiply top row by 1/4; multiply bottom row by $-1/7$

$$\left[\begin{array}{cc|cc} 1 & 0 & 2 & -4 \\ 0 & 1 & -1 & 4 \end{array}\right]$$

The systems corresponding to systems (i) and (ii) would be

$$\begin{array}{ll} 1x_1 + 0x_2 = 2 & 1x_3 + 0x_4 = -4 \\ 0x_1 + 1x_2 = -1 & 0x_3 + 1x_4 = 4 \end{array}$$

yielding

$$\begin{array}{ll} x_1 = 2 & x_3 = -4 \\ x_2 = -1 & x_4 = 4 \end{array}$$

and what appears magical about this process is that

$$\left[\begin{array}{cc} 2 & -4 \\ -1 & 4 \end{array}\right]$$

is the right half of the last augmented matrix and it is A^{-1}, which we wanted!

The previous discussion and example lends plausibility to the following definition and theorem.

Definition 9   Matrices A and B are *row equivalent*, and we write $A \sim B$, if B can be obtained from A using one or more of the following elementary row operations:

(i)   Interchanging any two rows

(ii)   Multiplying any row by a nonzero scalar

(iii)   Replacing any row by the sum of that row and a nonzero scalar multiple of some other row

Theorem 10   Given any square matrix A, let $[A|I]$ denote its augmented matrix. If by a sequence of elementary row operations $[A \mid I] \sim \cdots \sim [I \mid B]$, then $A^{-1} = B$. If it is not possible to find such a sequence of row operations, then A is singular.

We summarize the method for finding A^{-1} given A using the definition and theorem:

(i)   Form the augmented matrix $[A|I]$.

(ii)   Using elementary row operations try to transform $[A|I]$ into the row equivalent matrix $[I|B]$.

(iii)   Then $A^{-1} = B$.

Example 1

Using elementary row operations, find A^{-1}, where

$$A = \begin{bmatrix} 2 & 2 & 0 \\ 0 & 1 & 4 \\ 1 & -1 & 2 \end{bmatrix}$$

Solution

$$\left[\begin{array}{ccc|ccc} 2 & 2 & 0 & 1 & 0 & 0 \\ 0 & 1 & 4 & 0 & 1 & 0 \\ 1 & -1 & 2 & 0 & 0 & 1 \end{array}\right]$$

multiply the first row by $-1/2$ and add it to the bottom row

$$\sim \left[\begin{array}{ccc|ccc} 1 & 1 & 0 & 1/2 & 0 & 0 \\ 0 & 1 & 4 & 0 & 1 & 0 \\ 0 & -2 & 2 & -1/2 & 0 & 1 \end{array}\right]$$

multiply the middle row by 2 and add it to the bottom row

$$\sim \left[\begin{array}{ccc|ccc} 1 & 1 & 0 & 1/2 & 0 & 0 \\ 0 & 1 & 4 & 0 & 1 & 0 \\ 0 & 0 & 10 & -1/2 & 2 & 1 \end{array}\right]$$

multiply the middle row by (-5); and multiply the bottom row by 2

$$\sim \left[\begin{array}{ccc|ccc} 1 & 1 & 0 & 1/2 & 0 & 0 \\ 0 & -5 & -20 & 0 & -5 & 0 \\ 0 & 0 & 20 & -1 & 4 & 2 \end{array}\right]$$

add the bottom row to the middle r

$$\sim \left[\begin{array}{ccc|ccc} 1 & 1 & 0 & 1/2 & 0 & 0 \\ 0 & -5 & 0 & -1 & -1 & 2 \\ 0 & 0 & 20 & -1 & 4 & 2 \end{array}\right]$$

add the middle row to five times the top row

$$\sim \begin{bmatrix} 5 & 0 & 0 & \bigm| & 3/2 & -1 & 2 \\ 0 & -5 & 0 & \bigm| & -1 & -1 & 2 \\ 0 & 0 & 20 & \bigm| & -1 & 4 & 2 \end{bmatrix}$$ multiply the first row by 1/5
multiply the middle row by −1/5
multiply the bottom row by 1/20

$$\sim \begin{bmatrix} 1 & 0 & 0 & \bigm| & 3/10 & -1/5 & 2/5 \\ 0 & 1 & 0 & \bigm| & 1/5 & 1/5 & -2/5 \\ 0 & 0 & 1 & \bigm| & -1/20 & 2/10 & 1/10 \end{bmatrix}$$

where A^{-1} is the right half of the last augmented matrix. To check this more easily we can factor out 1/20, to obtain

$$A^{-1} = 1/20 \begin{bmatrix} 6 & -4 & 8 \\ 4 & 4 & -8 \\ -1 & 4 & 2 \end{bmatrix}$$

And AA^{-1} yields

$$1/20 \begin{bmatrix} 2 & 2 & 0 \\ 0 & 1 & 4 \\ 1 & -1 & 2 \end{bmatrix} \begin{bmatrix} 6 & -4 & 8 \\ 4 & 4 & -8 \\ -1 & 4 & 2 \end{bmatrix} =$$

$$1/20 \begin{bmatrix} 20 & 0 & 0 \\ 0 & 20 & 0 \\ 0 & 0 & 20 \end{bmatrix} = \begin{bmatrix} 1 & 0 & 0 \\ 0 & 1 & 0 \\ 0 & 0 & 1 \end{bmatrix}$$

Notice that during the row operations we tried to obtain zeros in the "lower triangular" part of the matrix in the order shown below; then we obtained zeros easily in the "upper triangular" portion of the matrix. Once we have entries in the main diagonal only, it is a simple matter to transform them into 1's.

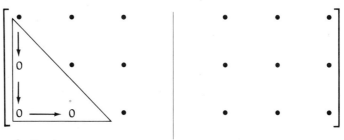

Example 2

Using elementary row operations show that A is singular where

$$A = \begin{bmatrix} 9 & 3 \\ 3 & 1 \end{bmatrix}$$

Solution
$$\begin{bmatrix} 9 & 3 \\ 3 & 1 \end{bmatrix} \begin{bmatrix} 1 & 0 \\ 0 & 1 \end{bmatrix} \sim \begin{bmatrix} 9 & 3 \\ 0 & 0 \end{bmatrix} \begin{bmatrix} 1 & 0 \\ 1 & -3 \end{bmatrix}$$

Since the first two entries of the second row are 0, it is impossible to achieve the form $[I | B]$; hence, A^{-1} does not exist.

Exercise 9.6 1. Find A^{-1} using elementary row operations.

a. $A = \begin{bmatrix} 2 & 0 \\ 0 & 7 \end{bmatrix}$

b. $A = \begin{bmatrix} 1 & -4 \\ 3 & 9 \end{bmatrix}$

c. $A = \begin{bmatrix} 1 & 1 & 3 \\ 0 & 2 & 4 \\ 0 & 0 & -1 \end{bmatrix}$

d. $A = \begin{bmatrix} 1 & 1 & 1 \\ 3 & -1 & -2 \\ -4 & -2 & 1 \end{bmatrix}$

e. $A = \begin{bmatrix} 0 & 1 & 2 & 0 \\ 0 & 0 & 0 & 1 \\ 1 & 1 & 3 & 0 \\ 2 & 4 & 0 & 0 \end{bmatrix}$

2. Show that matrices A and B are singular

$$A = \begin{bmatrix} 5 & 1 \\ -10 & -2 \end{bmatrix} \qquad B = \begin{bmatrix} 1 & 4 & 7 \\ -5 & 8 & -3 \\ 3 & -2 & 5 \end{bmatrix}$$

9.7 Solving Linear Systems with Matrix Methods

We begin with an example.

Example 1

Solve the system

$$2x - 3y = -4$$
$$2x + 5y = 12$$

by utilizing the inverse of the matrix of coefficients.

Solution First rewrite the system in matrix form:

$$\begin{bmatrix} 2 & -3 \\ 2 & 5 \end{bmatrix} \begin{bmatrix} x \\ y \end{bmatrix} = \begin{bmatrix} -4 \\ 12 \end{bmatrix}$$

Performing elementary row operations on the augmented matrix, it is easy to show that

$$\left[\begin{array}{cc|cc} 2 & -3 & 1 & 0 \\ 2 & 5 & 0 & 1 \end{array}\right] \sim \left[\begin{array}{cc|cc} 1 & 0 & 5/16 & 3/16 \\ 0 & 1 & -1/8 & 1/8 \end{array}\right]$$

Hence

$$\begin{bmatrix} x \\ y \end{bmatrix} = \begin{bmatrix} 2 & -3 \\ 2 & 5 \end{bmatrix}^{-1} \begin{bmatrix} -4 \\ 12 \end{bmatrix} = \begin{bmatrix} 5/16 & 3/16 \\ -1/8 & 1/8 \end{bmatrix} \begin{bmatrix} -4 \\ 12 \end{bmatrix} = \begin{bmatrix} 1 \\ 2 \end{bmatrix}$$

and it follows that $x = 1$ and $y = 2$.

Of course it may happen that a system of equations may have no solution (this is called an *inconsistent* system) or may have an infinite number of solutions (this is called a *dependent* system; one equation is some linear combination of the others). It would be revealing to examine such an example.

Example 2

Explain, in terms of matrices, why the following system is either inconsistent or dependent:

$$2x + 2y = a$$
$$x + y = b$$

Solution Simple row operations reveal that

$$\left[\begin{array}{cc|cc} 2 & 2 & 1 & 0 \\ 1 & 1 & 0 & 1 \end{array}\right] \sim \left[\begin{array}{cc|cc} 1 & 1 & 1/2 & 0 \\ 0 & 0 & 1 & -2 \end{array}\right]$$

Therefore, the matrix of coefficients is singular. Notice also that if $a = 2b$, the first equation is merely twice the second, which makes it possible to have an infinite number of solutions. If $a \neq 2b$, then the system is inconsistent and has no solutions. This leads to the following result.

> **Theorem 11**   If the matrix of coefficients of a linear $n \times n$ system is nonsingular, then the system has a unique solution. If the matrix of coefficients is singular, then the system is either inconsistent or dependent.

It will be useful to examine one last method of solving linear systems. It has several advantages: we can obtain the solution by direct use of elementary row operations; we can tell at a glance whether a system has a unique solution, infinitely many solutions, or no solution.

Gauss-Jordan Method for Solving a Linear System This method is similar to the method of finding general inverses of square matrices because it also utilizes elementary row operations. We already pointed out that elementary row operations on a system of equations were equivalent to "addition and subtraction" methods of the standard algebraic type. Therefore in solving a system such as

$$\begin{aligned} x + 2y - 4z &= -4 \\ y - z &= -2 \\ -8y + 15z &= 23 \end{aligned}$$

we could formulate the following augmented matrix:

$$\left[\begin{array}{ccc|c} 1 & 2 & -4 & -4 \\ 0 & 1 & -1 & -2 \\ 0 & -8 & 15 & 23 \end{array}\right]$$

This matrix is row-equivalent to the matrix

$$\left[\begin{array}{ccc|c} 1 & 0 & 0 & 2 \\ 0 & 1 & 0 & -1 \\ 0 & 0 & 1 & 1 \end{array}\right]$$

and thus $x = 2$, $y = -1$, $z = 1$. Notice that the method does not utilize the inverse of the coefficient matrix. It merely uses the fact that two row-equivalent augmented matrices correspond to linear systems that are equivalent (that is, have the same solution set).

Example 3

Solve the system

$$\begin{aligned} 3x + 3y &= 15 \\ x + y &= 10 \end{aligned}$$

by the Gauss-Jordan method.

Solution

$$\left[\begin{array}{cc|c} 3 & 3 & 15 \\ 1 & 1 & 10 \end{array}\right] \sim \left[\begin{array}{cc|c} 1 & 1 & 5 \\ 1 & 1 & 10 \end{array}\right] \sim \left[\begin{array}{cc|c} 1 & 1 & 5 \\ 0 & 0 & 5 \end{array}\right]$$

Since there is no x and y such that $0(x) + 0(y) = 5$, the system has no solution. Observe that the first two entries of the second row (in the last form of the augmented matrix) are zero while the last is nonzero.

Example 4

Solve the system

$$3x + 3y = 15$$
$$x + y = 5$$

by the Gauss-Jordan method.

Solution

$$\begin{bmatrix} 3 & 3 & | & 15 \\ 1 & 1 & | & 5 \end{bmatrix} \sim \begin{bmatrix} 1 & 1 & | & 5 \\ 1 & 1 & | & 5 \end{bmatrix} \sim \begin{bmatrix} 1 & 1 & | & 5 \\ 0 & 0 & | & 0 \end{bmatrix}$$

The equations therefore have an infinite number of solutions which can be obtained by assigning arbitrary values to x. Here observe that one complete row of entries are zeros in the augmented matrix.

We will not prove the following theorem. However the previous three examples help us to understand the logic behind it.

Theorem 12   Given any system of n linear equations with n unknowns:

$$a_{11}x_1 + a_{12}x_2 + \cdots + a_{1n}x_n = b_1$$
$$a_{21}x_1 + a_{22}x_2 + \cdots + a_{2n}x_n = b_2$$
$$\vdots \qquad\qquad\qquad\qquad \vdots$$
$$a_{n1}x_1 + a_{n2}x_2 + \cdots + a_{nn}x_n = b_n$$

and given A designating the matrix of coefficients and B designating the column matrix

$$B = \begin{bmatrix} b_1 \\ \vdots \\ b_n \end{bmatrix},$$

the following are true:
(i)   If $[A \,|\, B] \sim [I \,|\, C]$, where

$$C = \begin{bmatrix} c_1 \\ \vdots \\ c_n \end{bmatrix}$$

then the system has a unique solution set given by $x_1 = c_1$, $x_2 = c_2, \cdots, x_n = c_n$. This is called the *consistent* case.

(ii)   If $[A \,|\, B]$ is row-equivalent to a matrix in which at least one row has its first n entries equal to zero and the last entry nonzero, then the system has no solutions. This is called the *inconsistent* case.

(iii) If $[A \,|\, B]$ is row-equivalent to a matrix in which at least one row has all entries equal to zero but no row of the type described in (ii), then the system has infinitely many solutions. This is called the *dependent* case.

Example 5

In an election poll sample taken in Rochester, Minnesota, 940 people were interviewed, and of these, 713 voted for Carter. Of the females interviewed, 80% voted for Carter, and of the males, 70% voted for Carter. In Rochester, Minnesota, women outnumber men 2∶1. How many of each gender voted for Carter?

Solution One might argue that the above problem could be solved easily without matrices. We can imagine, however, that the addition of further variables and constraints might create a linear system in which matrix methods coupled with a computer program would be a superior method. Since the objective here is to improve our techniques for matrix formulation and solution of linear systems, we will solve the problem using matrices. At the outset we have

$$.80F + .70M = 713$$
$$F = 2M$$

which can be written in the following convenient form:

$$8F + 7M = 7130$$
$$F - 2M = 0$$

Now using the Gauss-Jordan method, we have the following equivalent augmented matrices:

$$\begin{bmatrix} 8 & 7 & | & 7130 \\ 1 & -2 & | & 0 \end{bmatrix}$$

$$\sim \begin{bmatrix} 8 & 7 & | & 7130 \\ 0 & 23 & | & 7130 \end{bmatrix}$$

$$\sim \begin{bmatrix} 8 & 0 & | & 4960 \\ 0 & 1 & | & 310 \end{bmatrix}$$

$$\sim \begin{bmatrix} 1 & 0 & | & 620 \\ 0 & 1 & | & 310 \end{bmatrix}$$

Hence the solution is $F = 620$ and $M = 310$.

Earlier, the inverse of a square matrix was introduced as a handy device to use in solving a system of n equations in n unknowns. In all fairness, the following should be pointed out.

a. It can only be so used in the unique solution case.

b. The work involved in finding the inverse of the coefficient matrix is generally greater than that involved in solving the system by the Gauss elimination method (also presented). Furthermore, the Gauss method will solve any system, even if it is not square. It handles at the same time the cases for which there are no solutions or an infinite number of solutions. Thus the inverse is important in solving systems mainly if you happen to have a large number of square systems, all having the same coefficient matrix.

Exercise 9.7 1. Using the Gauss-Jordan method solve each of the following linear systems.

a. $\quad 7x - 9y = \quad 23$
$\quad -3x + 4y = -10$

b. $\quad 2x + y \quad = \quad 3$
$\quad x - y + 2z = \quad 9$
$\quad y - z \quad = -4$

2. Using the theorem on P. 331, demonstrate that the following system is dependent and therefore must have infinitely many solutions.

$$4x - y - 9z = 7$$
$$2x - 3y + z = 1$$
$$x + y - 5z = 3$$

3. Show that the following system is inconsistent (has no solutions).

$$2x + 3y + z = 3$$
$$x + y - z = 2$$
$$- y - 3z = 0$$

4. Prove that the following linear system has a unique solution set. Can you find it?

$$2x - y + z = 0$$
$$x - y = 0$$
$$y + 2z = 0$$

5. Solve using matrix methods: In order to cure a certain influenza it is necessary to prescribe 66 units of serum A and 86 units of serum B. However the pharmacist can use commercial drug I, which contains 6 units of serum A and 2 units of serum B together with commercial drug II, which contains 3 units of serum A and 9 units of serum B. How much of each type of commercial drug should be used to obtain exactly the right proportions of serum needed?

*6.   Recall that $AX = B$ implies $X = A^{-1}B$, whenever A is nonsingular. Rewrite the following system in matrix form and use the following BASIC language computer program to solve the system. (Your method should be correct if it yields $x = 5$, $y = 2$, and $z = 1$.)

$$x - 3y + 4z = 3$$
$$x + y - 2z = 5$$
$$x + 2y + 3z = 12$$

The following is the BASIC computer program for solving the matrix equation $AX = B$, where $A = (a_{ij})_{3\times3}$, $X = (x_{ij})_{3,1}$, and $B = (b_{ij})_{3,1}$.

```
 10   DIM A(3,3),B(3,1),X(3,1)
 20   MAT READ A,B
 30   PRINT 'SOLVING THE MATRIX EQUATION AX = B '
 40   PRINT
 50   MAT X = (INV(A))*B
 60   PRINT 'MATRIX X = '
 70   PRINT
 80   MAT PRINT X:
 90   DATA 1,-3,4,1,1,-2,1,2,3,3,5,12
100   END
     RUN
```

*7.   The following system is extremely difficult to handle:

$$\sqrt{2}\, x + \sqrt{3}y + z = 1$$
$$x + y - z = 1/2$$
$$23x - \pi y - z = 9.532$$

Solve the system using the program in Problem 6. Use the following approximations: $\sqrt{2} = 1.414$, $\sqrt{3} = 1.732$, and $\pi = 3.142$.

8.   Solve by any matrix method: A man has $\$x$, $\$y$, and $\$z$ invested at 7.75%, 9.50%, and 11.50%, respectively. His total investments amount to $800,000. His annual income from the investments is $77,650, but the total earnings from the 7.75% and 9.50% investments amount to $66,150. Find the amounts invested at each rate.

9.8   Cryptography and Matrices

Clever elementary school children are known to create "secret" codes by which they can communicate private messages. One such code is devised by associating numbers with letters in the following fashion:

> basic alpha-numeric association
>
> A B C D E F G H I J K L M N O P
> 1 2 3 4 5 6 7 8 9 10 11 12 13 14 15 16
>
> Q R S T U V W X Y Z
> 17 18 19 20 21 22 23 24 25 26

and then the message "Fred is cute" could be translated into

F	R	E	D	I	S	C	U	T	E
6	18	5	4	9	19	3	21	20	5

The problem with using such a code for serious purposes is that certain statistical patterns concerning the letters used in the English language are well known. For example, it is a fact that the letter "e" occurs more frequently than any other letter. Such types of character-frequency information could be used by even a mediocre cryptographer to "break" such a code.

How to Encode a Message Using a Matrix Scrambler Suppose we wanted to encode the message "Jackal is armed." Using the basic alpha-numeric association in the figure above, we have

J	A	C	K	A	L	I	S	A	R	M	E	D
10	1	3	11	1	12	9	19	1	18	13	5	4

Now write the numeric message as a sequence of column matrices:

$$\begin{bmatrix} 10 \\ 1 \end{bmatrix}, \begin{bmatrix} 3 \\ 11 \end{bmatrix}, \begin{bmatrix} 1 \\ 12 \end{bmatrix}, \begin{bmatrix} 9 \\ 19 \end{bmatrix}, \begin{bmatrix} 1 \\ 18 \end{bmatrix}, \begin{bmatrix} 13 \\ 5 \end{bmatrix}, \begin{bmatrix} 4 \\ 0 \end{bmatrix}$$

in which we arbitrarily assign a zero (blank letter) to the second entry of the last matrix because we have an odd number of letters in our message. If we were to premultiply each 2×1 matrix by a nonsingular 2×2 matrix we could scramble or encode the message to a much deeper level of incomprehensibility. As an example we use

$$A = \begin{bmatrix} 3 & 5 \\ 1 & 2 \end{bmatrix}$$

as the coding premultiplier. Then the seven 2×1 column matrices above become

$$\begin{bmatrix} 35 \\ 12 \end{bmatrix}, \begin{bmatrix} 64 \\ 25 \end{bmatrix}, \begin{bmatrix} 63 \\ 25 \end{bmatrix}, \begin{bmatrix} 122 \\ 47 \end{bmatrix}, \begin{bmatrix} 93 \\ 37 \end{bmatrix}, \begin{bmatrix} 64 \\ 23 \end{bmatrix}, \begin{bmatrix} 12 \\ 4 \end{bmatrix}$$

and the encoded message could be delivered as

35	12	64	25	63	25	122	47	93	37	64	23	12	4
J	A	C	K	A	L	I	S	A	R	M	E	D	

This encoded message has two notable advantages: identical letters have different numbers associated with them, and identical numbers have different letters associated with them. A tough code to break!

Decoding the Message Using the Inverse of the Matrix Scrambler

If we premultiply each of the encoded 2×1 matrices by A^{-1}, we will "undo" the previous transformations and decipher the message. Note that

$$\text{If } A = \begin{bmatrix} 3 & 5 \\ 1 & 2 \end{bmatrix}, \text{ then } A^{-1} = \begin{bmatrix} 2 & -5 \\ -1 & 3 \end{bmatrix}$$

Now to unscramble the message, merely premultiply each of the pairs of numbers (each pair is written as a 2×1 column matrix again) by A^{-1}. Thus

$$\begin{bmatrix} 2 & -5 \\ -1 & 3 \end{bmatrix} \begin{bmatrix} 35 \\ 12 \end{bmatrix} = \begin{bmatrix} 10 \\ 1 \end{bmatrix}$$

$$\begin{bmatrix} 2 & -5 \\ -1 & 3 \end{bmatrix} \begin{bmatrix} 64 \\ 25 \end{bmatrix} = \begin{bmatrix} 3 \\ 11 \end{bmatrix}$$

etc., and write the resulting entries in a single horizontal line. Then we've returned to

10	1	3	11	1	12	9	19	1	18	13	5	4	0

which, when translated, is

J	A	C	K	A	L	I	S	A	R	M	E	D

Notice that we selected a 2×2 encoding matrix whose entries were integers and which had an inverse having integral entries also. Such a code might actually be broken by a fast computer program that could test large numbers of 2×2 integer matrices having inverses with integral entries. A thoughtful mathematician, however, might create a code that would be very difficult to break with high-speed computers.

We could have, for example, used a 3 × 3 matrix encoder and written the message in 3 × 1 column matrices associated with triplets of letters. If we really wanted to get fancy, we could encode once using a 3 × 3 matrix encoder and follow this by a second matrix transformation using a 4 × 4 matrix encoder; two separate inverses would then have to be found and applied in order to break the code and decipher the message. It is not difficult to imagine how we could devise a complicated sequence of encoding matrices that would push coding schemes to the furthest limits of impenetrability.

Exercise 9.8 1. Without using matrices, using only the alpha-numeric chart, decode the following messages.

a. 18 9 7 8 20 15 14 2 1 2 25
b. 12 15 22 5 9 19 18 5 1 12

2. Using only the alpha-numeric chart, encode the following messages.

a. Drop the bomb now   b. Close encounter third kind
c. Deliver the jewels

3. Using your results from Problem 2, encode the messages using the scrambling matrix

$$A = \begin{bmatrix} 1 & 2 \\ 3 & 7 \end{bmatrix}$$

Then, using the decoding matrix

$$A^{-1} = \begin{bmatrix} 7 & -2 \\ -3 & 1 \end{bmatrix}$$

unscramble the messages.

4. Given the 3 × 3 matrix decoder

$$A^{-1} = \begin{bmatrix} 2 & 3 & -1 \\ 1 & 2 & 1 \\ -1 & -1 & 3 \end{bmatrix}$$

Decode the following messages using A^{-1} and the alpha-numeric chart. (Also find the coding matrix A.)

a. 100 −56 21 54 −26 11
b. 27 −14 6 82 −45 17 4 2 7 28 −16 4

*5.   Find your own personal 3×3 integer matrix with an inverse having integer entries. Code and decode a message of your own choosing.

*6.   Using the decoding matrix

$$A^{-1} = \begin{bmatrix} -5 & 4 & -3 \\ 10 & -7 & 6 \\ 8 & -6 & 5 \end{bmatrix}$$

together with a slightly creative variation of the alpha-numeric chart, break the code and decipher the message contained in the dedication of this book.

9.9   Digraph Matrices Applied to Dominance and Communication Models

Many binary relationships exist in the social sciences, in business relationships, and in various types of human communication networks where we can use matrices to model certain diagrammatic representations of these relationships. The following are examples of *binary relationships* or "communications" between two entities split into two categories.

Unidirectional (one-way)

Person A dominates person B.
Person A passes gossip to person B.
Radio A can have one-way communication to radio B.
Person A considers person B a friend.
Person A dislikes person B.
Tennis player A beat tennis player B.

Bidirectional (two-way)

Person A exchanges gossip with person B.
Telephone A is connected to telephone B.
Radio A can have two-way communication with radio B.
Person A is a friend of person B.
Nation A has diplomatic relations with nation B.
Executive A exchanges memos with executive B.
Tennis player A had a match with tennis player B.

The above kinds of relationships will be referred to as communications. Given a set of entities (or "points"), it is possible that the binary relationships between them are exclusively one-way, exclusively two-way, or a mixture of both types. Thus the following terms will be helpful: A set of communications that is exclusively one-way will be referred to as a *dominance* relationship; one exclusively two-way will be referred to as a *perfect communication;* and one that is a mixture will be called a *friendly* relationship. It turns out that we can utilize a portion of a subject known as graph theory to represent communications. In particular we are interested in modeling communications using *digraphs* and their associated matrices.

> **Definition 10**   A *digraph* is a finite set of points $X_1, X_2, \ldots, X_n$ together with a finite number of directed edges $X_i \rightarrow X_j$ in which $i \neq j$.

Consider the example of a friendly digraph shown in the following figure.

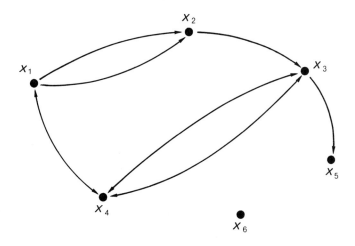

Notice that there are five basic types of direct relationships that exist between pairs of points in the above digraph.

(i)   A single one-way communication (as from X_2 to X_3)

(ii)   A double one-way communication (as from X_1 to X_2)

(iii)   A single two-way communication (as between X_1 and X_4)

(iv)   A double two-way communication (as between X_4 and X_3)

(v)   No communication (as between X_5 and X_6)

We will model the six-point digraph above using the following 6×6 matrix.

$$
\begin{bmatrix}
 & X_1 & X_2 & X_3 & X_4 & X_5 & X_6 \\
X_1 & 0 & 2 & 0 & 1 & 0 & 0 \\
X_2 & 0 & 0 & 1 & 0 & 0 & 0 \\
X_3 & 0 & 0 & 0 & 2 & 1 & 0 \\
X_4 & 1 & 0 & 2 & 0 & 0 & 0 \\
X_5 & 0 & 0 & 0 & 0 & 0 & 0 \\
X_6 & 0 & 0 & 0 & 0 & 0 & 0
\end{bmatrix} = M
$$

We can make several useful observations regarding the above matrix M and its associated digraph:

(i)   Each entry $m_{ij} = 0$ represents no communication between X_i and X_j

(ii)   Each entry $m_{ij} = 1$ represents one communication from X_i to X_j

(iii)   Each entry $m_{ij} = 2$ represents two communications from X_i to X_j

(iv)   Zeros along the main diagonal indicate that no element communicates directly with itself

(v)   The two 1's indicated in bold type are symmetric with respect to the main diagonal; this represents one two-way communication (in this case between X_4 and X_1)

(vi)   Some entries (as, for example, $m_{21} = 0$ and $m_{12} = 2$) are asymmetric with respect to the main diagonal

(vii)   In view of (v) and (vi), we call M a "friendly" communication matrix

(viii) The fifth row of zeros indicates that X_5 communicates to no one

(ix)   The fifth column has only one nonzero entry $m_{35} = 1$ which indicates that only X_3 communicates to X_5

(x)   The arithmetic total of all the matrix entries equals the number of arrowheads in the digraph

In short we assert that the matrix M represents each and every possible communication in the digraph. The matrix represents no more than the information given in the digraph.

Three illustrative digraphs are shown below with their associated matrices.

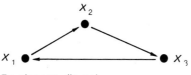

Dominance digraph

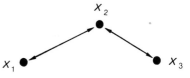

Perfect communication digraph

$$\begin{array}{c} & \begin{array}{ccc} X_1 & X_2 & X_3 \end{array} \\ \begin{array}{c} X_1 \\ X_2 \\ X_3 \end{array} & \left[\begin{array}{ccc} 0 & 1 & 0 \\ 0 & 0 & 1 \\ 1 & 0 & 0 \end{array} \right] \end{array}$$

$$\begin{array}{c} & \begin{array}{ccc} X_1 & X_2 & X_3 \end{array} \\ \begin{array}{c} X_1 \\ X_2 \\ X_3 \end{array} & \left[\begin{array}{ccc} 0 & 1 & 0 \\ 1 & 0 & 1 \\ 0 & 1 & 0 \end{array} \right] \end{array}$$

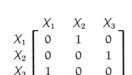

Friendly digraph

$$\begin{array}{c} & \begin{array}{ccc} X_1 & X_2 & X_3 \end{array} \\ \begin{array}{c} X_1 \\ X_2 \\ X_3 \end{array} & \left[\begin{array}{ccc} 0 & 1 & 1 \\ 1 & 0 & 1 \\ 0 & 1 & 0 \end{array} \right] \end{array}$$

Notice that dominance digraphs have associated matrices that are asymmetric, perfect communication matrices are symmetric, and friendly digraph matrices are neither symmetric nor asymmetric.

Some digraphs have more than one edge connecting a pair of points. However, most useful digraphs have either one edge or no edge connecting all pairs of points. The following definition will be useful for distinguishing between the two types.

Definition 11   Given a digraph and its associated matrix M, if M consists of entries which are 1's and 0's only, then M is called an *incidence* matrix.

Example 1

Four "unidirectional gossipers" pass information according to the digraph shown. The relationship is X_i passes gossip to X_j. Construct and interpret the associated matrix M. Do the same for M^2.

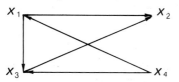

Solution

$$
\begin{array}{c}
\begin{array}{cccc} X_1 & X_2 & X_3 & X_4 \end{array} \\
\begin{array}{c} X_1 \\ X_2 \\ X_3 \\ X_4 \end{array}
\left[\begin{array}{cccc}
0 & 1 & 1 & 0 \\
0 & 0 & 0 & 0 \\
0 & 1 & 0 & 0 \\
1 & 0 & 1 & 0
\end{array} \right] = M
\end{array}
$$

Notice that the digraph shown is of the dominance type (exclusively one-way communications) and therefore has a characteristic asymmetric matrix (no nonzero elements are symmetric with respect to the main diagonal). Also the matrix M consists of only 1's and 0's and hence is an incidence matrix.

Observe that X_2 gossips to no one, and X_4 receives no gossip. The "biggest" gossipers are X_1 and X_4. The diagonal of 0's indicates that no one gossips directly to himself or herself. Notice also that although X_4 cannot gossip directly to X_2, the gossiping could be accomplished in two stages (possibly distorted) as follows:

$$X_4 \longrightarrow X_3 \longrightarrow X_2$$

Such a sequence is referred to as a two-stage communication. We could count the number of two-stage communications from the digraph. There are four of them (do you see them?):

$X_1 \longrightarrow X_3 \longrightarrow X_2 \Big\}$ one two-stage communication from X_1 to X_2

$X_4 \longrightarrow X_3 \longrightarrow X_2$
$X_4 \longrightarrow X_1 \longrightarrow X_3 \Big\}$ two two-stage communications from X_4 to X_2

$X_4 \longrightarrow X_1 \longrightarrow X_3 \Big\}$ one two-stage communication from X_4 to X_3

Now if we examine the matrix product $MM = M^2$, we see that

$$
\begin{array}{c}
\begin{array}{cccc} X_1 & X_2 & X_3 & X_4 \end{array} \\
\begin{array}{c} X_1 \\ X_2 \\ X_3 \\ X_4 \end{array}
\left[\begin{array}{cccc}
0 & 1 & 1 & 0 \\
0 & 0 & 0 & 0 \\
0 & 1 & 0 & 0 \\
1 & 0 & 1 & 0
\end{array} \right]
\end{array}
\begin{array}{c}
\begin{array}{cccc} X_1 & X_2 & X_3 & X_4 \end{array} \\
\left[\begin{array}{cccc}
0 & 1 & 1 & 0 \\
0 & 0 & 0 & 0 \\
0 & 1 & 0 & 0 \\
1 & 0 & 1 & 0
\end{array} \right]
\end{array}
=
\left[\begin{array}{cccc}
0 & 1 & 0 & 0 \\
0 & 0 & 0 & 0 \\
0 & 0 & 0 & 0 \\
0 & 2 & 1 & 0
\end{array} \right] = M^2
$$

The entries of M^2 correspond exactly to the number of two-stage communications. This makes sense when we realize that, for example, the entry c_{42} of M^2 (in bold type) derives from the product

$$c_{42} = m_{41}\,m_{12} + m_{42}\,m_{22} + m_{43}\,m_{32} + m_{44}\,m_{42}$$

or $\qquad 2 = (1)(1) + (0)(0) + (1)(1) + (0)(0)$

and in the previous expression a term $m_{4k}m_{k2} = 1$ if and only if both $m_{4k} = 1$ and $m_{k2} = 1$; this will occur when the following two-stage gossiping happens:

$$X_4 \longrightarrow X_k \longrightarrow X_2$$

The above will happen twice: when $k = 1$ and when $k = 3$. Thus $c_{42} = 2$.

We can extend this to the other elements of M^2 and say that for each two-stage communication there is a 1 in the c_{ij}th entry of the M^2 matrix, and for each 1 in the product of the ith row of M with the jth column of M there is a corresponding communication from X_i to X_j. This can be extended further to three-stage, four-stage, ..., and k-stage communications, which are either uni- or bidirectional or both. Although we omit the formal proof, mathematical induction can be used to prove the following result.

> **Theorem 13**   Given that M is an incidence matrix corresponding to the digraph formed from the points $X_1, X_2, \ldots X_k$, if we compute
>
> $$M^n = (c_{ij})_{k,k}$$
>
> then $c_{ij} =$ number of n-stage communications from X_i to X_j.

Example 2

Compute M^3 for the previous example and find all three-stage communications. Also discuss M^n, where $n \geq 4$.

Solution After computation we obtain

$$M^3 = \begin{bmatrix} 0 & 0 & 0 & 0 \\ 0 & 0 & 0 & 0 \\ 0 & 0 & 0 & 0 \\ 0 & 1 & 0 & 0 \end{bmatrix}$$

and entry $c_{42} = 1$. Thus there is one three-stage gossip communication from X_4 to X_2. From the digraph this will occur as follows:

Note that there are no other three-stage communications. A simple computation will show that $M^n = 0$ for $n \geq 4$; thus there are no multistage communications for n above 3.

Connected The following definition will be useful in the discussion to follow.
Digraphs

> **Definition 12**   A digraph is said to be *connected* if there is a path between X_i and X_j for all i and j, where $i \neq j$.

In a perfect communication digraph of n points and its associated incidence matrix M_{nxn}, the entries of the matrix sum S, where

$$S = M + M^2 + \cdots + M^{n-1}$$

represent the total number of communication paths between two distinct points X_i and X_j for 1, 2, 3, . . . , and $(n-1)$ stage communications. If and only if an entry $s_{ij} = 0$, is there no path along which X_i can communicate with X_j so that X_i and X_j are disconnected. Thus we have the following theorem.

> **Theorem 14**   An incidence matrix M for a perfect communication digraph involving n points is connected if and only if
>
> $$S = M + M^2 + \cdots + M^{n-1}$$

has all nonzero entries.

Example 3

Five towns are connected by telephone lines. The associated perfect communication incidence matrix is given by

$$
\begin{array}{cc}
 & \begin{array}{ccccc} X_1 & X_2 & X_3 & X_4 & X_5 \end{array} \\
\begin{array}{c} X_1 \\ X_2 \\ X_3 \\ X_4 \\ X_5 \end{array} &
\left[\begin{array}{ccccc}
0 & 1 & 0 & 0 & 1 \\
1 & 0 & 1 & 1 & 1 \\
0 & 1 & 0 & 1 & 0 \\
0 & 1 & 1 & 0 & 0 \\
1 & 1 & 0 & 0 & 0
\end{array} \right] = M
\end{array}
$$

Town X_2 is hit by a tornado that destroys all of its telephone linkages. Can the other towns still communicate with one another? Also suppose, instead, that town X_4 was struck by the tornado.

Solution Since X_2 is destroyed by a tornado, we delete the entire second row and second column of entries of matrix M and formulate the remaining towns into the 4×4 matrix

$$
N = \left[\begin{array}{cccc}
0 & 0 & 0 & 1 \\
0 & 0 & 1 & 0 \\
0 & 1 & 0 & 0 \\
1 & 0 & 0 & 0
\end{array} \right]
$$

Applying the theorem, we have that

$$N + N^2 + N^3 = \begin{bmatrix} 1 & 0 & 0 & 2 \\ 0 & 1 & 2 & 0 \\ 0 & 2 & 1 & 0 \\ 2 & 0 & 0 & 1 \end{bmatrix}$$

which has some zero entries. Therefore if we remove town X_2 from the original digraph, the remaining digraph is disconnected and towns X_1, X_3, X_4, and X_5 cannot all communicate with one another.

If, on the other hand, town X_4 is destroyed by a tornado, the deleted matrix becomes

$$P = \begin{bmatrix} 0 & 1 & 0 & 1 \\ 1 & 0 & 1 & 1 \\ 0 & 1 & 0 & 0 \\ 1 & 1 & 0 & 0 \end{bmatrix}$$

and

$$P + P^2 + P^3 = \begin{bmatrix} 4 & 6 & 2 & 5 \\ 6 & 5 & 4 & 6 \\ 2 & 4 & 1 & 2 \\ 5 & 6 & 2 & 4 \end{bmatrix}$$

Thus if town X_4 were destroyed, the remaining towns would be connected and could communicate with one another.

Finally, we note from the example above the following conjecture, which can be proved: powers of symmetric matrices are symmetric. A diagram digraph for the above five towns as originally interconnected follows. The hypothetical tornado destructions can easily be related to the previous matrix computations.

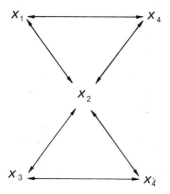

Example 4

For the following communication digraph, how many two- and three-stage feedback paths (from one point to at least one other point and back to itself) are there?

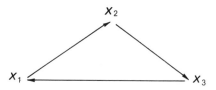

Solution Computation reveals that

$$M = \begin{bmatrix} 0 & 1 & 1 \\ 0 & 0 & 1 \\ 1 & 0 & 0 \end{bmatrix}, \quad M^2 = \begin{bmatrix} 1 & 0 & 1 \\ 1 & 0 & 0 \\ 0 & 1 & 1 \end{bmatrix}, \quad M^3 = \begin{bmatrix} 1 & 1 & 1 \\ 0 & 1 & 1 \\ 1 & 0 & 1 \end{bmatrix}$$

Now examine the diagonal entries of M^2 and M^3. Examination of M^2 reveals that there is one feedback path for X_1 and one feedback path for X_3; these are

$$X_1 \longrightarrow X_3 \longrightarrow X_1 \qquad \text{and} \qquad X_3 \longrightarrow X_1 \longrightarrow X_3$$

There are also feedback paths that occur in three stages, which can be seen by examining the diagonal entries of M^3, where we see that

$$X_1 \longrightarrow X_2 \longrightarrow X_3 \longrightarrow X_1$$

$$X_2 \longrightarrow X_3 \longrightarrow X_1 \longrightarrow X_2$$

$$X_3 \longrightarrow X_1 \longrightarrow X_2 \longrightarrow X_3$$

are three-stage feedbacks.

A Dominance Matrix Model for Leadership Identification

Example 5

Four vice-presidents who work together are being studied to determine which among them has the most influence over the others. It is known that X_1 has influence over X_2 and X_4, X_2 has influence over X_3 and X_4, X_3 has influence over X_1, and X_4 has influence over X_3. Who is the leader in terms of the strongest influences?

Solution In this problem we recognize that we have a dominance digraph with an associated asymmetric matrix:

$$
\begin{array}{c c c c c}
 & X_1 & X_2 & X_3 & X_4 \\
\begin{array}{c} X_1 \\ X_2 \\ X_3 \\ X_4 \end{array} &
\left[\begin{array}{cccc}
0 & 1 & 0 & 1 \\
0 & 0 & 1 & 1 \\
1 & 0 & 0 & 0 \\
0 & 0 & 1 & 0
\end{array}\right] &&&= M
\end{array}
$$

Notice that X_1 and X_2 each has a total of two one-stage dominances over certain other individuals. It is not clear which one of these two vice-presidents has the most influence over others. Normally a sociometric model would define the individual with the most one-stage dominances as the leader. In this case, however, we could also look at $M + M^2$ and define the most influential individual as the one with the most one- or two-stage dominances. (If need be, we could extend this to one- or two- or three-stage dominances.) In the above example we have that

$$
M + M^2 =
\left[\begin{array}{cccc}
0 & 1 & 0 & 1 \\
0 & 0 & 1 & 1 \\
1 & 0 & 0 & 0 \\
0 & 0 & 1 & 0
\end{array}\right]
+
\left[\begin{array}{cccc}
0 & 0 & 2 & 1 \\
1 & 0 & 1 & 0 \\
0 & 1 & 0 & 1 \\
1 & 0 & 0 & 0
\end{array}\right]
=
\left[\begin{array}{cccc}
0 & 1 & 2 & 2 \\
1 & 0 & 2 & 1 \\
1 & 1 & 0 & 1 \\
1 & 0 & 1 & 0
\end{array}\right]
$$

and in this case vice-president X_1 has the most one- or two-stage dominances and emerges as the leader. Note also that X_4 has the weakest degree of influence.

We should recognize, however, that this method of solution does not allow for varying strengths of influences over individuals. We therefore have to be aware of the limitations of the model and recognize that subjectivity is involved in assuming equal weights to the various influences involved. Using sophisticated interviewing techniques and psychological testing it might be possible to quantify several component factors (such as verbal persuasiveness, written persuasiveness, tenacity, etc.) and devise a more refined matrix model. Such a scheme could permit a unique composite numerical measure for each person's total influence over each other person. This probably would result in a more objective measurement for leadership identification.

Example 6

In a singles tennis tournament consisting of four players, these were the results:

MATT: three wins and zero losses
DANNY: three wins and zero losses
TOD: two wins and one loss
JORDAN: two wins and one loss

Matthew beat Danny, Tod, and Jordan
Danny beat Matthew, Tod, and Jordan
Tod beat Matthew and Jordan
Jordan beat Matthew and Danny.

Who should be delcared winner? How can we rank the players?

Solution First we examine the friendly matrix M:

$$M = \begin{array}{c} \\ M \\ D \\ T \\ J \end{array} \begin{array}{c} \begin{array}{cccc} M & D & T & J \end{array} \\ \begin{bmatrix} 0 & 1 & 1 & 1 \\ 1 & 0 & 1 & 1 \\ 1 & 0 & 0 & 1 \\ 1 & 1 & 0 & 0 \end{bmatrix} \end{array}$$

Here we see that there is no clear winner and we have two sets of ties. In this case we examine $M + M^2$ and we find that

$$M + M^2 = \begin{bmatrix} 3 & 2 & 2 & 3 \\ 3 & 2 & 2 & 3 \\ 2 & 2 & 1 & 2 \\ 2 & 2 & 2 & 2 \end{bmatrix}$$

and we declare a winning tie for Matthew and Danny. The number of one- or two-stage winnings is larger for Jordan than for Tod. Hence the rankings are

First place: Matthew and Danny
Second place: Jordan
Third place: Tod

The Identification of Cliques In studying various sociometric applications of friendly digraphs, it is sometimes useful to be able to determine which subsets of "points" have mutual (two-way) relationships between any pair of them. Below you will find two illustrations of three-element and four-element cliques and a formal definition of a clique.

Three-element clique (**ABD**)

Four-element clique (**ABCD**)

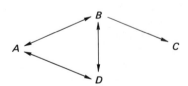

Three-element clique *(ABD)*

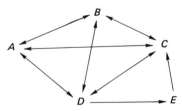

Four-element clique *(ABCD)*

> **Definition 13** In a digraph, a *clique* is the largest collection of three or more points with the property that any two of the points have one two-way communication between them.

When we looked at "feedback" we learned that if a diagonal element of M^3 is nonzero, then there is at least one three-stage path from the associated point back to itself. But for cliques we must limit ourselves to a path along bidirectional arrows only. What we could do therefore is eliminate unidirectional arrows (by replacing the corresponding matrix entries with zeros) and examine the symmetric matrix S thus formulated; then we look for nonzero entries in the main diagonal of the symmetric matrix S^3.

> **Theorem 15** Given a friendly incidence matrix $M_{n \times n}$, delete all the unidirectional entries and replace them with zeros to create a symmetric matrix S. Compute the matrix $T = S^3$. Then point X_i belongs to at least one clique if and only if $t_{ii} > 0$.

Example 7

Use Theorem 15 to verify the existence of a clique in the digraph shown.

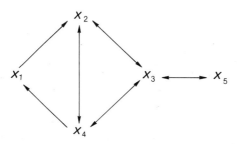

Solution First formulate the matrix M, where we have shown the unidirectional elements in bold type.

$$M = \begin{bmatrix} 0 & \mathbf{1} & 0 & 0 & 0 \\ 0 & 0 & 1 & 1 & 0 \\ 0 & 1 & 0 & 1 & 1 \\ \mathbf{1} & \mathbf{1} & 1 & 0 & 0 \\ 0 & 0 & \mathbf{1} & 0 & 0 \end{bmatrix}$$

Now replace the bold elements with zeros to form the associated symmetric matrix S; then compute $T = S^3$:

$$S = \begin{bmatrix} 0 & 0 & 0 & 0 & 0 \\ 0 & 0 & 1 & 1 & 0 \\ 0 & 1 & 0 & 1 & 1 \\ 0 & 1 & 1 & 0 & 0 \\ 0 & 0 & 1 & 0 & 0 \end{bmatrix}$$

$$T = S^3 = \begin{bmatrix} 0 & 0 & 0 & 0 & 0 \\ 0 & 2 & 4 & 3 & 1 \\ 0 & 4 & 2 & 4 & 3 \\ 0 & 3 & 4 & 2 & 1 \\ 0 & 1 & 3 & 1 & 0 \end{bmatrix}$$

Note that $t_{22} = t_{33} = t_{44} = 2 \neq 0$. Hence X_2, X_3, and X_4 belong to at least one clique. In this case we also see from the diagram that $X_2X_3X_4$ do form a clique.

Exercise 9.9 1. Construct a matrix for each of the following.

a.

b.

c.

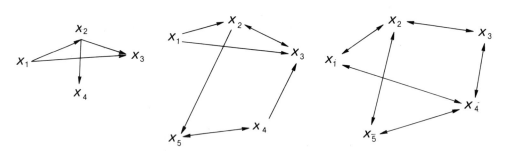

Which of the matrices is symmetric? asymmetric? neither symmetric nor asymmetric? Which digraph is a perfect communication? Which is a dominance relationship? Which is friendly?

2. Using each M (in Problem 1), compute M^2 and find the number of two-stage communications for each digraph. How many of these are two-stage feedback loops?

3. Using the friendly incidence matrix below, compute M^2, M^3, and M^4. How many two-, three-, and four-stage communications are there? Identify all feedback loops and verify by examining the associated digraph for M.

$$\begin{array}{c} \\ X_1 \\ X_2 \\ X_3 \\ X_4 \end{array} \begin{array}{cccc} X_1 & X_2 & X_3 & X_4 \\ \begin{bmatrix} 0 & 1 & 0 & 1 \\ 0 & 0 & 1 & 0 \\ 1 & 0 & 0 & 1 \\ 1 & 0 & 1 & 0 \end{bmatrix} \end{array} = M$$

4. A sociometric dominance relationship among five gang members is given below. Using $M + M^2$, find the leader and rank all of the gang members in terms of their one- and two-stage dominance strengths.

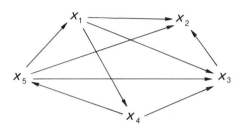

5. The following symmetric matrix corresponds to a perfect communications relationship representing diplomatic relations between five nations:

	US	USSR	Ethiopia	China	Mexico
US	0	1	0	0	1
USSR	1	0	1	1	1
Ethiopia	0	1	0	0	1
China	0	1	0	0	0
Mexico	1	1	1	0	0

a. Find the channels of communication open to each country if it is willing to speak through one intermediary.
b. If USSR cuts off diplomatic relations with Ethiopia, will it still be possible for all five countries to communicate with one another? Use the theorem on connected digraphs to verify your contention.

6. With no sexist innuendos intended, five two-way gossipers exchange gab according to the symmetric matrix below. Identify the cliques using appropriate matrix theorems and check by examining the digraph associated with the matrix M.

	Cathy	Rose	Mabel	Judy	Nina	
Cathy	0	1	1	0	1	
Rose	1	0	1	0	1	
Mabel	1	1	0	1	0	$= M$
Judy	0	0	1	0	1	
Nina	1	1	0	1	0	

*7. Solve using a computer program. (*Hint:* Make adjustments in the BASIC program found on P. 314.) Stephanie is a breakfast-food taster at General Foods. She prefers:

(a) *Krispies* over *Munchies, Snappies, Nudgies,* and *Posties*
(b) *Chockies* over *Krispies, Vities, Munchies,* and *Nudgies*
(c) *Vities* over *Krispies, Snappies, Nudgies,* and *Posties*
(d) *Snappies* over *Chockies, Munchies,* and *Posties*
(e) *Nudgies* over *Snappies* and *Posties*
(f) *Munchies* over *Nudgies, Posties,* and *Vities*
(g) *Posties* over *Chockies*

Which cereal does Stephanie like best? (Use $M + M^2$.)

9.10 Population Forecasting Models Using Matrices

At its best, population forecasting is a very difficult and complicated mathematical application. This is true because for a given geographical region a perfect model has to take into account

$$(\text{births} - \text{deaths}) + (\text{immigrants} - \text{emigrants})$$

Population forecasting models using matrix methods were first studied independently by H. Bernardelli, E. G. Lewis, and P. H. Leslie during the 1940s. Earlier methods were defective largely because birth and death rates are not consistent throughout various age levels. Matrix methods were thus developed in order to permit unique birth and death rates within each of several age groups. We will examine a simplified model for females only, and, in order to avoid overcomplications, we will ignore the effects of migrations. Suppose we consider the U.S. female population in 1975 split into three age groups:

FEMALES IN THREE AGE GROUPS

Group	1	2	3
Age-range	0–14	15–29	30–44
Population (in millions)	$p_1 = 32.8$	$p_2 = 22.7$	$p_3 = 20.4$

and an associated "Leslie" matrix

$$M = \begin{bmatrix} b_1 & b_2 & b_3 \\ s_1 & 0 & 0 \\ 0 & s_2 & 0 \end{bmatrix}$$

In the Leslie matrix

b_i = expected proportion of female births to females in group i ($i = 1$, 2, 3)

s_1 = expected proportion of females in group 1 who will survive over the next 15 years (and who will thus live to be in group 2)

s_2 = expected proportion of females in group 2 who will survive over the next 15 years (and who will thus live to be in group 3)

In actuality the birth and survivorship ratios given in a Leslie matrix should change from year to year due to varying sociological, economic, and medical influences. They would of course change radically if we were beset by some widespread disaster such as a nuclear holocaust or some terrible disease contagion. For simplification purposes, however, we will assume the ratios to be constant for each of several 15-year periods.

Let's form a column matrix for the initial (1975) female population:

$$P^{(1)} = \begin{bmatrix} 32.8 \\ 22.7 \\ 20.4 \end{bmatrix}$$

If we premultiply $P^{(1)}$ by the Leslie matrix M, we obtain

$$P^{(2)} = MP^{(1)} = \begin{bmatrix} b_1 & b_2 & b_3 \\ s_1 & 0 & 0 \\ 0 & s_2 & 0 \end{bmatrix} \begin{bmatrix} 32.8 \\ 22.7 \\ 20.4 \end{bmatrix}$$

$$= \begin{bmatrix} 32.8b_1 + 22.7b_2 + 20.4b_3 \\ \\ 32.8s_1 \\ \\ 22.7s_2 \end{bmatrix}$$

Births in previous three groups now become the new group 1 15 years later.

Survivors of old group 1 now become the new group 2 15 years later.

Survivors of old group 2 now become the new group 3 15 years later.

and the above generated column matrix $P^{(2)}$ represents the female population in the same age ranges in 1990. If we repeat the process, we have that

$$P^{(3)} = MP^{(2)} = M(MP^{(1)}) = M^2 P^{(1)} = \text{year 2005 female population column matrix}$$

This process can be continued indefinitely and we have the general result

$$P^{(k+1)} = M^k P^{(1)}$$

where

k = number of 15-year intervals projected
$P^{(1)}$ = initial female population column matrix in 1975
$P^{(k+1)}$ = future female population column matrix in the year (1975 + 15k)

Example 1

For the same 15-year intervals of age and time, assume the following Leslie matrix of birth and survivorship ratios:

$$M = \begin{bmatrix} 0.4271 & 0.8498 & 0.1273 \\ 0.9924 & 0 & 0 \\ 0 & 0.9826 & 0 \end{bmatrix}$$

Using the U.S. 1975 female column matrix

$$P^{(1)} = \begin{bmatrix} 32.8 \\ 22.7 \\ 20.4 \end{bmatrix}$$

forecast the female population for the year 2005.

Solution Here we have two 15-year intervals, hence $k = 2$. We therefore want

$$P^{(3)} = M^2 P^{(1)}$$

After computation we find that

$$M^2 = \begin{bmatrix} 1.0257 & 0.4880 & 0.0544 \\ 0.4238 & 0.8434 & 0.1264 \\ 0.9751 & 0 & 0 \end{bmatrix}$$

$$\text{and } P^{(3)} = M^2 \begin{bmatrix} 32.8 \\ 22.7 \\ 20.4 \end{bmatrix} = \begin{bmatrix} 45.8 \\ 35.6 \\ 32.0 \end{bmatrix}$$

which are the respective numbers of females alive in 2005.

Example 2

Using the same data as in Example 1, predict the female population for the year 2035.

Solution Here $k = 4$ and although a computer certainly would help, we observe that

$$M^4 = M^2M^2 = \begin{bmatrix} 1.3120 & 0.9122 & 0.1175 \\ 0.9154 & 0.9181 & 0.1296 \\ 1.0002 & 0.4759 & 0.0530 \end{bmatrix}$$

We obtain

$$P^{(5)} = M^4P^{(1)} = \begin{bmatrix} 66.1 \\ 53.5 \\ 44.7 \end{bmatrix}$$

corresponding to the year 2035.

Exercise 9.10 1. Assume the Leslie matrix in 1930 for England and Wales is given by

$$M = \begin{bmatrix} 0.2871 & 0.8241 & 0.1106 \\ 0.9836 & 0 & 0 \\ 0 & 0.9215 & 0 \end{bmatrix}$$

where we are using the same 15-year intervals of age and time as before. In 1930 the number of females in the three age categories were

$$P^{(1)} = \begin{bmatrix} 2.7 \\ 2.3 \\ 2.4 \end{bmatrix}$$

(each entry in millions). Project the female population to 1945, 1960, and 1990.

2. Locate demographic statistics on England and Wales for 1960 and compare to the results derived above.

*3. Solve the following problem using a BASIC language program. In 1964 the U.S. female population in 5-year age intervals was as follows:

0–4	10,136
5–9	10,006
10–14	9,065
15–19	8,045
20–24	6,546
25–29	5,614
30–34	5,632
35–39	6,193
40–44	6,345
45–49	5,796

where figures are in thousands. Use the Leslie matrix that follows to predict the populations for 1969, 1974, 1979, and 1984.

$$
\begin{bmatrix}
0 & 0.0010 & 0.0878 & 0.3487 & 0.4761 & 0.3377 & 0.1833 & 0.0761 & 0.0174 & 0.00 \\
0.9967 & 0 & 0 & 0 & 0 & 0 & 0 & 0 & 0 & 0 \\
0 & 0.9983 & 0 & 0 & 0 & 0 & 0 & 0 & 0 & 0 \\
0 & 0 & 0.9979 & 0 & 0 & 0 & 0 & 0 & 0 & 0 \\
0 & 0 & 0 & 0.9968 & 0 & 0 & 0 & 0 & 0 & 0 \\
0 & 0 & 0 & 0 & 0.9961 & 0 & 0 & 0 & 0 & 0 \\
0 & 0 & 0 & 0 & 0 & 0.9947 & 0 & 0 & 0 & 0 \\
0 & 0 & 0 & 0 & 0 & 0 & 0.9923 & 0 & 0 & 0 \\
0 & 0 & 0 & 0 & 0 & 0 & 0 & 0.9887 & 0 & 0 \\
0 & 0 & 0 & 0 & 0 & 0 & 0 & 0 & 0.9830 & 0
\end{bmatrix}
$$

*4. Compare the 1974 results against actual census data.

10

Applying Matrices to Linear Programming

> Of course . . . we cannot produce a minus number of products. But in mathematics the exclusion of negative values must be carefully noted. In fact, the successful development of the theory of linear programming required extensive study of the effects that this restriction would have on traditional methods of solving and analyzing equations.
>
> William W. Cooper and Abraham Charnes

10.1 The Simplex Method—Standard Linear Programming Problems

In Chapter 8 we examined a geometric method for solving linear programming problems having two variables x and y. In many applications we are certain to have more than two variables. When this occurs, it is not easy to find all of the feasible solutions so that an optimum point may be determined. In this chapter we will learn an algorithm called the *simplex method,* which will enable us to solve linear programming problems without having to determine the complete set of feasible solutions.

The simplex method was invented by George Dantzig during the late 1940s. It utilizes the matrix algebra developed in Chapter 9, and it can be applied to linear programming problems having any number of variables. It has the advantage of being readily adaptable for computer programming in case the number of variables is excessively large; this does in fact happen in real-world applications having many linear constraints.

We will introduce and illustrate the method by plunging directly into a simple example.

Example 1

Maximize $P = 5x - 2y$ subject to the constraints

$$x + 2y \leq 10$$
$$4x + y \leq 12$$
$$x \geq 0$$
$$y \geq 0$$

Solution The simplex method works with equations and not with inequalities. Thus our first procedure will be to convert each of the stated inequalities into equalities. This is accomplished by introducing some additional variables called slack variables. Examining the first constraint

$$x + 2y \le 10$$

we observe that for each pair of numbers (x, y) satisfying the inequality there must be a number u such that

$$x + 2y + u = 10$$

Thus u is the number that we would have to add to $x + 2y$ in order to increase its value to 10. Thus u "takes up the slack" in the original inequality. Similarly, we transform the second inequality $4x + y \le 12$ into the equality $4x + y + v = 12$. By introducing the slack variables u and v, we have transformed the constraints to the following system.

Constraints with Slack Variables Introduced

$$
\begin{aligned}
x + 2y + u \quad\quad\;\; &= 10 \\
4x + y \quad\quad + v \;\; &= 12
\end{aligned}
$$

with $x \ge 0$
     $y \ge 0$
     $u \ge 0$
     $v \ge 0$

Now we observe that the objective function $P = 5x - 2y$ can be written in the form $-5x + 2y + P = 0$, and the complete problem can be viewed as an attempt to find a solution to the system shown below.

We want P to be the largest possible number (where $x \ge 0$, $y \ge 0$, $u \ge 0$, and $v \ge 0$), such that

$$
\begin{aligned}
x + 2y + u \quad\quad\quad &= 10 \\
4x + y \quad\quad + v \quad\quad &= 12 \\
-5x + 2y \quad\quad\quad + P &= 0
\end{aligned}
$$

The above system is written in matrix form as

$$
\begin{bmatrix}
1 & 2 & 1 & 0 & 0 & 10 \\
4 & 1 & 0 & 1 & 0 & 12 \\
-5 & 2 & 0 & 0 & 1 & 0
\end{bmatrix}
$$

which we will refer to as the initial simplex tableau. The simplex algorithm consists of a special sequence of elementary row operations performed on the initial simplex tableau and resulting in a final simplex tableau. When correctly performed, this sequence of elementary row operations will yield an optimal solution to our problem.

Simplex Algorithm

1. Locate the smallest negative entry in the last row other than the last element. If two or more such entries have this property, select any one of them arbitrarily. If all such entries are nonnegative, the tableau is in final form.

2. Divide each positive entry, in the column defined above, into the corresponding entry of the last column.

3. Select as the *pivot* element the divisor yielding the smallest quotient.

4. Make the pivot a 1 and create 0's elsewhere in the pivot column.

5. Repeat this sequence until all such negative elements are eliminated from the last row.

The above sequence of steps guarantees (under circumstances to be described later) that we will obtain—in a very efficient manner—an equivalent final simplex tableau which represents our solution. Now we are ready to apply these steps to our example.

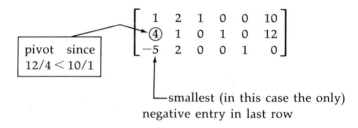

$$\begin{bmatrix} 1 & 2 & 1 & 0 & 0 & 10 \\ ④ & 1 & 0 & 1 & 0 & 12 \\ -5 & 2 & 0 & 0 & 1 & 0 \end{bmatrix}$$

pivot since
$12/4 < 10/1$

smallest (in this case the only) negative entry in last row

Once the PIVOT has been located we then make it a 1. In the example we can do this by performing the elementary row operation $(1/4)R_2$.

objective: make the PIVOT a 1 by performing $(1/4)R_2$.

$$\text{done} \rightarrow \begin{bmatrix} 1 & 2 & 1 & 0 & 0 & 10 \\ ① & 1/4 & 0 & 1/4 & 0 & 3 \\ -5 & 2 & 0 & 0 & 1 & 0 \end{bmatrix}$$

Now we can create 0's elsewhere in the pivot column by performing elementary row operations.

objective: make the entry above the PIVOT a 0 by performing
$-R_2 + R_1$

$$\text{done} \begin{bmatrix} 0 & 7/4 & 1 & -1/4 & 0 & 7 \\ ① & 1/4 & 0 & 1/4 & 0 & 3 \\ -5 & 2 & 0 & 0 & 1 & 0 \end{bmatrix}$$

objective: make the entry below the PIVOT a 0 by performing
$5R_2 + R_3$

$$\text{done} \begin{bmatrix} 0 & 7/4 & 1 & -1/4 & 0 & 7 \\ 1 & 1/4 & 0 & 1/4 & 0 & 3 \\ 0 & 13/4 & 0 & 5/4 & 1 & 15 \end{bmatrix}$$

Observe that we wanted zeros for all entries in the pivot column other than the pivot itself. This has been accomplished.

Now we ask ourselves, are there any remaining negative entries in the last row? In this case, since the answer is no, our last matrix is the final simplex tableau.

$$\begin{bmatrix} 0 & 7/4 & 1 & -1/4 & 0 & 7 \\ 1 & 1/4 & 0 & 1/4 & 0 & 3 \\ 0 & 13/4 & 0 & 5/4 & 1 & 15 \end{bmatrix}$$

no negative entries in last row

This final simplex tableau is equivalent to the following system of equations:

$$(7/4)y + u - (1/4)v = 7$$
$$x + (1/4)y + (1/4)v = 3$$
$$(13/4)y + (5/4)v + P = 15 \quad \text{MAX}(P)$$

The last equation indicates that P is a maximum of 15, which occurs when $y = v = 0$. On substituting these back into the system, we have that $x = 3$ and $u = 7$. Thus the optimal feasible solution is:

$$\max(P) = 15 \text{ when } x = 3 \text{ and } y = 0$$

Observe that the last entry of the last row in the final tableau is the maximum value of P.

Let us go through at least one more example to be sure that we understand the steps that are involved. We will analyze the procedure step-by-step in the next example.

Example 2

Maximize $P = 7x + 4y$ subject to the constraints

$$2x + y \leq 8$$
$$x + y \leq 5$$
$$x \geq 0$$
$$y \geq 0$$

Solution First we transform the constraints by introducing the slack variables u and v. The inequalities are now inequalities:

$$2x + y + u \quad\;\; = 8$$
$$x + y \quad\;\; + v = 5$$

and x, y, u, v are all non-negative. Secondly, rewrite the objective function in the form $-7x - 4y + P = 0$ and observe that the signs of the coefficients in the objective function have been reversed. Our system can now be written as

$$2x + \;y + u \qquad\quad = 8$$
$$x + \;\;y \qquad + v \qquad = 5$$
$$-7x - 4y \qquad\qquad + P = 0$$

The matrix of the above system is now our *initial simplex tableau:*

$$\begin{bmatrix} 2 & 1 & 1 & 0 & 0 & 8 \\ 1 & 1 & 0 & 1 & 0 & 5 \\ -7 & -4 & 0 & 0 & 1 & 0 \end{bmatrix}$$

We are now ready to perform our simplex algorithm.

(i)   Locate the smallest negative entry in the last row other than the last element.

$$\begin{bmatrix} 2 & 1 & 1 & 0 & 0 & 8 \\ 1 & 1 & 0 & 1 & 0 & 5 \\ -7 & -4 & 0 & 0 & 1 & 0 \end{bmatrix}$$

(ii)   Divide each positive entry, in the column defined above [in step (i)], into the corresponding entry of the last column.

$$\frac{8}{2} = 4$$ ——— divisor yielding the smallest quotient.

$$\frac{5}{1} = 5$$

(iii) Select as the pivot element the divisor yielding the smallest quotient. (The pivot is circled below.)

$$\begin{bmatrix} ② & 1 & 1 & 0 & 0 & 8 \\ 1 & 1 & 0 & 1 & 0 & 5 \\ -7 & -4 & 0 & 0 & 1 & 0 \end{bmatrix}$$

(iv) Make the pivot a 1 and create zeros elsewhere in the pivot column. (This is done by using elementary row operations.) We want the pivot to be a 1, so we perform $(1/2)R_1$.

$$\begin{bmatrix} ① & 1/2 & 1/2 & 0 & 0 & 4 \\ 1 & 1 & 0 & 1 & 0 & 5 \\ -7 & -4 & 0 & 0 & 1 & 0 \end{bmatrix}$$

Now we want zeros elsewhere in the pivot column, so we perform $-R_1 + R_2$ and then $7R_1 + R_3$.

$$\begin{bmatrix} 1 & 1/2 & 1/2 & 0 & 0 & 4 \\ 0 & 1/2 & -1/2 & 1 & 0 & 1 \\ 0 & -1/2 & 7/2 & 0 & 1 & 28 \end{bmatrix}$$

(v) Now we must repeat this sequence until all negative elements are eliminated from the last row. (Note that since we do have one negative entry in the last row, we must select a new pivot.)

(i)–(iv) repeated

$$\frac{4}{1/2} = 8$$

$$\frac{1}{1/2} = 2$$

Since $2 < 8$, the new pivot is indicated below by a circle.

$$\begin{bmatrix} 1 & 1/2 & 1/2 & 0 & 0 & 4 \\ 0 & ⑴/2 & -1/2 & 1 & 0 & 1 \\ 0 & -1/2 & 7/2 & 0 & 1 & 28 \end{bmatrix}$$

Make the new pivot into a 1.

$$\begin{bmatrix} 1 & 1/2 & 1/2 & 0 & 0 & 4 \\ 0 & ① & -1 & 2 & 0 & 2 \\ 0 & -1/2 & 7/2 & 0 & 1 & 28 \end{bmatrix}$$

Create zeros elsewhere in the new pivot column. To accomplish this we perform $(-1/2)R_2 + R_1$ and then $(1/2)R_2 + R_3$. We now have the matrix

$$\begin{bmatrix} 1 & 0 & 1 & -1 & 0 & 3 \\ 0 & 1 & -1 & 2 & 0 & 2 \\ 0 & 0 & 3 & 1 & 1 & 29 \end{bmatrix}$$

Since we now have no negative entries in the last row, this is our final simplex tableau. This final tableau is equivalent to the system of equations shown below.

$$\begin{array}{rcl} x + u - v &=& 3 \\ y - u + 2v &=& 2 \\ 3u + v + P &=& 29 \end{array}$$

The last equation indicates that P is a maximum of 29 which occurs when $u = v = 0$. On substituting these back into the system we have that $x = 3$ and $y = 2$. Thus the optimal feasible solution is

$$\max(P) = 29 \text{ when } x = 3 \text{ and } y = 2.$$

Comments: Observe that the simplex algorithm yields a final tableau that will have columns of an identity matrix above the last row as indicated

$$I_{2\times2} \quad \begin{array}{cccccc} x & y & u & v & P & \text{Solution column} \end{array}$$
$$\begin{bmatrix} \begin{pmatrix} 1 & 0 \\ 0 & 1 \end{pmatrix} & 1 & -1 & 0 & 3 \\ & -1 & 2 & 0 & 2 \\ 0 & 0 & 3 & 1 & 1 & 29 \end{bmatrix}$$

In the above example the identity matrix columns correspond to the x and y variables. This permits us to obtain an immediate answer by inspection: $x = 3$ and $y = 2$ (by noting the corresponding values in the last column), and $\max(P) =$ the last entry of the last row.

Why the Simplex Method Works Essentially the simplex method has allowed us to shift from one vertex to another in such a way that the objective function is increased the most. At each stage there may be a negative entry in the bottom row; this informs us that this vertex is not optimal and the process is to be repeated. The various shifts in the previous example are indicated below.

$$\begin{bmatrix} 2 & 1 & 1 & 0 & 0 & 8 \\ 1 & 1 & 0 & 1 & 0 & 5 \\ -7 & -4 & 0 & 0 & 1 & 0 \end{bmatrix}$$

vertex $(x, y) = (0, 0)$
(not optimal)

$$\begin{bmatrix} 1 & 1/2 & 1/2 & 0 & 0 & 4 \\ 0 & 1/2 & -1/2 & 1 & 0 & 1 \\ 0 & -1/2 & 7/2 & 0 & 1 & 28 \end{bmatrix}$$

vertex $(x, y) = (4, 0)$
(not optimal)

$$\begin{bmatrix} 1 & 0 & 1 & -1 & 0 & 3 \\ 0 & 1 & -1 & 2 & 0 & 2 \\ 0 & 0 & 3 & 1 & 1 & 29 \end{bmatrix}$$

vertex $(x, y) = (3, 2)$
(optimal)

We will accept without proof that the above-described method will always work on a standard linear programming problem as defined below.

Definition 10.1   A standard linear programming problem consists of maximizing a function $P = b_1 x_1 + \cdots + b_n x_n$

having n variables subject to the m constraints

$$a_{11} x_1 + \cdots + a_{1n} x_n \leq c_1$$
$$\vdots \qquad \qquad \vdots \qquad \vdots$$
$$a_{m1} x_1 + \cdots + a_{mn} x_n \leq c_m$$

in which all the c's are non-negative and in which all the variables are constrained to be non-negative.

Thus the simplex method will work nicely provided:

1. All the inequalities point to the left
2. All the constants on the right sides of the inequalities are non-negative
3. The variables are always non-negative
4. The objective function is to be maximized

Even if all of the above conditions are satisfied, there are a few complications that may arise.

(i)   There may be more than one "smallest negative entry in the last row." If this should happen, arbitrarily pick one of them as the pivot column.

(ii)   When the quotients are formed to determine the pivot, two or more quotients may be *equal*. If this should happen, arbitrarily pick any of the entries corresponding to a tied quotient as your pivot. It is possible to construct a few peculiar examples in which this may not work. If this happens, select one of the other entries corresponding to a tied quotient as the pivot.

The following flow chart summarizes the basic simplex method

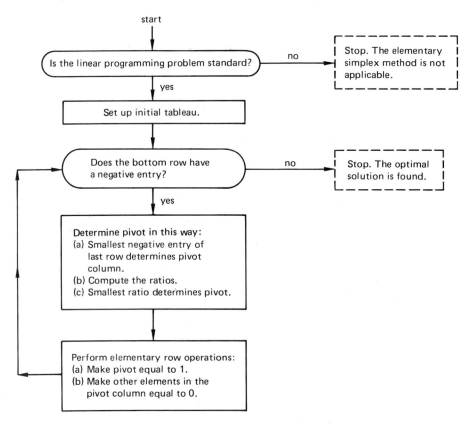

In the previous discussion we have limited ourselves to examples that are standard linear programming problems and that have unique optimal solutions. Examples that have more than one optimal solution and nonstandard linear programming problems will be considered in the last section of this chapter.

Exercise 10.1   1.   Solve this problem by inspection. Given the objective function

$$P = 4 - 2u - 5v$$

subject to the constraints

$$x = 6 - 7u - 5v$$
$$y = 8 + 2u - v$$
$$x \geq 0$$
$$y \geq 0$$
$$u \geq 0$$
$$v \geq 0$$

a. What values of u, v, x, and y will maximize P?
b. What is the maximum value of P?

2. Solve this problem by inspection. Given the simplex matrix

$$
\begin{array}{ccccc}
x & y & u & v & P \\
\end{array}
$$
$$
\begin{bmatrix}
5 & 0 & -7 & 1 & 0 & 15 \\
3 & 1 & 6 & 0 & 0 & 14 \\
-3 & 0 & -9 & 0 & 1 & 36
\end{bmatrix}
$$

a. What values of x, u, y, and v will maximize P?
b. What is the maximum value of P?

In Problems 3–10 the simplex method should be used.

3. Maximize $P = 4x + 2y$ subject to

$$x + y \leq 4$$
$$x - y \leq 2$$
$$x \geq 0$$
$$y \geq 0$$

4. Maximize $P = 20x + 30y$ subject to

$$x + 3y \leq 5$$
$$4x + y \leq 9$$
$$x \geq 0$$
$$y \geq 0$$

5. Maximize $P = x - y$ subject to

$$2x + y \leq 17$$
$$3x + 5y \leq 50$$
$$x \geq 0$$
$$y \geq 0$$

6. Maximize $P = x + y$ subject to

$$x + y \leq 9$$
$$3x - 2y \leq 6$$
$$-x + y \leq 3$$
$$x \geq 0$$
$$y \geq 0$$

7. Maximize $P = x + 2y$ subject to

$$x + y \le 4$$
$$x - y \le 2$$
$$y \le 3$$
$$x \ge 0$$
$$y \ge 0$$

8. Maximize $P = 2x + 5y$ subject to

$$x + y + z \le 2$$
$$y - z \le 0$$
$$x \le 1$$
$$x \ge 0$$
$$y \ge 0$$
$$z \ge 0$$

9. Maximize $P = 2x - 3y + 10z$ subject to

$$x + 2y + 2z \le 8$$
$$x + y + z \le 6$$
$$y - z \le 0$$
$$x \ge 0$$
$$y \ge 0$$
$$z \ge 0$$

10. (Difficult) Maximize $P = 3x + y + z$ subject to

$$2x - y + 3z \le 3$$
$$3x + y - 2z \le 2$$
$$2x + 3y - 5z \le 12$$
$$x, y, z \ge 0$$

10.2 Standard Applications

Sophisticated applications of the simplex method might utilize a computer; still, some person will have to interpret an applied situation, convert each practical constraint into an inequality, and render the problem adaptable to the simplex method before the problem can be fed into a computer.

We will illustrate the simplex method with a simple application.

Example 1

A mining company owns three mines A, B, and C, which each produce high- and low-grade coal according to the production schedule below:

Tons of coal produced each day

	High grade	Low grade
Mine A	3	2
Mine B	2	4
Mine C	4	2

The company can sell up to 960 tons of high-grade ore and up to 720 tons of low-grade ore. The net profit per day of operation is $600 per day at mine A, $300 per day at mine B, and $900 per day at mine C. How many days should each mine be operating in order to maximize profits within the company's ability to sell the ore it produces?

Solution (simplex) Let

$x =$ the number of days mine A is in operation
$y =$ the number of days mine B is in operation
$z =$ the number of days mine C is in operation

Then we want to maximize the function $P = 600x + 300y + 900z$ subject to

$$3x + 2y + 4z \leq 960$$
$$2x + 4y + 2z \leq 720$$
$$x \geq 0$$
$$y \geq 0$$
$$z \geq 0$$

Now we introduce non-negative slack variables u and v, and an initial simplex matrix is given by

$$\begin{bmatrix} 3 & 2 & ④ & 1 & 0 & 0 & 960 \\ 2 & 4 & 2 & 0 & 1 & 0 & 720 \\ -600 & -300 & -900 & 0 & 0 & 1 & 0 \end{bmatrix}$$

where the pivot is circled. For convenience we multiply the last row by 1/100:

$$\begin{bmatrix} 3/4 & 1/2 & ① & 1/4 & 0 & 0 & 240 \\ 2 & 4 & 2 & 0 & 1 & 0 & 720 \\ -6 & -3 & -9 & 0 & 0 & 0.01 & 0 \end{bmatrix}$$

Now we perform the operations $-2R_1 + R_2$, and $9R_1 + R_3$.

$$
\begin{array}{cccccc}
x & y & z & u & v & P \\
\end{array}
$$

$$
\begin{bmatrix}
3/4 & 1/2 & 1 & 1/4 & 0 & 0 & 240 \\
1/2 & 3 & 0 & -1/2 & 1 & 0 & 240 \\
3/4 & 3/2 & 0 & 9/4 & 0 & 0.01 & 2160
\end{bmatrix}
$$

This is the final simplex tableau, and it follows that $\max(P) = 216{,}000$, which occurs when $x = y = u = 0$ and $z = v = 240$. Thus mine C should be run for 240 days; mines A and B should not be run at all under the given restrictions.

Example 2

A small tax accountant firm, the Aibel tax service, wishes to determine how to allocate time between standard form tax returns and nonstandard tax returns. There are 70 h per week available for reviewing returns by a tax specialist; there are 110 h per week available for reviewing returns by a nonspecialist. Each standard form brings in $30 in revenue but requires 10 min of review time by a specialist and 30 min of review time by a nonspecialist. Each nonstandard return brings in $90 in revenue but requires 1 h of review time by a specialist and 1 h of review time by a nonspecialist. Find the optimal mix of standard and nonstandard tax returns for the Aibel tax service.

Solution Let

$x =$ the number of standard tax returns and
$y =$ the number of nonstandard tax returns

We then want to maximize $P = 30x + 90y$ subject to

$$(1/6)x + y \leq 70 = \text{total specialist hours available}$$

$$(1/2)x + y \leq 110 = \text{total nonspecialist hours available}$$

$$x \geq 0$$
$$y \geq 0$$

The initial tableau is given by

$$
\begin{array}{ccccc}
x & y & u & v & P \\
\end{array}
$$

$$
\begin{bmatrix}
1/6 & ① & 1 & 0 & 0 & 70 \\
1/2 & 1 & 0 & 1 & 0 & 110 \\
-30 & -90 & 0 & 0 & 1 & 0
\end{bmatrix}
$$

where the pivot is circled. We then have

$$\begin{bmatrix} 1/6 & 1 & 1 & 0 & 0 & 70 \\ 1/3 & 0 & -1 & 1 & 0 & 40 \\ -15 & 0 & 90 & 0 & 1 & 6300 \end{bmatrix}$$

(The $1/6$ and $1/3$ and -15 at the left; $1/3$ is circled.)

The new pivot is circled above. Pivoting again, we have

$$\begin{bmatrix} 0 & 1 & 3/2 & -1/2 & 0 & 50 \\ 1 & 0 & -3 & 3 & 0 & 120 \\ 0 & 0 & 45 & 45 & 1 & 8100 \end{bmatrix}$$

which is the final tableau. Thus the maximum weekly revenue is $8100 when the mix is optimal. The optimal mix is given by

$$x = 120 \text{ standard form tax returns}$$
$$y = 50 \text{ nonstandard tax returns}$$

It can happen that very small changes in one or more of the parameters may cause drastic changes in the solution. (See Problems 5 and 6 in Exercise 10.2 as illustrations of this.) When this occurs, we describe the situation by saying that the linear programming problem is sensitive to changes in the parameters. When the simplex method is used by scientists, business decision-makers, or economists, the subject of sensitivity analysis becomes important, especially because price fluctuations, measurement errors in cost or price, and deviations from expected distributions of resources available are often factors in realistic situations. An applied linear programming problem that is quite sensitive to small changes is a warning flag that caution must be observed by the user. A student who is interested in how sensitivity measures are developed and used in actual applications should consult an advanced reference source on linear programming.

Exercise 10.2 1. A manufacturer makes bicycles and tricycles. Her machines are in operation 75 h per week. To produce a tricycle requires 3 h of work on machine A and 1 hr of work on machine B. To produce a bicycle requires 6 h of work on machine A and 7 h on machine B. She makes $20 profit on each tricycle and $44 profit on each bicycle. How many of each should she make in order to maximize profits?

2. An ice-cream producer has the following supplies available: 12 gal of chocolate, 8 gal of vanilla, and 6 gal of strawberry. For each gallon of fudgie-mix flavor, he uses 2/3 gal of chocolate and 1/3 gal of vanilla. For each gallon of rainbow-mix flavor, he uses 1/3 gal each of vanilla, chocolate, and strawberry. He can sell rain-

bow at $2 per gallon and fudgie at $3 per gallon. How many of each type should he make to maximize his return?

3. A manufacturer has on hand 240, 420, and 300 units of raw materials A, B, and C, respectively. The manufacturer produces three products, which require the following number of units of each raw material:

		Raw materials		
		A	B	C
	I	1	3	1
Product	II	2	2	1
	III	1	2	2

Product I sells for $1, product II sells for $2, and product III sells for $3. How many of each product should be made if the manufacturer wishes to maximize his gross income?

4. A corporation manufactures products A, B, and C. The weekly production requirements are given below in numbers of hours per unit per process.

Product	Profit per unit	Milling	Drilling	Finishing
A	$80	2	2	2
B	$90	6	4	2
C	$50	4	4	6
Number Hours Per Week Available Per Process		64	24	48

a. Find the objective function for weekly production of each unit.
b. Maximize the objective function.

5. The C & S Heating Company does servicing and repair jobs which, for the purpose of this problem, are divided into minor and major jobs. The company is small. There are 40 man-hours per week available for work done by a specialist (the boss himself), and 100 man-hours per week available for work done by nonspecialists (repairmen). Each minor job brings in $26 of revenue; each major job brings in $55. Time requirements for each type of job are given in hours.

Time Requirements

	Specialist	Nonspecialist
Minor job	1/2	1/2
Major job	1	4

Assuming no other factors are relevant, determine the optimal mix for major and minor jobs. What is the maximum revenue?

6. Show that if the revenue taken in for each minor job (in Problem 5) is $28, the results are drastically different.

10.3 Special and Nonstandard Problems Using the Simplex Method—Duality

Certain difficulties can arise when we examine special situations and nonstandard problems. We will enlarge our use of the simplex method to include problems of the following types.

(A) Problems having more than one solution
(B) *Minimizing* the objective function P
(C) Maximizing objective functions of the type

$$P = b_1 x_1 + \cdots + b_n x_n + R$$

where R is a constant.
(D) Maximizing P where some of the constants on the right side of the constraint inequalities are negative.
(E) Maximizing P with mixed inequalities.
(F) Problems having no feasible points (no solution)
(G) Problems having unbounded solutions

(Problem with more than one solution)

Maximize $P = x + y$ subject to

$$2x + y \leq 8$$
$$x + y \leq 5$$
$$x \geq 0$$
$$y \geq 0$$

Solution The initial and final tableaux are shown with pivots circled.

$$\begin{bmatrix} ② & 1 & 1 & 0 & 0 & 8 \\ 1 & 1 & 0 & 1 & 0 & 5 \\ -1 & -1 & 0 & 0 & 1 & 0 \end{bmatrix} \sim \cdots$$

$$\begin{array}{cccccc} x & y & u & v & P & \\ \begin{bmatrix} 1 & 0 & 1 & -1 & 0 & 3 \\ 0 & ① & -1 & 2 & 0 & 2 \\ 0 & 0 & 0 & 1 & 1 & 5 \end{bmatrix} \end{array}$$

Note the equation resulting from the last row:

$$v + P = 5$$

P is clearly a maximum when $v = 0$. Substituting this into the first two equations, we have that

$$x = 3 - u$$
$$y = 2 + u$$

Thus $\max(P) = 5$ when $v = 0$ and when u is arbitrary within the limitation that (since x and y cannot be negative)

$$0 \le u \le 3$$

Equating the u's in the two equations above, we have that any point (x,y) satisfying $3 - x = y - 2$ will yield $\max(P) = 5$. Our solution set is therefore all x and y such that

$$x + y = 5$$

with $0 \le x \le 3$.

Minimizing the Objective Function P

Without going into all of the details, we merely point out that if we wish to minimize $P = b_1 x_1 + \cdots + b_n x_n$, we can create an equivalent problem by seeking to maximize the value of $-P$. Thus if we wanted to minimize $P = 3x - 6y$ subject to a set of linear inequalities, we could change the objective function to $C = -3x + 6y$ and our objective would then be equivalently satisfied if we maximize C.

Maximizing an Objective Function of the Type Where R Is a Constant

$$P = b_1 x_1 + \cdots + b_n x_n + R$$

Example

Maximize $P = 2x - 3y + 2$ subject to

$$-x + 2y \le 4$$
$$3x + 5y \le 21$$
$$x \ge 0$$
$$y \ge 0$$

Solution Actually the addition of a constant (either positive or negative) to the objective function will present no special difficulties. The objective function is interpreted as

$$-2x + 3y + P = 2$$

The tableaux are shown below.

$$
\begin{bmatrix}
-1 & 2 & 1 & 0 & 0 & 4 \\
③ & 5 & 0 & 1 & 0 & 21 \\
-2 & 3 & 0 & 0 & 1 & 2
\end{bmatrix}
$$

$$
\begin{bmatrix}
-1 & 2 & 1 & 0 & 0 & 4 \\
① & 5/3 & 0 & 1/3 & 0 & 7 \\
-2 & 3 & 0 & 0 & 1 & 2
\end{bmatrix}
$$

$$
\begin{bmatrix}
0 & 11/3 & 1 & 1/3 & 0 & 11 \\
① & 5/3 & 0 & 1/3 & 0 & 7 \\
0 & 19/3 & 0 & 2/3 & 1 & 16
\end{bmatrix}
$$

where the last row is equivalent to the equation

$$\frac{19}{3}y + \frac{2}{3}v + P = 16$$

Clearly P is a maximum when $y = v = 0$. When these are substituted into the equations of the first two rows, we have that $u = 11$ and $x = 7$. Thus $\max(P) = 16$ when $x = 7$ and $y = 0$ is our solution.

When a constraint constant is negative

When a Constraint Constant Is Negative

Example

Maximize $P = 2x + y + 3$ subject to

$$
\begin{aligned}
-x + 2y &\leq 4 \\
x - y &\leq -1 \\
x &\geq 0 \\
y &\geq 0
\end{aligned}
$$

Solution by the "big M" method Converting the inequalities into equalities, we have

$$
\begin{aligned}
-x + 2y + u &= 4 \\
x - y \quad + v &= -1
\end{aligned}
$$

Multiplying the second equation by -1 yields

$$-x + 2y + u \quad\quad = 4$$
$$-x + y \quad\quad - v = 1$$

The difficulty here is that there is no initial feasible solution, which is necessary for an initial tableau in the standard simplex algorithm presented in the previous section. (Note that $x = y = 0$, $u = 4$, $v = -1$ is not feasible.) To get around this problem we introduce what is called an artificial variable w and reconstruct the problem as

$$-x + 2y + u \quad\quad\quad = 4$$
$$-x + y \quad\quad - v + w = 1$$

where $w \geq 0$. (Note that $x = y = v = 0$, $u = 4$, and $w = 1$ is feasible.) Now let M be thought of as an extremely large number (say 10^9). We now let our objective function be modified using M in the following way:

Modified objective function $P' = 2x + y + 3 - Mw$

Notice that P' reduces to P when $w = 0$. Putting M into our equation in this way (M assumed very large) guarantees that P' will attain its maximum only if $w = 0$. Thus the maximum point of P' can be used to determine the maximum point of P. This method has the advantage of being adaptable to computer methods. Our generalization of the original problem now looks like the following.

Maximize $P' = 2x + y + 3 - Mw$ subject to

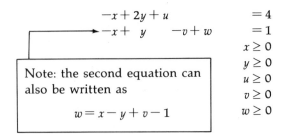

$$\begin{aligned}
-x + 2y + u \quad\quad\quad &= 4 \\
-x + y \quad\quad -v + w &= 1 \\
x &\geq 0 \\
y &\geq 0 \\
u &\geq 0 \\
v &\geq 0 \\
w &\geq 0
\end{aligned}$$

Note: the second equation can also be written as

$$w = x - y + v - 1$$

The variable w now should be eliminated from the objective function. This is easily accomplished using a rearrangement of the second equation above (boxed).

$$P' = 2x + y + 3 - M(x - y + v + 1)$$
$$= (2 - M)x + (1 + M)y - Mv - M + 3$$

Now the tableaux are generated as follows:

$$
\begin{bmatrix}
x & y & u & v & w & P' & \\
-1 & 2 & 1 & 0 & 0 & 0 & 4 \\
-1 & ① & 0 & -1 & 1 & 0 & 1 \\
-(2-M) & -(1+M) & 0 & M & 0 & 1 & -M+3
\end{bmatrix} \sim
$$

$$
\begin{bmatrix}
① & 0 & 1 & 2 & -2 & 0 & 2 \\
-1 & 1 & 0 & -1 & 1 & 0 & 1 \\
-3 & 0 & 0 & -1 & 1+M & 1 & 4
\end{bmatrix} \sim
$$

$$
\begin{bmatrix}
1 & 0 & 1 & 2 & -2 & 0 & 2 \\
0 & 1 & 1 & 1 & -1 & 0 & 3 \\
0 & 0 & 3 & 5 & -5+M & 1 & 10
\end{bmatrix}
$$

Thus the maximum value of P' is 10 and will occur when $u = v = w = 0$. This can be seen if we convert the last row into the form

$$
P = 10 - 3u - 5v - (M - 5)w
$$

The first two rows yield $x = 2$ and $y = 3$ as the optimum solution. Thus when M is large,

$$
\max(P) = \max(P') = 10
$$

when $x = 2$ and $y = 3$. Observe that we have not defined just how "large" M needs to be, but on a computer, using $M = 10^9$ will suffice in most problems in which coefficients and constants in the problem are not excessively large.

Maximizing with Mixed Inequalities

This situation can always be altered so that it can be solved as in the previous case. For example, if we had to maximize an objective function subject to the constraints

$$
\begin{aligned}
-x + 2y &\leq 6 \\
-3x + y &\geq 4
\end{aligned}
$$

we could merely multiply the second inequality by -1 to obtain the system

$$
\begin{aligned}
-x + 2y &\leq 6 \\
3x - y &\leq -4
\end{aligned}
$$

We then would proceed as in the previous case.

Problems with No Feasible Points (No Solution)

Example

Maximize $P = 2x + y$ subject to

$$x + y \leq 1$$
$$-x - y \leq -2$$

where $x \geq 0$ and $y \geq 0$.

Attempted Solution As before, introduce slack variables u and v and the artificial variable w. The problem is that of maximizing $P' = 2x + y - Mw$ subject to

$$x + y + u \qquad\quad = 1$$
$$x + y \qquad - v + w = 2$$

where u, v, and w are non-negative.

Now eliminating w in the P' equation, we have

$$P' = 2x + y - M(2 - x - y + v)$$
$$= (2 + M)x + (1 + M)y - Mv - 2M$$

The tableaux are shown below.

$$
\begin{bmatrix}
x & y & u & v & w & P & \\
① & 1 & 1 & 0 & 0 & 0 & 1 \\
1 & 1 & 0 & -1 & 1 & 0 & 2 \\
-(2+M) & -(1+M) & 0 & M & 0 & 1 & -2M
\end{bmatrix}
$$

$$
\sim
\begin{bmatrix}
1 & 1 & 1 & 0 & 0 & 0 & 1 \\
0 & 0 & -1 & -1 & 1 & 0 & 1 \\
0 & 1 & M+2 & M & 0 & 1 & -M+2
\end{bmatrix}
$$

Although it may appear that $-M + 2$ is a maximum that occurs when $x = 1$, $w = 1$, and $y = u = v = 0$, since $P' = 2x + y - Mw$, it cannot be true that P' is maximized when $w = 1$. The problem here is that the artificial variable has not been forced to zero. Thus $-M + 2$ is a pseudo-maximum. Whenever any artificial variable has a nonzero value in the final tableau, there is no feasible solution.

The above example has a very clear geometric interpretation when the constraints are graphed as in Chapter 8. We see the region obtained is entirely empty of feasible points in the figure that follows.

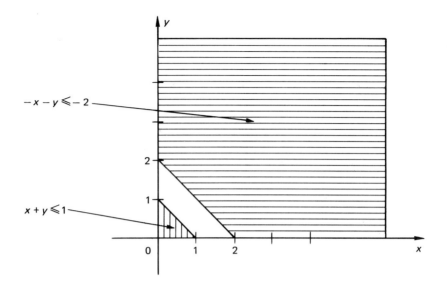

A Problem Having an Unbounded Solution

Maximize $P = 2x + y$ subject to

$$y \le 3$$
$$-x + y \le 0$$
$$x \ge 0$$
$$y \ge 0$$

Solution Observe the initial tableau:

$$\begin{bmatrix} 0 & 1 & 1 & 0 & 0 & 3 \\ -1 & 1 & 0 & 1 & 0 & 0 \\ -2 & -1 & 0 & 0 & 1 & 0 \end{bmatrix}$$

Note that it is impossible to select a pivot properly, since all of the entries in the pivot column are non-negative. (In this case this means that the variable x can be increased infinitely without the variables u and v becoming negative.)

A geometric interpretation of the above problem is given in the following figure. Note that $P = 2x + y$ does not attain a maximum on the unbounded region shown.

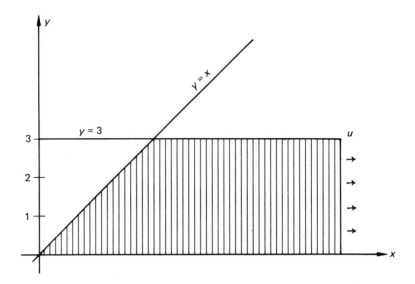

The following criteria describe unbounded situations in general:

> If, at any stage in the simplex process, a matrix tableau contains a column with no positive entries, the solution is unbounded.

Commentary: Actually the simplex method can also be adapted to handle two other special nonstandard linear programming problems: (i) cases where some of the variables can be negative, if need be, and (ii) cases in which some of the constraints are equalities rather than inequalities. These situations are beyond the scope of this text, but they can be found in the literature on linear programming at an advanced level.

Minimization and the Dual Problem Every linear programming problem has an associated dual problem. Consider the following problem:

Problem A

Maximize

$$P = 12x + 5y$$

subject to

$$
\begin{array}{ll}
5x + y \leq 26 & \text{optimal solution} \\
2x + 3y \leq 39 & (x, y) = (3, 11) \\
x \geq 0 & \\
y \geq 0 &
\end{array}
$$

The dual of this original (sometimes called the primal) problem is formulated as follows:

Problem B

Minimize

$$C = 26u + 39v$$

subject to

$$5u + 2v \geq 12 \qquad \text{optimal solution}$$
$$u + 3v \geq 5 \qquad (u,\ v) = (2,\ 1)$$
$$u \geq 0$$
$$v \geq 0$$

Now examine both problems very closely. Observe that the constants in the primal (Problem A) are "transposed" in the dual (Problem B).

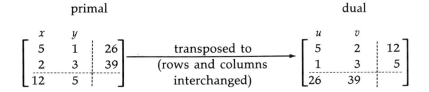

primal   dual

What is truly remarkable about the above two problems is that

$$\max(P) = \min(C)$$

which is easily verified since

$$\max(P) = 12(3) + 5(11) = 91$$
$$\min(C) = 26(2) + 39(1) = 91$$

If we had originally wanted to solve Problem B (the minimization problem), we can solve its dual (the dual of Problem B is Problem A) by the simplex method, but observe what happens:

The initial simplex tableau for Problem A is

$$\begin{bmatrix} 5 & 1 & 1 & 0 & 0 & 26 \\ 2 & 3 & 0 & 1 & 0 & 39 \\ -12 & -5 & 0 & 0 & 1 & 0 \end{bmatrix}$$

The final tableau is

$$\begin{bmatrix} 1 & 0 & 2/65 & -5/65 & 0 & 3 \\ 0 & 1 & -2/13 & 5/13 & 0 & 11 \\ 0 & 0 & 2 & 1 & 1 & 91 \end{bmatrix} \text{—solution Problem A}$$

solution Problem B

and the optimal solution to Problem B appears in the bottom row of its dual!

In more advanced work these results are generalized. Essentially, once we solve either the primal or the dual, the other is also solved because the final tableau will give the optimal solutions to both problems. Moreover, this means that we can select whichever form is the easiest to solve. This can result in considerable savings of computer time if the most economical choice (of the primal or dual) is made.

Exercise 10.3 Solve using the simplex method.

1. This problem has more than one optimal solution. Characterize all optimal solutions. Maximize

$$P = 3x + 2y$$

subject to

$$\begin{aligned} x + y &\le 5 \\ 3x + 2y &\le 12 \\ x &\ge 0 \\ y &\ge 0 \end{aligned}$$

2. This is a minimization problem. Transform the problem to an equivalent maximization problem and solve. Minimize

$$C = x - 2y$$

subject to

$$\begin{aligned} x + 3y &\le 5 \\ 4x + y &\le 9 \\ x &\ge 0 \\ y &\ge 0 \end{aligned}$$

3. Maximize the function

$$P = x + 7y + 4$$

subject to

$$\begin{aligned} 4x + 3y &\le 18 \\ 2x - y &\le 4 \\ x &\ge 0 \\ y &\ge 0 \end{aligned}$$

4. In this problem the right side of one of the inequalities is negative. Solve using the "big M" method. Maximize

$$P = 3x + 4y$$

subject to

$$
\begin{aligned}
x + 2y &\le 40 \\
-x + 3y &\le -20 \\
x &\ge 0 \\
y &\ge 0
\end{aligned}
$$

5. In this problem we have "mixed" inequalities. Convert to a problem in which the first two inequalities point $\le$, and then solve by the "big M" method. Maximize

$$P = 3x + 9y$$

subject to

$$
\begin{aligned}
-3x + 2y &\le 4 \\
-2x + y &\ge 1 \\
x &\ge 0 \\
y &\ge 0
\end{aligned}
$$

6. This problem is a combination of two types. Minimize the function

$$C = 6x + 4y$$

subject to

$$
\begin{aligned}
2x + y &\ge 3 \\
x + y &\ge 2 \\
x &\ge 0 \\
y &\ge 0
\end{aligned}
$$

7. This problem has no feasible solution. Maximize

$$P = x - 2y$$

subject to

$$
\begin{aligned}
3x + 2y &\le 6 \\
5x + 2y &\ge 20 \\
x &\ge 0 \\
y &\ge 0
\end{aligned}
$$

8. This problem has unbounded solutions. Maximize

$$P = 2x - y + 3$$

subject to

$$3x + y \geq 6$$
$$y - x \leq 2$$
$$4y - x \leq 14$$
$$x \geq 0$$
$$y \geq 0$$

9. This problem has more than one optimal solution. Characterize all optimal solutions. (An application yielding administrative options) A company owns two mines: mine A produces 1 ton of high-grade ore, 3 tons of medium-grade ore, and 2-tons of low-grade ore each day; mine B produces 3 tons of high-grade ore, 2 tons of medium-grade ore, and 1 ton of low-grade ore each day. The company needs 90 tons of high-grade ore, 130 tons of medium-grade ore and 70 tons of low-grade ore. How many days should each mine be operated if it costs $300 per day to operate mine A, and $200 per day to operate mine B?

10. This is a minimization problem. A motorcycle engine manufacturing company has an inventory of 100 engines at warehouse I and 160 engines at warehouse II. Motorcycle shops A, B, and C order 60, 80, and 120 of these engines, respectively. The costs, in dollars, of shipping one of these engines to each of the shops from I and II are as follows:

	To A	To B	To C
From I	3	2	4
From II	4	2	2

How should the orders be filled such that the shipping costs are minimized?

11. Using the simplex method on its dual, solve the following problem. Minimize

$$C = x + y$$

subject to

$$x + 2y \geq 10$$
$$2x + y \geq 14$$
$$x \geq 0$$
$$y \geq 0$$

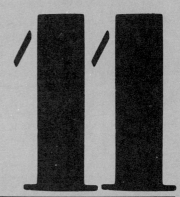

Matrix Games with
Applications

> The decision makers in our society are over-whelmingly preoccupied with power conflict, be it in business, in politics or in the military. Game theory is a science of conflict. What could this new science be but a reservoir of power for those who get there fastest with the mostest? A thorough understanding of game theory should dim these greedy hopes. Its strength derives from . . . the strategic analysis of certain conflict situations. The limitations are those inherent in the range of conflicts to which this analysis can be success-fully applied.
>
> Anatol Rapoport

11.1 Strictly Determined Zero-Sum Matrix Games

The game of *morra* is a particularly well-known pastime, especially among first-generation Italians. In it two persons simultaneously throw out one or two or three fingers each and, at the same time, each person calls out the sum total that he or she thinks will be the result. For example, the following might be the result of one game.

Person I calls out 4 and throws three fingers
Person II calls out 2 and throws one finger

Person I has won this game because he called the correct total. It is a remarkable fact that an optimal strategy exists for playing this game. In order to be able to appreciate such a strategy, we must learn the mathematics of game theory.

This theory was originally developed by J. Von Neumann, who, together with other mathematicians, dealt with optimal behavior in situations involving conflicting interests. The "game" must include a clear statement of the possible courses of action available to each player and the outcomes possible from each of the combinations of players' actions. Situations arise naturally in various recreational games, but the theory can be applied to economic problems, business decisions, and political and military strategies.

To simplify the presentation of the theory we will explain what is meant by a two-person zero-sum game. We will first consider an example that consists of an elementary form of the game of *morra*.

Elementary morra

Player I throws out one or two fingers and, simultaneously, player II throws out one or two fingers.

(i)   If the sum is 2, player I pays $10 to player II
(ii) If the sum is 4, player II pays $20 to player I
(iii) If the sum is odd, player I pays $5 to player II

If the ordered pair (x, y) represents the "finger throws" of player I and II, respectively, we then have four outcomes: $(1, 1)$, $(1, 2)$, $(2, 1)$, and $(2, 2)$.

(1, 1)	(1, 2)
I loses $10 II wins $10	I loses $5 II wins $5
(2, 1)	**(2, 2)**
I loses $5 II wins $5	I wins $20 II loses $20

The situation can be described by a simple matrix in which player I picks a row and player II picks a column.

		player II	
		column 1	column 2
player I	row 1	−10	−5
	row 2	−5	+20

Each entry in the 2×2 matrix

$$\begin{bmatrix} -10 & -5 \\ \text{\textcircled{-5}} & +20 \end{bmatrix}$$

represents the outcome with reference to player I. Thus the −10 entry is situated in row 1, column 1 (both players threw 1's) and player I lost $10 while player II won $10. The +20 entry is located in row 2 column 2 (both players threw 2's) and in this case player I wins $20 while player II loses $20.

Notice that the game can be interpreted as player I picking a row and player II (not knowing which row was picked by player I) picking a column. If this game is played repeatedly, various strategies might be tried by each player. At the outset, player I might decide to always pick row 2 to improve the chances of winning $20 in case player II picks the second column. But player II (realizing this) could always pick column 1, which would guarantee a win regardless of what player I does. Seeing what is happening, player I might decide to minimize losses by continually picking row 2. Notice that this particular game favors player II. The optimum strategies are

Player I: play row 2 (to minimize losses)
Player II: play column 1 (to guarantee a win)

The existence of these optimal strategies is guaranteed because of the nature of one of the entries in the matrix, namely, the -5 in the second row and first column. This element is the minimum in its row and the maximum in its column. When this happens, such games are called strictly determined.

In the discussion that follows, we will restrict ourselves to matrix games in which whatever is gained by player I (in any outcome) is lost by player II and vice versa; such games are called *two-person zero-sum* games.

> Definition 1   If, in a two-person game, whatever is gained by player A is lost by player B (and vice versa), then we call such a game a *zero-sum* game.

A matrix game in which one player's knowledge of his opponent's strategy does not alter his own strategy is said to be *strictly determined*. We will accept the following theorem without proof.

> Theorem 1   A zero-sum matrix game is strictly determined if and only if there exists at least one entry a_{ij} that is the minimum in row i and the maximum in column j. Moreover, this entry determines the optimum strategy for both players and
>
> If $a_{ij} > 0$, the game favors player I
> If $a_{ij} < 0$, the game favors player II
> If $a_{ij} = 0$, the game is fair

If such an entry exists, it is called a *saddle point* and it determines the *value of the game.*

Example 1

Consider the game in which player I picks a row and player II simultaneously picks a column. Each of the entries denotes the "payoff" to player I, where we interpret the game as a zero-sum game. Show that the game is strictly determined and give the best strategies for each player. Also state the value of the game.

$$\begin{bmatrix} 1 & -4 \\ 5 & -3 \end{bmatrix}$$

Solution −3 is a minimum in the second row, and a maximum in the second column. Thus the game is strictly determined. The best strategies are

Player I should always pick the second row
Player II should always pick the second column

The value of the game is −3, which is the saddle point, and thus the game favors player II.

$$\begin{bmatrix} 1 & -4 \\ 5 & -3 \end{bmatrix}$$ saddle point

Observe that player II will always pick column 2 to guarantee a win. Player I, realizing this, will pick the second row to minimize his losses.

Example 2

Analyze the matrix game below, where entries are payoffs to player I and where player I picks a row and player II picks a column.

$$\begin{bmatrix} 5 & 1 & 4 \\ 6 & -1 & 2 \\ 2 & 1 & 3 \end{bmatrix}$$

Solution We list the minimum of each row and the maximum of each column.

$$\begin{bmatrix} 5 & 1 & 4 \\ 6 & -1 & -2 \\ 2 & 1 & 3 \end{bmatrix}$$

	row minima
	1
	−2
	1

column maxima   6   1   4

In this case there are two saddle points (circled). The value of the game is +1, which favors player I. These are the optimum strategies.

Player I should pick either row 1 or row 3 (it does not matter which)
Player II should pick column 2

With a little thought the student will be able to see that if there is more than one saddle point, the value of the game must still be the same, that is, the saddle point entries must be identical.

Example 3

Show that the following game is not strictly determined.

$$\begin{bmatrix} -3 & 2 \\ 5 & -1 \end{bmatrix}$$

Solution The matrix has no saddle point, as can be seen in the following analysis.

$$\begin{array}{cc} & \text{row minima} \\ \begin{bmatrix} -3 & 2 \\ 5 & -1 \end{bmatrix} & \begin{array}{c} -3 \\ -1 \end{array} \end{array}$$

$$\begin{array}{ccc} \text{column maxima} & 5 & 2 \end{array}$$

Thus the game is not strictly determined.

Example 4

Two northeastern power companies, A and B, can each develop one new installation in any one of three counties: Putnam, Dutchess, and Westchester. Although each installation will stimulate new customers for both companies, they will be in competition against one another. Each entry in the matrix below represents the difference between the number of additional customers gained by company A and the number of additional customers gained by company B for the various location options available to each company. What is the best strategy for company A to follow if it wishes to maximize its opportunity for a competitive advantage over company B? Knowing all the same facts, what is the best counterstrategy for company B?

		Company *B*		
		Putnam	Dutchess	Westchester
Company *A*	Putnam	3000	2000	1000
	Dutchess	1000	−4000	−3000
	Westchester	−2000	−1000	500

Solution Note the saddle point in the matrix below (circled).

$$\begin{bmatrix} 3000 & 2000 & \boxed{1000} \\ 1000 & -4000 & -3000 \\ -2000 & -1000 & 500 \end{bmatrix} \quad \text{saddle point}$$

Thus these are the optimum strategies:

Company A should locate in Putnam
Company B should locate in Westchester

The "game" favors company A, however. Thus company A will have 1000 *more* additional customers than company B.

Exercise 11.1 In examples 1–7, Determine if the game is strictly determined or not. For those that are, state the value of the game.

1. $\begin{bmatrix} 2 & -2 \\ 5 & -1 \end{bmatrix}$

2. $\begin{bmatrix} -2 & 0 \\ 0 & 5 \end{bmatrix}$

3. $\begin{bmatrix} -2 & 1 \\ 1 & -6 \end{bmatrix}$

4. $\begin{bmatrix} x & 5 \\ x & -2 \end{bmatrix}$

5. $\begin{bmatrix} 1 & -1 & -1 \\ -2 & 2 & -2 \\ -3 & -3 & 3 \end{bmatrix}$

6. $\begin{bmatrix} 1 & -1 & -1 \\ 2 & -2 & -2 \\ -3 & -3 & 3 \end{bmatrix}$

7. $\begin{bmatrix} 1 & -1 & 3 & -4 \\ 2 & -3 & 2 & 0 \\ -2 & -1 & 1 & 3 \\ -1 & 0 & 1 & 2 \end{bmatrix}$

8. Consider the familiar game of "once-twice-three-shoot," in which each of two players simultaneously throws out either one or two fingers. If the sum is even, player I pays 1¢ to player II. If the sum is odd, player II pays 1¢ to player I. Show that this game is not strictly determined.

9. Consider the game of "patsy," in which each of two players simultaneously throws out either one or two or three fingers. If the

product of the fingers shown is even, player II must pay the number of dollars indicated by that product to player I. If the product of the fingers shown is odd, player I must pay the number of dollars indicated by that product to player II. Show that this game is strictly determined. Who has the advantage and what is the value of the game? What is each player's optimum strategy?

10. Show that if the word "product" (in the previous example) were replaced with the word "sum," the game would not be strictly determined.

11. Fastfood and Quiktrix can each put up new stores in any one of three towns: Rye, Scarsdale, and Harrison. Although new stores will stimulate new customers for both companies, they will be in competition against one another. Each entry in the matrix below represents the difference between the number of additional hamburgers sold by Fastfood and the number of additional hamburgers sold by Quiktrix for the various location options available to each company. What is the best strategy for Fastfood to follow if it wishes to maximize its opportunity for a competitive hamburger advantage over Quiktrix? Knowing all the same facts, what is the best counterstrategy for Quiktrix?

Quiktrix

		Rye	Scarsdale	Harrison
	Rye	6000	2000	4000
Fastfood	Scarsdale	2000	−6000	−8000
	Harrison	−4000	1000	−2000

(Each entry is on a monthly basis.)

12. Show that Fastfood would have a definite disadvantage if the data were as shown below. Discuss the optimal location options for each company.

Quiktrix

		Rye	Scarsdale	Harrison
	Rye	−2000	2000	1000
Fastfood	Scarsdale	−4000	3000	−1000
	Harrison	−2000	−1000	0

*13. Find necessary and sufficient conditions for the matrix

$$\begin{bmatrix} a & b \\ b & c \end{bmatrix}$$

to be strictly determined.

11.2 Mixed Strategies for Nonstrictly Determined Matrix Games

Consider the following matrix game. It does not have a saddle point.

$$M = \begin{bmatrix} 3 & -1 \\ -2 & 4 \end{bmatrix}$$

The entries are dollar gains or losses. Suppose once again that player I picks a row, player II picks a column, and the entries of matrix M are the payoffs relative to player I. Player I, hoping to maximize possible gains, picks row 2. Player II, knowing his opponent's strategy, picks column 1 for a win of $2. But if player I was going to pick row 1, and player II knew it, player II would alter his former strategy and pick column 2 for a win of $1.

If the above game were to be played repeatedly, it would be very unwise for player I to pick consistently one row only. Likewise it would be disadvantageous for player II to pick consistently one column only. Some kind of a mixed strategy is required for each player.

The Value of a Now suppose that each player decides on a certain specific mixed strat-
Game for a egy. For example, player I might decide to pick a row randomly by
Particular Mix picking the first row 50% of the time and the second row 50% of the time. Player II might decide to pick his columns randomly by picking the first column 80% of the time and the second 20% of the time. (Player II might reason that it is to his advantage to "lean more heavily" in favor of column 1 because in that column he stands to win more and lose less.) Both players will have to do their selecting *randomly:* no pattern of plays that would reveal subsequent plays should be discernible. There are four possible situations that can arise during each play:

row 1–column 1   row 1–column 2

row 2–column 1   row 2–column 2

The probabilities of each of the events can be listed as entries in the matrix below.

$$\begin{bmatrix} (1/2)(4/5) & (1/2)(1/5) \\ (1/2)(4/5) & (1/2)(1/5) \end{bmatrix} = \begin{bmatrix} .4 & .1 \\ .4 & .1 \end{bmatrix}$$

Note that the sum of the probability entries is 1. We can now compute the expectation of each possible outcome by multiplying each payoff by its respective probability. The result is given below in the form of a matrix.

$$\begin{bmatrix} .4(\$3) & .1(-\$1) \\ .4(-\$2) & .1(\$4) \end{bmatrix} = \begin{bmatrix} \$1.20 & -\$0.10 \\ -\$0.80 & \$0.40 \end{bmatrix}$$

The total of the expectations is $\$1.20 - \$0.10 - \$0.80 + \$0.40 = + \$0.70$, which is positive, making the game favorable to player I. Using matrix multiplication, we could have computed the above result using the product form:

$$[1/2 \quad 1/2] \begin{bmatrix} 3 & -1 \\ -2 & 4 \end{bmatrix} \begin{bmatrix} 4/5 \\ 1/5 \end{bmatrix} = \$0.70$$

The idea developed in the previous example can be generalized to any $m \times n$ matrix.

> **Definition 2**   Given a matrix game defined by the payoff matrix P, the row matrix S_1, and the column matrix S_2 defining the strategic probabilities of row player I and column player II, respectively, the *value of the game* is the sum of the expectations given by the matrix product
>
> $$V = S_1 P S_2$$

Example 1

Find the value of the matrix game given by the payoff matrix

$$P = \begin{bmatrix} 4 & -2 \\ -3 & 1 \end{bmatrix}$$

where the strategies employed are as follows:

$$\text{Player I: } S_1 = [1/4 \quad 3/4]$$
$$\text{Player II: } S_2 = \begin{bmatrix} 1/3 \\ 2/3 \end{bmatrix}$$

Interpret your results.

Solution The value of the game is

$$V = S_1 P S_2 = [1/4 \quad 3/4] \begin{bmatrix} 4 & -2 \\ -3 & 1 \end{bmatrix} \begin{bmatrix} 1/3 \\ 2/3 \end{bmatrix}$$

$$= [-5/4 \quad 1/4] \begin{bmatrix} 1/3 \\ 2/3 \end{bmatrix} = -\$0.25$$

V is negative and the game is favorable to player II, who will have, in the long run, expected winnings averaging $0.25 per game played.

Example 2

Find the value of the matrix game defined by the payoff matrix

$$P = \begin{bmatrix} 5 & 1 & 4 \\ 6 & -1 & 2 \\ 2 & 1 & 3 \end{bmatrix}$$

where the strategies employed by players I and II, respectively, are given by

$$S_1 = [0 \quad 0 \quad 1]$$

$$S_2 = \begin{bmatrix} 0 \\ 1 \\ 0 \end{bmatrix}$$

Solution First observe that player I intends to pick row 3 *always* and player II intends to pick column 2 *always*. The value V of the game is (not surprisingly, as we shall see) 1:

$$V = [0 \quad 0 \quad 1] \begin{bmatrix} 5 & 1 & 4 \\ 6 & -1 & 2 \\ 2 & ① & 3 \end{bmatrix} \begin{bmatrix} 0 \\ 1 \\ 0 \end{bmatrix} = 1$$

This is not surprising because 1 also happens to be an entry in the P matrix that is a saddle point (circled above). Thus the game is strictly determined and matrices S_1 and S_2 as they are given represent the optimum strategies that should be followed by each player. The game favors player I, who will win $1 on each play.

Example 3

Given the matrix game with payoffs given by

$$\begin{bmatrix} 4 & -2 \\ -1 & 3 \end{bmatrix}$$

where player I has the strategy $S_1 = [1/16 \quad 15/16]$, what strategy would player II have to follow for the game to be exactly fair?

Solution Here we want the value of the game to be $V = 0$. We can write

$$S_2 = \begin{bmatrix} a \\ 1 - a \end{bmatrix}$$

where we require that $S_1 P S_2 = 0$, so that we must have

$$[1/16 \quad 15/16] \begin{bmatrix} 4 & -2 \\ -1 & 3 \end{bmatrix} \begin{bmatrix} a \\ 1-a \end{bmatrix} = 0$$

which yields $a = 43/54$ as a solution. Hence a strategy for player II that would make the game fair is given by

$$S_2 = \begin{bmatrix} 43/54 \\ 11/54 \end{bmatrix}$$

Example 4

An aircraft carrier detects an enemy warship 50 mi away. It is known that the enemy ship is either a battleship or a destroyer, but the radar instruments cannot distinguish between the two types of ships. The aircraft carrier plans an attack on the enemy ship. The carrier has three types of armaments to use: long-range torpedoes, rockets, and fighter planes. The probabilities for a lethal hit with each of these devices against either type of ship are given below. For example, the probability of a lethal hit with a rocket against a destroyer is .04. Assuming there is a 50% probability the enemy ship is a battleship and 50% probability the enemy ship is a destroyer, find the "value of the game" for two types of mixed barrage attacks under consideration:

attack A: $S_1 = [1/8 \quad 1/4 \quad 5/8]$,
attack B: $S_1 = [1/8 \quad 3/8 \quad 1/2]$.

Here each entry is the relative proportion of torpedoes, rockets, and fighter planes directed against the enemy ship.

		enemy ship	
		destroyer	battleship
aircraft carrier	long-range torpedo	.01	.03
	rocket	.04	.01
	fighter plane	.05	.02

Which attack is the optimum strategy for the aircraft carrier?

Solution First observe that since there are equal likelihoods that the enemy ship is a battleship or a destroyer, the "strategy matrix" for the enemy ship (player II) is

$$S_2 = \begin{bmatrix} 1/2 \\ 1/2 \end{bmatrix}$$

The value of attack A is given by

$$V_A = [1/8 \quad 1/4 \quad 5/8] \begin{bmatrix} .01 & .03 \\ .04 & .01 \\ .05 & .02 \end{bmatrix} \begin{bmatrix} 1/2 \\ 1/2 \end{bmatrix} = .030625$$

The value of attack B is given by

$$V_B = [1/8 \quad 3/8 \quad 1/2] \begin{bmatrix} .01 & .03 \\ .04 & .01 \\ .05 & .02 \end{bmatrix} \begin{bmatrix} 1/2 \\ 1/2 \end{bmatrix} = .05$$

These results may be interpreted in the following way. Suppose a total of 100 torpedoes, rockets, and fighter planes are launched against the enemy ship. Using strategy A, the probability of a lethal hit would be

$$1 - (1 - .030625)^{100} = 95.5\%$$

Using strategy B, the probability of a lethal hit would be

$$1 - (1 - .05)^{100} = 99.4\%$$

Thus the optimum (of the two strategies) is strategy B. Notice that the respective value of each game strategy is the expected probability of a hit if one device could theoretically be divided up in the given proportions and launched "fractionally" against the enemy.

Notice that in the above problem the question remains, what is the optimal mixed strategy that could be devised for player I if all possible strategies were under consideration. This is the subject of the next section.

Exercise 11.2 1. Find the value of the matrix game

$$\begin{bmatrix} 1 & -5 \\ -2 & 3 \end{bmatrix}$$

   a. If player I plays the first row 30% of the time and the second row 70% of the time and player II plays the first column 20% of the time and the second column 80% of the time
   b. If the players play according to

$$S_1 = [1/2 \quad 1/2]$$

and

$$S_2 = \begin{bmatrix} 1/2 \\ 1/2 \end{bmatrix}$$

2. Given the matrix game below, where

$$S_1 = \begin{bmatrix} 1/3 & 1/3 & 1/3 \end{bmatrix}$$

$$S_2 = \begin{bmatrix} 1/4 \\ 1/4 \\ 1/2 \end{bmatrix}$$

Show that the game is not strictly determined.
Find the value of the game.

$$\begin{bmatrix} 1 & 2 & 3 \\ 2 & -6 & -3 \\ 0 & 1 & -2 \end{bmatrix}$$

*3. Find criteria for a, b, c and d so that the game below is strictly determined.

$$\begin{bmatrix} a & b \\ c & d \end{bmatrix}$$

4. Given the matrix game below in which the strategies are

$$S_1 = \begin{bmatrix} p & 1-p \end{bmatrix} \quad \text{and} \quad S_2 = \begin{bmatrix} 1/2 \\ 1/2 \end{bmatrix}$$

$$\begin{bmatrix} 2 & 0 \\ -6 & 1 \end{bmatrix}$$

Find the value of p so the game is fair (that is, the value is 0).

5. Show that if

$$S_2 = \begin{bmatrix} 1/8 \\ 7/8 \end{bmatrix}$$

then no matter what strategy player I follows, the game can never be fair. Who has the advantage?

$$\begin{bmatrix} -3 & 2 \\ 1 & 0 \end{bmatrix}$$

6. Player I and player II decide to play a coin matching game several hundred times. In each game a player uses a dime, a nickel, and

a quarter. Each player selects one coin and places it under a cup (unseen by the opponent). At a given signal, both cups are lifted and the coins are revealed. If they match, player I keeps both coins. If they do not match, player II keeps both coins. Both players decide to select each of the three coins in a random sequence but to include pennies, nickels, and quarters each one-third of the time. Does either player have an advantage?

player II

		penny	nickel	quarter
	penny	1	−1	−1
Player I	nickel	−5	5	−5
	quarter	−25	−25	25

7. Two antiviral serums mycin A and mycin B have the probabilities of destroying flu viruses flu 1 and flu 2 given in the matrix below. For example, the probability of serum mycin A killing flu 1 is .7. From medical and statistical studies it is known that those infected with flu either have flu 1 or flu 2 in the ratio of 2 to 1, respectively. However, it is prohibitively expensive for a doctor to perform tests on every infected patient to determine which serum would be best. Doctors are considering a mixed serum of two types:

$$S_1 = [1/2 \quad 1/2] \quad \text{and} \quad S_2 = [3/8 \quad 5/8]$$

where each entry is the relative proportion of the type of mycin drug to be included in the serum mixture. Which of the two mixed strategies would give the greater expected probability of being effective?

viruses

		flu 1	flu 2
serums	mycin A	.7	.1
	mycin B	.4	.6

Which strategy would be correct if, during the following year, the infected flu patients had flu 1 or flu 2 in the ratio of 1 to 1?

11.3   Optimal Mix in Nonstrictly Determined 2 × 2 Matrix Games

In cases where the matrix game is strictly determined, we know how to optimize the strategies for each player: choose a saddle point. It is clear that in nonstrictly determined games that will be repeatedly played, some kind of mix might be determined that would maximize the expectation for player I. Also it might be possible to determine a mix that would minimize the expected losses of player II.

Example 1

Consider the nonstrictly determined matrix game

$$\begin{bmatrix} \$3 & -\$1 \\ -\$2 & \$4 \end{bmatrix}$$

with strategies

$$S_1 = \begin{bmatrix} x & 1-x \end{bmatrix} \quad \text{and} \quad S_2 = \begin{bmatrix} z \\ 1-z \end{bmatrix}$$

Find x so that player I will achieve maximum expected gains; and find z so that player II will achieve minimum expected losses.

Solution If player II chooses column 1, then player I can expect to earn y dollars, where

$$y = \begin{bmatrix} x & 1-x \end{bmatrix} \begin{bmatrix} 3 \\ -2 \end{bmatrix} = 3x - 2(1-x) = 5x - 2$$

Similarly if player II chooses column 2, then player I can expect to earn y dollars, where

$$y = \begin{bmatrix} x & 1-x \end{bmatrix} \begin{bmatrix} -1 \\ 4 \end{bmatrix} = -x + 4(1-x) = -5x + 4$$

Both of these equations are graphed below. Player I wishes to maximize a guaranteed expected return. This occurs at the intersection point $(3/5, 1)$.

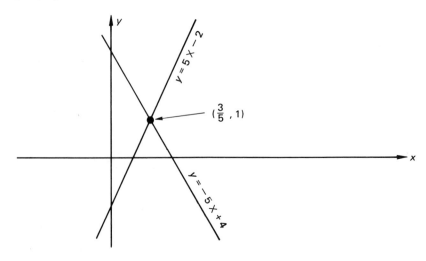

The optimal strategic mix for player I is thus

$$S_1 = [x \quad 1 - x] = [3/5 \quad 2/5]$$

Now consider the reasoning of player II. If player I chooses row 1, then player II can expect to earn y dollars, where

$$y = [3 \quad -1] \begin{bmatrix} z \\ 1 - z \end{bmatrix} = 3z - (1 - z) = 4z - 1$$

Similarly if player I chooses row 2, then player II can expect to earn y dollars where

$$y = [-2 \quad 4] \begin{bmatrix} z \\ 1 - z \end{bmatrix} = -2z + 4(1 - z) = -6z + 4$$

Both of these equations are graphed below. Player II wishes to minimize expected losses (or maximize a guaranteed expected value y) which occurs at the intersection point $(1/2, 1)$.

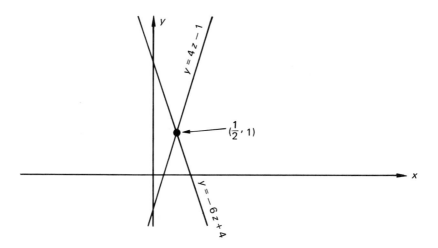

The optimal strategic mix for player II is thus

$$S_2 = \begin{bmatrix} z \\ 1 - z \end{bmatrix} = \begin{bmatrix} 1/2 \\ 1/2 \end{bmatrix}$$

The value of the game is

$$V = S_1 P S_2 = [3/5 \quad 2/5] \begin{bmatrix} 3 & -1 \\ -2 & 4 \end{bmatrix} \begin{bmatrix} 1/2 \\ 1/2 \end{bmatrix} = 1$$

Von Neumann showed that in games such as the above, the expected winnings for the row player are the same (in absolute value) as the expected losses for the column player. The method used in the above problem can be generalized to any 2×2 zero-sum matrix game. This is given in the theorem below, which is not only capable of being proved by any student, but is a truly remarkable result!

Theorem 2 (optimum mix for any 2×2 zero-sum matrix game)
Given a payoff matrix P given by

$$P = \begin{bmatrix} a & b \\ c & d \end{bmatrix}$$

where $a + d - b - c \neq 0$, the optimal mix for player I is given by

$$S_1 = \begin{bmatrix} p & 1-p \end{bmatrix}$$

and the optimal mix for player II is given by

$$S_2 = \begin{bmatrix} q \\ 1-q \end{bmatrix}$$

where

$$p = \frac{d-c}{a+d-b-c} \text{ and } q = \frac{d-b}{a+d-b-c}.$$

The expected value V of the game is then given by

$$V = \frac{ad-bc}{a+d-b-c}$$

Example 2

Determine the optimal mix for each player in the matrix game

$$P = \begin{bmatrix} 5 & -2 \\ -1 & 3 \end{bmatrix}$$

and find the value V of the game.

Solution Using Theorem 2, we find

$$p = \frac{3-(-1)}{5+3-(-2)-(-1)} = \frac{4}{11}$$

and

$$q = \frac{3 - (-2)}{5 + 3 - (-2) - (-1)} = 5/11$$

Thus the optimal mix for each player will be

$$S_1 = [4/11 \quad 7/11]$$

for player I and

$$S_2 = \begin{bmatrix} 5/11 \\ 6/11 \end{bmatrix}$$

for player II. The value V of the game is

$$V = \frac{(5)(3) - (-1)(-2)}{11} = \frac{13}{11} > 0$$

which means the game favors player I.

Example 3

Elia and Lou decide to play a coin game 300 times. Here's how the game works: each person must have a nickel and a quarter. Each person will select one of the coins (secretly) and place it under a cup. At a given signal, both cups are lifted. If they match, Elia keeps both coins. If they do not match, Lou keeps both coins. Determine the optimum strategies for both Elia and Lou. Determine the value of this game.

Solution The game can be represented by the matrix below

Lou

$$\begin{array}{c} \\ \text{Elia} \end{array} \begin{array}{cc} & \begin{array}{cc} \text{nickel} & \text{quarter} \end{array} \\ \begin{array}{c} \text{nickel} \\ \text{quarter} \end{array} & \begin{bmatrix} 5 & -5 \\ -25 & 25 \end{bmatrix} \end{array}$$

in which Elia "picks a row" and Lou "picks a column." Note that each entry is the amount won (or lost) relative to Elia. First we observe that the game is not strictly determined because there is no saddle point. Using the theorem, we have

$$p = \frac{25 - (-25)}{5 + 25 - (-5) - (-25)} = \frac{50}{60} = 5/6,$$

Hence $1 - p = 1/6$. Thus Elia's optimal strategy is

$$S_1 = [5/6 \quad 1/6]$$

For Lou, we have

$$q = \frac{25 - (-5)}{60} = \frac{30}{60} = 1/2$$

Hence $1 - q = 1/2$.

Thus Lou's optimal strategy is

$$S_2 = \begin{bmatrix} 1/2 \\ 1/2 \end{bmatrix}.$$

If 300 games are to be played, Lou and Elia should have a random "mix" that results in the given proportions. Elia should play 250 nickels and 50 quarters; Lou should play 150 nickels and 150 quarters. Both players must be sure that no determinable "pattern" can be perceived in the distribution. If a pattern could be observed, then an opponent could alter the strategy and improve his or her expectation. The value V in the above game is

$$V = \frac{(5)(25) - (-5)(-25)}{60} = 0$$

and the game is fair.

What to Do   Consider again the game in Example 3.
When an
Opponent's   Lou
Strategy is
Known   nickel   quarter

$$\begin{array}{c} \\ \text{Elia} \end{array} \begin{array}{c} \text{nickel} \\ \\ \text{quarter} \end{array} \begin{bmatrix} 5 & -5 \\ -25 & 25 \end{bmatrix}$$

in which it was determined that the optimal strategies are

$$S_1 = (5/6 \quad 1/6) \quad \text{and} \quad S_2 = \begin{bmatrix} 1/2 \\ 1/2 \end{bmatrix}$$

It would give us insight into the meaning of these "strategies" to ask the following question, what should you (Elia) do if your opponent's strategy is known?

Example 4

What should you do if you know your opponent's strategy is optimal? In this case it is known that Lou intends to stick to

$$S_2 = \begin{bmatrix} 1/2 \\ 1/2 \end{bmatrix}$$

It turns out that for *any* p, where $S_1 = [p \quad 1 - p]$, the value of the game is unchanged, for

$$V = [p \quad 1 - p] \begin{bmatrix} 5 & -5 \\ -25 & 25 \end{bmatrix} \begin{bmatrix} 1/2 \\ 1/2 \end{bmatrix} = 0$$

If Lou sticks to optimal strategy, then Elia can use *any* strategy, and the value of the game will be the same as the value when both players used optimal strategies!

Example 5

If Elia maintains optimal strategy at

$$S_1 = [5/6 \quad 1/6]$$

and Lou alters his strategy to

$$S_2 = \begin{bmatrix} q \\ 1 - q \end{bmatrix}$$

where $q \neq 1/2$, what will the value of the game be? Here again

$$V = [5/6 \quad 1/6] \begin{bmatrix} 5 & -5 \\ -25 & 25 \end{bmatrix} \begin{bmatrix} q \\ 1 - q \end{bmatrix} = 0$$

and the game is *still* fair!

Example 6

What could happen if both players depart from optimal strategies? The answer to this is that one of the players might have an advantage. Suppose, for example,

$$S_1 = [1/4 \quad 3/4] \quad \text{and} \quad S_2 = \begin{bmatrix} 1/3 \\ 2/3 \end{bmatrix}$$

Then we have

$$V = [1/4 \quad 3/4] \begin{bmatrix} 5 & -5 \\ -25 & 25 \end{bmatrix} \begin{bmatrix} 1/3 \\ 2/3 \end{bmatrix} = +35/6$$

which is a decided advantage for Elia.

Example 7

Suppose you (Elia) *know* that Lou will depart from optimal strategy and that he will use

$$S_2 = \begin{bmatrix} 1/3 \\ 2/3 \end{bmatrix}$$

What will Elia's new optimal strategy be? Here Elia wants to select p for $S_1 = [p \quad 1 - p]$ so that V will be a maximum in the expression

$$V = [p \quad 1 - p] \begin{bmatrix} 5 & -5 \\ -25 & 25 \end{bmatrix} \begin{bmatrix} 1/3 \\ 2/3 \end{bmatrix} = \frac{-30p + 25}{3}$$

Thus maximum V will occur when $p = 0$, which will result in $\max(V) = 25/3$. To produce this maximum V, Elia must follow the strategy

$$S_1 = [0 \quad 1]$$

In other words, *she should always play quarters!*

It is possible to make certain general statements concerning illustrations of the 2×2 type above:

1. It does not matter what you do if your opponent sticks to optimal strategy; the value of the game is unchanged
2. If both players depart from optimal strategies, the value of the game may change
3. If your opponent departs from optimal strategy, then your best strategy is only one of the following: either $[0 \quad 1]$ or $[1 \quad 0]$

The above statements are embodied in the following theorem, the proof of which is left as a classroom exercise.

Theorem 2:   Given a non-strictly determined 2×2 matrix game with payoff matrix $P = \begin{bmatrix} a & b \\ c & d \end{bmatrix}$, optimal strategies $S_1 = [p \quad 1 - p]$ and $S_2 = \begin{bmatrix} q \\ 1 - q \end{bmatrix}$ and value V_0 of the game. Then

(i) if player II chooses strategy $S_2^* = \begin{bmatrix} r \\ 1-r \end{bmatrix}$ with $r \neq q$ then the revised *optimal strategy* S_1^* for player I is only one of the following: either [0 1] or [1 0];

(ii) for *any* strategies T_1 and T_2, $T_1 P S_2 = S_1 P T_2 = V_0$.

Example 8

In the previously described coin-matching game

$$\begin{bmatrix} 5 & -5 \\ -25 & 25 \end{bmatrix}$$

player II (Lou) decides to depart from optimal strategy and use

$$S_2^* = \begin{bmatrix} 7/8 \\ 1/8 \end{bmatrix}.$$

Find player I's optimal strategy and the value of the game with best strategy.

Solution Recall that the game was fair when player II used his optimal strategy

$$S_2 = \begin{bmatrix} 1/2 \\ 1/2 \end{bmatrix}.$$

In this case, therefore, $7/8 \neq 1/2$. Checking [1 0] and [0 1], we have

$$[1 \quad 0] \begin{bmatrix} 5 & -5 \\ -25 & 25 \end{bmatrix} \begin{bmatrix} 7/8 \\ 1/8 \end{bmatrix} = +3.75 \text{ and}$$

$$[0 \quad 1] \begin{bmatrix} 5 & -5 \\ -25 & 25 \end{bmatrix} \begin{bmatrix} 7/8 \\ 1/8 \end{bmatrix} = -18.75.$$

Thus player I's optimal strategy is [1 0] and she should always play nickels (row 1).

Exercise 11.3   1. Explain why the following matrix games are not strictly determined.

a. $\begin{bmatrix} 6 & 2 \\ 1 & 7 \end{bmatrix}$

b. $\begin{bmatrix} 5 & -4 \\ -3 & 10 \end{bmatrix}$

c. $\begin{bmatrix} -5 & 3 \\ 1 & 0 \end{bmatrix}$

2. Find the optimal strategy for both players in each of the above games. Find the value of each game, and state which player has the advantage.

3. Played repeatedly, the following game is a losing proposition for player I:

$$\begin{bmatrix} -3 & 2 \\ 1 & 4 \end{bmatrix}$$

   a. What optimal mix should player I maintain if she has absolutely no idea what strategy will be used by player II?
   b. Suppose player II sticks to the strategy

   $$S_2 = \begin{bmatrix} 3/5 \\ 2/5 \end{bmatrix}$$

   and this fact is known to player I. Show that player I can maintain *any* mix but her losses will be the same.
   c. Suppose player II sticks to the strategy

   $$S_2 = \begin{bmatrix} 4/7 \\ 3/7 \end{bmatrix}$$

   and this fact is known to player I. What is the best strategy for player I? Find the value of the game.
   d. Suppose player II sticks to the strategy

   $$S_2 = \begin{bmatrix} 3/4 \\ 1/4 \end{bmatrix}$$

   and this fact is known to player I. What is the best strategy for player I? Find the value of the game.

4. Don and Judy decide to play a coin-matching game several hundred times. In each game each person must use a dime and quarter. Each player selects one coin and places it (without being seen) under a cup. At a given signal, both cups are lifted and the coins are revealed. If they match, Don keeps both coins. If they do not match, Judy keeps both coins. Show that this game is fair. Determine optimal mixes for each player.

5. Using a dime and a half-dollar coin, analyze the game in Problem 4.

6. A "warrant hedge" occurs when a person buys long on a stock and short on the corresponding warrant. If the stock price goes up, he wins on the stock and loses on the warrant. If the stock price goes down, he loses on the stock and wins on the warrant. An investor has information which leads him to believe that if the market trend is upward during the next year, he will gain $30 per share on the price of the stock and loose $10 per share on the price of the warrant. If the market trend is downward, he feels he will lose only $5 per share on the stock and gain $40 per share on the warrant.

$$
\begin{array}{c}
\text{market} \\[4pt]
\begin{array}{cc}
\text{up} & \text{down}
\end{array} \\
\text{investor} \quad
\begin{array}{c}
\text{stock} \\
\text{warrant}
\end{array}
\begin{bmatrix}
30 & -5 \\
-10 & 40
\end{bmatrix}
\end{array}
$$

   a. Assuming the investor has no idea what the market trend will be, how should he apportion his investments among long stocks and short warrants for maximum guaranteed return? If he buys 8500 shares (in total) of stocks and warrants combined, what profit can he expect at the end of the year?

   b. Assuming the investor feels there is 50% probability the market will go up and 50% probability the market will go down, what is the investor's optimum strategy?

   c. Assuming the investor feels there is a 65% chance the market will go up and 35% chance the market will go down, what is his optimum strategy?

7. For the "warrant hedge" in Problem 6, but in which the matrix is given by

$$
\begin{bmatrix}
40 & -50 \\
-30 & 35
\end{bmatrix}
$$

   and the investor has no idea about the general market trend, show that the game is disadvantageous to the investor. Also show that if there is a 50% chance the market trend is up, the investor can have an advantage with the best strategy.

8. In a local political battle, there are two main issues: taxes and law and order. The units given to each candidate's strategy are entries in the matrix below. Positive entries indicate a weighted political advantage for the Republican (and a concomitant and

equal disadvantage to the Democrat), while negative entries indicate a disadvantage for the Republican (and a concomitant advantage for the Democrat). What is the best strategy for each candidate?

Democrat

taxes   law-and-order

$$\text{Republican}\quad \begin{matrix}\text{taxes}\\ \text{law-and-order}\end{matrix}\quad \begin{bmatrix} 1 & -2 \\ -2 & -4 \end{bmatrix}$$

9. Discuss the optimum strategy for the Republican if the Democrat deviates from optimum strategy.

10. Two antivirul serums mycin A and mycin B have the probabilities of destroying flu viruses flu C and flu D given in the matrix below. For example, the probability of serum mycin A killing flu C is .7. Assume it is not known in what proportions the viruses are infecting the population. In what ratio should the serums be mixed so as to maximize the probability of being effective?

viruses

flu C   flu D

$$\text{serums}\quad \begin{matrix}\text{mycin A}\\ \text{mycin B}\end{matrix}\quad \begin{bmatrix} .7 & .1 \\ .2 & .8 \end{bmatrix}$$

11. In Problem 10 what would the best strategy be if the following are known?

   a. 100% of the infected flu patients have flu C?
   b. 10% of the infected flu patients have flu C and 90% of the infected flu patients have flu D?
   c. 75% have flu C and 25% have flu D?

12. An aircraft carrier detects an enemy warship 50 mi away. It is known that the enemy ship is either a battleship or a destroyer, but the radar instruments cannot distinguish between the two types of ships. The aircraft carrier plans an attack on the enemy ship. The carrier has rockets and fighter planes it will use in the attack. The probabilities for a lethal hit with each of these devices against either type of ship are given below. For example, the probability of a lethal hit with a rocket against a destroyer is .01. The carrier plans a mixed strategy using both devices. Find the optimum proportions of rockets and fighter planes to be used for the following situations.

    a.   It is not known in what proportion the enemy has battleships and destroyers.

    b.   It is equally likely

$$S_2 = \begin{bmatrix} 1/2 \\ 1/2 \end{bmatrix}$$

that the ship is a battleship or a destroyer.

    c.   The ratio of enemy battleships to destroyers is 1 to 5.

    d.   The ratio of enemy battleships to destroyers is 4 to 1.

enemy ship

		battleship	destroyer
carrier	rocket	.01	.04
	fighter plane	.03	.02

*13.   A total of 100 rockets and fighter planes are launched against the enemy ship (see Problem 12). Find the probability of a lethal hit if the optimum proportions are used in each of the cases (a), (b), (c), and (d) above. (*Hint:* See Example 4.)

**14.   (Very difficult) Find the optimal strategy for the game of *little morra:* two persons simultaneously throw out one or two fingers each, and, at the same time, each person calls out the sum total of that he thinks will be the result. In a case where only one person makes the correct call, he wins; otherwise it's a tie. In the case of a win, the winner gets $1 from the loser.

*15.   An optimal strategy exists for the game of *big morra:* two persons simultaneously throw out one or two or three fingers each, and, at the same time, each person simultaneously calls out the sum total that he thinks will be the result. In a case where only one person makes the correct call, he wins $1 from the loser; otherwise it's a tie. An optimal strategy for both players is

> Always call out 4 and for every 12 games throw out one finger five times, two fingers four times, and three fingers *three* times.

If this optimal strategy is played by either (or both) players, the game will be fair ($V = 0$). Write a BASIC language computer program that will play *big morra* 1728 times and test the previous assertion by keeping a record of wins and losses for both players. Allow both players to play optimal strategy. Also allow only one player to use optimal strategy. Finally, permit both players to deviate from optimal strategy.

'12

Essentials of Precalculus

> Descartes contemptuously rejected the idea that the only curves we should consider were plane and solid loci, that is to say lines, circles and conics, and maintained that we were at liberty to make use of any smooth curve which has a recognizable equation.
>
> J. L. Coolidge

12.1 Absolute Value and the Definition of a Function

Increasingly, many business and social science students take calculus courses and end up feeling very uncomfortable with the subject. If you have successfully completed a course in intermediate-level algebra with some trigonometry, you may still be unsure whether you are prepared to take calculus. This chapter is aimed at strengthening a student's background with the essentials needed to move more successfully into a calculus course.

Many students know how to factor, solve simple equations, and find the value of $\sqrt[3]{56.78}$ using base 10 logarithms. However, as soon as the word *function* is mentioned, the anxiety level goes up because this word, the symbol $f(x)$, etc., are all surrounded by mystery and confusion.

Each section of this chapter is essential to a proper study of calculus. Great emphasis is placed on the graphing of functions, and many examples are given. The list of topics we could have included would certainly have been too long. We assume that a student knows something about sets, real numbers, and the rudiments of algebra.

It often happens that courses such as "Calculus for business students" and the like exclude the topic of trigonometric functions. If the calculus course you intend to study does include trigonometric functions (and you should check on this), then you will have to study or review basic trigonometry of right triangles and trigonometric functions on your own.

It is very important that the student examine each of the examples worked out in this chapter. Each example has been included for an important reason. Some examples contain essential new ideas that are not otherwise discussed in detail in the chapter.

Absolute Value The concept of absolute value is useful in calculus. It is an invaluable aid in the analysis of inequalities and in a study of basic functions. To express absolute value we need a symbol that will not alter the sign of a non-negative number, but that will change the sign of a negative number to a positive one.

> **Definition 1**   The absolute value of x, written $|x|$, is given by
>
> $$|x| = \begin{cases} x & \text{if } x \geq 0 \\ -x & \text{if } x < 0 \end{cases}$$
>
> **Definition 2** $$|x| = \sqrt{x^2}$$

The following illustrate:

$$|6| = 6$$
$$|-7| = 7$$
$$|-2.1| = 2.1$$
$$|0| = 0$$

In terms of the geometry of a real number line, we can use the absolute value symbol to measure the distance between two points x_1 and x_2. The distance between two x values on the real line is given by the formula

$$d = |x_1 - x_2|$$

where it is unimportant which of the two numbers x_1 or x_2 is the larger of the two. Suppose, for example, that $x_1 = 3$ and $x_2 = -4$; then $|(3) - (-4)| = 7$ and $|(-4) - (3)| = |-7| = 7$.

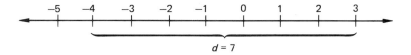

$$d = 7$$

A number of properties of absolute value, all of which are capable of being proved algebraically, will be stated without proof for the sake of brevity. You will find these properties useful in solving problems. In all the following theorems a and b are real.

Theorem 1	$|a - b| = |b - a|$

Theorem 2   If $a > 0$, then $|x| \leq a$ if and only if $-a \leq x \leq a$

Theorem 3   If $a > 0$, then $|x| \geq a$ if and only if $x \geq a$ or $x \leq -a$

(Note that in Theorems 2 and 3 the results also hold if the inequality signs $\leq$ and $\geq$ are replaced with the strict inequality signs $<$ and $>$, respectively.)

Theorem 4 $|ab| = |a||b|$

Theorem 5 $\left|\dfrac{a}{b}\right| = \dfrac{|a|}{|b|}, \; b \neq 0$

Theorem 6
(triangle inequality) $|a + b| \leq |a| + |b|$

Theorem 7 $|a - b| \leq |a| + |b|$

Theorem 8 $|a| - |b| \leq |a - b|$

Example 1

Find the solution set of the inequality

$$|x - 7| < 3$$

and illustrate it on the real number line.

Solution By Theorem 2 we know that $|x - 7| < 3$ is equivalent to

$$-3 < x - 7 < 3$$

Now we add 7 to each member of the inequality, obtaining

$$4 < x < 10$$

This is illustrated in the diagram

Notice that in this case the original form of the problem uses the absolute value symbol to measure the distance between x and 7; if this distance is to be less than 3 units, our answer makes sense.

Example 2

Find the solution set of the inequality

$$|2x - 5| \leq 17$$

Solution
$$-17 \leq 2x - 5 \leq 17$$
$$-12 \leq 2x \leq 22$$
$$-6 \leq x \leq 11$$

Example 3

Given the relation $y = 3x + 6$. Find the value d such that

$$|y - 15| < 0.1 \qquad \text{whenever} \qquad |x - 3| < d.$$

Solution Substituting $3x + 6$ for y in the first inequality, we have

$$|3x + 6 - 15| < 0.1$$
$$|3x - 9| < 0.1$$
$$|3||x - 3| < 0.1$$
$$3|x - 3| < 0.1$$
$$|x - 3| < 1/30$$

Hence $d = 1/30$

Definition of a Function In mathematics we often speak of one variable being a function of some other variable. Precisely what does this mean? Essentially we are saying that y is a function of x if there is some equation or rule that assigns a unique value of y for each x value. This can be formalized as follows.

> **Definition 3**   A function f is set of ordered pairs (x, y) of real numbers such that to each allowable x value there corresponds one and only one y value.

Consider the following simple illustrations:

y is a function of x for these equations:

$$y = 3x + 17 \qquad (-4, 5), (0, 17), (4, 29), \ldots$$
$$y = |x| \qquad (-2, 2), (-1, 1), (0, 0), (1, 1), (2, 2), \ldots$$
$$y = \sqrt{x} \qquad (0, 0), (1, 1), (4, 2), (9, 3), (16, 4), \ldots$$

where to the right of each function we have listed some of the ordered pairs associated with each equation. Notice that in each sample of ordered pairs we do not have more than one y value for some x value. y is not a function of x for these equations:

$$y = \pm\sqrt{x} \qquad (0, 0), (4, 2), (4, -2), (9, 3), 9, -3), \ldots$$
$$|y| = x \qquad (0, 0), (1, 1), (1, -1), (2, 2), (2, -2), \ldots$$

Note that associated with each equation there are two pairs having different y values for the same x value.

There are many cases in mathematics where it is useful to have a special notational form for functions. The equation

$$y = -4x + 9$$

defines y as a function of x. Such equations are often written using the notation

$$f(x) = -4x + 9$$

where the symbol $f(x)$ is read "f of x," which is an abbreviated way of saying "the value of the function f at x." This notation is tremendously useful in making our symbols and statements very compact. This will be clear if we consider the following two equivalent problems:

Problem A: Find the value of y, where $y = -4x + 9$ and $x = 7$
Problem B: Find $f(7)$, where $f(x) = -4x + 9$

Thus we may think of a function f as a rule, equation, or "machine" that "produces" $f(x)$ or y values for some acceptable set of x values. In the following diagram x must be a value acceptable to f

must be a value
acceptable to f $x \longrightarrow$ f $\longrightarrow$ $f(x) = y$

The totality of all the ordered pairs $[x, f(x)]$ that result from the "substitution" of acceptable x values is such that no two distinct ordered pairs will have the same first number x.

The "acceptable" x values and the resulting y values are given names.

> Definition 4   The *domain D* of a function *f* is the set of *x* values that are allowable.

> Definition 5   The *range R* of a function *f* is the resulting set of values that *y* can assume for a given domain.

Example 4

For the functions listed below, find $f(3)$, $f(5)$, $g(-3)$, $g(4)$, $h(-3)$, $h(2)$, $F(2)$, $F(3)$.

$$f(x) = \sqrt{x^2 - 9}$$
$$g(x) = |x| + 3$$
$$h(x) = 2x^2 + 5$$
$$F(x) = \begin{cases} 4x - 2 & \text{if } 1 \le x \le 2 \\ x^3 & \text{if } 2 < x \le 4 \end{cases} \longrightarrow \begin{array}{l} F \text{ has its domain} \\ \text{split into two parts} \end{array}$$

Solution

$$\begin{aligned} f(3) &= \sqrt{3^2 - 9} = 0 \\ f(5) &= \sqrt{5^2 - 9} = 4 \\ g(-3) &= |-3| + 3 = 6 \\ g(4) &= |4| + 3 = 7 \\ h(-3) &= 2(-3)^2 + 5 = 23 \\ h(2) &= 2(2)^2 + 5 = 13 \\ F(2) &= 4(2) - 2 = 6 \\ F(3) &= 3^3 = 27 \end{aligned}$$

Remark concerning domains: Notice that in the function *f* (in Example 4), the domain is not explicitly stated. When this occurs the student must assume that *x* can take on any and all values for which *y* is defined (that is, is a real number). Thus for $f(x)$ to be a real number, $x^2 - 9 \ge 0$, which is the same as $x^2 \ge 9$. Therefore the domain of $f(x)$ is the set of *x* values such that either $x \ge 3$ or $x \le -3$. The domains of the other functions are therefore listed below:

Function	Domain
f	$x \ge 3$ or $x \le -3$
g	$(-\infty, \infty)$
h	$(-\infty, \infty)$
F	$1 \le x \le 4$ sometimes written [1, 4]

When the *x* values of each of the domains are substituted into the respective functions, the range may be computed. Without drawing a graph of a function, it is sometimes very difficult to compute the precise range.

The range for the function f in Example 4 is all values of y such that $y \geq 0$. This can be seen intuitively because the smallest value of y is 0, which occurs when $x = 3$; as x becomes unboundedly large, y can become unboundedly large. The ranges for all four functions are given below, but some thought must be given to each case to see that they are correct. See if you can verify each case.

Function	Range
$f(x) = \sqrt{x^2 - 9}$	$y \geq 0$
$g(x) = \|x\| + 3$	$y \geq 3$
$h(x) = 2x^2 + 5$	$y \geq 5$
$F(x) = \begin{cases} 4x - 2 & \text{if } 1 \leq x \leq 2 \\ x^3 & \text{if } 2 < x \leq 4 \end{cases}$	$2 \leq y \leq 6$ or $8 < y \leq 64$

Exercise 12.1 1. Find the distance $d = |x_2 - x_1|$ between each pair of points on the real line.

    a.   2 and 17
    b. -7 and 14
    c. -10 and 0
    d. -18 and -5
    e.   0 and 45
    f. x and -5
    g. $-x$ and x
    h. $x = a$ and $x = b$

2. Find the solution set, expressed as an interval, for each inequality and graph the resulting interval on the real line.

    a. $|x| \leq 5$ d. $|3x - 1| < 11$
    b. $|x - 5| < 2$ e. $|4x + 1| \geq 13$
    c. $|x + 5| \leq 2$ f. $|4x + 1| \geq 0$

3. Express each statement as an absolute value inequality.

    a. The distance between x and 7 is less than or equal to 2.
    b. The distance between x and -3 is less than or equal to 1.
    c. The distance between $2x$ and 5 is greater than 23.

Also graph each of the above on a separate real line.

4. Express each inequality in words (in terms of distance).

    a. $|x - 4| \leq 8$ d. $|x + 6| \leq 1/2$
    b. $|x - 3| < 5$ e. $|x| \geq 4$
    c. $|x - 7| \geq 1$

Also graph each of the above on a separate real line.

5. Given the equation $y = 6x - 7$, find the value of d such that

$$|y - 5| < 0.2 \quad \text{whenever} \quad |x - 2| < d$$

6. Consider the set of points (x, y) defined by each of the cases below. In each case specify whether or not y is a function of x.

   a. $\{(1, 1), (2, 1), (3, 1), (4, 2), (5, 2)\}$
   b. $\{(1, 1), (1, 2), (1, 3), (2, 4), (2, 5)\}$
   c. $y = x^2$
   d. $x = y^2$
   e. $y = |x| + 3$
   f. $x = |y| + 3$
   g. $y = 2x + 1$
   h. $x = 2y + 1$
   i. $y = x^3$
   j. $x = y^3$

7. Given the two functions

$$f(x) = x^3 - 2x - 19$$
$$g(x) = \frac{5|x|}{x - 2}$$

   answer each question.

   a. Compute $f(-1)$, $f(0)$, $f(1)$, $f(2)$, $f(3)$.
   b. Compute $g(-1)$, $g(0)$, $g(1)$, $g(3)$, $g(4)$.
   c. By finding the innermost value first, compute $f[g(3)]$.
   d. Explain why it is not possible to compute $g[f(3)]$.

8. Show that $f(-x) = f(x)$ for values of $x = -2, -1, 0, 1, 2, 3$ in the function

$$f(x) = x^4 - 5|x|$$

9. Show that $g(-x) = -g(x)$ for values of $x = -2, -1, 0, 1, 2, 3$ in the function

$$g(x) = x^3 + 7x$$

10. Given the functions

$$f(x) = x^2 - 3$$
$$g(x) = |6 - x|$$
$$h(x) = \sqrt{x - 4}$$
$$u(x) = \frac{1}{\sqrt{x}}$$
$$v(x) = \frac{x}{(x + 2)(x - 1)}$$

Compute the following.

a. $f(-4)$ b. $f(\sqrt{2})$ c. $f(h)$ d. $f(x+2)$
e. $f(x+h)$ f. $g(-3)$ g. $g(0)$ h. $g(3)$
i. $h(4)$ j. $h(40)$ k. $u(4)$ l. $u(.01)$
m. $v(0)$ n. $v(2)$ o. $v(-1)$

11. State the implied domains for the functions f, g, h, u, and v above.

12. Find the ranges for the functions f, g, and h above.

13. Given the function

$$f(x) = \begin{cases} x+3 \text{ if } 1 \leq x \leq 4 \\ \sqrt{x+45} \text{ if } 4 < x \leq 99 \end{cases}$$

a. Compute values of $f(2)$, $f(4)$, $f(19)$, $f(99)$.
b. Find the domain and range of f.

14. Find the domain of the function g, where

$$g(x) = \frac{\sqrt{x-3}\,\sqrt{x+1}}{x^2 - 6x - 7}$$

12.2 Graphing Simple Functions and Basic Terminology

Since a function consists of a set of ordered pairs, it is of course possible to obtain a pictorial representation of the function on a Cartesian x–y coordinate system. If we are given a function written in the form

$$y = f(x)$$

we can assign to the variable x any values we choose in the domain of f. These, together with the respective y values generated, determine a set of points in the x–y plane. The set of all points formulated in this way constitute a picture of the functional relationship between x and y.

> **Definition 6**   The graph of a function f is the set of all points $[x, f(x)]$ in the plane such that x is in the domain of f.

The following definitions are sometimes useful when discussing the graph of a function.

> **Definition 7** $x = a$ is a *zero* (or an *x intercept*) of a function f if it is true that $f(a) = 0$.

The zero(s) of a function, if they exist, locate the point(s) where the graph touches or crosses the x axis.

Definition 8   If $x=0$ is in the domain of f, then we call $f(0)=b$ the y *intercept* of the graph for f.

Example 1

Graph the following example of a *constant function* $f(x) = 3$.

Solution Since nothing is explicitly stated concerning the domain, we assume it to be $(-\infty, \infty)$. Thus we can arbitrarily select any real numbers we choose for x. The table below indicates some representative ordered pairs for the function. Note that there is no x intercept, since in this case $f(x) \neq 0$ for any x in the domain.

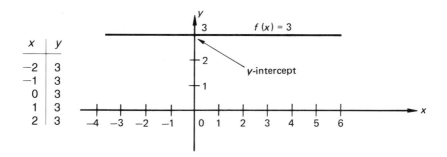

Example 2

Graph the *linear function* given by $f(x) = \frac{1}{2}x - 2$ and note the intercepts on the graph.

Solution Again the domain is $(-\infty, \infty)$, so we are free to choose any x values we wish for our table. Three points should suffice to ensure our straight-line graph is correct.

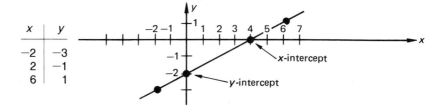

To find the x intercept we merely set $f(x) = 0$ and solve for x. We obtain

$$\tfrac{1}{2}x - 2 = 0$$
$$\tfrac{1}{2}x = 2$$
$$x = 4$$

which is indicated on the diagram. To find the y intercept we set $x = 0$ and find that $f(0) = -2$.

Both Examples 1 and 2 are elementary representatives of a much wider class of functions called *polynomial functions*. Some of these are listed below, where it is understood that letters a, b, c, and d represent constants.

Constant function	$f(x) = a$
Linear function	$g(x) = ax + b$
Quadratic function	$h(x) = ax^2 + bx + c, \qquad a \neq 0$
Cubic function	$s(x) = ax^3 + bx^2 + cx + d, \qquad a \neq 0$

It is obvious that this class could be enlarged to a polynomial function of any degree n, where n is the positive integral exponent of largest order among the terms of the functions. Thus a *quartic function* (degree 4) could be written as

$$t(x) = ax^4 + bx^3 + cx^2 + dx + e, \qquad a \neq 0$$

All of the above functions f, g, h, s, and t are members of a class defined as follows.

Definition 9   A *polynomial function* p is any function of the form

$$p(x) = a_0 x^n + a_1 x^{n-1} + a_2 x^{n-2} + \cdots + a_{n-1}x + a_n$$

where $n \geq 0$ and the coefficients a_i (for each $i = 0, 1, 2, \ldots, n$) are real constants. If $a_0 \neq 0$, the polynomial function is said to be of degree n.

Monomial Functions— Odd and Even Functions   A special subset of the polynomial functions is a type of function called a *monomial function*. This is any function of the form

$$y = ax^n, \qquad a \neq 0$$

These functions are very easy to graph. It is understood that n is a positive integer and a is a nonzero real number. For these functions, the x intercept and the y intercept coincide at the origin $(0, 0)$. Unless otherwise specified by some special case, the domain is the set of all real numbers $(-\infty, \infty)$. The range depends on whether n is odd or even and whether a is positive or negative.

Range of ax^n

If $a > 0$ and n is even	$y \geq 0$
If $a < 0$ and n is even	$y \leq 0$
If $a \neq 0$ and n is odd	$(-\infty, \infty)$

Some examples follow.

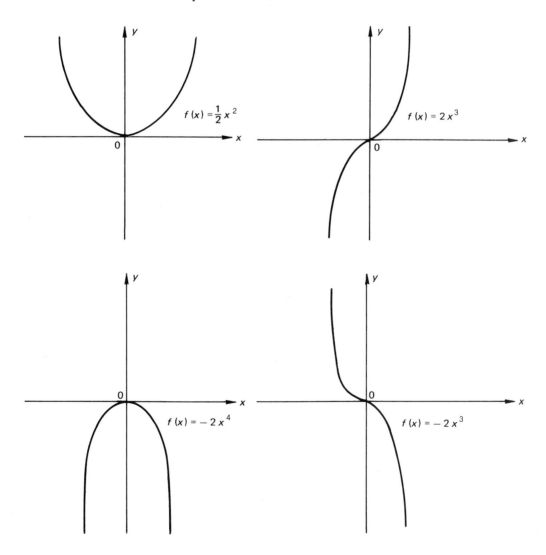

These functions have certain symmetries obvious from the graphs. These properties of symmetry are formally expressed in the following definitions.

Definition 10 f is an *even function* (and has symmetry with respect to the y axis) if $f(-x) = f(x)$ for all x and $-x$ in the domain of f.

Definition 11 f is an *odd function* (and has symmetry with respect to the origin) if $f(-x) = -f(x)$ for all x and $-x$ in the domain of f.

Example 3

Show that $f(x) = -3x^4$ is an even function and illustrate the symmetry involved by drawing a graph.

Solution First note that $f(-x) = -3(-x)^4 = -3(x)^4 = -3x^4 = f(x)$. A table of values is included to illustrate further the kind of symmetry that is involved, namely, symmetry with respect to the y axis.

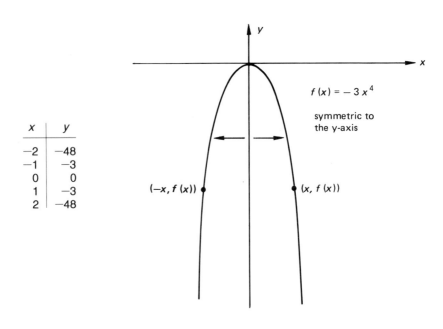

x	y
-2	-48
-1	-3
0	0
1	-3
2	-48

Example 4

Show that $f(x) = x^3$ is an odd function and illustrate the symmetry involved by drawing a graph.

Solution In this case $f(-x) = (-x)^3 = (-x)(-x)(-x) = -x^3 = -f(x)$

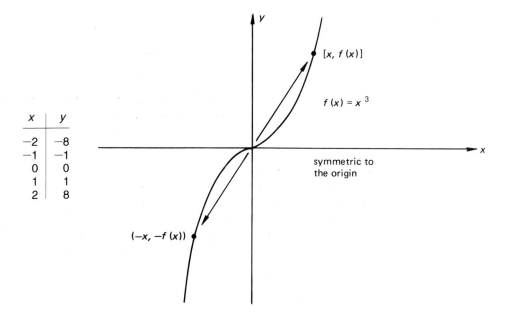

x	y
−2	−8
−1	−1
0	0
1	1
2	8

A function does not have to be a monomial function in order to be odd or even. Functions can be neither odd nor even. The following examples will illustrate.

Example 5

Graph the absolute value function $y = |x|$ and show that it is an even function.

Solution For all real x, $|-x| = |x|$; hence $|x|$ is an even function. The appropriate symmetry is seen on the graph.

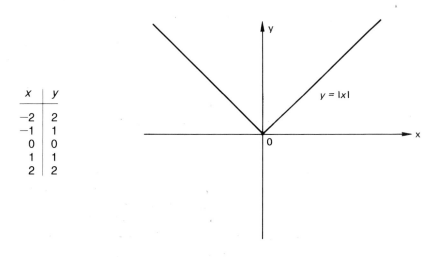

x	y
−2	2
−1	1
0	0
1	1
2	2

Example 6

Graph the cube root function $f(x) = \sqrt[3]{x}$ and show that it is an odd function.

Solution For all real x, $\sqrt[3]{-x} = -\sqrt[3]{x}$. Note that this is not a monomial function because the exponent involved is 1/3, which is not a positive integer.

$$f(x) = \sqrt[3]{x} = x^{1/3}$$

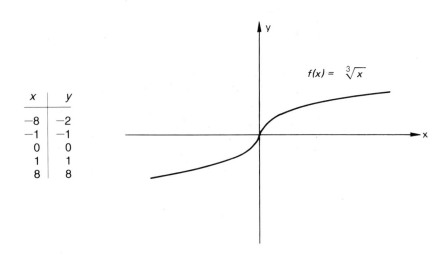

x	y
−8	−2
−1	−1
0	0
1	1
8	8

Example 7

Graph the function $f(x) = 6\,|x| + x^3$ on the closed interval $[-3, 3]$. Show that it is neither odd nor even.

Solution We see that

$$f(-x) = 6\,|-x| + (-x)^3 = 6\,|x| - x^3$$

but

$$f(x) = 6\,|x| + x^3$$
$$-f(x) = -6\,|x| - x^3$$

It is clear that neither of the following holds for all x:

$$f(-x) = f(x)$$
$$f(-x) = -f(x)$$

Thus the function is neither odd nor even.

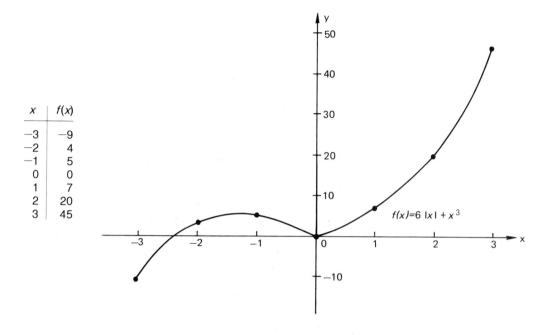

x	f(x)
-3	-9
-2	4
-1	5
0	0
1	7
2	20
3	45

$f(x)=6\ |x|+x^3$

Finally we note that all monomial functions of the form $f(x) = ax^n$ are either even or odd functions according to whether n is even or odd.

Exercise 12.2 1. Graph each of the following functions. It is assumed that each function has the domain $-3 \leq x \leq 3$. Find and label on your graph the x intercept (if any) and the y intercept.

     a.   The constant function $f(x) = -5$
     b.   The constant function $g(x) = 0$
     c.   The linear function $h(x) = 2x + 3$
     d.   The linear function $s(x) = -\frac{1}{2}x - 2$
     e.   The monomial function $t(x) = 4x^3$
     f.   The monomial function $u(x) = -5x^2$

2. Which of the following are examples of polynomial functions and which are not?

     a. $f(x) = 7x^3 - 2x^2 + 7x - 4$ b. $f(x) = 3x^{-3} + 7x^2 + 4x - 5$
     c. $f(x) = 6x^{1/2} - 4x^{1/4} - 3$ d. $y = 7x^2 - 5x + 3$
     e. $y = 4x + 5$ f. $y = 6$

3. Graph the relation $x = |y|$ by first assigning arbitrary values to y and then computing the corresponding x values. Is it true that y is a function of x? Is it true that x is a function of y?

4. Quickly graph each of the following linear functions by finding the x and y intercepts.

    a. $2x - 3y = 12$ b. $-2x - 3y = 6$
    c. $2x + 3y = 24$ d. $x - 7y = -14$

    Also express each of the above in the form $y = f(x) = mx + b$, where we recall that m is the slope and b is the y intercept. See that your results agree with the graphs you have made.

5. Which of the following are even functions? odd functions? neither?

    a. $f(x) = x^6$ b. $f(x) = 4x^5$ c. $f(x) = 6|x|$
    d. $f(x) = x^2 + 7x^4$ e. $f(x) = x^3 - x$ f. $f(x) = -7x + |x|$
    g. $f(x) = \sqrt{x}$ h. $f(x) = x^4 + x^2 + 7$ i. $f(x) = x^3 - x + 1$

6. For what values of m and b is the general linear function $y = mx + b$

    a. An even function?
    b. An odd function?
    c. Neither?

7. Quickly sketch graphs of each of the following monomial functions, and, assuming the domain in all real x, state the range for each.

    a. $y = 4x$ b. $y = 7x^3$ c. $y = -2x^3$
    d. $y = 5x^2$ e. $y = -5x^2$ f. $y = x^4$
    g. $y = \tfrac{1}{2}x^3$ h. $y = -\tfrac{1}{4}x^8$ i. $y = x$

8. Prove each of the following.

    a. The sum and product of two even functions is an even function.
    b. The sum of two odd functions is an odd function.
    c. The product of two odd functions is an even function.

12.3 Quadratic Polynomial Functions

The student is probably already familiar with solving quadratic equations of the form $ax^2 + bx + c = 0$, $a \neq 0$ by various methods, including factoring. For example, we can solve $2x^2 - x - 6 = 0$ by factoring the left side into two binomials.

$$(x - 2)\,(2x + 3) = 0$$
$$x - 2 = 0 \quad \text{or} \quad 2x + 3 = 0$$
$$x = 2 \quad \text{or} \quad x = -3/2$$

Each solution (or *root*) will satisfy the equation. Whether or not the quadratic equation can be factored, we can always solve such equations by *completing the square*, which is demonstrated on the general quadratic equation below.

$$ax^2 + bx + c = 0$$

$$x^2 + \frac{b}{a}x = -\frac{c}{a}$$

We add the quantity $(b/2a)^2$ to both sides.

$$x^2 + \frac{b}{a}x + \frac{b^2}{4a^2} = \frac{b^2}{4a^2} - \frac{c}{a}$$

The left side factors into two identical binomials.

$$\left(x + \frac{b}{2a}\right)^2 = \frac{b^2 - 4ac}{4a^2}$$

Then we have

$$x + \frac{b}{2a} = \frac{\pm\sqrt{b^2 - 4ac}}{2a}$$

and

$$x = \frac{-b \pm \sqrt{b^2 - 4ac}}{2a}$$

This double-valued result is the well-known *quadratic formula*. If $b^2 - 4ac > 0$, the roots are real and distinct. If $b^2 - 4ac = 0$, the roots are identical. If $b^2 - 4ac < 0$, the roots are not real numbers but are called *complex*.

In this section we wish to emphasize the distinction between the quadratic *equation* $ax^2 + bx + c = 0$ and the quadratic *function* $f(x) = ax^2 + bx + c$, $a \neq 0$. The quadratic equation merely has two solutions in x. The quadratic function is not solvable because it is not an equation in x; it has infinitely many "points," or pairs of real numbers $[x, f(x)]$ that satisfy it. In general, its domain is $(-\infty, \infty)$ and its graph is always a parabola that opens upward if $a > 0$ and downward if $a < 0$.

Suppose, for example, $a > 0$, and the parabola opens upward. We might want to find the coordinates of the *minimum* point of this parabola. If we modify, slightly, the appearance of the function, we can deduce the coordinates of the minimum point.

$$f(x) = ax^2 + bx + c, \qquad a > 0$$

$$= a\left(x^2 + \frac{b}{a}x\right) + c$$

$$= a\left(x^2 + \frac{b}{a}x + \frac{b^2}{4a^2}\right) + c - \frac{b^2}{4a}$$

$$= a\left(x + \frac{b}{2a}\right)^2 + c - \frac{b^2}{4a}.$$

Since $a > 0$, it can easily be seen that the smallest value of $f(x)$ will occur when $x = -b/2a$. For this latter value of x, the resulting minimum value of the function is

$$f\left(\frac{-b}{2a}\right) = a\left(\frac{-b}{2a} + \frac{b}{2a}\right)^2 + c - \frac{b^2}{4a}$$

$$= c - \frac{b^2}{4a} = \frac{4ac - b^2}{4a}$$

Since it is true that $f(-b/2a + x) = f(-b/2a - x)$ for all real x, the function is symmetric with respect to the vertical line $x = -b/2a$, called the *axis of symmetry* of the parabola. If $a > 0$ and $b^2 - 4ac > 0$, the graph might appear as follows:

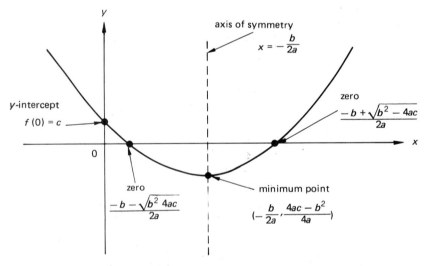

Observe that the roots of the quadratic equation $ax^2 + bx + c = 0$ are the zeros or x intercepts of the quadratic function $f(x) = ax^2 + bx + c$. If $a > 0$ and $b^2 - 4ac < 0$, the zeros will be imaginary and the graph of the parabola will lie entirely above the x axis.

An argument similar to the one above can be used to show that if $a < 0$, then the parabola opens downward, and the same formulas can be used to find the maximum point of the curve, which will be

$$\left(\frac{-b}{2a}, \frac{4ac - b^2}{4a}\right)$$

Example 1

Analyze the quadratic polynomial function $f(x) = -2x^2 + 4x + 3$. Graph the function using appropriate values of x. Show the y intercept on the graph, the x intercepts, the axis of symmetry, and the coordinates of the turning point. State the domain and range of the function.

Solution To compute the zeros of the function (or the x intercepts), we must use the quadratic formula since the function cannot be factored into two binomials with integral coefficients.

$$x = \frac{-b \pm \sqrt{b^2 - 4ac}}{2a} = \frac{-4 \pm \sqrt{16 - 4(-2)(3)}}{-4}$$

$$= \frac{-4 \pm \sqrt{10}}{-4} = \frac{-4 \pm 2\sqrt{10}}{-4} = \frac{-2 \pm \sqrt{10}}{-2}$$

$$= \begin{cases} -0.58 \text{ (rounded)} \\ 2.58 \text{ (rounded)} \end{cases}$$

The axis of symmetry is given by $x = -b/2a = -4/2(-2) = +1$, which we observe to be midway between the two x intercepts. Since the axis of symmetry also gives us the x coordinate of the turning point, the maximum value of the function will occur at $x = 1$. Thus $f(1) = -2(1)^2 + 4(1) + 3 = 5$ is the y value of the maximum point. To construct our graph, we will need a table of values; for the table we choose integral values of x on both sides of the axis of symmetry.

A table of values is given, where we note the y intercept $f(0) = 3$. Since the leading coefficient $a = -2 < 0$, the parabola opens downward and has a maximum point.

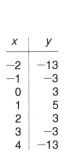

x	y
-2	-13
-1	-3
0	3
1	5
2	3
3	-3
4	-13

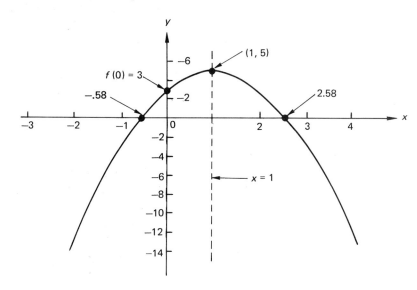

The domain of the function is $(-\infty, \infty)$, and the range is all real y such that $y \leq 5$.

Example 2

An apartment house owner has 60 apartments available for renting. From a marketing survey she knows she can rent all 60 if she charges $500 per month rent for each apartment. However, for each $25 increase in rent, she will rent two less apartments. What rent should she charge per month in order to maximize her return? How many apartments will be rented? What is her maximum gross profit?

Solution Let $n =$ the number of $25 increases she should charge. Then the rent $R = (500 + 25n)$ in dollars. The number of apartments that will be rented is given by $N = (60 - 2n)$. The profit P is thus $P = RN = (500 + 25n)(60 - 2n) = -50n^2 + 500n + \$30,000$ which is a quadratic function of n. Since $a < 0$, the function has a maximum at

$$x = -b/2a = \frac{-500}{2(-50)} = 5$$

which is the number of $25 increases. Thus the rent charged should be $625 per month, and 50 apartments will be rented. The maximum gross profit will be $P = \$31,250$. The situation is illustrated by letting $n = 0, 1, 2, 3, 4, 5, 6, 7, 8, 9, 10$ and examining the resulting return P.

n	Rent R $(500 + 25n)$	Apartments rented N $(60 - 2n)$	Gross profit P $(-50n^2 + 500n + \$30,000)$	
0	500	60	$30,000	
1	525	58	$30,450	
2	550	56	$30,800	
3	575	54	$31,050	
4	600	52	$31,200	
5	625	50	$31,250	maximum
6	650	48	$31,200	
7	675	46	$31,050	
8	700	44	$30,800	
9	725	42	$30,450	
10	750	40	$30,000	

Exercise 12.3   1.   Solve the following quadratic equations by factoring.

   a. $2x^2 - 11x - 6 = 0$ b. $6x^2 + 16x - 6 = 0$
   c. $2x^2 + 5x = 0$ d. $x^2 - 16 = 0$

2.   Solve the following quadratic equations by either completing the square or by use of the quadratic formula.

    a. $3x^2 - 2x - 2 = 0$ b. $x^2 - x = 1$

    c. $x^2 - 2x - 8 = 0$ d. $4x^2 - 12x + 9 = 0$

3. Sketch a graph of each of the quadratic polynomial functions given below. Find the axis of symmetry, the x and y intercepts, and the coordinates of the turning point. In each case state whether the turning point is a maximum or a minimum point.

    a. $f(x) = x^2 - 2x - 15$ b. $g(x) = -x^2 + 4x + 12$

    c. $h(x) = x^2 - 6x + 1$ d. $u(x) = 4x^2 - 16x - 9$

    e. $v(x) = x^2 - 8x$ f. $w(x) = -x^2 + 8$

4. The width of a rectangle is x and the length is $x + 3$. If the area is 10 in², find the width and length.

5. Show algebraically that the function $f(x) = 3x^2 - 2x + 1$ has no x intercepts. Illustrate with a graph of the function. State the domain and range of this function.

6. A cattle rancher has 1200 ft of fencing material and wishes to enclose a rectangular grazing area. Find the dimensions of the rectangle that will maximize the grazing area if one side of the rectangle is bordered naturally by a stone wall. (*Hint:* Let $x =$ width and $1200 - 2x =$ length.)

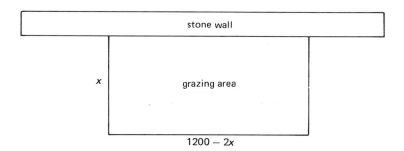

7. A merchandiser can sell all of 20 table lamps of a certain type at $60 per lamp. For each $5 increase in price, he will sell one less lamp.

    a. What price should he charge to maximize his return?

    b. How many lamps will he sell?

    c. What is his maximum return?

    Illustrate with a table of values similar to the one given in Example 2.

8. Find a quadratic polynomial function having $x = -2$ and $x = 5$ as x intercepts. Is there more than one answer to this question?

9. In a manufacturing plant, the price function $P(x) = 5 - 0.001x$ gives the price charged per unit where $x =$ number of units manu-

factured daily. Daily production costs are given by the cost function $C(x) = 1000 + 2x$. Find x so that the manufacturer can maximize the daily profit $R(x)$ given by the function

$$R(x) = xP(x) - C(x).$$

Also find

a. The price of each unit
b. The daily profit if it is to be a maximum?

10. Find two numbers whose difference is 16 and whose product is a minimum.

12.4 Graphing Factorable Polynomial Functions

In the preceding section we studied the parabolic graphs of quadratic functions $f(x) = ax^2 + bx + c$. These functions constitute a subset of the general polynomial functions:

$$p(x) = a_0x^n + a_1x^{n-1} + a_2x^{n-2} + \cdots + a_n$$

Using more advanced results it is possible to show that all polynomial functions are *continuous* (the graphs have no breaks in them), and if the polynomial function is of degree n, the graph can have at most $(n-2)$ *reverse bends* (or changes in concavity). When a polynomial function can be expressed as a product of linear factors, a rough qualitative picture of the graph can be constructed quickly.

Consider the example given by

$$f(x) = (x-1)(x-1)(x-3) = (x-1)^2(x-3)$$

Suppose we wish to find the x intercepts. Since a product equals 0 if and only if one of the factors is 0, $f(x) = 0$ when $x = 1$ or $x = 3$. Thus the graph must touch (or perhaps cross) the x axis at 1 and at 3. Consider the three intervals determined by these intercepts:

$$x < 1 \qquad 1 < x < 3 \qquad x > 3$$

On each of these intervals, $f(x)$ cannot change sign (for if it did, there would have to be an additional x intercept). Let us examine the sign pattern of $f(x)$ on each interval.

	$x < 1$	$1 < x < 3$	$x > 3$
$(x-1)^2$	+	+	+
$(x-3)$	−	−	+
$f(x) = (x-1)^2(x-3)$	−	−	+

no sign change   sign change

Since $f(x)$ does not change sign at $x = 1$, $x = 1$ is a "touching point" on the x axis. But $f(x)$ does change sign at $x = 3$, so the graph of $f(x)$ crosses the x axis at $x = 3$.

It is useful to observe that $f(x)$ becomes unboundedly large as x approaches infinity and $f(x)$ becomes unbounded in a negative sense as x approaches negative infinity. This will be a bit clearer if we select a few values of x that are of large magnitude (both in a positive and negative sense) for inclusion in a table of values.

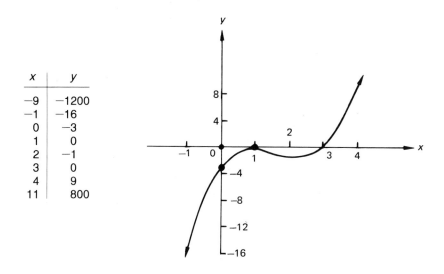

x	y
−9	−1200
−1	−16
0	−3
1	0
2	−1
3	0
4	9
11	800

Since $f(x)$ is of degree 3, there can be at most one reverse bend in the curve. It might appear from the graph that $x = 2$ is a minimum point on the interval $1 < x < 3$, but methods developed in calculus itself are needed to determine precisely such points (actually it occurs at $x = 7/3$).

Some of the preceding results can be generalized in a theorem we will accept without formal proof.

Theorem 9   If $(x − a)$ occurs m times as a factor of a real polynomial function $p(x)$, then

(i) $x = a$ is a *touching point* if m is even.
(ii) $x = a$ is a *crossing point* if m is odd.

Example 1

Sketch a qualitative graph of the polynomial function

$$f(x) = (x + 3)^2 \, (x + 1) \, (x − 1)^4 \, (x − 3)^2 \, (x − 5)^3$$

Solution First observe that this is a polynomial function of degree 12, and the leading term is x^{12}. For a large value of x (say, $x = 10$ or above), it is clear that $f(x)$ must be positive. However, even if x is large in a negative sense (say, $x = -10$ or below), $f(x)$ in this case will be positive. So extreme values of x will produce a positive $f(x)$. The zeros are indicated below together with the indicated multiplicity of their respective factors.

Zero (x intercept)	Multiplicity	Type of intercept
$x = -3$	2	touching
$x = -1$	1	crossing
$x = 1$	4	touching
$x = 3$	2	touching
$x = 5$	3	crossing

Now we can quickly sketch the graph realizing, of course, that our picture is crude since the y values may be greatly distorted.

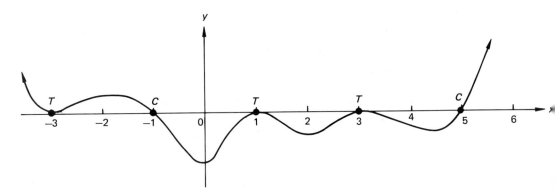

The discussion we have just had concerned polynomial functions that are *factored*. But what of polynomial functions that are not factored? Although we will not go into detail concerning this topic, the student might have some time to review the subject of synthetic division in a good high school algebra text. This, together with the brief summary of theorems given below, should enable the thoughtful student to analyze many polynomial functions.

Theorem 10   If $p(x)$ is a real polynomial and c is any real number, then there exists a unique real polynomial $Q(x)$ and a real number r such that

$$P(x) = (x - c)Q(x) + r$$

Although this theorem does not explicitly involve the quotient

$$\frac{P(x)}{x - c}$$

it does assure us that, for $x \neq c$,

$$\frac{P(x)}{x - c} = Q(x) + \frac{r}{x - c}$$

Theorem 11   (remainder theorem) If $P(x)$ is a real polynomial function, then for every real number c there exists a unique real polynomial $Q(x)$ such that

$$P(x) = (x - c)Q(x) + P(c)$$

This theorem asserts that the remainder, when $P(x)$ is divided by $(x - r)$ is the value $P(r)$. Since sometimes synthetic division offers a rapid means of obtaining this remainder, we may be able to find values of $P(r)$ more rapidly by synthetic division than by actual direct substitution.

Theorem 12   (factor theorem) $x = c$ is a zero of the real polynomial function $p(x)$ if and only if $(x - c)$ is a factor of $p(x)$.

Theorem 13   (rational root theorem) If a/b is a rational zero (reduced) of the polynomial function $p(x) = a_0 x^n + a_1 x^{n-1} + \cdots + a_n$ in which the coefficients are *integers*, then
(i) a is an integral factor of the constant term a_n
(ii) b is an integral factor of the leading coefficient a_0

Exercise 12.4 1. Factor each of the following cubic polynomial functions into the product of three linear factors:

a. $f(x) = x^3 - 2x^2 + x$
b. $g(x) = x^3 + 2x^2 - 4x - 8$

2. Show that the given polynomial function cannot be factored into the product of three linear factors with real coefficients.

$$p(x) = x^3 + x^2 + x$$

3. Sketch a graph of each of the following factored polynomial functions.

    a. $f(x) = (x+3)(x-1)(x-4)$
    b. $g(x) = (x+2)^2(x-1)$
    c. $h(x) = (x+1)^3(x-5)^2(x-7)$
    d. $u(x) = (x+1)^4(x-2)^3(x-4)^2(x-6)$
    e. $v(x) = x^3(x^2 - 8x + 16)(x+1)$

4. Prove that on the interval $-1 < x < 1$,

$$f(x) \le g(x)$$

where $f(x) = x^6$ and $g(x) = x^4$.

5. Given that $(x + 3)$ is a factor of $p(x)$, where $p(x) = x^3 + 6x^2 + 11x + 6$, find the remaining pair of linear factors for p.

6. Divide the polynomial function $p(x) = x^3 - 4x^2 + 7x + 1$ by the divisor $(x - 4)$ to find the quotient and the remainder r. Show that $p(4) = r$.

7. Factor the polynomial function $f(x) = 2x^3 + x^2 - 7x - 6$

8. Find the domain of the indicated function:

$$g(x) = [(x-3)(x-1)^2(x+4)^3(x+2)^5]^{1/2}$$

9. Explain why it is true that every polynomial function of odd degree must have at least one real zero.

12.5 Composite and Inverse Functions

Suppose we are given two functions $y = f(x)$ and $y = g(x)$ and we wish to combine them and form a new function in the following way:

$$y = f[g(x)]$$

Here the understanding is that we are substituting the value of $g(x)$ into the function f.

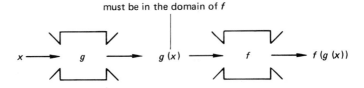

must be in the domain of f

When it can be done, such a function is called the *composite of f and g.* Of course we have to be careful that the value of $g(x)$ is acceptable (that is, is in the domain) to the function f.

Example 1

Given the two functions

$$f(x) = \frac{1}{(2x-1)^{1/2}} \text{ and } g(x) = |x| + 1$$

form the composite function $f[g(x)]$ and state its domain.

Solution First we observe that the domain of f is all x such that $x > 1/2$. Next, we see that the range of $g(x)$ is given by $g(x) \geq 1$. In this case (this does not always happen) the value of $g(x)$ must be acceptable to f because the range of g is a subset of the domain of f. The composite is simply obtained thus:

$$f[g(x)] = \frac{1}{[2g(x)-1]^{1/2}} = \frac{1}{(2|x|+2-1)^{1/2}}$$
$$= \frac{1}{(2|x|+1)^{1/2}}$$

which has the same domain as the function g, namely, all x such that $-\infty < x < \infty$.

Example 2

Given the functions $f(x) = 1/x$ and $g(x) = \sqrt{x} - 1$, form each of the composite functions indicated and state their domains:

a. $f[g(x)]$
b. $g[f(x)]$

Solution a. Note that the domain of g is all x such that $x \geq 0$:

$$f[g(x)] = \frac{1}{g(x)} = \frac{1}{\sqrt{x}-1}$$

We see that $g(x) = 0$ is not acceptable to f. Therefore we must also require that $g(x) = \sqrt{x} - 1 \neq 0$. Thus $x \neq 1$. Thus the domain of the composite function $f[g(x)]$ consists of the set

$$\{x \mid x \geq 0 \text{ and } x \neq 1\}$$

b. The domain of f is all $x \neq 0$:

$$g[f(x)] = \sqrt{f(x)} - 1 = \sqrt{1/x} - 1 = \frac{1}{\sqrt{x}} - 1$$

But $x < 0$ is not acceptable to g; thus, the domain of $g[f(x)]$ is all x such that $x > 0$. We also observe that in general $f[g(x)] \neq g[f(x)]$.

The domain of the composite function $f[g(x)]$ consists of all those elements $a \in D_g$ such that $g(a) \in D_f$.

Example 3   (two functions that "undo" each other)

Given the two functions f and g on the specified domains:

$$f(x) = \sqrt{x} + 1$$

where D_f is $x \geq 0$

$$g(x) = (x - 1)^2$$

where D_g is $x \geq 1$

show that $f[g(x)] = x$ for all x in the domain of g and $g[f(x)] = x$ for all x in the domain of f. Also explain, by means of ordered pairs and a graph, in what sense these functions "undo" each other.

Solution   First observe that the range of g is given by $g(x) \geq 0$. These values are certainly acceptable to f. Thus

$$f[g(x)] = [(x - 1)^2]^{1/2} + 1 = x - 1 + 1 = x$$

for $x \geq 1$. Next observe that the range of f is given by $f(x) \geq 1$. These values are acceptable to g. Then

$$g[f(x)] = (\sqrt{x} + 1 - 1)^2 = x$$

for $x \geq 0$.

In a certain sense these functions "undo" each other. Suppose we substitute the values $x = 0, 1, 4, 9, 16$ into the function f and look at the associated ordered pairs. We have

$$(0, 1), (1, 2), (4, 3), (9, 4), (16, 5)$$

Now let us see what would happen if we used the y values in the above pairs as x values for the function g. We have

$$(1, 0), (2, 1), (3, 4), (4, 9), (5, 16)$$

All of the ordered pairs of f are the *reverse* of the ordered pairs of g. The following graph illustrates the two functions on the same coordinate system. Notice that the domain and range of f are precisely the reverse of the domain and range for g.

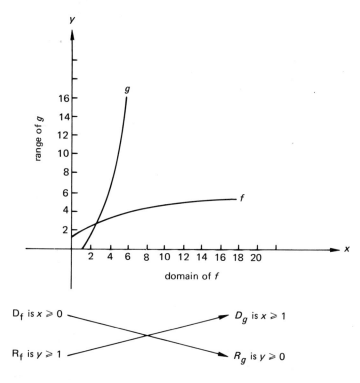

D_f is $x \geqslant 0$ D_g is $x \geqslant 1$

R_f is $y \geqslant 1$ R_g is $y \geqslant 0$

The preceding example was demonstrated in order to motivate and illustrate the following definition.

> **Definition 12**   If $f[g(x)] = x$ for every x in the domain of g and $g[f(x)] = x$ for every x in the domain of f, then f and g are said to be *inverse functions* of each other. We write $f(x) = g^{-1}(x)$ and $g(x) = f^{-1}(x)$. The notation $g^{-1}(x)$ is read "g inverse of x" and the -1 symbol should not be confused with the exponent -1.

Example 4

Show that $f(x) = x^3$ and $g(x) = \sqrt[3]{x}$ are inverse functions of each other and illustrate with a graph.

Solution $f[g(x)] = (\sqrt[3]{x})^3 = x$ and $g[f(x)] = \sqrt[3]{x^3} = x$. Here we have no problem with domains because the domain and range of both functions is all real numbers. Thus

$$f(x) = x^3 \quad \text{and} \quad f^{-1}(x) = \sqrt[3]{x}$$
$$g(x) = \sqrt[3]{x} \quad \text{and} \quad g^{-1}(x) = x^3$$

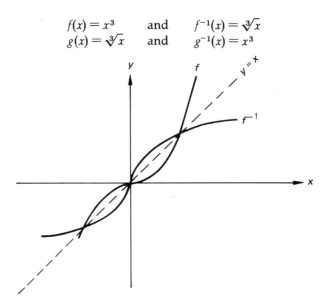

The graphs of $f(x)$ and $f^{-1}(x)$ are reflections about the 45° line $y = x$. This will always be the case because of the role interchange of x and y.

As it happens, merely interchanging the roles of x and y in a function $y = f(x)$ guarantees that the newly formulated equation $x = f(y)$ will yield a graph that is a reflection of the graph of $y = f(x)$ about the 45° line $y = x$. However, we have to be cautious. Merely doing this does not always guarantee that $x = f(y)$ is a function of x.

> **Definition 13**   Given the function $y = f(x)$, we call the equation $x = f(y)$ the *inverse relation*. It may or may not be a function of x.

Example 5

Given the function $y = x^2$, find its inverse relation and show that it is not a function of x. Illustrate with a graph.

Solution $y = f(x) = x^2$. Interchanging the roles of x and y, we have the inverse relation

$$x = y^2$$

which can be written in the equivalent form

$$y = \pm\sqrt{x}$$

which is not a function of x because for $x \neq 0$ there are two values

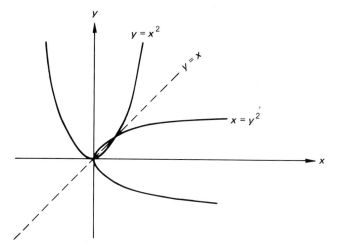

of y for every x. The graphs, however, are reflections about the 45°
line $y = x$.

Because of the interchange of domain and range between a function
and its inverse relation, we can use x-y role interchange to find the
range of a function $y = f(x)$. All we have to do is observe the domain
of the inverse relation $x = f(y)$.

Example 6

Find the range of the function $y = x/(x - 2)$

Solution The inverse relation is

$$x = \frac{y}{y-2}$$

Rewritten, this becomes $xy - 2x = y$ or $xy - y = 2x$. If we solve this
latter equation for y in terms of x, we have

$$y(x - 1) = 2x$$

or

$$y = \frac{2x}{x-1}$$

which has the domain $x \neq 1$. Our conclusion is that the range of f is
all y such that $y \neq 1$.

The reason that some functions do not have inverse *functions* is that
we can have situations such as $y = x^2$, in which (i) for each x there
is one and only one y, but (ii) for each y there is more than one x,
such as (2, 4) and (−2, 4) in the example cited. When these pairs are
interchanged, we have (4, 2) and (4, −2), which does not indicate y
as a function of x.

If $y = f(x)$ were an *increasing* function (on some domain), we would see intuitively that for each x there is one and only one y, and for each y there is one and only one x. (The same holds for *decreasing* functions.) Such functions will have *inverse functions* which, it turns out, will be increasing or decreasing in the same sense as f is either increasing or decreasing. This is illustrated below:

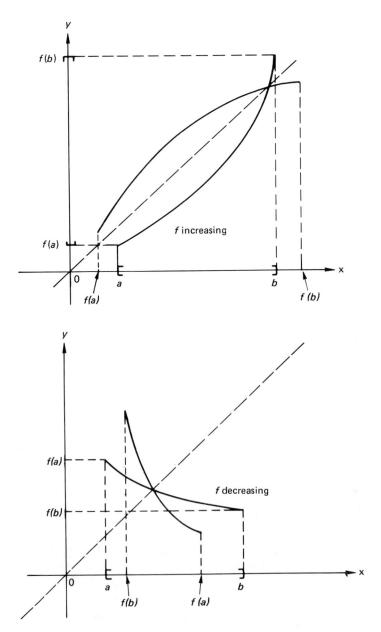

The above diagrams do not prove, but suffice to motivate the following theorem which we accept:

> Theorem 4   If $f(x)$ is increasing on the closed interval $[a, b]$, then f has an inverse function f^{-1}, which is increasing on the closed interval between $f(a)$ and $f(b)$.

The theorem holds as well if the word "increasing," wherever it appears, is replaced with the word "decreasing."

Example 7

Show that $f(x) = x^2$ is increasing on the interval $[0, 2]$ and find f^{-1}. Illustrate with a graph.

Solution We are given $f(x) = x^2$ with domain $[0, 2]$ and range $0 \leq y \leq 4$. Arbitrarily we pick x_1 and x_2 such that $0 \leq x_1 < x_2 \leq 2$. Then we need to show that $x_1^2 < x_2^2$. This will be true if $x_2^2 - x_1^2 > 0$ or if $(x_2 + x_1)(x_2 - x_1) > 0$.

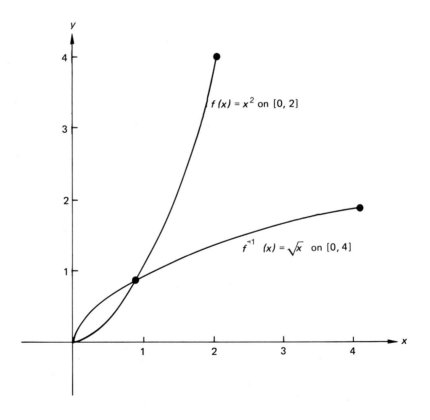

$f(x) = x^2$ on $[0, 2]$

$f^{-1}(x) = \sqrt{x}$ on $[0, 4]$

But both of these factors are positive on the interval [0, 2]. The steps are clearly reversible, so that

$$f(x_1) < f(x_2)$$

and thus f is increasing.

The inverse relation $x = y^2$ with range $0 \le y \le 2$ requires that we take the positive square root. Thus

$$y = f^{-1}(x) = \sqrt{x}$$

is the inverse function on the domain $0 \le x \le 4$.

An illustration appears on p. 447.

Exercise 12.5   1.   Formulate and simplify the indicated composite functions.

      a. $f[g(x)]$, where $f(x) = x - 1$ and $g(x) = x^2 + 3$.
      b. $g[f(x)]$ for the same two functions as in (a).

  2.   State the domain of f and the range of g. Formulate the composite function $f[g(x)]$ and state its domain.

$$f(x) = \frac{1}{(x-1)^{1/2}} \qquad g(x) = |x| + 5$$

  3.   State the domain of u and the range of v. Formulate the composite function $u[v(x)]$ and state its domain.

$$u(x) = \frac{1}{x-1} \qquad v(x) = \sqrt{x} - 2$$

  4.   Verify that $f(x) = 3x - 2$ and $g(x) = \frac{1}{3}x + \frac{2}{3}$ are inverses of one another.

  5.   Given the function $s(x) = \sqrt[5]{x}$, with domain $[-32, 32]$, find the inverse function s^{-1} expressed as a function of x and state its domain and range. Illustrate with a graph.

  6.   For each pair of relations, construct graphs on the same set of axes.

      a. $y = x^4$ and $x = y^4$ b. $x - y = 7$ and $y - x = 7$

      c. $y = \sqrt{x} - 2$ and $x = \sqrt{y} - 2$ d. $y = \dfrac{1}{x+1}$ and $x = \dfrac{1}{y+1}$

      Are both members of each pair functions of x?

  7.   Find the range of each of the following functions by finding the domain of each inverse relation.

      a. $y = \dfrac{1}{x-3}$ b. $y = \dfrac{-3x}{x+5}$ c. $x^2 = y + 5$ d. $y = \dfrac{x^2}{x+1}$

8. Which of the following functions are increasing in the interval [0, 1]? Which are decreasing? Which are neither increasing nor decreasing?

    a. $f(x) = x^2$ b. $g(x) = 1/x$ c. $h(x) = -1/x^2$ d. $y = x - x^2$

9. The function $f(x) = x^3 + 2$ is increasing on the domain [0, 2]. Find $f^{-1}(x)$ and graph both f and f^{-1} on the same set of axes. Indicate the domain and range for both functions.

10. In Problem 9, show that $f^{-1}[f(x)] = x$ and $f[f^{-1}(x)] = x$ for values of x restricted to the domains and ranges indicated.

11. The function $f(x) = 1/(x - 1)$ is decreasing on the domain $x \geq 2$. Find $f^{-1}(x)$ and graph both f and f^{-1} on the same set of axes. Indicate the domain and range for both functions.

*12. Prove that $f(x) = \dfrac{x}{1 - x^2}$ is increasing for all x such that $|x| < 1$.

    Find $f^{-1}(x)$. State the domain and range of f and f^{-1}.

*13. Given the functions $f(x) = \sqrt[3]{x}$ and $g(x) = x - 3$, show that

$$\{f[g(x)]\}^{-1} = g^{-1}[f^{-1}(x)]$$

14. Given the linear function $f(x) = mx + b$ and $m \neq 0$, find $f^{-1}(x)$. What would happen if $m = 0$?

12.6 Illustrations of Rational Functions

The previous sections virtually dictate that we discuss the subject of *rational functions,* which consist of quotients of polynomial functions, such as

$$\frac{1}{x}, \quad \frac{x}{x - 5}, \quad \frac{x^3 - x}{x^2 + 1}, \quad \frac{2x^3 - 3x^2 + 4x - 3}{3x^4 - 6x^2 - x + 1}$$

A complete discussion of such functions would be a very tedious and complicated affair. We will try, however, to give some of the essential ideas necessary for analyzing such functions and examine a few examples.

Definition 14   A rational function f is any function of the form

$$f(x) = \frac{N(x)}{D(x)}$$

where N and D are polynomials and $D(x) \neq 0$.

It will be difficult to discuss such functions without using some special new notations. Intuitively, we introduce a notation that is precisely defined in calculus.

Notation	Meaning
$x \to 3^+$	"x approaches the value 3 from the right" (x might, for example, take on the values 4, 3½, 3¼, 3⅛, etc.)
$x \to 1^-$	"x approaches $+1$ from the left" (½, ¾, ⅞, ¹⁵⁄₁₆, ³¹⁄₃₂, etc.)
$x \to 0$	"x approaches 0 from either side" (½, ¼, ⅛, ¹⁄₁₆, etc., or $-½, -¼, -⅛, -¹⁄₁₆$, etc.)
$x \to \infty$	"x becomes unboundedly large" (10, 1000, 10,000, 100,000, etc.)

We may also write statements such as $f(x) \to 3$ as $x \to -\infty$, which means that $f(x)$ becomes arbitrarily close to 3 as x becomes unboundedly large in a negative sense. We will try to supply a nonrigorous explanation of each of the following illustrations:

Example 1

$$1/x \to \infty \quad \text{as} \quad x \to 0^+$$

Solution Here we are saying that $1/x$ increases without bound as x approaches 0 from the left. This can be seen by examining each of the following cases:

$$\frac{1}{1/10} = 10, \qquad \frac{1}{1/100} = 100, \qquad \frac{1}{1/1000} = 1000$$

Example 2

$$1/x \to 0^- \quad \text{as} \quad x \to -\infty$$

Solution In this case $1/x$ approaches 0 from the left as x becomes unbounded in a negative sense.

$$\frac{1}{-10} = -.1, \qquad \frac{1}{-100} = -.01, \qquad \frac{1}{-1000} = -.001$$

Example 3

$$\frac{1}{2-x} \to \infty \quad \text{as} \quad x \to 2^-$$

Solution This says $1/(2 - x)$ becomes unboundedly large as x approaches 2 from the left.

$$\frac{1}{2 - 1.9} = 10, \qquad \frac{1}{2 - 1.99} = 100, \qquad \frac{1}{2 - 1.999} = 1000$$

The following example is an important one, since from it we will try to justify partly some important generalizations. This example will also help illustrate a step-by-step procedure for analyzing and graphing a rational function.

Example 4

Analyze and graph the rational function

$$f(x) = \frac{x^2 - 4}{x^2 - 1}$$

Solution (i)   (An illustrative table of values) First note that the domain is all real x such that $x \neq \pm 1$.

Compute a few ordered pairs and plot them. (Do *not* connect the points.)

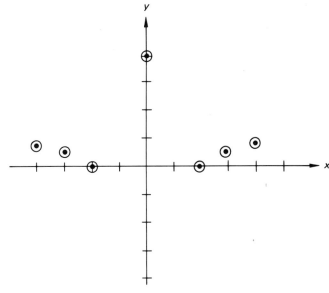

x	y
−4	4/5
−3	5/8
−2	0
−1	undefined
0	4
1	undefined
2	0
3	5/8
4	4/5

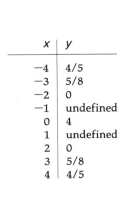

(ii)   (y intercept) From the table we see that (0,4) is a point on the curve. We also could see this by computing $f(0) = -4/-1 = 4$.

(iii)   [x intercept(s)] As long as $D(x) \neq 0$, $N(x)/D(x) = 0$ if and only if $N(x) = 0$. So by setting the numerator equal to 0 we can find the x intercepts. $x^2 - 4 = 0$ yields $x = 2$ and $x = -2$. Moreover, since $x^2 - 4 = (x - 2)(x + 2)$, we see that these zeros are of odd order, so that they are crossing points on the x axis.

(iv) (behavior for large x) (Is there a horizontal asymptote?) Here we want to see what will happen to $f(x)$ as $x \to \infty$. To observe the behavior of $f(x)$ when x is large, we divide $N(x)$ and $D(x)$ by x^n, where n is the largest exponent appearing in any of the terms of polynomials N and D.

$$f(x) = \frac{x^2 - 4}{x^2 - 1} = \frac{x^2/x^2 - 4/x^2}{x^2/x^2 - 1/x^2} = \frac{1 - 4/x^2}{1 - 1/x^2}$$

Observe that as $x \to \infty$, the expressions $1/x^2$ and $4/x^2$ both approach 0. This means that $f(x) \to 1$ for $x \to \infty$. (The same will be true for $x \to -\infty$.) This implies that $f(x)$ (or y) is arbitrarily close to the value $y = 1$ when x is sufficiently large. In this case the horizontal line $y = 1$ is called a *horizontal asymptote*.

(v) (behavior of $f(x)$ near values of x excluded from the domain) Suppose x is very close to but slightly smaller than 1 (such as 0.999). Then $N(x) \approx -3$, but $D(x)$ will be close to 0 and its sign will be negative. This means that the ratio $N(x)/D(x)$ "explodes" in a positive sense for values of x approaching 1 from the left. We write

$$\frac{x^2 - 4}{x^2 - 1} \to \infty \qquad \text{as} \qquad x \to 1^-$$

In this case the vertical line $x = 1$ is a *vertical asymptote* of the function $f(x)$.

Similar lines of reasoning lead us to see that

$$f(x) \to -\infty \qquad \text{as} \qquad x \to \ 1^+$$
$$f(x) \to \ \ \infty \qquad \text{as} \qquad x \to -1^-$$
$$f(x) \to -\infty \qquad \text{as} \qquad x \to -1^+$$

Thus we have two vertical asymptotes $x = 1$ and $x = -1$. We indicate all the asymptotes with dotted lines on our graph.

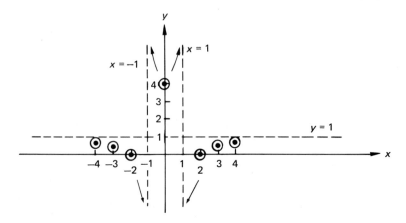

(vi) [does the graph of $f(x)$ cross the horizontal asymptote?] It is
not clear yet whether the graph approaches $y = 1$ from above
or from below. Since we already have points on the graph of
the function that are below $y = 1$, if the function approached y
$= 1$ from above, then the graph would have to intersect the
horizontal asymptote. In some problems this will occur. To find
out where or if this occurs, set $f(x) = 1$ and solve the resulting
equation:

$$\frac{x^2 - 4}{x^2 - 1} = 1 \Rightarrow x^2 - 4 = x^2 - 1$$

Clearly this equation has no solutions. Thus $f(x)$, in this case,
does not intersect the horizontal asymptote and we conclude
that the graph must approach $y = 1$ from below.

Finally, we observe that this particular rational function is an
even function since

$$f(-x) = \frac{(-x)^2 - 4}{(-x)^2 - 1} = f(x)$$

so we have symmetry with respect to the y axis. This, together
with the addition of a few more x values on our table, gives us
the following, complete picture of the graph of the function.

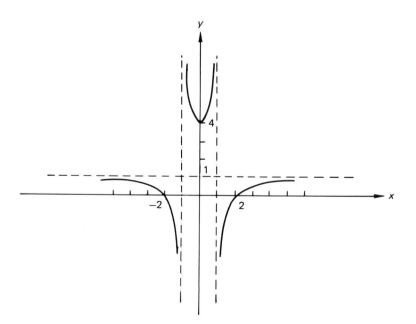

A consideration of the previous example leads us to the following definitions:

Definition 15   If $N(x)/D(x) \to h$ as $x \to \infty$, then the line $y = h$ is a *horizontal asymptote*.

Definition 16   If $D(v) = 0$ and $N(v) \neq 0$, then the line $x = v$ is a *vertical asymptote* of the rational function $N(x)/D(x)$.

A few more examples are given below in which the analysis is condensed. The student should take the time to consider each of these carefully.

Example 5

Analyze and graph

$$r(x) = \frac{2x - 1}{x + 1}$$

Solution Intercepts: y intercept at $(0, -1)$
x intercept at $(1/2, 0)$
Horizontal asymptote: $y = 2$ since $r(x) \to 2$ as $x \to \infty$
Vertical asymptote: $x = -1$
Cross horizontal asymptote?:   No since $r(x) = 2$ has no solution

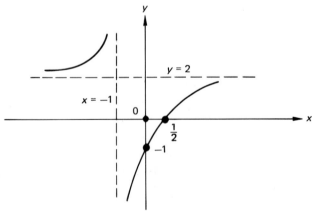

$$r(x) = \frac{2x - 1}{x + 1}$$

Example 6

Analyze and graph

$$s(x) = \frac{2x^2 - 8}{x}$$

Solution Intercepts: no y intercept

x intercepts at $(-2, 0)$ and $(2, 0)$

Horizontal asymptote: none, since $s(x) \to \infty$ as $x \to \infty$
Vertical asymptote: $x = 0$

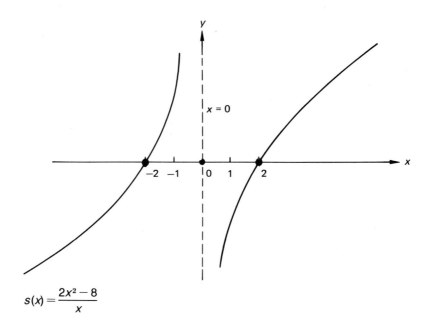

$$s(x) = \frac{2x^2 - 8}{x}$$

Example 7

Analyze and graph

$$t(x) = \frac{x}{x^2 - 9}$$

Solution Intercepts: x and y intercepts coincide at $(0, 0)$
Horizontal asymptote: $y = 0$ since $t(x) \to 0$ as $x \to \infty$
Vertical asymptotes: $x = 3$ and $x = -3$
Cross horizontal asymptote?: Yes since $t(x) = 0$ yields the solution
$x = 0$

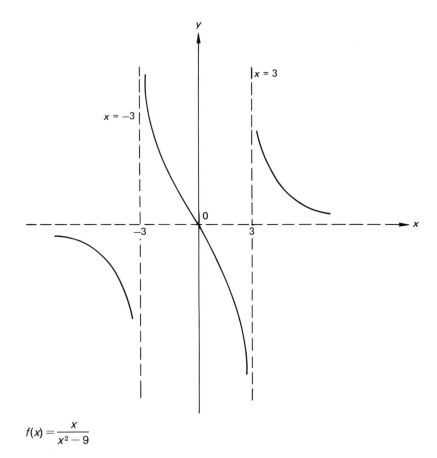

$$f(x) = \frac{x}{x^2 - 9}$$

Sometimes the following theorem is useful regarding horizontal asymptotes:

Theorem 15   Given the rational function

$$f(x) = \frac{a_0 x^n + \cdots + a_n}{b_0 x^m + \cdots + b_m}$$

(i)   If $n > m$, f has no horizontal asymptote

(ii)   If $n = m$, the horizontal asymptote is given by $x = \dfrac{a_0}{b_0}$

(iii)   If $n < m$, the horizontal asymptote is $y = 0$

Exercise 12.6 1.   Analyze and graph each rational function.

a. $f(x) = \dfrac{2x + 4}{x - 3}$ b. $g(x) = \dfrac{2x^2 - 18}{x}$

c. $h(x) = \dfrac{-3x}{x^2 - 25}$ d. $r(x) = \dfrac{x^2 - 9}{x^2 - 16}$

e. $s(x) - \dfrac{x^3 - 27}{x^2 - 2x + 1}$ f. $t(x) = \dfrac{2x^2 + x - 1}{x^2 + 2x - 3}$

2. Find A and B so that

$$\frac{13 - x}{x^2 - x - 6} \equiv \frac{A}{x - 3} + \frac{B}{x + 2}$$

3. Prove that the following rational functions are inverses of each other. Graph both functions on the same set of axes.

$$f(x) = \frac{x + 1}{x - 2} \qquad g(x) = \frac{2x + 1}{x - 1}$$

4. Given the function $y = 1/(x - 3)$, explain the ambiguity in the following statement, "y is large when x is close to 3."

*5. Construct a careful graph of

$$y = \frac{x^3 + 1}{x}$$

and explain why it is true that the equation $y = x^2$ is a nonlinear asymptote for this function.

12.7 Exponential and Logarithmic Functions

In this section we are going to study some completely new types of functions. Before we begin to discuss exponential functions, we will review some of the basic properties of exponents.

We list some of the basic definitions of elementary algebra.

Definition 17 $x^n = \underbrace{x \cdot x \cdot x \cdot \cdots \cdot x}_{n \text{ factors of } x}$, where n is a positive integer n

Definition 18 $x^0 = 1$ for $x \neq 0$

Definition 19 $x^{-n} = 1/x^n$, where n is any integer and $x \neq 0$

Definition 20 $x^{1/n} = \sqrt[n]{x}$, where n is a positive integer and where $x \geq 0$ if n is even

Definition 21 $x^{m/n} = (\sqrt[n]{x})^m$ where m/n is rational, $n > 0$, and $x \geq 0$ if n is even

In more advanced work it is possible to show that expressions of the form $3^{\sqrt{2}}$ can be defined in such a way that 3^a can be made arbitrarily close to $3^{\sqrt{2}}$ by choosing a rational number a sufficiently close to $\sqrt{2}$. Thus for convenience, we shall assume that all expressions of the form x^a can be meaningfully defined for $x > 0$ and for any real number a. It then becomes possible to prove each of the theorems below (which hold for all real a and b and where imaginary or undefined expressions are avoided).

Theorem 16 $x^a x^b = x^{a+b}$

Theorem 17 $(x^a)^b = x^{ab}$

Theorem 18 $(xy)^a = x^a y^a$

Theorem 19 $\left(\dfrac{x}{y}\right)^a = \dfrac{x^a}{y^a}$

Theorem 20 $\dfrac{x^a}{x^b} = x^{a-b}$

We are now ready to begin discussing exponential functions of the type $f(x) = b^x$, where the positive constant $b \neq 1$. (Sometimes the constant b is referred to as a *base*.) From what we have said earlier the domain of this function is $(-\infty, \infty)$. For convenience we will also use without proof the fact that for any positive real y, there exists an x such that $y = b^x$. Thus the range of b^x is all positive real numbers.

Example 1

Graph and state the domain and range of $y = 2^x$.

Solution

x	y
-2	1/4
-1	1/2
0	1
1	2
2	4

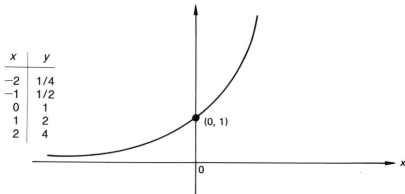

We observe the domain to be all real x and the range to be all positive real y. Notice also that $2^x \to 0$ as $x \to -\infty$, so that the x axis is a horizontal asymptote for the function.

Example 2

Graph and state the domain and range for the exponential function $y = (1/2)^x$.

Solution We note that the function can be equivalently expressed as $y = (1/2)^x = 2^{-x}$

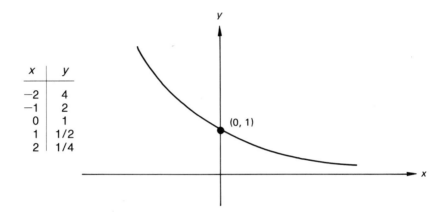

x	y
-2	4
-1	2
0	1
1	1/2
2	1/4

(0, 1)

The domain is all real x and the range is all $y > 0$.

In calculus and in other branches of mathematics (both pure and applied) it is useful to use a certain base number e, which is named after the mathematician Leonhard Euler. One way of defining the number e is to say that it is the number "approached" by the expression

$$\left(1 + \frac{1}{x}\right)^x$$

as x becomes unboundedly large and positive. Although this may seem peculiar, the student can verify with a calculator that

$$\left(1 + \frac{1}{10,000}\right)^{10,000} = 2.71815 \text{ (rounded)}$$

It turns out that e is an irrational number and equals, to the nearest ten-millionth,

$$e = 2.7182818$$

Although it may not seem significant until a student has studied calculus, the function $f(x) = e^x$ has the property that for any point (x, e^x) on the graph, the *rate of increase* of the function is precisely equal to the ordinate e^x.

Example 3

The number of certain bacteria present in a culture is related to time by the formula

$$N = N_0 e^{0.03 t}$$

where N_0 is the amount of bacteria present at time $t = 0$ and t is time in hours. If 500 bacteria are present when the clock is started, how many are present after 5 h? 10 h? 100h? Illustrate with a graph and use a calculator for your computations.

Solution First observe that $N_0 = 500$, so that $N = 500$ when $t = 0$. Then we have at

$$t = 0, \qquad N = 500 e^{0.03(5)} = 500 e^{0.15} = 581$$
$$t = 10, \qquad N = 500 e^{0.03(10)} = 500 e^{0.30} = 675$$
$$t = 100, \qquad N = 500 e^{0.03(100)} = 500 e^3 = 10{,}040$$

Note the following graph.

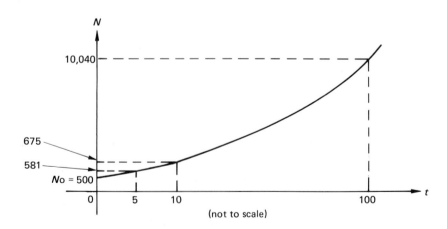

Example 4

Given the function $f(x) = 2 - 2e^{-x}$ on the domain $x \geq 0$, compute values of $f(x)$ for $x = 0, 1, 2, 3, 4, 5$ using a calculator. Analyze and graph, and from your graph, state the range. Use $e = 2.718$.

Solution

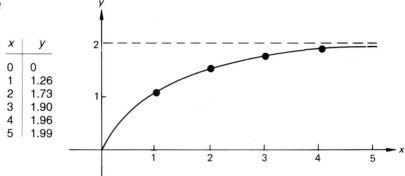

x	y
0	0
1	1.26
2	1.73
3	1.90
4	1.96
5	1.99

Note that as $x \to \infty$, $2e^{-x} \to 0$ and hence $f(x) \to 2$, which is a horizontal asymptote. The range is all y such that $0 \le y < 2$.

A simple application of exponential functions is in the area of compound interest. For example, if the sum of P dollars is earning interest at a rate r per year compounded annually, the amount A

After 1 year: $A = P + Pr = P(1 + r)$
After 2 years: $A = P(1 + r) + Pr(1 + r) = P(1 + r)(1 + r) = P(1 + r)^2$
After 3 years: $A = P(1 + r)^2 + Pr(1 + r)^2 = P(1 + r)^3$
After n years: $A = P(1 + r)^n$

Example 5

$5000 is invested at 8.45% annually. Find A after 5 years and after 10 years. Use a calculator and illustrate with a graph.

Solution $n = 0,$ $A = \$5000(1 + .0845)^0 = \$5000$
$n = 5,$ $A = \$5000(1.0845)^5 \approx \$7501$
$n = 10,$ $A = \$5000(1.0845)^{10} \approx \$11{,}253$

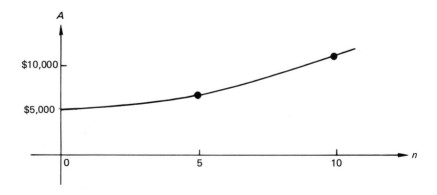

Before going any further we will state and accept without proof the following theorem:

> **Theorem 21**   If $f(x) = b^x$, with the positive constant $b \neq 1$, then
>
> (i)   If $b > 1$, $f(x)$ is an increasing function for all real x
> (ii)   If $0 < b < 1$, $f(x)$ is a decreasing function for all real x

The Inverse of an Exponential Function—The Log Function

Suppose we try to find inverses of exponential functions

$$y = b^x, \qquad b > 1$$

We already know that such functions are increasing for all real x, and hence the inverse relation $x = b^y$ is a function of x. Since there is no simple way to rewrite the equation $x = b^y$ in the form $y = f(x)$ (you should try to do it to convince yourself that it is virtually impossible), we make the following definition.

> **Definition 22**   For $b > 1$, $y = \log_b x$ if and only if $x = b^y$.

The logarithm of a number x is an exponent y to which a fixed base $b > 0$ must be raised in order to equal x.

Although we recognize that there is a certain artificiality in merely rewriting $x = b^y$ as $y = \log_b x$, it will be useful to do so, because certain exponential forms need to be written explicitly as functions of x. We have created a new notation to accomplish this. Thus each of the following pairs of statements are equivalent to each other:

$$
\begin{array}{lll}
1000 = 10^3 & \text{and} & \log_{10} 1000 = 3 \\
8 = 2^3 & \text{and} & \log_2 8 = 3 \\
e = e^1 & \text{and} & \log_e e = 1 \\
1/4 = 2^{-2} & \text{and} & \log_2 1/4 = -2
\end{array}
$$

Since there is an interchange of domain and range between $y = b^x$ and its inverse $x = b^y$, we formally state the domain and range of each function below:

	Domain	Range
$y = b^x$	$-\infty < x < \infty$	$y > 0$
$y = \log_b x$ (or $x = b^y$)	$x > 0$	$-\infty < y < \infty$

The graph of a typical exponential function and its inverse follow. Notice that we have a reflection in the 45° line $y = x$.

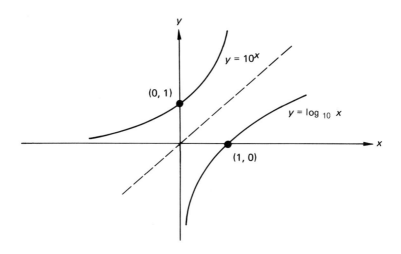

There are some extremely useful properties of logarithms that some readers may already be familiar with. We will only prove the first one. The student who works at it should be able to prove the rest. All are true for any base $b > 1$.

Theorem 22	If x and y are positive, $\log(xy) = \log x + \log y$
Theorem 23	If x and y are positive, $\log (x/y) = \log x - \log y$
Theorem 24	If x is positive and y is real, $\log x^y = y(\log x)$
Theorem 25	$\log_b b = 1$
Theorem 26	(change of base formula) $\log_a x = \log_b x / \log_b a$

Proof of Theorem 22   Let $u = \log_b x$ and $v = \log_b y$. Then $b^u = x$ and $b^v = y$.

$$b^u b^v = b^{u+v} = xy$$

and it follows that

$$u + v = \log_b xy$$

or $\log x + \log y = \log xy$

Common Although they have been rendered somewhat obsolete by electronic
Logarithms calculators, common logarithms (or base 10 logarithms) are sometimes
useful. Tables are usually available that list the logarithms of numbers
between 1 and 10. We can write any decimal number as the product
of a number between 1 and 10 times some integral power of 10. For
example, we can write

$$\begin{array}{lll} 2340 & \text{as} & 2.34 \times 10^3 \\ 0.00000234 & \text{as} & 2.34 \times 10^{-6} \end{array}$$

Since $\log_{10} 10 = 1$, we can evaluate log 2340 as follows (we are omitting
the base as is the custom with common logs):

$$\log 2340 = \log (2.34)(10^3) = \log(2.34) + 3 \log 10$$

$$= \underset{\text{mantissa}}{\underbrace{.3692}} + \underset{\text{characteristic}}{\underbrace{3}} = 3.3692$$

Similarly, we can write

$$\log 0.00000234 = \log (2.34)(10^{-6}) = .3692 + (-6)$$

which, for calculation purposes, might be written $4.3692 - 10$ to avoid
a negative mantissa.

Example 6

The formula $A = Pe^{rt}$ gives the amount A of money compounded
continuously at an annual rate r for t years, on a principal of P dollars.
At an annual rate of 7%, continuously compounded, how long does
it take for an initial principal of P dollars to double? Use logs base
10.

Solution Here we want t such that $Pe^{rt} = 2P$, with $r = 0.07$. We want to solve
$e^{0.07t} = 2$. Taking the log of both sides, we have

$$\log(e^{0.07t}) = \log 2$$
$$0.07t \log e = \log 2$$

$$t = \frac{\log 2}{0.07 \log e} = \frac{0.3010}{0.07(0.4343)} = 9.90 \text{ years}$$

Example 7

The amount of a radioactive substance remaining at any time t is
given by $y = y_0 e^{-0.004432t}$, where t is measured in years and y_0 is the

amount present initially. How long would it take for an initial amount y_0 to be halved (this is called the *half-life* of the substance)? Use logs base e.

Solution (It is a conventional notation to write $\log_e x$ as $\ln x$, which is sometimes referred to as the *natural* logarithm of x.) We want t such that

$$y_{0/2} = y_0 e^{-0.00432\,t}$$

A direct method of solving this is to write

$$0.5 = e^{-0.00432\,t}$$

and take the natural log of both sides, which yields

$$\ln(0.5) = -0.00432t\,(\ln e)$$

But since $\ln e = \log_e e = 1$, we can easily solve using the natural log table in the back of the book:

$$t = \frac{\ln(0.5)}{-0.00432} = \frac{-0.6931}{-0.00432} = 160 \text{ years}$$

Examples 6 and 7 show that the choice of a base is really dependent on the log tables or calculator buttons that happen to be available.

Exercise 12.7   1.   Graph and state the domain and range of each function.

   a. $y = 3^x$ b. $y = 3^{-x}$ c. $y = 3^{-x} + 2$
   d. $y = 4(1 - e^{-x})$ e. $y = 5e^{-x}$

2.   Graph and state the domain and range for each function and its inverse function.

   a. $y = 5^x$ b. $y = \log_2 x$ c. $y = e^{-x}$

3.   Demonstrate that $\log_{\sqrt 2} 2 = 2$ and that $\log_{\sqrt 2} 4 = 4$.

4.   Explain why $y = \log_x x$ for $x > 1$ defines a function. What is its domain? its range? Graph the function.

5.   Explain why it is not possible to find a real number $\log x$ for a value of x that is real but negative. (Note: base b must be positive)

6.   Show that for every positive real number u, $e^{\ln u} = u$.

7.   Show that for every real number u, $\ln(e^u) = u$.

8.   What do Problems 6 and 7 show concerning the exponential (base e) function and the logarithmic function (base e)?

9.   Two banks offer different savings plans:

a.   14% compounded daily

b. $14\frac{1}{4}$% compounded semi-annually

How much would an initial deposit of $1 amount to at the end of five years at each bank?

10.   How much should be invested at 8% compounded annually to amount to $30,000 in 15 years?

11.   If the student population at your institution went from 5000 in 1960 to 15,000 in 1980, find the average annual growth rate during this 20-year period.

12.   A simple population growth model can be written as

$$N = N_0 e^{kt}$$

where

k = a proportionality constant
N_0 = the initial population at time $t = 0$
N = the population at time t (in years)

For the city of Fertilityville the 1940 population was 25,000 and the 1980 population was 75,000. Assuming the model to be correct, predict the population for the year 2000.

13.   Prove the following property of logs: For positive x and y,

$$\log(x/y) = \log x - \log y$$

14.   Solve using base 10 logs: $2^{3x-5} = 3^{x+3}$. Also solve using base e logs.

15.   At an earnings rate of $i = 7\%$ compounded annually, deposits of $1 made at the end of each year for n years will amount to A dollars, where

$$A = \frac{(1+i)^n - 1}{i}$$

Find A after 10 years. Do the same problem for the rate $i = 8.45\%$.

Answers to Odd-Numbered Problems

Exercise 1.1 **1.** *a, b, c, f, h, i*

3. "Some metals are abundant" is true, while "All metals are abundant" is false.

Exercise 1.2 **3.** **(a)** We will not study, and we will not go to the movies.
(b) Harold is not dashing, or Cheryl is not charming.
(c) Joe Smith is not a socialist, or he is a communist.
(d) Some astronauts are not brave.
(e) No buses are made in Italy.
(f) No vehicles made in Italy are buses (equivalent to answer **(e)**).
(g) All positive numbers are rational.
(h) Some fathers are mothers.

5. **(a)** $p \wedge \sim q$
(b) $p \wedge q$
(c) $q \vee p$
(d) $(q \vee \sim p) \wedge \sim (q \wedge \sim p)$
(e) $\sim(p \wedge q)$; alternatively, $\sim p \vee \sim q$
(f) $\sim(\sim p \vee q)$; alternatively, $p \wedge \sim q$
(g) $\sim(\sim(\sim(\sim p)))$; alternatively, p

Exercise 1.3 **1.** If $4 = 3$ then by subtracting 1 from both sides it follows that $3 = 2$. Equals multiplied by equals gives us $4 \cdot 3 = 3 \cdot 2$ or $12 = 6$.

3.

p	q	$p \to q$	$q \to p$
T	T	T	T
T	F	F	T
F	T	T	F
F	F	T	T

not identical

5.

p	q	$p \wedge q$	$p \vee (p \wedge q)$
T	T	T	T
T	F	F	T
F	T	F	F
F	F	F	F

identical

7.

p	q	r	$\sim p$	$\sim q$	$\sim r$	$(\sim p \to q)$	$\wedge$	$(\sim r \to \sim q)$	$\sim[(\sim q \to \sim p)$	$\wedge$	$(q \to \sim r)]$
T	T	T	F	F	F	T	T	T	T	T	F	F
T	T	F	F	F	T	T	F	F	F	T	T	T
T	F	T	F	T	F	T	T	T	T	F	F	T
T	F	F	F	T	T	T	T	T	T	F	F	T
F	T	T	T	F	F	T	T	T	T	T	F	F
F	T	F	T	F	T	T	F	F	F	T	T	T
F	F	T	T	T	F	F	F	T	F	T	T	T
F	F	F	T	T	T	F	F	T	F	T	T	T

identical

9. **(a)** $H \to D$
(b) $\sim D \to \sim H$
(c) $H \to D$
(d) $D \to H$
(e) $D \to \sim H$
(f) $H \to \sim D$
(g) $\sim D \to H$
(h) $\sim H \to \sim D$
(i) $D \to H$
(j) $\sim H \to \sim D$

equivalent

a, b, c are converses of d, h, i, j
e, f are converses of g

Exercise 1.4 **1.** **(a)**

p	q	~q	[(p → q)	∧	~q]	→	~p
T	T	F	T	F	F	(T)	F
T	F	T	F	F	T	(T)	F
F	T	F	T	F	F	(T)	T
F	F	T	T	T	T	(T)	T

(b)

p	q	r	[(p → q)	∧	(q → r)]	→	(p → r)
T	T	T	T	T	T	(T)	T
T	T	F	T	F	F	(T)	F
T	F	T	F	F	T	(T)	T
T	F	F	F	F	T	(T)	F
F	T	T	T	T	T	(T)	T
F	T	F	T	F	F	(T)	T
F	F	T	T	T	T	(T)	T
F	F	F	T	T	T	(T)	T

3. **(a)**

p	∧	(~p	∧	q)
T	(F)	F	F	T
T	(F)	F	F	F
F	(F)	T	T	T
F	(F)	T	F	F

(b)

(p	→	q)	∧	(p	∧	~q)
T	T	T	(F)	T	F	F
T	F	F	(F)	T	T	T
F	T	T	(F)	F	F	F
F	T	F	(F)	F	F	T

5. **(a)** $(p \lor t) \land (p \lor C) \equiv$
   $t \land (p \lor C) \equiv$
   $p \lor C \equiv$
   p

(b) $(p \to q) \lor p \equiv$
   $\sim p \lor q) \lor p \equiv$
   $q \lor (\sim p \lor p)$
   $q \lor t \equiv$
   t

(c) $\sim(\sim p \land q) \equiv p \land \sim q$

(d) $\sim(p \to q) \land q \equiv$
   $(p \land \sim q) \land q \equiv$
   $p \land C \equiv C$

(e) $p \land (\sim p \lor q) \equiv (p \land \sim p) \lor (p \land q)$
   $\equiv C \lor (p \land q)$
   $\equiv p \land q$

5. **(f)** $\sim(p \leftrightarrow q) \lor (q \land \sim p) \equiv$
   $[(p \land \sim q) \lor (q \land \sim p)] \lor (q \land \sim p) \equiv$
   $(p \land \sim q) \lor p \equiv p \lor (p \land \sim q) \equiv p$
(g) $(p \lor q) \land (p \lor \sim r) \equiv p \lor (q \land \sim r)$
(h) $(p \land r) \lor (p \land \sim r) \equiv p \land (r \lor \sim r)$
   $\equiv p \land t$
   $\equiv p$

7. $p \cdot (q + r) = pq + pr$

Exercise 1.5 **1.** **(a)** $p \to q$
$\underline{q \to r}$
$p \to r$

(b) $p \to q$
$\underline{\sim p}$
no valid conclusion

(c) $p \to (q \lor r)$
$\underline{\sim q \land \sim r}$
$\sim p$

(d) $p \to (q \land r)$
$\underline{\sim r}$
$\sim p$

3. **(a)** valid, **(b)** valid, **(c)** valid, **(d)** valid, **(e)** valid, **(f)** valid
5. invalid
7. invalid
9. yes
11. No female students at Yale are persons who never have guilty feelings.
13. $\sim[(p \land q) \to r] \equiv$
$\sim[\sim(p \land q) \lor r] \equiv$
$\sim[\sim p \lor (\sim q \lor r)] \equiv$
$\sim[\sim p \lor (q \to r)] \equiv$
$\sim[p \to (q \to r)]$
15. Use truth tables.
17. $[(M \to H) \to C] \equiv [(\sim M \lor H) \to C]$
$\sim T \lor A$
$\sim(M \land \sim T)$
$\sim H \to A$

$\overline{}$
C
From the last three premises, it follows that $A \lor (\sim M \land H)$, but this does *not* necessarily imply $(\sim M \lor H)$. The argument is invalid.
19. **(a)** yes
(b) yes

Exercise 2.1 **1.**

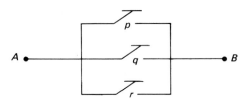

3.

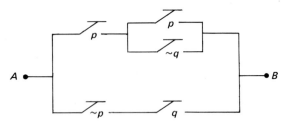

5. $p \lor (q \land r) \lor p \lor (\sim q \land r) \equiv$
$p \lor (r \land q) \lor (r \land \sim q) \equiv$
$p \lor [r \land (q \lor \sim q)] \equiv$
$p \lor (r \land t) \equiv p \lor r$

7. $[(p \rightarrow q) \land p] \rightarrow q$ is equivalent to
$(p \land \sim q) \lor \sim p \lor q$, represented by the circuit shown.

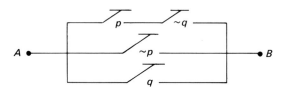

Current always flows, thus the original conditional statement is a tautology, and the argument is valid.

9.

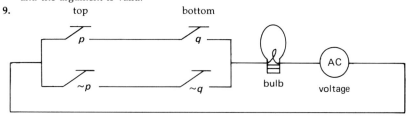

Exercise 2.2 **1.**

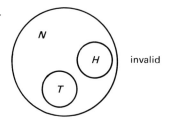

3.

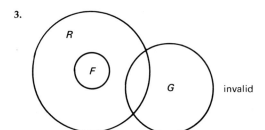

5.

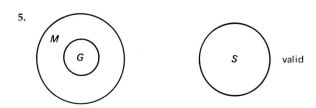

7.

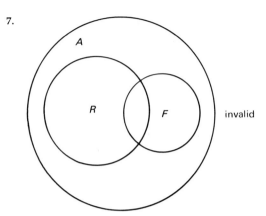

invalid

9. **(1)** "Neutralize stomach acids" is undistributed in both premises—invalid.
    (3) "Red" is undistributed in both premises—invalid.
    (5) All rules satisfied—valid.
    (7) "Animals" is distributed in the conclusion but not in the premises—invalid.
11. **(a)** Some wise persons are not dishonest.
    (b) Some fliers are black.
13. Babies cannot manage crocodiles.
15. No M.P. should ride in a donkey-race, unless he has perfect self-command.
17. No showy talkers are well-informed.

Exercise 2.3 **1.** Implied conclusion: You are a born thief. Valid.
    3. Implied premise: Anything that improves your reading skills will also improve mine. Implied conclusion: My reading skills will be improved. Logic is valid, but the truth of the implied premise is certainly questionable.
    5. Implied conclusion: So-and-so is a communist. Invalid.
    7. Implied conclusion: Brenda will end up unhappy. Valid.

Exercise 3.1 **1.** **(a)** not well-defined   **(b)** well defined
    (c) not well-defined   **(d)** not well defined
    (e) not well-defined unless some precise criteria for obesity are stipulated
    (f) well-defined   **(g)** well defined and empty
    3. **(a)** $\{x|x = 2a,\ 1 \le a \le 10,\ a$ an integer$\}$
    (b) $\{x|x$ is a non-zero real number$\}$
    (c) empty set   **(d)** $\{-2, -1, 0, 1, 2\}$
    (e) $\{$Mars, Jupiter, Saturn, Uranus, Neptune, Pluto$\}$
    (f) $\{n|n$ is an odd integer$\} = \{\ldots, -5, -3, -1, 1, 3, 5, \ldots\}$
    (g) $\{x|x = 4n + 2,\ n \ge 0,\ n$ an integer$\}$
    5. Subsets of A: $\emptyset$, $\{1\}$, $\{2\}$, $\{1,2\}$
    Subsets of B: $\emptyset$, $\{a\}$, $\{b\}$, $\{c\}$, $\{d\}$, $\{a,\ b\}$, $\{b,\ c\}$, $\{c,\ d\}$, $\{a,\ c\}$, $\{b,\ d\}$, $\{a,\ d\}$, $\{a,\ b,\ c\}$, $\{b,\ c,\ d\}$, $\{a,\ c,\ d\}$, $\{a,\ b,\ d\}$, $\{a,\ b,\ c,\ d\}$
    7. $2/5 = .4\overline{0000}\ldots$
    $2/7 = .\overline{285714}\ \overline{285714}\ldots$
    $3/13 = .\overline{230769}\ \overline{230769}\ldots$
    $1/11 = .\overline{09}\,\overline{09}\,\overline{09}\,\overline{09}\ldots$

9. **(a)** unequal   **(d)** equal
     (b) equal   **(e)** unequal
     (c) equal

Exercise 3.2 **1.** **(a)** $\{1, 2, 6\}$ **(c)** $\{1\}$ **(e)** $\{3, 6\}$
     (g) $\{1, 4, 5\}$ **(i)** $\{3\}$

3. **(a)** $\{1, 3, 5, 7, 9, 11, 13, 15, 17, 19, \ldots\}$
     (c) $\{4, 8, 12, 16, 20, 24, 28, 32, 36, 40, \ldots\}$
     (e) $\{20, 40, 60, 80, 100, 120, 140, 160, 180, 200, \ldots\}$
     (f) empty set

5. **(a)** Let $x \in (A \cup B)'$. Then
$x \in A \cup B \Rightarrow x \in A$ and $x \in B \Rightarrow x \in A'$ and $x \in B \Rightarrow x \in A' \cap B'$; thus
$(A \cup B)' \subset (A' \cap B')$. Let $x \in A' \cap B'$. Then
$x \in A'$ and $x \in B' \Rightarrow x \in A$ and $x \in B \Rightarrow x \in (A \cup B) \Rightarrow x \in (A \cup B)'$; thus $(A' \cap B') \subset (A \cup B)'$.
Now it follows that $(A \cup B)' = A' \cap B'$.

(b) Let $x \in A \cap (B \cup C)$. Then
$x \in A$ and $x \in (B \cup C)$, so that $x \in A$ and $x \in B$ or $x \in A$ and $x \in C$. If $x \in A$ and $x \in B$, then $x \in (A \cap B)$ and so $x \in (A \cap B) \cup (A \cap C)$; similarly, if $x \in A$ and $x \in C$, then $x \in A \cap C$ and so $x \in [(A \cap B) \cup (A \cap C)]$. Thus $A \cap (B \cup C) \subset [(A \cap B) \cup (A \cap C)]$. Let $x \in (A \cap B) \cup (A \cap C)$, so that $x \in (A \cap B)$ or $x \in (A \cap C)$. If $x \in (A \cap B)$, then $x \in A$ and $x \in B$ so that $x \in A$ and $x \in B \cup C$; similarly, if $x \in (A \cap C)$, then $x \in A$ and $x \in C$ so that $x \in A$ and $x \in (B \cup C)$. Thus $x \in A \cap (B \cup C)$ and $[(A \cap B) \cup (A \cap C)] \subset [A \cap (B \cup C)]$.
Now it follows that $A \cap (B \cup C) = (A \cap B) \cup (A \cap C)$.

7. **(a)** $(A \cap B) \cup (A \cap B') =$ **(b)** $A \cap (B \cup C' \cup A') =$
     $A \cap (B \cup B') =$ $A \cap (B \cup A' \cup C') =$
     $A \cap U =$ $A \cap (A' \cup B \cup C') =$
     A $(A \cap A') \cup (A \cap B) \cup (A \cap C') =$
                                     $\phi \cup (A \cap B) \cup (A \cap C') =$
                                     $(A \cap B) \cup (A \cap C')$

(c) $(A \cap B) \cap (C \cup D) =$
     $((A \cap B) \cap C) \cup ((A \cap B) \cap D) =$
     $(A \cap B \cap C) \cup (A \cap B \cap D)$

9. **(a)** $A \cap B$ **(b)** $B \cap C$ **(c)** $A \cap C$
     (d) $B' \cap A'$ **(e)** $B' \cap A' \cap C'$ **(f)** $C - B$
     (g) $A \cap B \cap C$ **(h)** $C - (A \cap B)$

11. $A \cap B \cap D$

Exercise 3.3 **1.** $a(a + b) = a$ false;
     $a(b - c) = b(a - c)$ false;
     $(a - b) + (b - a) = (a + b) - (ab)$ false.

3. $C(S_0) = C(S_7)$
     $C(S_1) = C(S_6)$
     $C(S_2) = C(S_5)$
     $C(S_3) = C(S_4)$
     $\{1, 2\}, \{1, 3\}, \{1, 4\} \{1, 5\}, \{1, 6\}, \{1, 7\}$
     $\{2, 3\}, \{2, 4\}, \{2, 5\}, \{2, 6\}, \{2, 7\}$
     $\{3, 4\}, \{3, 5\}, \{3, 6\}, \{3, 7\}, \{4, 5\}, \{4, 6\}, \{4, 7\}, \{5, 6\}, \{5, 7\}, \{6, 7\}$

Exercise 3.4 **1.** 90
3. 5% read Playmacho and Snob's but not Scandal's; 20% read Snob's who do not read Playmacho.
5. Eight possibilities:

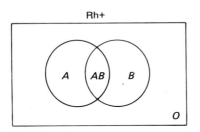
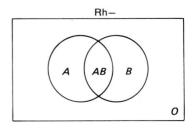

7. $n(A) + n(B) + n(C) + n(D)$
$-n(A \cap B) - n(A \cap C) - n(B \cap C) - n(A \cap D) - n(B \cap D) - n(C \cap D)$
$+n(A \cap B \cap C) + n(A \cap B \cap D) + n(A \cap C \cap D) + n(B \cap C \cap D)$
$-n(A \cap B \cap C \cap D)$

Exercise 4.1 **1.** 15 ways
3. 6 combinations
5. $9! = 362,880$ batting orders
7. **(a)** 72 possible daily doubles outcomes
(b) 504 possible exacta outcomes
(c) 36 possible quinella outcomes
9. 12
11. $7! = 5040$
13. 6 cross pollinations
15. 9
17. **(a)** $6!$ **(b)** $\dfrac{5!}{2!}$ **(c)** $\dfrac{6!}{3!}$

19. 720

Exercise 4.2 **1.** **(a)** 3,628,800 **(b)** 2880 **(c)** 336 **(d)** 6720
3. $_{12}P_9 = 79,833,600$
5. $6! = 720$; 240 if two people must stand together
7. **(a)** $x = 3$ **(b)** $x = 5$ **(c)** $x = 2$
9. 2652
11. $4! = 24$
13. **(a)** $5!$ **(b)** $\dfrac{10!}{2!2!}$ **(c)** $\dfrac{12!}{3!4!3}$ **(d)** $\dfrac{11!}{7!}$

15. $2^{10} = 1024$
17. 24 with no repetitions permitted; 256 if repetitions are permitted
19. 2520 ways
21. 13! has 2, 5, and 10 as separate factors
23. **(b)** three at a time

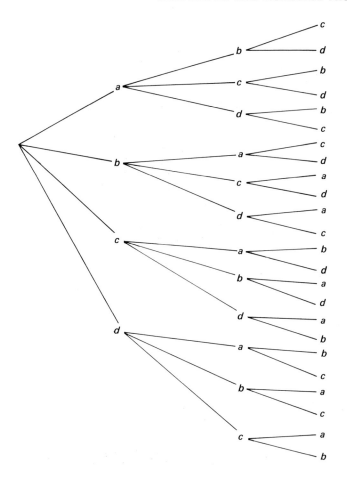

25. **(a)** $13! = 6,227,020,800$

   (b) Stirling Formula approximation: $6,187,239,476$

Exercise 4.3   **1.** **(a)** 28   **(b)** 28   **(c)** 1225   **(d)** 5   **(e)** 1   **(f)** 1

   3. $_4C_2 = 6$ **5.** 226

   7. $_3C_0 + _3C_1 + _3C_2 + _3C_3 = 8$

   $_5C_0 + _5C_1 + _5C_2 + _5C_3 + _5C_4 + _5C_5 = 32$

   9. 15 if you can hear every click.

   11. **(a)** $_{12}P_9$ **(b)** $_{12}C_9$

   13. $$\frac{n!}{(r+1)!(n-r-1)!} + \frac{n!}{r!(n-r)!} =$$

   $$\frac{n!(n-r) + n!(r+1)}{(r+1)!(n-r)!} =$$

   $$\frac{(n+1)!}{(r+1)!(n-r)!} = {}_{(n+1)}C_{(r+1)}$$

15. Two people: $(_6C_2)(_4C_2)(_2C_2) = 90$
    Three people: $(_6C_3)(_3C_3) = 20$
17. $_{40}C_{10} \approx 8.48 \times 10^8$
19. There are 15 different lines.

Exercise 5.1   1. (H)(H) ; (H)(T) ; (T)(H) ; (T)(T)
    $P(E_1) = 1/4;\ P(E_2) = 1/4;\ P(E_3) = 1/2$
3. $P(E_1) = 1/2;\ P(E_2) = 1;\ P(E_3) = 0$
5. The event-pairs are not equally likely.
7. One deck: $P(\text{blackjack}) = \dfrac{4 \cdot 16}{_{52}C_2} = .04827$

    Four decks: $P(\text{blackjack}) = \dfrac{16 \cdot 64}{_{208}C_2} = .04757$

9. 1/3
11. $P(\text{blackjack}) = \dfrac{2 \cdot 12}{_{46}C_2} = .02319$

Exercise 5.2   1. $P(\text{Mon}) = .069 \quad P(\text{Tues}) = .021 \quad P(\text{Wed.}) = .017$
    $P(\text{Thur}) = .018 \quad P(\text{Fri}) = .034$
3. For reasons that are not clear, more people select 3 than any of the other numbers.
5. (a) .69816   (b) .14471   (c) .92197   (d) .49396
    (e) .37510   (f) .00004   (g) .22641

Exercise 5.3   1. (a) $P(a_1) = P(a_2) = P(a_3) = P(a_4) = 1/4$
    (b) $P(a_1) = P(a_3) = 1/4;\ P(a_2) = 1/8;\ P(a_4) = 3/8$
3. $\dfrac{19}{36} = .5278$ 5. 2/9
7. (a) $1 - \dfrac{4}{52} = \dfrac{12}{13}$ (b) 1/6   (c) .10

    (d) $\dfrac{60}{105} = .5714$ (e) $\dfrac{18}{38} = .4737$ (f) $\dfrac{8}{26} = .3077$

9. 1/5!   11. 3/8
13. (a) 1/2   (b) 1/2   (c) 1/4
15. $P(A \cap B) = 0$

Exercise 5.4
1. $\dfrac{_7C_4}{_{15}C_4} = \dfrac{1}{39}$

3. $\dfrac{365 \cdot 364 \cdot 363}{(365)^3} = .9918$

5. $\dfrac{13(_4C_2)}{_{52}C_2}$ for one deck; $\dfrac{13(_{16}C_2)}{_{208}C_2}$ for four decks

7. $\dfrac{(_{13}C_1)(_4C_3)(_{12}C_2)(_4C_1)^2}{_{52}C_5} = .0211$

9. (a) $\dfrac{{}_5C_3}{{}_{15}C_3}$ **(b)** $\dfrac{({}_5C_2)({}_5C_1)}{{}_{15}C_3}$ **(c)** $\dfrac{{}_{10}C_3}{{}_{15}C_3}$

Exercise 5.5 **1. (a)** .9
      (b) .7
     3. $P(A) = 1/4$; $P(B) = 1/2$; A and B are mutually exclusive.
     5. (a) .1   **(b)** .4   **(c)** .9
     7. (a) .85   **(b)** 0   **(c)** .15

Exercise 5.6 **1. (a)** 1/13   **(b)** 1/2   **(c)** 1/26   **(d)** 7/13   **(e)** 1/13
      (f) 1/2
     3. $P(H1) = 1/4$

$$P(T1) = \frac{1}{26}$$

$$P(T2 \mid T1) = \frac{1}{51}$$

$$P(T2) = \frac{1}{26}$$

$$P(H2 \mid T1) = \frac{100}{663}$$

     5. 1/2
     7. (i) 3/4   **(ii)** 7/16

Exercise 5.7 **1.** $P(A) = \dfrac{3}{13}$; $P(B) = 1/4$; $P(A \cap B) = \dfrac{3}{52}$; $P(A \cap B) = P(A)\,P(B)$

     3. (a) 1/18   **(b)** 5/18   **(c)** 1/9   **(d)** 5/9
     7. (a) .2642
      (b) .4996
      (c) .3852
     9. (a) .16
      (b) .48
      (c) .36
    11. (a) .04
      (b) .81
      (c) .64
      (d) .01
      (e) .32
      (f) .18
    13. .44

    15. $P(\text{none will pay by check}) = \left(\dfrac{3}{4}\right)^{10} = .06$ (rounded)

    17. 1/4
    19. It doesn't matter.
    21. .3625

Exercise 6.1 **1.** ${}_4C_4 a^4 b^0 + {}_4C_1 a^3 b + {}_4C_2 a^2 b^2 + {}_4C_3 ab^3 + {}_4C_4 a^0 b^4$
     3. ${}_9C_3 = {}_9C_6 = 84$

5. (a) 1

   (b) 4

   (c) 6 $\quad$ and $1 + 4 + 6 + 4 + 1 = 2^4$.

   (d) 4

   (e) 1

7. $(1 + 4)^n = \sum_{k=0}^{n} {}_nC_k 4^k$

Exercise 6.2 1. (a) $P\left(2, 5, \dfrac{1}{2}\right) = \dfrac{5}{16}$ $\qquad$ (b) $P\left(2, 5, \dfrac{1}{6}\right) = \dfrac{25}{3888}$ (c) $P\left(1, 5, \dfrac{1}{4}\right) = \dfrac{405}{1024}$

$\qquad$ (d) $P\left(0, 5, \dfrac{1}{4}\right) = \dfrac{243}{1024}$ $\qquad$ (e) $P\left(5, 5, \dfrac{1}{4}\right) = \dfrac{1}{1024}$

3. .1550 $\qquad\qquad$ 5. .1615

7. (a) .8320 $\qquad\qquad$ (b) .4718 $\qquad\qquad$ (c) .1631

   (d) .0308 $\qquad\qquad$ (e) .0024 $\qquad\qquad$ (f) .1989

9. .09126

11. Participant P_3 presents stronger evidence in favor of ESP powers. All participants present evidence of being better able to identify triangles.

13. $P(5, 8, .4) + P(6, 8, .4) + P(7, 8, .4) + P(8, 8, .4) = .1738$
   The sample is too small to reflect voting preferences of a Typical City.

15. $\dfrac{1}{7} + \left(\dfrac{6}{7}\right)\left(\dfrac{1}{7}\right) + \left(\dfrac{6}{7}\right)^2\left(\dfrac{1}{7}\right) + \left(\dfrac{6}{7}\right)^3\left(\dfrac{1}{7}\right) + \left(\dfrac{6}{7}\right)^4\left(\dfrac{1}{7}\right) = .5373$

19. Jones. $\quad P(B) = .3$

   $P(\overline{B} \cap J) = .42$

   $P(\overline{B} \cap \overline{J} \cap S) = .28$

21. second ring radius $= \sqrt{3}$
   third ring radius $= 2\sqrt{2}$

Exercise 6.3 1. (a) $\dfrac{35}{72}$ (b) $\dfrac{27}{35}$

3. $\dfrac{60}{61}$ or about 98%

5. .5627

7. (a) $\dfrac{3}{4}$ (b) $\dfrac{3}{8}$

9. $P(A|H) = .3562$; $P(B|H) = .0742$; $P(C|H) = .1187$; $P(D|H) = .1855$; $P(E|H) = .0056$; $P(F|H) = .0371$; $P(G|H) = .2226$

   Ranked Diagnosis: 1. brain tumor

   $\qquad\qquad\qquad\quad$ 2. other

   $\qquad\qquad\qquad\quad$ 3. migraine

   $\qquad\qquad\qquad\quad$ 4. cervical spine problem

   $\qquad\qquad\qquad\quad$ 5. psychosomatic ailment

   $\qquad\qquad\qquad\quad$ 6. optical problem

   $\qquad\qquad\qquad\quad$ 7. sinusitis

Exercise 6.4 1. (a) $E = 250$ $\qquad$ (b) $E = 36$ $\qquad$ (c) $E = 30$

   3. 1999 $\qquad$ 5. $-\$.15$ $\qquad$ 7. \$50 $\qquad$ 9. $E = .6667$

Exercise 6.5 1. $P(A) = 1/38$ $\qquad$ $P(B) = 1/19$ $\qquad$ $P(C) = 3/38$ $\qquad$ $P(F) = 3/19$

   $\qquad\qquad$ $P(G) = 6/19$ $\qquad$ $P(H) = 6/19$ $\qquad$ $P(J) = 9/19$ $\qquad$ $P(K) = 9/19$

3. Assuming the payoffs are the same as with an American roulette wheel, the expectations are each 2.70% against the player, except for the five-number bet which would be 5.41% against the player.

5. $789   7. −11.11%   9. −9.09%

11. $\dfrac{976 - 1004}{976 + 1004 + 1320} = \dfrac{-28}{3300} = -.008484$

15. For each $5 wager, there is an expectation of $.39 against the player.

Exercise 7.1   **1.**

(a)

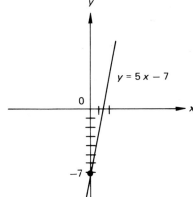

(c)

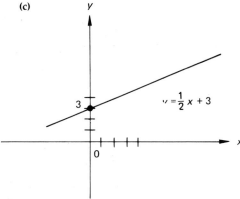

(b)

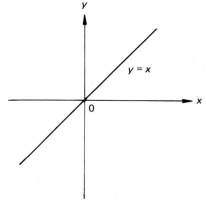

(d)

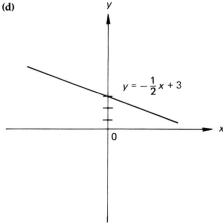

(e)

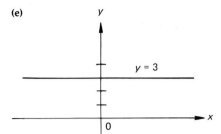

(f)

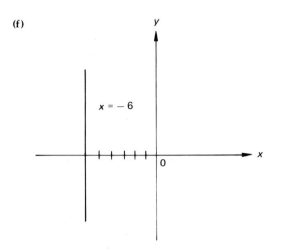

3.

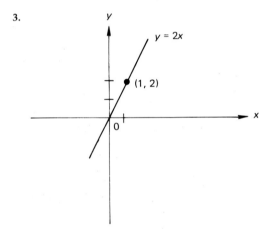

5.

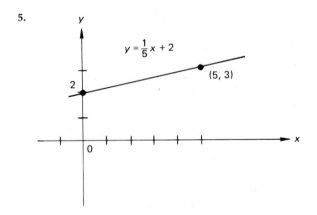

7. $y = -20x + 90$

y	-30	-60
x	6	8

9.

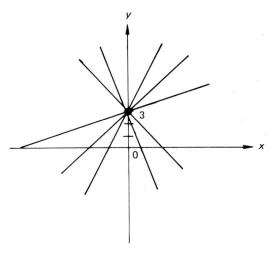

11. $y = 3x - 4$
13. Estimate $y \approx 2.3$
15. **(a)** $C = .50x + 350$ dollars
     (b) $x = 100$ miles
     (c) $C = .5x + 45y + 80$ dollars
     (d) graph shown below

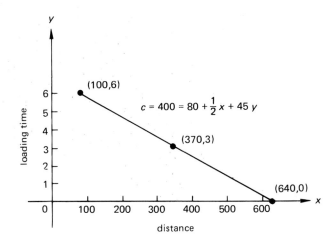

Exercise 7.2   **1.**   *a, b,* and *c* are equivalent and therefore represent the same straight line.
3.

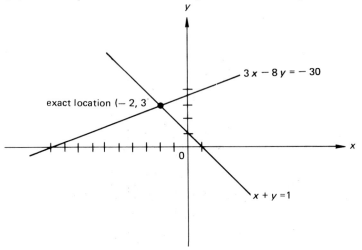

5.   The equations are equivalent.
7.   addition: $-3x - 21y = 33$ $3x + 16 = 25$
              $\underline{3x - 8y = 25}$ $3x = 9$
                 $-29y = 58$ $x = 3$
                     $y = -2$
     substitution: $x = -7y - 11$
                $3(-7y - 11) - 8y = 25$
                $-21 - 33 - 8y = 25$
                $-29y = 58$
                  $y = -2$

9. $y = \dfrac{4}{3}x - \dfrac{20}{3}$

11.

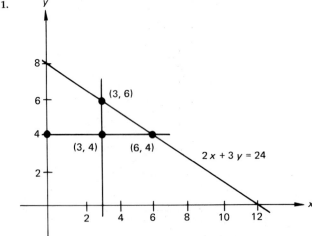

13. $6x + y = 54$
$4x + 9y = 86$
solution: $x = 8$ of compound I
$y = 6$ of compound II

15.   The lines are parallel (distinct but have the same slope) if and only if $\frac{A}{D} = \frac{B}{E} \neq \frac{C}{F}$.

Exercise 7.3 **1.** **(a)**

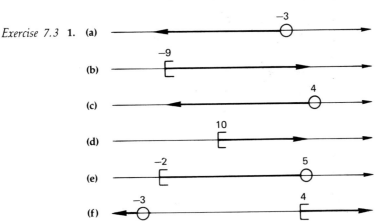

3.   Solution set is all x such that $x < 6$.

5.   if $x > 0$ if $x < 0$
$\Rightarrow 2 < 8x$ $\Rightarrow 2 > 8x$

$x > \dfrac{1}{4}$ $x < \dfrac{1}{4}$

               thus $x < 0$

Inequality is thus satisfied by all x such that either $x > \dfrac{1}{4}$ or $x < 0$ which can be

written: $\{x \mid x > 1/4\} \cup \{x \mid x < 0\}$

7.   **(a)** $a < b$ is equivalent to $b - a > 0$. Hence $a + c < b + c$ since $b + c - (a + c) = b - a > 0$

    (b) $bc - ac = c(b - a) > 0$ when $c > 0$ and $a < b$.   **(c)** $a < b \Rightarrow b - a > 0$
        Hence $ac < bc$. $b < c \Rightarrow c - b > 0$
                                                           thus $c - a > 0$ and $a < c$

Exercise 7.4 **1.** **(a)**

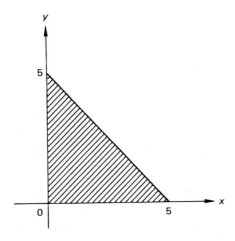

(c)

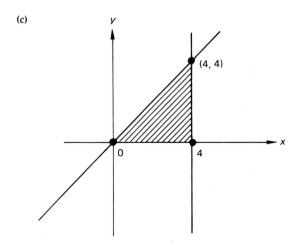

(e)

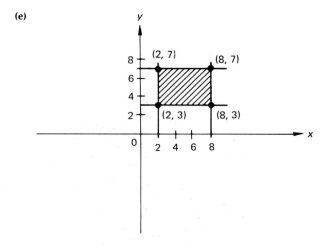

(g)

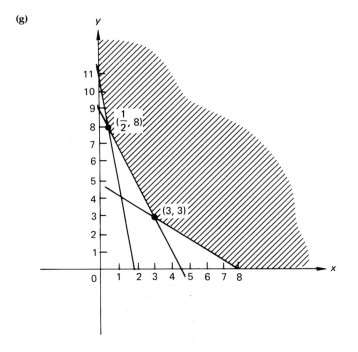

(i)

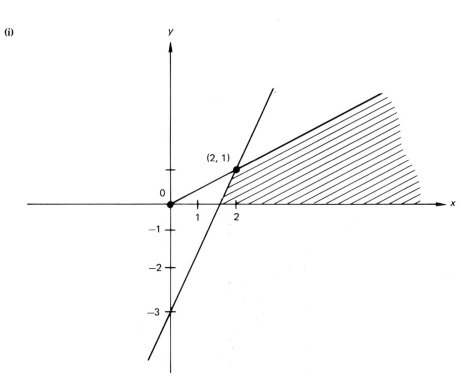

3. **(a)** $W \geq 1$ **(b)** $S \leq 15$
    (c) $W + S < 18$ **(d)** $S \geq W$

5. **(a)**   **(b)** $y \leq \frac{1}{2}x$
    $3x + 4y \leq 12$ $y \geq 0$
    $x \geq 0$
    $y \geq 0$

    (c) $y \leq 5$ **(d)** $y \leq x$
         $y \geq 2$ $x \leq 4$
         $x \leq 8$ $y \geq 2$
         $x \geq 3$

    (e) $y \geq 2$ **(f)** $y \leq 4x - 2$
         $y \leq 6$ $3x + 2y \leq 18$
         $x \geq 0$ $3y - x \geq 5$
         $y \geq 2x - 12$

7. $6x + 6y \leq 600$
    $4x + 2y \leq 360$
    $2x + 6y \leq 420$
        $x \geq 0$
        $y \geq 0$
    (graph shown below)

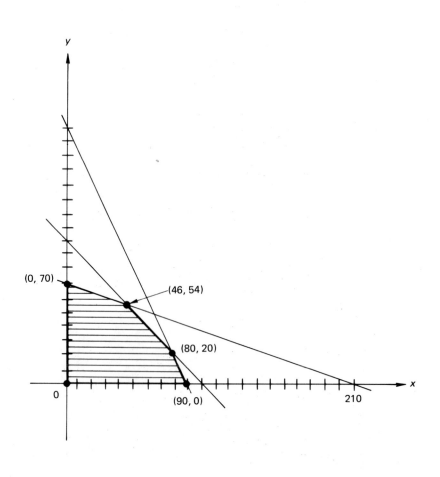

Exercise 8.1   **1.**   max $(z) = 6$ at $(2, 3)$
min $(z) = -4$ at $(10, 1)$
3.   max $(z) = 19$ at $(4, -1)$

min $(z) = \dfrac{20}{3}$ at $\left(\dfrac{4}{3}, \dfrac{4}{3}\right)$

5.

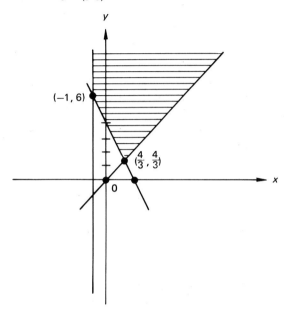

7.

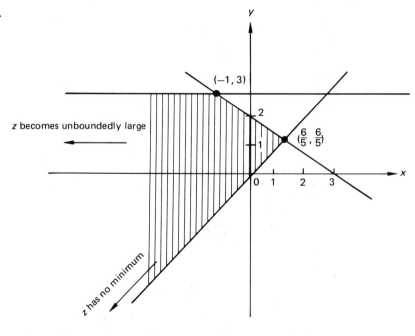

9.

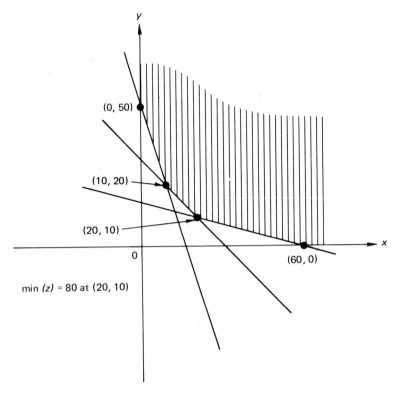

(0, 50)

(10, 20)

(20, 10)

0

(60, 0)

x

y

min (z) = 80 at (20, 10)

11. The graph of the objective function $z = Ax + By + C$ could not be a plane.

Exercise 8.2 **1.** max profit = $3800 for 40 shepherds, 20 poodles, and 40
Irish setters.

3. Program I twice, and
Program II eight times.

5. 500 T.V. sets; 100 washing machines; 400 dryers.

7.

	A	B	C
I	60	40	0
II	0	40	120

9. any point is optimal on the line segment defined by $3x + 2y = 60$ and where
$12 \leq x \leq 18$. max $(I) = \$600$

Exercise 8.3 **1.** max $(w) = 2470$ at (332.5, 95, 0)
min $(w) = 30$ at (0, 0, 0)

3. mine A: 125 days
mine B: 0 days
mine C: 50 days

Exercise 9.1 **1.** **(a)** 3×1; $a_{21} = -2$ **(b)** 3×3; $b_{32} = 3$; $b_{23} = 7$

   (c) 2×4; $c_{14} = c_{22} = 2$ **(d)** 4×3; $d_{42} = 0$; $d_{41} = 0$

3. **(a)** $\begin{bmatrix} 8 & 10 & -2 \\ -2 & 3 & 22 \end{bmatrix}$ **(b)** $\begin{bmatrix} 8 & 10 & -2 \\ -2 & 3 & 22 \end{bmatrix}$

   (c) $\begin{bmatrix} -2 & 0 & -12 \\ 6 & -15 & -4 \end{bmatrix}$ **(d)** $\begin{bmatrix} -2 & 0 & -12 \\ 6 & -15 & -4 \end{bmatrix}$

   (e) $\begin{bmatrix} 7 & -1 & -21 \\ 4 & -15 & -1 \end{bmatrix}$ **(f)** $\begin{bmatrix} 14 & 20 & -16 \\ 2 & -9 & 40 \end{bmatrix}$

   (g) $\begin{bmatrix} 21 & -6 & 3 \\ -15 & 27 & 6 \end{bmatrix}$ **(h)** $\begin{bmatrix} 21 & -6 & 3 \\ -15 & 27 & 6 \end{bmatrix}$

5.

	from cities in		
	US	Europe	Africa
A	100,000	10,000	0
B	4000	50,000	2000

7. $x = 2$, $y = 5$

9. $A + C = B + C$
$A + C + (-C) = B + C + (-C)$
$A + O = B + O$
$A = B$

Exercise 9.2 **1.** addition of real numbers is associative

5. $6A + 12A = (6 + 12)A = 18A$ by theorem (1, (ix))

Exercise 9.3 **1.** $AB = BA = \begin{bmatrix} 2 & 0 \\ 0 & 2 \end{bmatrix}$; $CD = \begin{bmatrix} 11 & 4 \\ 23 & 8 \end{bmatrix}$; $DC = \begin{bmatrix} 1 & 2 \\ 11 & 18 \end{bmatrix}$

3. $A(B + C) = \begin{bmatrix} 1 & 2 \\ 0 & -1 \end{bmatrix} \begin{bmatrix} 8 & 8 \\ 1 & 7 \end{bmatrix} = \begin{bmatrix} 10 & 22 \\ -1 & -7 \end{bmatrix}$

5. Associativity: $n = p$ and $q = r$
   Distributivity: $n = p = r$ and $q = s$

7. $A = \begin{bmatrix} 0 & a & b \\ 0 & 0 & c \\ 0 & 0 & 0 \end{bmatrix}$

$A^2 = \begin{bmatrix} 0 & 0 & ac \\ 0 & 0 & 0 \\ 0 & 0 & 0 \end{bmatrix}$

$A^3 = A^2 \cdot A = \begin{bmatrix} 0 & 0 & 0 \\ 0 & 0 & 0 \\ 0 & 0 & 0 \end{bmatrix}$

9. $\begin{bmatrix} 2 & 3 & 4 \\ 1 & -1 & -2 \\ 1 & 1 & 1 \end{bmatrix} \begin{bmatrix} x \\ y \\ z \end{bmatrix} = \begin{bmatrix} 5 \\ 3 \\ 1 \end{bmatrix}$

11. Because matrix multiplication is not, in general, commutative.

13. Show that $\begin{bmatrix} a & b \\ c & d \end{bmatrix} \left(\begin{bmatrix} e & f \\ g & h \end{bmatrix} + \begin{bmatrix} i & j \\ k & l \end{bmatrix} \right) =$

$\begin{bmatrix} a & b \\ c & d \end{bmatrix} \begin{bmatrix} e & f \\ g & h \end{bmatrix} + \begin{bmatrix} a & b \\ c & d \end{bmatrix} \begin{bmatrix} i & j \\ k & l \end{bmatrix}$

Exercise 9.4

1. (a) $\begin{bmatrix} -8 & -6 \\ 4 & 3 \end{bmatrix} \begin{bmatrix} a & b \\ c & d \end{bmatrix} = \begin{bmatrix} 1 & 0 \\ 0 & 1 \end{bmatrix}$

inconsistent
$\begin{array}{l} -8a - 6c = 1 \\ -8b - 6d = 0 \\ 4a + 3c = 0 \\ 4b + 3d = 1 \end{array}$
inconsistent

(b) $\begin{bmatrix} 1 & 1 & -2 \\ 0 & 3 & 8 \\ 0 & 0 & 0 \end{bmatrix} \begin{bmatrix} a & b & c \\ d & e & f \\ g & h & i \end{bmatrix} = \begin{bmatrix} 1 & 0 & 0 \\ 0 & 1 & 0 \\ 0 & 0 & 1 \end{bmatrix}$

impossible to produce the entry shown

3. $\begin{bmatrix} x_1 \\ x_2 \end{bmatrix} = \frac{1}{14} \begin{bmatrix} 4 & 2 \\ -1 & 3 \end{bmatrix} \begin{bmatrix} 0 \\ 14 \end{bmatrix} = \frac{1}{14} \begin{bmatrix} 28 \\ 42 \end{bmatrix} = \begin{bmatrix} 2 \\ 3 \end{bmatrix}$

5. (a) $\begin{bmatrix} 2 & 3 & -1 \\ 1 & 2 & 1 \\ -1 & -1 & 3 \end{bmatrix} \begin{bmatrix} x \\ y \\ z \end{bmatrix} = \begin{bmatrix} 7 \\ 8 \\ 6 \end{bmatrix}$

(b) $\begin{bmatrix} x \\ y \\ z \end{bmatrix} = \begin{bmatrix} 7 & -8 & 5 \\ -4 & 5 & -3 \\ 1 & -1 & 1 \end{bmatrix} \begin{bmatrix} 7 \\ 8 \\ 6 \end{bmatrix} = \begin{bmatrix} 15 \\ -6 \\ 5 \end{bmatrix}$

Exercise 9.5 **1. (a)**
$$AXA^{-1} = B$$
$$A^{-1}(AXA^{-1}) = A^{-1}B$$
$$(A^{-1}A)XA^{-1} = A^{-1}B$$
$$IXA^{-1} = A^{-1}B$$
$$XA^{-1} = A^{-1}B$$
$$X = A^{-1}BA$$

(b) let $\quad (A^{-1})^{-1} = A^*$
$$(A^{-1})^{-1}(A^{-1}) = A^*A^{-1}$$
$$I = A^*A^{-1}$$
$$IA = (A^*A^{-1})A$$
$$A = A^*$$

(c) $A(A^{-1} + B) - (B^{-1}A^{-1})^{-1} = I + AB - AB = I$

3. For simplicity suppose that (x, y) is at unit distance from the origin; further

suppose $\psi = \text{Arctan} \dfrac{x}{y}$ as shown.

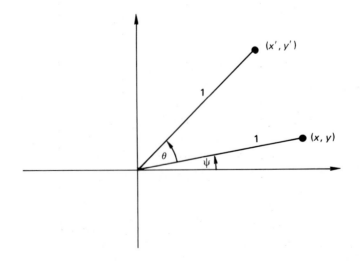

then for a rotation of θ,

$$x' = \cos(\psi + \theta) = \cos\psi\cos\theta - \sin\psi\sin\theta$$
$$y' = \sin(\psi + \theta) = \sin\psi\cos\theta + \cos\psi\sin\theta$$

or

$$x' = x\cos\theta - y\sin\theta$$
$$y' = x\sin\theta + y\cos\theta$$

which in matrix form is

$$\begin{bmatrix} x' \\ y' \end{bmatrix} = \begin{bmatrix} \cos\theta & -\sin\theta \\ \sin\theta & \cos\theta \end{bmatrix} \begin{bmatrix} x \\ y \end{bmatrix}$$

Exercise 9.6 (a) $\begin{bmatrix} 1/2 & 0 \\ 0 & 1/7 \end{bmatrix}$

(c). $\begin{bmatrix} 1 & -1/2 & 1 \\ 0 & 1/2 & 2 \\ 0 & 0 & -1 \end{bmatrix}$

(e) $\dfrac{1}{10}\begin{bmatrix} -12 & 0 & 8 & 1 \\ 6 & 0 & -4 & 2 \\ 2 & 0 & 2 & -1 \\ 0 & 10 & 0 & 0 \end{bmatrix}$

Exercise 9.7 **1.** (a) $x = 2, y = -1$

(b) $x = 2, y = -1, z = 3$

3. $\begin{bmatrix} 2 & 3 & 1 & | & 3 \\ 1 & 1 & -1 & | & 2 \\ 0 & -1 & -3 & | & 0 \end{bmatrix} \sim \begin{bmatrix} 1 & 0 & -4 & | & 2 \\ 0 & 1 & 3 & | & -1 \\ 0 & 0 & 0 & | & -1 \end{bmatrix}$

third row has first three entries equal to zero; hence the system has no solutions. (inconsistent)

5. $\begin{bmatrix} 6 & 3 & | & 66 \\ 2 & 9 & | & 86 \end{bmatrix} \sim \begin{bmatrix} 1 & 1/2 & | & 11 \\ 0 & 8 & | & 64 \end{bmatrix} \sim \begin{bmatrix} 1 & 1/2 & | & 11 \\ 0 & 1 & | & 8 \end{bmatrix} \sim \begin{bmatrix} 1 & 0 & | & 7 \\ 0 & 1 & | & 8 \end{bmatrix}$

Hence $x = 7$ (type I), $y = 8$ (type II)

Exercise 9.8 **1.** (a) RIGHTONBABY

(b) LOVEISREAL

Exercise 9.9 **1.** (a)

	x_1	x_2	x_3	x_4
x_1	0	1	1	0
x_2	0	0	1	1
x_3	0	0	0	0
x_4	0	0	0	0

(b)

	x_1	x_2	x_3	x_4	x_5
x_1	0	1	1	0	0
x_2	0	0	1	0	1
x_3	0	1	0	0	0
x_4	0	0	1	0	1
x_5	0	0	0	1	0

(c)

	x_1	x_2	x_3	x_4	x_5
x_1	0	1	0	1	0
x_2	1	0	1	0	1
x_3	0	1	0	1	0
x_4	1	0	1	0	1
x_5	0	1	0	1	0

(a)   is asymmetric (dominance).

(b)   is neither symmetric nor asymmetric (friendly).

(c)   is symmetric (perfect communication).

3. $M^2 = \begin{bmatrix} 1 & 0 & 2 & 0 \\ 1 & 0 & 0 & 1 \\ 1 & 1 & 1 & 1 \\ 1 & 1 & 0 & 2 \end{bmatrix}$ (non-zero entries indicate 2-stage communications)

non-zero entries in main diagonal indicate feed-back loops:

$$x_1 \to x_4 \to x_1$$
$$x_3 \to x_4 \to x_3$$
$$x_4 \to x_1 \to x_4$$
$$x_4 \to x_3 \to x_4$$

diagraph shown:

5.   (a)   Use M^2

(b)   Yes, since $S = M + M^2 + M^3 + M^4$ has all non-zero entries; also verified using diagraph.

7.   Hint: find $M + M^2$

Exercise 9.10   1.   1945 $\begin{bmatrix} 2.9 \\ 2.7 \\ 2.1 \end{bmatrix}$;   1960 $\begin{bmatrix} 3.3 \\ 3.0 \\ 2.4 \end{bmatrix}$;   1990 $\begin{bmatrix} 4.0 \\ 3.6 \\ 3.0 \end{bmatrix}$

3.   Modify the program on page 314 (powers of a matrix).

Exercise 10.1   1.   (a) $u = v = 0$

$x = 6$

$y = 8$

(b) $\max(P) = 4$

3. $\max(P) = 14$ at the point $(3, 1)$

5. $\max(P) = 8.5$ at the point $(5, 7)$

7. $\max(P) = 7$ at the point $(1, 3)$

9. $\max(P) = 40$ at the point $(0, 0, 4)$

Exercise 10.2   1. $\max(P) = \$540$ with 5 tricycles and 10 bicycles

3.   Final tableau

$$\begin{bmatrix} 1/3 & 1 & 0 & 2/3 & 0 & -1/3 & 0 & 60 \\ 1/3 & 0 & 1 & -1/3 & 0 & 7/6 & 0 & 120 \\ 5/3 & 0 & 0 & -2/3 & 1 & -2/3 & 0 & 60 \\ 2/3 & 0 & 0 & 1/3 & 0 & 4/3 & 1 & 480 \end{bmatrix}$$

$\max(\text{income}) = 480$ when $x = 0$ (type I)

$y = 60$ (type II)

$z = 120$ (type III)

5. $\max(R) = \$2140$ for 40 minor jobs and 20 major jobs.

Exercise 10.3   1. $3x + 2y = 12$ with $2 \le x \le 4$

3. $\max(P) = 46$ at $(0, 6)$

5. $\max(P) = 51$ at the point $(2, 5)$

7. Final tableau

$$\begin{bmatrix} 1 & 2/3 & 1/3 & 0 & 0 & 0 & 2 \\ 0 & -4/3 & -5/3 & -1 & \textcircled{1} & 0 & 10 \\ 0 & 4M+8 & 5M+1 & M & 0 & 0 & 2-10M \end{bmatrix}$$

Artificial variable w not forced to zero; therefore no solution.

9. Where $x =$ the number of days for mine A and

$y =$ the number of days for mine B,

optimal solutions are all points (x, y) satisfied by $3x + 2y = 130$ subject to $10 \le x \le 30$.

11. Dual Problem: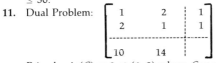

$$\begin{bmatrix} 1 & 2 & \vdots & 1 \\ 2 & 1 & \vdots & 1 \\ \hline 10 & 14 & \vdots & \end{bmatrix}$$

Primal: $\min(C) = 8$ at $(6, 2)$ where $C = x + y$

Dual: $\max(P) = 8$ at $(1/3, 1/3)$ where $P = 10u + 14v$

Exercise 11.1   **1.** Strictly determined. Value $= -1$

3. Not strictly determined

5. Not strictly determined

7. Not strictly determined

9. "PATSY"

II

$$\begin{array}{cc} & \begin{array}{ccc} 1 & 2 & 3 \end{array} \\ \text{I} \begin{array}{c} 1 \\ 2 \\ 3 \end{array} & \begin{bmatrix} -1 & 2 & -3 \\ \textcircled{2} & 4 & 6 \\ -3 & 6 & -9 \end{bmatrix} \end{array}$$

Saddle point is circled; $V = 2$; Player I has the advantage.

Optimal strategies are:

Player I : 2 fingers

Player II : 1 finger

11. Fastfood: locate in Rye

Quiktrix: locate in Scarsdale

13. The only non strictly determined games are those for which either

(i) $a > b, c > b$

(ii) $a < b, c < b$ or

All others are strictly determined.

Exercise 11.2 **1.** **(a)** $V = \dfrac{13}{50}$ **(b)** $V = -\dfrac{3}{4}$

3. Nonstrictly determined if and only if each of the entries on one of the diagonals is greater than each of the entries on the other diagonal.

5. $V = \begin{bmatrix} p & 1-p \end{bmatrix} \begin{bmatrix} -3 & 2 \\ 1 & 0 \end{bmatrix} \begin{bmatrix} 1/8 \\ 7/8 \end{bmatrix} = \dfrac{10p+1}{8} > 0$

For all p, $V > 0$, hence Player I has the advantage.

7.

Ratio of Flu-1 to Flu-2	Superior strategic mix
2:1	$S = \begin{bmatrix} 1/2 & 1/2 \end{bmatrix}$
1:1	$S = \begin{bmatrix} 3/8 & 5/8 \end{bmatrix}$

Exercise 11.3   **1.**   No saddle point in each matrix (i.e., no entry which is a minimum in its row and a maximum in its column).

3.   **(a)** $S_1 = [1/2 \quad 1/2]$

(b)   For all p

$$[p \quad 1-p] \begin{bmatrix} -3 & 2 \\ 1 & -4 \end{bmatrix} \begin{bmatrix} 3/5 \\ 2/5 \end{bmatrix} = -1$$

(c)   Optimal strategy for Player I:
$S_1^* = [1 \quad 0]$. value $V = -6/7$

(d)   Optimal strategy for Player I:
$S_1^* = [0 \quad 1]$. value $V = -1/4$

5.
$$\text{Judy(II)}$$

$$\begin{array}{c} \\ \text{Don(I)} \end{array} \begin{array}{cc} & \text{dime} \qquad\qquad 50¢ \\ \begin{array}{c} \text{dime} \\ 50¢ \end{array} \begin{bmatrix} 10 & -10 \\ -50 & 50 \end{bmatrix} \end{array}$$

Don's optimal: $S_1 = [5/6 \quad 1/6]$

Judy's optimal: $S_2 = \begin{bmatrix} 1/2 \\ 1/2 \end{bmatrix}$; $V = \dfrac{ad - bc}{a + d - b - c} = 0$

and the game is fair.

7.   With unknown market trend and optimal strategy

$$V = \frac{ad - bc}{a + d - b - c} = \frac{-100}{145} = -.69 \text{ (against the investor).}$$

With 50% chance the market trend is up, investor's best strategy is

$$S_1 = [0 \quad 1]$$

which can be interpreted as purchase warrants only; in this case, $V = 2.5$ (favoring the investor).

9.   If the Democrat spends less than two-thirds of his time on the tax issue, then the Republican should spend 100% of his time on the law-and-order issue. If the Democrat spends more than two-thirds of his time on the tax issue, then the Republican should spend 100% of his time on the tax issue.

11.   **(a)**   Use only Mycin-A
(b)   Use only Mycin-B
(c)   Use only Mycin-A

13.   In each of the cases (a) and (b), $V = .025$, which can be interpreted as the probability of a hit if one device could theoretically be divided into the given proportions and launched fractionally against the enemy; thus for 100 devices,

$$P(\text{hit}) = 1 - P(\text{miss}) = 1 - (.975)^{100} = 92\%.$$

(c) $P(\text{hit}) = 1 - (.965)^{100} = 97\%$ **(d)** $P(\text{hit}) = 1 - (.972)^{100} = 94\%$

Exercise 12.1   **1.**   **(a)**   15
(b)   21
(c)   10
(d)   13
(e)   45
(f) $|x + 5|$
(g) $2|x|$
(h) $|a - b|$

3. **(a)** $|x-7| \le 2$
 (b) $|x+3| \le 1$
 (c) $|2x-5| > 23$

5. $d = \dfrac{1}{30}$

7. **(a)** $f(-1) = -18$ **(b)** $g(-1) = \dfrac{-5}{3}$

$f(0) = -19$ $g(0) = 0$
$f(1) = -20$ $g(1) = -5$
$f(2) = -15$ $g(3) = 15$
$f(3) = 2$ $g(4) = 10$

 (c) $f[g(3)] = 3326$
 (d) $f(3)$ is not in the domain of the function g.
9. Observe that $g(-x) = -x^3 - 7x = -g(x)$.

11. function   implied domain

function	implied domain
f	all real x
g	all real x
h	all real x such that $x \ge 4$
u	all real x such that $x > 0$
v	all x such that $x \ne -2$, $x \ne 1$

13. **(a)** $f(2) = 5$ **(b)** domain: $1 \le x \le 99$
$f(4) = 7$ range: $\;\;1 \le y \le 12$
$f(19) = 8$
$f(99) = 12$

Exercise 12.2   **1.** **(a)**

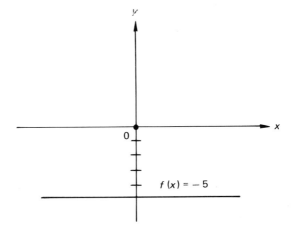

(b)

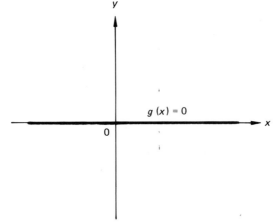

(c)

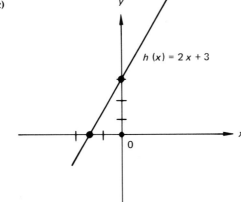

(d)

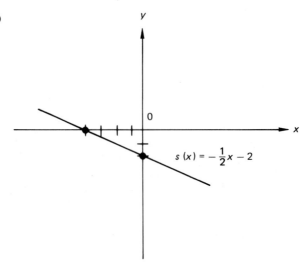

(e)

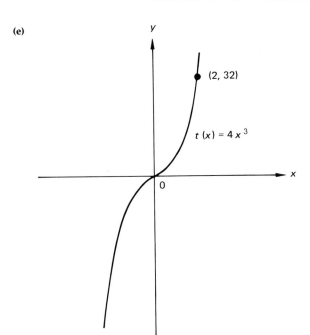

(f)

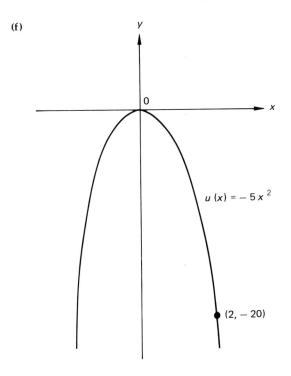

3. $x = |y|$

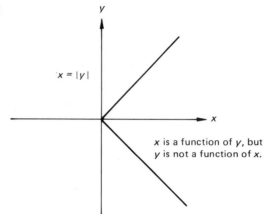

x is a function of y, but
y is not a function of x.

5.   even: a, c, d, h
odd: b, e
neither: f, g, i

7.

(a)

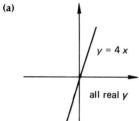

$y = 4x$

all real y

(d)

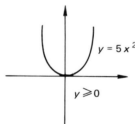

$y = 5x^2$

$y \geqslant 0$

(g)

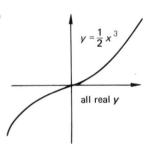

$y = \frac{1}{2}x^3$

all real y

(b)

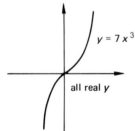

$y = 7x^3$

all real y

(e)

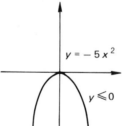

$y = -5x^2$

$y \leqslant 0$

(h)

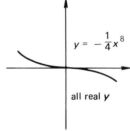

$y = -\frac{1}{4}x^8$

all real y

(c)

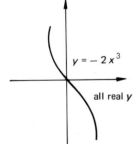

$y = -2x^3$

all real y

(f)

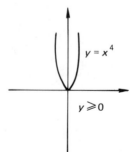

$y = x^4$

$y \geqslant 0$

(i)

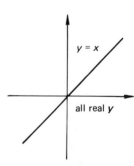

$y = x$

all real y

Exercise 12.3 **1.** **(a)** $x = -1/2, x = 6$ **(b)** $x = -3, x = 1/3$
(c) $x = 0, x = -5/2$ **(d)** $x = -4, x = 4$

3.

function	axis of symmetry	turning point	x-intercepts	y-intercept
$x^2 - 2x - 15$	$x = 1$	$(1, -16)$	$x = -3, 5$	$y = -15$
$-x^2 + 4x + 12$	$x = 2$	$(2, 16)$	$x = -2, 6$	$y = 12$
$x^2 - 6x + 1$	$x = 3$	$(3, -8)$	$x = 3 \pm 2\sqrt{2}$	$y = 1$
$4x^2 - 16x - 9$	$x = 2$	$(2, -25)$	$x = -1/2, 9/2$	$y = -9$
$x^2 - 8x$	$x = 4$	$(4, -16)$	$x = 0, 8$	$y = 0$
$-x^2 + 8$	$x = 0$	$(0, 8)$	$x = \pm 2\sqrt{2}$	$y = 8$

5. Roots are not real numbers since the quadratic formula yields

$$x = \frac{2 \pm \sqrt{-8}}{6}$$

domain: all real x
range: $y \geq 2/3$

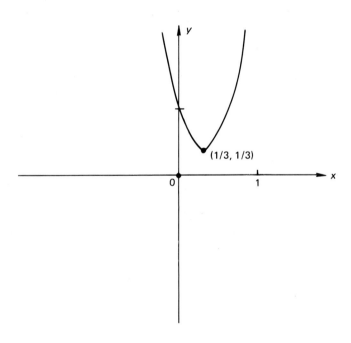

(1/3, 1/3)

7. **(a)** $80 per lamp
(b) 16 lamps $R = (20 - x)(60 + 5x)$
(c) $1280 max. return
9. $x = 1500$
price per unit = $3.50
max daily profit = $1250

Exercise 12.4 **1.** **(a)** $f(x) = x(x - 1)(x - 1)$
(b) $g(x) = (x - 2)(x + 2)^2$

3.

(a)

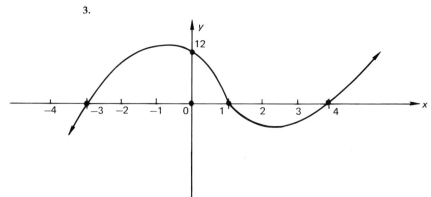

(b)

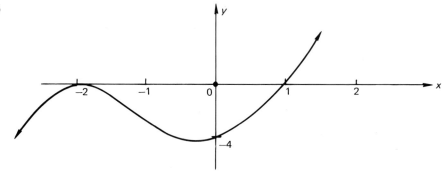

(c)

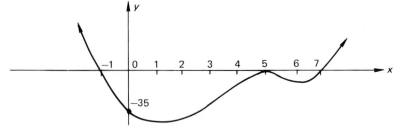

(d)

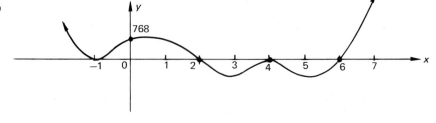

(e)

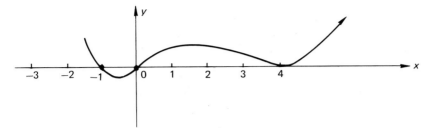

5. $P(x) = (x + 3)(x + 1)(x + 2)$
7. $f(x) = (2x + 3)(x + 1)(x - 2)$
9. Suppose $A_0 > 0$ and n is odd in the polynomial function $f(x) = A_0x^n + A_1x^{n-1} + A_2x^{n-2} + \cdots + A_n$. Then for sufficiently large x, $f(x) > 0$; and for sufficiently small (negative) x, $f(x) < 0$. Hence the graph of $f(x)$ must cross the x-axis at least once.

Exercise 12.5

1. **(a)** $f(g(x)) = x^2 + 2$
    (b) $g(f(x)) = x^2 - 2x + 4$
3. domain of u: all real $x \neq 1$
    range of v: all $v(x) \geq -2$
    $u(v(x)) = \dfrac{1}{\sqrt{x - 3}}$ with $x \geq 0$ and $x \neq 9$

5.

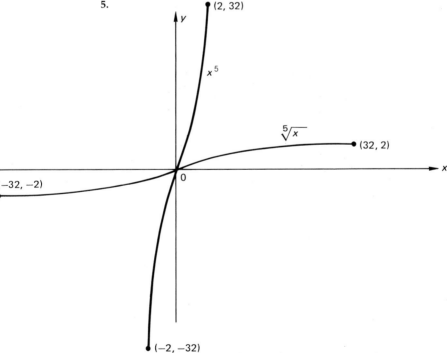

7. Range of each of the given functions:
    (a) $y \neq 0$ **(b)** $y \neq -3$ **(c)** $y \geq -5$
    (d) $y \geq 0$ *or* $y \leq -4$

9. $f^{-1}(x) = \sqrt[3]{x - 2}$

domain and range for f and f^{-1} are as follows:

domain: $-\infty < x < \infty$

range: $-\infty < y < \infty$

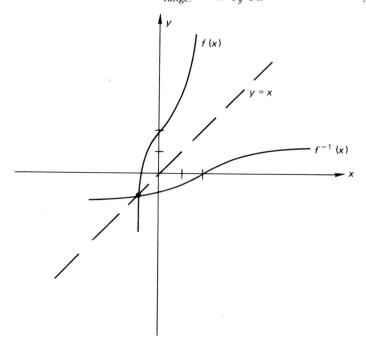

11. $f(x) = \dfrac{1}{x - 1}$ domain $x \geq 2$

$f^{-1}(x) = \dfrac{x + 1}{x}$ domain $0 < x \leq 1$

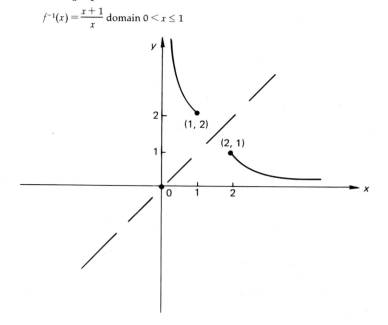

13. $f(g(x)) = \sqrt[3]{x - 3}$
$(f(g(x)))^{-1} = x^3 + 3$
$f^{-1}(x) = x^3$
$g^{-1}(x) = x + 3$
$g^{-1}(f^{-1}(x)) = x^3 + 3$

identical functions

Exercise 12.6 **1.**

function	x-intercept(s)	y-intercept	horizontal asymptote	vertical asymptote	Does graph intersect horizontal asymptote?
$f(x)$	$x = -2$	$y = \dfrac{-4}{3}$	$y = 2$	$x = 3$	yes, at $x = 13$
$g(x)$	$x = \pm 3$	none	none	$x = 0$	----------
$h(x)$	$x = 0$	$y = 0$	$y = 0$	$x = \pm 5$	yes, at $x = 0$
$r(x)$	$x = \pm 3$	$y = \dfrac{9}{16}$	$y = 1$	$x = \pm 4$	no
$s(x)$	$x = 3$	$y = -27$	none	$x = 1$	----------
$t(x)$	$x = 1/2$, $x = -1$	$y = \dfrac{1}{3}$	$y = 2$	$x = -3$, $x = 1$	yes, at $x = 5/3$

3. $f(g(x)) = \dfrac{\dfrac{2x + 1}{x - 1} + 1}{\dfrac{2x + 1}{x - 1} + 2} = x$

Similarly, $g(f(x)) = x$ and hence f and g are inverses of each other.

5. $y = x^2$ is a non-linear (in this case, quadratic) asymptote in the sense that

$$\left[\frac{x^3 + 1}{x} - x^2 \right] \to 0$$

as $x \to \infty$.

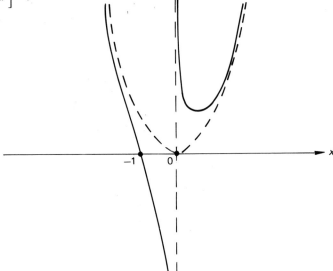

Exercise 12.7   **1.**   **(a)**

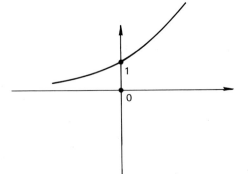

domain: all real x
range: $y > 0$

(b)

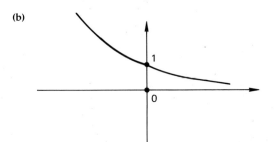

domain: all real x
range: $y > 0$

(c)

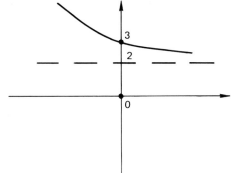

domain: all real x
range: $y > 2$

(d)

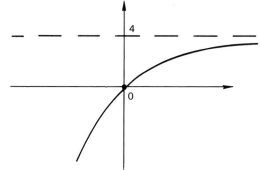

domain: all real x
range: $y < 4$

(e)

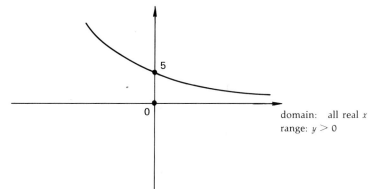

domain: all real x
range: $y > 0$

3. $(\sqrt{2})^2 = 2$ and $(\sqrt{2})^4 = 4$
5. $\log_b x = L$ means $b^L = x$. If $b > 0$ and $\log_b x$ is real, then $b^L > 0$.
7. $\ln(e^u) = u \ln(e) = u$
9. **(a)**   \$2.01
      (b)   \$1.99

11. $\sqrt[20]{\dfrac{15,000}{5,000}} - 1 = 5.65\%$

13. Let $M = \log_b x$ and $N = \log_b y$.

Then $x = b^M$ and $y = b^N$. It follows that $\dfrac{x}{y} = b^{M-N}$ and thus $M - N = \log_b\left(\dfrac{x}{y}\right)$.

15. 7% rate: $A = \$13.82$
8.45% rate: $A = \$14.80$

Table 1

Binomial Probabilities
$P(k,n,p)$ = probability of exactly k successes in n trials

n	k	.05	.10	.15	.20	.25	.30	.35	.40	.45	.50
1	0	.9500	.9000	.8500	.8000	.7500	.7000	.6500	.6000	.5500	.5000
	1	.0500	.1000	.1500	.2000	.2500	.3000	.3500	.4000	.4500	.5000
2	0	.9025	.8100	.7225	.6400	.5625	.4900	.4225	.3600	.3025	.2500
	1	.0950	.1800	.2550	.3200	.3750	.4200	.4550	.4800	.4950	.5000
	2	.0025	.0100	.0225	.0400	.0625	.0900	.1225	.1600	.2025	.2500
3	0	.8574	.7290	.6141	.5120	.4219	.3430	.2746	.2160	.1664	.1250
	1	.1354	.2430	.3251	.3840	.4219	.4410	.4436	.4320	.4084	.3750
	2	.0071	.0270	.0574	.0960	.1406	.1890	.2389	.2880	.3341	.3750
	3	.0001	.0010	.0034	.0080	.0156	.0270	.0429	.0640	.0911	.1250
4	0	.8145	.6561	.5220	.4096	.3164	.2401	.1785	.1296	.0915	.0625
	1	.1715	.2916	.3685	.4096	.4219	.4116	.3845	.3456	.2995	.2500
	2	.0135	.0486	.0975	.1536	.2109	.2646	.3105	.3456	.3675	.3750
	3	.0005	.0036	.0115	.0256	.0469	.0756	.1115	.1536	.2005	.2500
	4	.0000	.0001	.0005	.0016	.0039	.0081	.0150	.0256	.0410	.0625
5	0	.7738	.5905	.4437	.3277	.2373	.1681	.1160	.0778	.0503	.0312
	1	.2036	.3280	.3915	.4096	.3955	.3602	.3124	.2592	.2059	.1562
	2	.0214	.0729	.1382	.2048	.2637	.3087	.3364	.3456	.3369	.3125
	3	.0011	.0081	.0244	.0512	.0879	.1323	.1811	.2304	.2757	.3125
	4	.0000	.0004	.0022	.0064	.0146	.0284	.0488	.0768	.1128	.1562
	5	.0000	.0000	.0001	.0003	.0010	.0024	.0053	.0102	.0185	.0312
6	0	.7351	.5314	.3771	.2621	.1780	.1176	.0754	.0467	.0277	.0156
	1	.2321	.3543	.3993	.3932	.3560	.3025	.2437	.1866	.1359	.0938
	2	.0305	.0984	.1762	.2458	.2966	.3241	.3280	.3110	.2780	.2344
	3	.0021	.0146	.0415	.0819	.1318	.1852	.2355	.2765	.3032	.3125
	4	.0001	.0012	.0055	.0154	.0330	.0595	.0951	.1382	.1861	.2344
	5	.0000	.0001	.0004	.0015	.0044	.0102	.0205	.0369	.0609	.0938
	6	.0000	.0000	.0000	.0001	.0002	.0007	.0018	.0041	.0083	.0156
7	0	.6983	.4783	.3206	.2097	.1335	.0824	.0490	.0280	.0152	.0078
	1	.2573	.3720	.3960	.3670	.3115	.2471	.1848	.1306	.0872	.0547
	2	.0406	.1240	.2097	.2753	.3115	.3177	.2985	.2613	.2140	.1641
	3	.0036	.0230	.0617	.1147	.1730	.2269	.2679	.2903	.2918	.2734
	4	.0002	.0026	.0109	.0287	.0577	.0972	.1442	.1935	.2388	.2734
	5	.0000	.0002	.0012	.0043	.0115	.0250	.0466	.0774	.1172	.1641
	6	.0000	.0000	.0001	.0004	.0013	.0036	.0084	.0172	.0320	.0547
	7	.0000	.0000	.0000	.0000	.0001	.0002	.0006	.0016	.0037	.0078
8	0	.6634	.4305	.2725	.1678	.1001	.0576	.0319	.0168	.0084	.0039
	1	.2793	.3826	.3847	.3355	.2670	.1977	.1373	.0896	.0548	.0312
	2	.0515	.1488	.2376	.2936	.3115	.2965	.2587	.2090	.1569	.1094
	3	.0054	.0331	.0839	.1468	.2076	.2541	.2786	.2787	.2568	.2188
	4	.0004	.0046	.0185	.0459	.0865	.1361	.1875	.2322	.2627	.2734
	5	.0000	.0004	.0026	.0092	.0231	.0467	.0808	.1239	.1719	.2188
	6	.0000	.0000	.0002	.0011	.0038	.0100	.0217	.0413	.0703	.1094
	7	.0000	.0000	.0000	.0001	.0004	.0012	.0033	.0079	.0164	.0312
	8	.0000	.0000	.0000	.0000	.0000	.0001	.0002	.0007	.0017	.0039

Table 1 (continued)

n	k	.05	.10	.15	.20	.25	.30	.35	.40	.45	.50
9	0	.6302	.3874	.2316	.1342	.0751	.0404	.0207	.0101	.0046	.0020
	1	.2985	.3874	.3679	.3020	.2253	.1556	.1004	.0605	.0339	.0176
	2	.0629	.1722	.2597	.3020	.3003	.2668	.2162	.1612	.1110	.0703
	3	.0077	.0446	.1069	.1762	.2336	.2668	.2716	.2508	.2119	.1641
	4	.0006	.0074	.0283	.0661	.1168	.1715	.2194	.2508	.2600	.2461
	5	.0000	.0008	.0050	.0165	.0389	.0735	.1181	.1672	.2128	.2461
	6	.0000	.0001	.0006	.0028	.0087	.0210	.0424	.0743	.1160	.1641
	7	.0000	.0000	.0000	.0003	.0012	.0039	.0098	.0212	.0407	.0703
	8	.0000	.0000	.0000	.0000	.0001	.0004	.0013	.0035	.0083	.0176
	9	.0000	.0000	.0000	.0000	.0000	.0000	.0001	.0003	.0008	.0020
10	0	.5987	.3487	.1969	.1074	.0563	.0282	.0135	.0060	.0025	.0010
	1	.3151	.3874	.3474	.2684	.1877	.1211	.0725	.0403	.0207	.0098
	2	.0746	.1937	.2759	.3020	.2816	.2335	.1757	.1209	.0763	.0439
	3	.0105	.0574	.1298	.2013	.2503	.2668	.2522	.2150	.1665	.1172
	4	.0010	.0112	.0401	.0881	.1460	.2001	.2377	.2508	.2384	.2051
	5	.0001	.0015	.0085	.0264	.0584	.1029	.1536	.2007	.2340	.2461
	6	.0000	.0001	.0012	.0055	.0162	.0368	.0689	.1115	.1596	.2051
	7	.0000	.0000	.0001	.0008	.0031	.0090	.0212	.0425	.0746	.1172
	8	.0000	.0000	.0000	.0001	.0004	.0014	.0043	.0106	.0229	.0439
	9	.0000	.0000	.0000	.0000	.0000	.0001	.0005	.0016	.0042	.0098
	10	.0000	.0000	.0000	.0000	.0000	.0000	.0000	.0001	.0003	.0010
11	0	.5688	.3138	.1673	.0859	.0422	.0198	.0088	.0036	.0014	.0005
	1	.3293	.3835	.3248	.2362	.1549	.0932	.0518	.0266	.0125	.0054
	2	.0867	.2131	.2866	.2953	.2581	.1998	.1395	.0887	.0513	.0269
	3	.0137	.0710	.1517	.2215	.2581	.2568	.2254	.1774	.1259	.0806
	4	.0014	.0158	.0536	.1107	.1721	.2201	.2428	.2365	.2060	.1611
	5	.0001	.0025	.0132	.0388	.0803	.1321	.1830	.2207	.2360	.2256
	6	.0000	.0003	.0023	.0097	.0268	.0566	.0985	.1471	.1931	.2256
	7	.0000	.0000	.0003	.0017	.0064	.0173	.0379	.0701	.1128	.1611
	8	.0000	.0000	.0000	.0002	.0011	.0037	.0102	.0234	.0462	.0806
	9	.0000	.0000	.0000	.0000	.0001	.0005	.0018	.0052	.0126	.0269
	10	.0000	.0000	.0000	.0000	.0000	.0000	.0002	.0007	.0021	.0054
	11	.0000	.0000	.0000	.0000	.0000	.0000	.0000	.0000	.0002	.0005
12	0	.5404	.2824	.1422	.0687	.0317	.0138	.0057	.0022	.0008	.0002
	1	.3413	.3766	.3012	.2062	.1267	.0712	.0368	.0174	.0075	.0029
	2	.0988	.2301	.2924	.2835	.2323	.1678	.1088	.0639	.0339	.0161
	3	.0173	.0852	.1720	.2362	.2581	.2397	.1954	.1419	.0923	.0537
	4	.0021	.0213	.0683	.1329	.1936	.2311	.2367	.2128	.1700	.1208
	5	.0002	.0038	.0193	.0532	.1032	.1585	.2039	.2270	.2225	.1934
	6	.0000	.0005	.0040	.0155	.0401	.0792	.1281	.1766	.2124	.2256
	7	.0000	.0000	.0006	.0033	.0115	.0291	.0591	.1009	.1489	.1934
	8	.0000	.0000	.0001	.0005	.0024	.0078	.0199	.0420	.0762	.1208
	9	.0000	.0000	.0000	.0001	.0004	.0015	.0048	.0125	.0277	.0537
	10	.0000	.0000	.0000	.0000	.0000	.0002	.0008	.0025	.0068	.0161
	11	.0000	.0000	.0000	.0000	.0000	.0000	.0001	.0003	.0010	.0029
	12	.0000	.0000	.0000	.0000	.0000	.0000	.0000	.0000	.0001	.0002

Table 1 (continued)

n	k	.05	.10	.15	.20	.25	.30	.35	.40	.45	.50
13	0	.5133	.2542	.1209	.0550	.0238	.0097	.0037	.0013	.0004	.0001
	1	.3512	.3672	.2774	.1787	.1029	.0540	.0259	.0113	.0045	.0016
	2	.1109	.2448	.2937	.2680	.2059	.1388	.0836	.0453	.0220	.0095
	3	.0214	.0997	.1900	.2457	.2517	.2181	.1651	.1107	.0660	.0349
	4	.0028	.0277	.0838	.1535	.2097	.2337	.2222	.1845	.1350	.0873
	5	.0003	.0055	.0266	.0691	.1258	.1803	.2154	.2214	.1989	.1571
	6	.0000	.0008	.0063	.0230	.0559	.1030	.1546	.1968	.2169	.2095
	7	.0000	.0001	.0011	.0058	.0186	.0442	.0833	.1312	.1775	.2095
	8	.0000	.0000	.0001	.0011	.0047	.0142	.0336	.0656	.1089	.1571
	9	.0000	.0000	.0000	.0001	.0009	.0034	.0101	.0243	.0495	.0873
	10	.0000	.0000	.0000	.0000	.0001	.0006	.0022	.0065	.0162	.0349
	11	.0000	.0000	.0000	.0000	.0000	.0001	.0003	.0012	.0036	.0095
	12	.0000	.0000	.0000	.0000	.0000	.0000	.0000	.0001	.0005	.0016
	13	.0000	.0000	.0000	.0000	.0000	.0000	.0000	.0000	.0000	.0001
14	0	.4877	.2288	.1028	.0440	.0178	.0068	.0024	.0008	.0002	.0001
	1	.3593	.3559	.2539	.1539	.0832	.0407	.0181	.0073	.0027	.0009
	2	.1229	.2570	.2912	.2501	.1802	.1134	.0634	.0317	.0141	.0056
	3	.0259	.1142	.2056	.2501	.2402	.1943	.1366	.0845	.0462	.0222
	4	.0037	.0349	.0998	.1720	.2202	.2290	.2022	.1549	.1040	.0611
	5	.0004	.0078	.0352	.0860	.1468	.1963	.2178	.2066	.1701	.1222
	6	.0000	.0013	.0093	.0322	.0734	.1262	.1759	.2066	.2088	.1833
	7	.0000	.0002	.0019	.0092	.0280	.0618	.1082	.1574	.1952	.2095
	8	.0000	.0000	.0003	.0020	.0082	.0232	.0510	.0918	.1398	.1833
	9	.0000	.0000	.0000	.0003	.0018	.0066	.0183	.0408	.0762	.1222
	10	.0000	.0000	.0000	.0000	.0003	.0014	.0049	.0136	.0312	.0611
	11	.0000	.0000	.0000	.0000	.0000	.0002	.0010	.0033	.0093	.0222
	12	.0000	.0000	.0000	.0000	.0000	.0000	.0001	.0005	.0019	.0056
	13	.0000	.0000	.0000	.0000	.0000	.0000	.0000	.0001	.0002	.0009
	14	.0000	.0000	.0000	.0000	.0000	.0000	.0000	.0000	.0000	.0001
15	0	.4633	.2059	.0874	.0352	.0134	.0047	.0016	.0005	.0001	.0000
	1	.3658	.3432	.2312	.1329	.0668	.0305	.0126	.0047	.0016	.0005
	2	.1348	.2669	.2856	.2309	.1559	.0916	.0476	.0219	.0090	.0032
	3	.0307	.1285	.2184	.2501	.2252	.1700	.1110	.0634	.0318	.0139
	4	.0049	.0428	.1156	.1876	.2252	.2186	.1792	.1268	.0780	.0417
	5	.0006	.0105	.0449	.1032	.1651	.2061	.2123	.1859	.1404	.0916
	6	.0000	.0019	.0132	.0430	.0917	.1472	.1906	.2066	.1914	.1527
	7	.0000	.0003	.0030	.0138	.0393	.0811	.1319	.1771	.2013	.1964
	8	.0000	.0000	.0005	.0035	.0131	.0348	.0710	.1181	.1647	.1964
	9	.0000	.0000	.0001	.0007	.0034	.0116	.0298	.0612	.1048	.1527
	10	.0000	.0000	.0000	.0001	.0007	.0030	.0096	.0245	.0515	.0916
	11	.0000	.0000	.0000	.0000	.0001	.0006	.0024	.0074	.0191	.0417
	12	.0000	.0000	.0000	.0000	.0000	.0001	.0004	.0016	.0052	.0139
	13	.0000	.0000	.0000	.0000	.0000	.0000	.0001	.0003	.0010	.0032
	14	.0000	.0000	.0000	.0000	.0000	.0000	.0000	.0000	.0001	.0005
	15	.0000	.0000	.0000	.0000	.0000	.0000	.0000	.0000	.0000	.0000

Table 1   (continued)

n	k	.05	.10	.15	.20	.25	.30	.35	.40	.45	.50
16	0	.4401	.1853	.0743	.0281	.0100	.0033	.0010	.0003	.0001	.0000
	1	.3706	.3294	.2097	.1126	.0535	.0228	.0087	.0030	.0009	.0002
	2	.1463	.2745	.2775	.2111	.1336	.0732	.0353	.0150	.0056	.0018
	3	.0359	.1423	.2285	.2463	.2079	.1465	.0888	.0468	.0215	.0085
	4	.0061	.0514	.1311	.2001	.2252	.2040	.1553	.1014	.0572	.0278
	5	.0008	.0137	.0555	.1201	.1802	.2099	.2008	.1623	.1123	.0667
	6	.0001	.0028	.0180	.0550	.1101	.1649	.1982	.1983	.1684	.1222
	7	.0000	.0004	.0045	.0197	.0524	.1010	.1524	.1889	.1969	.1746
	8	.0000	.0001	.0009	.0055	.0197	.0487	.0923	.1417	.1812	.1964
	9	.0000	.0000	.0001	.0012	.0058	.0185	.0442	.0840	.1318	.1746
	10	.0000	.0000	.0000	.0002	.0014	.0056	.0167	.0392	.0755	.1222
	11	.0000	.0000	.0000	.0000	.0002	.0013	.0049	.0142	.0337	.0667
	12	.0000	.0000	.0000	.0000	.0000	.0002	.0011	.0040	.0115	.0278
	13	.0000	.0000	.0000	.0000	.0000	.0000	.0002	.0008	.0029	.0085
	14	.0000	.0000	.0000	.0000	.0000	.0000	.0000	.0001	.0005	.0018
	15	.0000	.0000	.0000	.0000	.0000	.0000	.0000	.0000	.0001	.0002
	16	.0000	.0000	.0000	.0000	.0000	.0000	.0000	.0000	.0000	.0000
17	0	.4181	.1668	.0631	.0225	.0075	.0023	.0007	.0002	.0000	.0000
	1	.3741	.3150	.1893	.0957	.0426	.0169	.0060	.0019	.0005	.0001
	2	.1575	.2800	.2673	.1914	.1136	.0581	.0260	.0102	.0035	.0010
	3	.0415	.1556	.2359	.2393	.1893	.1245	.0701	.0341	.0144	.0052
	4	.0076	.0605	.1457	.2093	.2209	.1868	.1320	.0796	.0411	.0182
	5	.0010	.0175	.0668	.1361	.1914	.2081	.1849	.1379	.0875	.0472
	6	.0001	.0039	.0236	.0680	.1276	.1784	.1991	.1839	.1432	.0944
	7	.0000	.0007	.0065	.0267	.0668	.1201	.1685	.1927	.1841	.1484
	8	.0000	.0001	.0014	.0084	.0279	.0644	.1134	.1606	.1883	.1855
	9	.0000	.0000	.0003	.0021	.0093	.0276	.0611	.1070	.1540	.1855
	10	.0000	.0000	.0000	.0004	.0025	.0095	.0263	.0571	.1008	.1484
	11	.0000	.0000	.0000	.0001	.0005	.0026	.0090	.0242	.0525	.0944
	12	.0000	.0000	.0000	.0000	.0001	.0006	.0024	.0081	.0215	.0472
	13	.0000	.0000	.0000	.0000	.0000	.0001	.0005	.0021	.0068	.0182
	14	.0000	.0000	.0000	.0000	.0000	.0000	.0001	.0004	.0016	.0052
	15	.0000	.0000	.0000	.0000	.0000	.0000	.0000	.0001	.0003	.0010
	16	.0000	.0000	.0000	.0000	.0000	.0000	.0000	.0000	.0000	.0001
	17	.0000	.0000	.0000	.0000	.0000	.0000	.0000	.0000	.0000	.0000
18	0	.3972	.1501	.0536	.0180	.0056	.0016	.0004	.0001	.0000	.0000
	1	.3763	.3002	.1704	.0811	.0338	.0126	.0042	.0012	.0003	.0001
	2	.1683	.2835	.2556	.1723	.0958	.0458	.0190	.0069	.0022	.0006
	3	.0473	.1680	.2406	.2297	.1704	.1046	.0547	.0246	.0095	.0031
	4	.0093	.0700	.1592	.2153	.2130	.1681	.1104	.0614	.0291	.0117
	5	.0014	.0218	.0787	.1507	.1988	.2017	.1664	.1146	.0666	.0327
	6	.0002	.0052	.0301	.0816	.1436	.1873	.1941	.1655	.1181	.0708
	7	.0000	.0010	.0091	.0350	.0820	.1376	.1792	.1892	.1657	.1214
	8	.0000	.0002	.0022	.0120	.0376	.0811	.1327	.1734	.1864	.1669
	9	.0000	.0000	.0004	.0033	.0139	.0386	.0794	.1284	.1694	.1855
	10	.0000	.0000	.0001	.0008	.0042	.0149	.0385	.0771	.1248	.1669
	11	.0000	.0000	.0000	.0001	.0010	.0046	.0151	.0374	.0742	.1214
	12	.0000	.0000	.0000	.0000	.0002	.0012	.0047	.0145	.0354	.0708
	13	.0000	.0000	.0000	.0000	.0000	.0002	.0012	.0045	.0134	.0327
	14	.0000	.0000	.0000	.0000	.0000	.0000	.0002	.0011	.0039	.0117
	15	.0000	.0000	.0000	.0000	.0000	.0000	.0000	.0002	.0009	.0031
	16	.0000	.0000	.0000	.0000	.0000	.0000	.0000	.0000	.0001	.0006
	17	.0000	.0000	.0000	.0000	.0000	.0000	.0000	.0000	.0000	.0001
	18	.0000	.0000	.0000	.0000	.0000	.0000	.0000	.0000	.0000	.0000

Table 1 (continued)

n	k	.05	.10	.15	.20	.25	.30	.35	.40	.45	.50
19	0	.3774	.1351	.0456	.0144	.0042	.0011	.0003	.0001	.0000	.0000
	1	.3774	.2852	.1529	.0685	.0268	.0093	.0029	.0008	.0002	.0000
	2	.1787	.2852	.2428	.1540	.0803	.0358	.0138	.0046	.0013·	.0003
	3	.0533	.1796	.2428	.2182	.1517	.0869	.0422	.0175	.0062	.0018
	4	.0112	.0798	.1714	.2182	.2023	.1491	.0909	.0467	.0203	.0074
	5	.0018	.0266	.0907	.1636	.2023	.1916	.1468	.0933	.0497	.0222
	6	.0002	.0069	.0374	.0955	.1574	.1916	.1844	.1451	.0949	.1518
	7	.0000	.0014	.0122	.0443	.0974	.1525	.1844	.1797	.1443	.0961
	8	.0000	.0002	.0032	.0166	.0487	.0981	.1489	.1797	.1771	.1442
	9	.0000	.0000	.0007	.0051	.0198	.0514	.0980	.1464	.1771	.1762
	10	.0000	.0000	.0001	.0013	.0066	.0220	.0528	.0976	.1449	.1762
	11	.0000	.0000	.0000	.0003	.0018	.0077	.0233	.0532	.0970	.1442
	12	.0000	.0000	.0000	.0000	.0004	.0022	.0083	.0237	.0529	.0961
	13	.0000	.0000	.0000	.0000	.0001	.0005	.0024	.0085	.0233	.0518
	14	.0000	.0000	.0000	.0000	.0000	.0001	.0006	.0024	.0082	.0222
	15	.0000	.0000	.0000	.0000	.0000	.0000	.0001	.0005	.0022	.0074
	16	.0000	.0000	.0000	.0000	.0000	.0000	.0000	.0001	.0005	.0018
	17	.0000	.0000	.0000	.0000	.0000	.0000	.0000	.0000	.0001	.0003
	18	.0000	.0000	.0000	.0000	.0000	.0000	.0000	.0000	.0000	.0000
	19	.0000	.0000	.0000	.0000	.0000	.0000	.0000	.0000	.0000	.0000
20	0	.3585	.1216	.0388	.0115	.0032	.0008	.0002	.0000	.0000	.0000
	1	.3774	.2702	.1368	.0576	.0211	.0068	.0020	.0005	.0001	.0000
	2	.1887	.2852	.2293	.1369	.0669	.0278	.0100	.0031	.0008	.0002
	3	.0596	.1901	.2428	.2054	.1339	.0716	.0323	.0123	.0040	.0011
	4	.0133	.0898	.1821	.2182	.1897	.1304	.0738	.0350	.0139	.0046
	5	.0022	.0319	.1028	.1746	.2023	.1789	.1272	.0746	.0365	.0148
	6	.0003	.0089	.0454	.1091	.1686	.1916	.1712	.1244	.0746	.0370
	7	.0000	.0020	.0160	.0545	.1124	.1643	.1844	.1659	.1221	.0739
	8	.0000	.0004	.0046	.0222	.0609	.1144	.1614	.1797	.1623	.1201
	9	.0000	.0001	.0011	.0074	.0271	.0654	.1158	.1597	.1771	.1602
	10	.0000	.0000	.0002	.0020	.0099	.0308	.0686	.1171	.1593	.1762
	11	.0000	.0000	.0000	.0005	.0030	.0120	.0336	.0710	.1185	.1602
	12	.0000	.0000	.0000	.0001	.0008	.0039	.1036	.0355	.0727	.1201
	13	.0000	.0000	.0000	.0000	.0002	.0010	.0045	.0146	.0366	.0739
	14	.0000	.0000	.0000	.0000	.0000	.0002	.0012	.0049	.0150	.0370
	15	.0000	.0000	.0000	.0000	.0000	.0000	.0003	.0013	.0049	.0148
	16	.0000	.0000	.0000	.0000	.0000	.0000	.0000	.0003	.0013	.0046
	17	.0000	.0000	.0000	.0000	.0000	.0000	.0000	.0000	.0002	.0011
	18	.0000	.0000	.0000	.0000	.0000	.0000	.0000	.0000	.0000	.0002
	19	.0000	.0000	.0000	.0000	.0000	.0000	.0000	.0000	.0000	.0000
	20	.0000	.0000	.0000	.0000	.0000	.0000	.0000	.0000	.0000	.0000

Table 2

Common Logarithms (Base 10)*

N.	0	1	2	3	4	5	6	7	8	9
10	0000	0043	0086	0128	0170	0212	0253	0294	0334	0374
11	0414	0453	0492	0531	0569	0607	0645	0682	0719	0755
12	0792	0828	0864	0899	0934	0969	1004	1038	1072	1106
13	1139	1173	1206	1239	1271	1303	1335	1367	1399	1430
14	1461	1492	1523	1553	1584	1614	1644	1673	1703	1732
15	1761	1790	1818	1847	1875	1903	1931	1959	1987	2014
16	2041	2068	2095	2122	2148	2175	2201	2227	2253	2279
17	2304	2330	2355	2380	2405	2430	2455	2480	2504	2529
18	2553	2577	2601	2625	2648	2672	2695	2718	2742	2765
19	2788	2810	2833	2856	2878	2900	2923	2945	2967	2989
20	3010	3032	3054	3075	3096	3118	3139	3160	3181	3201
21	3222	3243	3263	3284	3304	3324	3345	3365	3385	3404
22	3424	3444	3464	3483	3502	3522	3541	3560	3579	3598
23	3617	3636	3655	3674	3692	3711	3729	3747	3766	3784
24	3802	3820	3838	3856	3874	3892	3909	3927	3945	3962
25	3979	3997	4014	4031	4048	4065	4082	4099	4116	4133
26	4150	4166	4183	4200	4216	4232	4249	4265	4281	4298
27	4314	4330	4346	4362	4378	4393	4409	4425	4440	4456
28	4472	4487	4502	4518	4533	4548	4564	4579	4594	4609
29	4624	4639	4654	4669	4683	4698	4713	4728	4742	4757
30	4771	4786	4800	4814	4829	4843	4857	4871	4886	4900
31	4914	4928	4942	4955	4969	4983	4997	5011	5024	5038
32	5051	5065	5079	5092	5105	5119	5132	5145	5159	5172
33	5185	5198	5211	5224	5237	5250	5263	5276	5289	5302
34	5315	5328	5340	5353	5366	5378	5391	5403	5416	5428
35	5441	5453	5465	5478	5490	5502	5514	5527	5539	5551
36	5563	5575	5587	5599	5611	5623	5635	5647	5658	5670
37	5682	5694	5705	5717	5729	5740	5752	5763	5775	5786
38	5798	5809	5821	5832	5843	5855	5866	5877	5888	5899
39	5911	5922	5933	5944	5955	5966	5977	5988	5999	6010
40	6021	6031	6042	6053	6064	6075	6085	6096	6107	6117
41	6128	6138	6149	6160	6170	6180	6191	6201	6212	6222
42	6232	6243	6253	6263	6274	6284	6294	6304	6314	6325
43	6335	6345	6355	6365	6375	6385	6395	6405	6415	6425
44	6435	6444	6454	6464	6474	6484	6493	6503	6513	6522
45	6532	6542	6551	6561	6571	6580	6590	6599	6609	6618
46	6628	6637	6646	6656	6665	6675	6684	6693	6702	6712
47	6721	6730	6739	6749	6758	6767	6776	6785	6794	6803
48	6812	6821	6830	6839	6848	6857	6866	6875	6884	6893
49	6902	6911	6920	6928	6937	6946	6955	6964	6972	6981
50	6990	6998	7007	7016	7024	7033	7042	7050	7059	7067
51	7076	7084	7093	7101	7110	7118	7126	7135	7143	7152
52	7160	7168	7177	7185	7193	7202	7210	7218	7226	7235
53	7243	7251	7259	7267	7275	7284	7292	7300	7308	7316
54	7324	7332	7340	7348	7356	7364	7372	7380	7388	7396
N.	0	1	2	3	4	5	6	7	8	9

* This table gives the mantissas of numbers with the decimal point omitted in each case. Characteristics are determined from the numbers by inspection.

Table 2 (*continued*)

N.	0	1	2	3	4	5	6	7	8	9
55	7404	7412	7419	7427	7435	7443	7451	7459	7466	7474
56	7482	7490	7497	7505	7513	7520	7528	7536	7543	7551
57	7559	7566	7574	7582	7589	7597	7604	7612	7619	7627
58	7634	7642	7649	7657	7664	7672	7679	7686	7694	7701
59	7709	7716	7723	7731	7738	7745	7752	7760	7767	7774
60	7782	7789	7796	7803	7810	7818	7825	7832	7839	7846
61	7853	7860	7868	7875	7882	7889	7896	7903	7910	7917
62	7924	7931	7938	7945	7952	7959	7966	7973	7980	7987
63	7993	8000	8007	8014	8021	8028	8035	8041	8048	8055
64	8062	8069	8075	8082	8089	8096	8102	8109	8116	8122
65	8129	8136	8142	8149	8156	8162	8169	8176	8182	8189
66	8195	8202	8209	8215	8222	8228	8235	8241	8248	8254
67	8261	8267	8274	8280	8287	8293	8299	8306	8312	8319
68	8325	8331	8338	8344	8351	8357	8363	8370	8376	8382
69	8388	8395	8401	8407	8414	8420	8426	8432	8439	8445
70	8451	8457	8463	8470	8476	8482	8488	8494	8500	8506
71	8513	8519	8525	8531	8537	8543	8549	8555	8561	8567
72	8573	8579	8585	8591	8597	8603	8609	8615	8621	8627
73	8633	8639	8645	8651	8657	8663	8669	8675	8681	8686
74	8692	8698	8704	8710	8716	8722	8727	8733	8739	8745
75	8751	8756	8762	8768	8774	8779	8785	8791	8797	8802
76	8808	8814	8820	8825	8831	8837	8842	8848	8854	8859
77	8865	8871	8876	8882	8887	8893	8899	8904	8910	8915
78	8921	8927	8932	8938	8943	8949	8954	8960	8965	8971
79	8976	8982	8987	8993	8998	9004	9009	9015	9020	9025
80	9031	9036	9042	9047	9053	9058	9063	9069	9074	9079
81	9085	9090	9096	9101	9106	9112	9117	9122	9128	9133
82	9138	9143	9149	9154	9159	9165	9170	9175	9180	9186
83	9191	9196	9201	9206	9212	9217	9222	9227	9232	9238
84	9243	9248	9253	9258	9263	9269	9274	9279	9284	9289
85	9294	9299	9304	9309	9315	9320	9325	9330	9335	9340
86	9345	9350	9355	9360	9365	9370	9375	9380	9385	9390
87	9395	9400	9405	9410	9415	9420	9425	9430	9435	9440
88	9445	9450	9455	9460	9465	9469	9474	9479	9484	9489
89	9494	9499	9504	9509	9513	9518	9523	9528	9533	9538
90	9542	9547	9552	9557	9562	9566	9571	9576	9581	9586
91	9590	9595	9600	9605	9609	9614	9619	9624	9628	9633
92	9638	9643	9647	9652	9657	9661	9666	9671	9675	9680
93	9685	9689	9694	9699	9703	9708	9713	9717	9722	9727
94	9731	9736	9741	9745	9750	9754	9759	9763	9768	9773
95	9777	9782	9786	9791	9795	9800	9805	9809	9814	9818
96	9823	9827	9832	9836	9841	9845	9850	9854	9859	9863
97	9868	9872	9877	9881	9886	9890	9894	9899	9903	9908
98	9912	9917	9921	9926	9930	9934	9939	9943	9948	9952
99	9956	9961	9965	9969	9974	9978	9983	9987	9991	9996
N.	0	1	2	3	4	5	6	7	8	9

Table 3

The Exponential Functions e^x, and e^{-x}

x	e^x	e^{-x}	x	e^x	e^{-x}
0.00	1.0000	1.0000	2.5	12.182	0.0821
0.05	1.0513	0.9512	2.6	13.464	0.0743
0.10	1.1052	0.9048	2.7	14.880	0.0672
0.15	1.1618	0.8607	2.8	16.445	0.0608
0.20	1.2214	0.8187	2.9	18.174	0.0550
0.25	1.2840	0.7788	3.0	20.086	0.0498
0.30	1.3499	0.7408	3.1	22.198	0.0450
0.35	1.4191	0.7047	3.2	24.533	0.0408
0.40	1.4918	0.6703	3.3	27.113	0.0369
0.45	1.5683	0.6376	3.4	29.964	0.0334
0.50	1.6487	0.6065	3.5	33.115	0.0302
0.55	1.7333	0.5769	3.6	36.598	0.0273
0.60	1.8221	0.5488	3.7	40.447	0.0247
0.65	1.9155	0.5220	3.8	44.701	0.0224
0.70	2.0138	0.4966	3.9	49.402	0.0202
0.75	2.1170	0.4724	4.0	54.598	0.0183
0.80	2.2255	0.4493	4.1	60.340	0.0166
0.85	2.3396	0.4274	4.2	66.686	0.0150
0.90	2.4596	0.4066	4.3	73.700	0.0136
0.95	2.5857	0.3867	4.4	81.451	0.0123
1.0	2.7183	0.3679	4.5	90.017	0.0111
1.1	3.0042	0.3329	4.6	99.484	0.0101
1.2	3.3201	0.3012	4.7	109.95	0.0091
1.3	3.6693	0.2725	4.8	121.51	0.0082
1.4	4.0552	0.2466	4.9	134.29	0.0074
1.5	4.4817	0.2231	5	148.41	0.0067
1.6	4.9530	0.2019	6	403.43	0.0025
1.7	5.4739	0.1827	7	1096.6	0.0009
1.8	6.0496	0.1653	8	2981.0	0.0003
1.9	6.6859	0.1496	9	8103.1	0.0001
2.0	7.3891	0.1353	10	22026	0.00005
2.1	8.1662	0.1225			
2.2	9.0250	0.1108			
2.3	9.9742	0.1003			
2.4	11.023	0.0907			

Table 4

Natural Logarithms of Numbers: $\log_e x$ (or $\ln x$)

n	$\log_e n$	n	$\log_e n$	n	$\log_e n$
0.0	*	4.5	1.5041	9.0	2.1972
0.1	7.6974	4.6	1.5261	9.1	2.2083
0.2	8.3906	4.7	1.5476	9.2	2.2192
0.3	8.7960	4.8	1.5686	9.3	2.2300
0.4	9.0837	4.9	1.5892	9.4	2.2407
0.5	9.3069	5.0	1.6094	9.5	2.2513
0.6	9.4892	5.1	1.6292	9.6	2.2618
0.7	9.6433	5.2	1.6487	9.7	2.2721
0.8	9.7769	5.3	1.6677	9.8	2.2824
0.9	9.8946	5.4	1.6864	9.9	2.2925
1.0	0.0000	5.5	1.7047	10	2.3026
1.1	0.0953	5.6	1.7228	11	2.3979
1.2	0.1823	5.7	1.7405	12	2.4849
1.3	0.2624	5.8	1.7579	13	2.5649
1.4	0.3365	5.9	1.7750	14	2.6391
1.5	0.4055	6.0	1.7918	15	2.7081
1.6	0.4700	6.1	1.8083	16	2.7726
1.7	0.5306	6.2	1.8245	17	2.8332
1.8	0.5878	6.3	1.8405	18	2.8904
1.9	0.6419	6.4	1.8563	19	2.9444
2.0	0.6931	6.5	1.8718	20	2.9957
2.1	0.7419	6.6	1.8871	25	3.2189
2.2	0.7885	6.7	1.9021	30	3.4012
2.3	0.8329	6.8	1.9169	35	3.5553
2.4	0.8755	6.9	1.9315	40	3.6889
2.5	0.9163	7.0	1.9459	45	3.8067
2.6	0.9555	7.1	1.9601	50	3.9120
2.7	0.9933	7.2	1.9741	55	4.0073
2.8	1.0296	7.3	1.9879	60	4.0943
2.9	1.0647	7.4	2.0015	65	4.1744
3.0	1.0986	7.5	2.0149	70	4.2485
3.1	1.1314	7.6	2.0281	75	4.3175
3.2	1.1632	7.7	2.0412	80	4.3820
3.3	1.1939	7.8	2.0541	85	4.4427
3.4	1.2238	7.9	2.0669	90	4.4998
3.5	1.2528	8.0	2.0794	95	4.5539
3.6	1.2809	8.1	2.0919	100	4.6052
3.7	1.3083	8.2	2.1041		
3.8	1.3350	8.3	2.1163		
3.9	1.3610	8.4	2.1282		
4.0	1.3863	8.5	2.1401		
4.1	1.4110	8.6	2.1518		
4.2	1.4351	8.7	2.1633		
4.3	1.4586	8.8	2.1748		
4.4	1.4816	8.9	2.1861		

* Subtract 10 from $\log_e n$ entries for $n < 1.0$.

Index